Industrial Conflict

STUDIES IN INDUSTRIAL RELATIONS

Hoyt N. Wheeler and Roy J. Adams, *Editors*

INDUSTRIAL CONFLICT

An Integrative Theory

by Hoyt N. Wheeler

 University of South Carolina Press

Library of Congress Cataloging-in-Publication Data

Wheeler, Hoyt N.
    Industrial conflict.

    (Studies in industrial relations)
    Includes index.
    1. Labor disputes.   2. Industrial relations.
3. Conflict management.   I. Title.   II. Series.
HD5306.W48   1985   658.3'154   85-16411
ISBN 0-87249-459-4

This, my song, is dedicated to my first-born son, Alan, who never got to sing his, to my mother, who helped me to learn how to sing, to Janice, who made the song possible, and to Jeff and Jon, who made it seem worthwhile to keep on singing.

CONTENTS

PREFACE

It is quite appropriate that the chain of events that led to the writing of this book began when the author, having completed an arbitration hearing in a labor-management dispute, wandered into the University of Wisconsin bookstore and purchased a copy of Carl Sagan's *The Dragons of Eden*. It was Sagan's discussion of the social dominance behavior of monkeys that suggested to me the importance of human social dominance behavior in industrial relations. Speculation about, and eventually study of, this analogy and ideas related to it produced several working papers, presentations to scholarly audiences in the Netherlands, England, and the United States, two published papers, and this book. That this was initiated by ideas made available to me by my graduate alma mater, Wisconsin, always a rich storehouse of challenging thoughts, is fitting indeed.

It is also appropriate that one of the functions this book may serve is to repay in small part the intellectual debt that this author owes to the "Wisconsin School" institutional labor economists. Although somewhat out of fashion these days, they have furnished many penetrating insights and sound, usable descriptions and policy prescriptions competing schools of thought have yet to match. Yet, the current marketplace for ideas, which places a high premium upon "Theory," seems to be dominated by mechanical and absolutist approaches that are singularly uncongenial to both the spirit and the methodology of institutional work. The theory presented in this book will more than exceed its author's expectations if it serves as a building block for theories that are more compatible with the realism, richness, and true rigor long characteristic of institutional studies.

It is also hoped that the presentation of this theory will cause other students of industrial relations to be sensitized to the new possibilities of building theory in our field. Biological ideas, properly used, hold out considerable promise. They provide a truly scientific base not found elsewhere; they may help to breathe some new life into industrial relations as a field of study.

In addition to my intellectual debt to the Wisconsin School and its current proponents, such as Jack Barbash and Everett Kassalow, a number of other debts need to be acknowledged. An invitation by Dick Petersen (University of Washington) and Gerard Bomers (Nijenrode) to present a paper on industrial conflict at the Netherlands School of Business (Nijenrode) prompted me to first put together some of these ideas. In the early stages, Leonard Berkowitz (University of Wisconsin), George Strauss (University of California), and John Lawler (University of Illinois) were very helpful in guiding me into new areas of literature. Others who took the time and trouble to give me very extensive comments on various versions of the theory were Tom Kochan (MIT), Angelo DeNisi (University of South Carolina), Tom Mahoney (Vanderbilt University), and Craig Pinder (University of British Columbia). Useful comments were provided by Howard Miller, Ross Azevedo, Mike Bognanno, Ken Gagala, and Jim Scoville of the University of Minnesota, Joe Ullman and Terry Shimp of the University of South Carolina, Roy Adams (McMaster University), Tom Bergmann (University of Wisconsin, Eau Claire), Jim Kuhn (Columbia University), Greg Bamber (Durham University), Joep Bolweg (University of Tilburg), and Allen Ponak (University of Calgary). Extensive comments on the book manuscript were provided by Bob Rosen (University of South Carolina), Charles Greer (Oklahoma State University), Steven Paulson (University of North Florida), Stuart Schmidt (Temple University) and Phil LaPorte (Georgia State University).

Some special thanks are due Don Cullen (Cornell University), editor of *Industrial and Labor Relations Review,* for accepting for publication my critique of the macrolevel strike literature, which is included in this book, and to Ken Rowland (University of Illinois) and Jerry Ferris (Texas A & M University) for including a paper summarizing the theory in their volume, *Research in Personnel and Human Resources Management,* Vol. 3 (1985), published by JAI Press. The permission of *Industrial and Labor Relations Review*, Vol. 37, No. 2 (reprinted by permission, all rights reserved), and JAI Press to reprint portions of these pieces is gratefully acknowledged.

Many of those listed here made substantial contributions to this work. Of course, some of their advice went unheeded. In consequence, the responsibility for the weaknesses and heresies contained in the final product rests solely with the author.

Many people contributed to the production of this manuscript. The Division of Research of the College of Business Administration, University of South Carolina, directed by Dr. Randolph Martin, provided nearly all of the typing. Queen Armstrong, Michele Bergen, Linda Doar, Regina Sandsted, Carmen Santana, Jeannette Strauss, and Franke Taylor did the hard labor of typing with good grace and a high degree of skill. My wife, Janice, has read much of this manuscript to judge its readability and sense. Frances Donnelly also did some of the typing. I thank all of them for their help.

The problem of pronoun gender is one of some difficulty in this book. In the author's opinion, it is necessary to use the term *man* to denote *Homo sapiens.* and the pronouns "he" and "she" in order to both clear and readable. Insofar as the use of pronouns is concerned, *he or she/his or her* are usually used to recognize the necessity to be evenhanded as to sexual referents. The generic *he* and *man* are used only where unavoidable.

I wish the reader at least a small part of the pleasure and challenge in reading this book that the author experienced in writing it.

Hoyt N. Wheeler
Columbia, South Carolina
January 15, 1985

Industrial Conflict

CHAPTER 1

Introduction to a Theory of Industrial Conflict

If we . . . wish to make a theoretical analysis of union behavior, we must operate within a broader frame of reference. . . . What is needed is to break down the walls between the separate disciplines of social science which have hitherto dealt with separate aspects of social behavior. Arthur M. Ross,
Trade Union Wage Policy
In matters of philosophy and science authority has ever been the great opponent of truth. A despotic calm is usually the triumph of error. In the republic of the sciences sedition and even anarchy are beneficial in the long-run to the greatest happiness to the greatest number. W. Stanley Jevons,
Classics of Economic Theory.

Industrial conflict has been one of the central subjects of industrial relations since the inception of the field. Collective worker action has provided high drama, martyrs, and rousing songs. It has provided the spark for social reforms and been a major force in the achievement of industrial justice. It has provoked bloody oppression. It has created major economic, political, and social disturbances. It has served as the instrument of orderly and peaceful dealings between employers and workers. It has been a matter of vital concern to policymakers in all Western nations at one time or another. As one of its lesser results, it has occupied the working lives of several generations of industrial relations scholars who have labored resolutely to penetrate its mysteries.

Although partial answers have been provided to some of the questions to which industrial conflict gives rise, we have not so far succeeded in the development of a theory that is capable of providing a general explanation of the phenomenon. This has not been for lack of trying. Economists, political scientists, sociologists, psychologists, and industrial relationists have all attacked the problem from their various perspectives. Given the number and variety of efforts at explaining and predicting industrial conflict, one would expect a high degree of success. Yet this has not been the case. Microeconomic the-

1

ory, powerful for some purposes, has not been as useful in dealing with important questions about industrial conflict. Marxists, whose class perspective still holds much promise, have not really done much better. Psychologists who have examined the collective action of organizing have achieved some interesting results but have not developed a general explanation. Sociologists and political scientists have mainly directed their attention to other forms of social conflict, perhaps thereby preventing themselves from developing theory that best fits this peculiar form of collective action.

To those familiar with the institution, industrial conflict has always appeared to be a complex, multifaceted, phenomenon that defies simplistic theoretical analysis. Perhaps the institutional scholars of the Wisconsin School best captured and described the various aspects of the labor problem. Because of their detailed knowledge of the incredible complexity of industrial reality, these scholars wisely declined to attempt to capture it in a single, simple theoretical system. Indeed, they often implied that theorizing was of very little use. Yet, inevitably, such scholars as John R. Commons[1] and Selig Perlman[2] tried to generalize about industrial relations. When the institutionalists did attempt to theorize, they tended to try to capture relatively enduring characteristics of institutions, workers, or human beings generally and build theory from that point. Perlman attempted this with his notion of "scarcity consciousness," which, although based only on general historical observation, provided a penetrating insight into the behavior of workers and trade unions. Thorstein Veblen's positing of certain "instincts," such as the instinct of workmanship, was an attempt to grasp the essence of working life.[3] Unfortunately, the psychological and biological knowledge upon which Perlman and Veblen drew was not very far advanced.

The dialectical materialism of Karl Marx provides a powerful and complex structure for theorizing about industrial conflict. The "class angle" of the Marxists has often permitted them to see clearly what others neglect. Yet one of Marx's chief explainers of the "breakdown" and its concommitant industrial conflict, the theory of progressive immiseration, has proved false and has been virtually abandoned by modern Marxists.[4] There remain valuable Marxist ideas regarding the importance of solidarity and class-consciousness, but Marxist theory is left without a clear explanation of why trade unions form and act. It is true, of course, that the provision of such an explanation is not the primary purpose of Marxist theory. It is also true that the depth of Marxist theory has remained unmatched by non-Marxist scholars. Marxism is a complete philosophical system that begins with basic statements about human nature and human society. It does appear that anyone who wishes to explain these industrial relations phenomena must, like Marx, grope for some of the basic springs of human behavior.

One of the difficulties of working in an essentially practical, problem-oriented field such as industrial relations is the necessity of relying upon more basic and scientific disciplines for theory. It has simply not been in our realm to discover new theories of human social behavior, although our ability to do our work is heavily dependent upon the existence of such theories. Until the last decade or so, the more basic scientific disciplines had not provided us with theories of human behavior usable as tools for industrial relations theorizing. Microeconomic theory, with its exclusive focus on the calculative, was virtually the only theoretical base available. Yet it stuck in the craw of those industrial relations scholars who, largely from their own experience, believed it to be fundamentally inadequate to explain the phenomena of interest.

One of the most dramatic developments in the modern history of the knowledge of human beings about ourselves is the solid establishment of grounds for the application to humans of some simple tenets of general biological theory. Beginning with the work of ethologists, such as Konrad Lorenz,[5] a body of knowledge has been building for perhaps twenty years. This work has ranged from the enchanting, but badly flawed, work of Robert Ardrey[6] to the more rigorous sociobiology of Edward O. Wilson.[7] Although hotly besieged by critics, this strain of work has provided a strong link between the hard scientific work of the biologists and the study of human behavior. It has identified, and made a case for, the usefulness for social scientific analysis of some enduring characteristics of the human animal.

We have long had available from economic theory sound and well-tested notions relating to the calculative side of human behavior. What has been lacking has been theory of comparable quality dealing with aspects of human nature that have nothing to do with cost-benefit calculations. Without consideration of this, there is surely little hope of understanding or predicting human behavior. Sociobiology and ethology are of considerable assistance in this regard. Added to the help we can receive from these disciplines, we have the assistance of social psychological frustration-aggression theory in its modern form and other fairly recent advances in psychological knowledge. Also of considerable use is relative deprivation theory, developed by political scientists. Taken together, these theoretical threads from basic disciplines can be woven into a multidisciplinary theory of individual behavior that can serve as a foundation for a theory of industrial conflict. With some assistance from the sociologists and political scientists, who have articulated theories of collective behavior, it is feasible to construct a theory of collective worker action to explain and predict industrial conflict better than existing theories.

A careful review of the most popular current strategies for studying industrial conflict shows that their failures are mainly attributable to the inadequacy of their theoretical groundings. Theories developed by students of social conflict in general have not proved equal to the task of understanding and predicting industrial conflict. The peculiar phenomenon of industrial conflict seems to demand some theory of its own and will probably continue to defy explanation until sound theories about it can be developed. This book is an attempt to create such a theory about industrial conflict as it has traditionally been defined in the industrial relations literature, i.e., strikes, union organizing, and similar worker collective action. The theory is labeled *integrative* because it brings together a number of different approaches into a single conceptual model.

A DEFINITION OF INDUSTRIAL CONFLICT

The term *industrial conflict* is susceptible of many definitions. For the purposes of this theory, it is defined as collective aggressive action by employees in opposition to their employers. This rather traditional definition includes collective action in its most advanced form: employees acting through formal organizations—unions.[8] It also applies to spontaneous collective action. Specifically, it includes: (1) organizing for purposes of collective bargaining; (2) striking, or utilizing a strike substitute to resolve an impasse in collective bargaining, or to organize; and (3) other, generally more spontaneous, collective actions such as wildcat strikes, overtime bans, working to rule, slowdowns, filing numerous grievances, and "sick-outs."[9]

To be more specific about the definition of industrial conflict, it is necessary to define what is meant by the terms *strike* and *organizing*. A strike, as the term is used here, is a collective withholding of labor from an employer by a group of that employer's employees. Organizing refers to collective action by a group of employees that establishes a labor organization, a union. It is considered to take place whenever a group not previously unionized becomes legally and practically able to operate as a union. In the American context this means having at least a majority of the members of the worker group become members or at least supporters of the labor organization. Implicit in this definition is the character of the labor organization in the American context—an organization of employees that has the function of pursuing their work-related interests by dealing with their employer on their behalf. Of course, such an organization ordinarily does other things as well; however, only an organization that has such a character is considered a union.

The traditional definition of industrial conflict as used here obviously does not include all of the conflict that occurs in an industrial setting. It takes a collective bargaining perspective, causing the analysis to be framed in a way that is of greatest interest to students of unions and collective bargaining. It is a theory *about* industrial conflict. It is a theory *of* industrial conflict only in the limited sense in which the term is here defined. What it is labeled is, of course, largely a matter of semantics. What is important to understand is that it refers to collective aggressive action by employees against their employers—organizing, striking, and similar activity. It does not, therefore, deal with political strikes aimed at overturning a government or influencing government policy, which are fairly common outside the United States. It might be possible to structure a theory broad enough to cover these activities of groups of workers. However, the "economic" strike and organizing is more than enough to occupy our attention and sufficiently distinctive to warrant separate treatment.

Another limitation upon the theory imposed by this definition is that it does not attempt to explain aggressive action by employers against workers. It would perhaps be possible to produce a theory of industrial conflict that simultaneously considered both employee and managerial aggression. It might well be a good idea to do so. Perhaps this theory will stimulate such a theory's development. However, it was chosen not to do so in the integrative theory because of the focus implied by its central aim, to understand and predict particular phenomena that are at the heart of the field of industrial relations—strikes and organizing. These are *actions by employees*. The focus upon employee actions does not imply that it is only their behavior, and not that of managers, which leads to industrial conflict. This is not the case. Managerial actions are important influences upon industrial conflict as it is here defined. Indeed, we will find the impact of managerial activity at every stage of the model proposed by the integrative theory.

SUMMARY OF THE THEORY

The integrative theory holds that the occurrence of "industrial conflict" is a highly complex matter. This phenomenon involves aggressive action by employees against their employers, not something employees readily do. It requires a very special set of conditions and dynamics. The theory attempts to delineate these.

The integrative theory starts with the proposition that human behavior is best understood when the nature of human beings is taken into account. It is founded in major part upon the biological notion that human beings have innate predispositions toward particular behaviors. It goes on to hold that tendencies to pursue material resources and social dominance are among these predispositions.

The employment relationship, from which industrial conflict arises, is seen as one of employee acceptance of a subordinate social dominance relationship in exchange for the employer's promise of material rewards for reasonable efforts. Those predispositions that pertain to social dominance and material resources are, therefore, considered to be crucial to our inquiry.

Each employee is believed to constantly pursue social dominance relative to his or her employer, and material resources at work. This pursuit may be accelerated by a gap between the employee's expectations and achievements. This gap can move the employee to a readiness for aggressive action against the employer in one of three ways: through calculating that aggressive action's benefits outweigh its costs; the employer attacking expected levels of these outcomes, or threatening to do so; and, most commonly, when the employee's peaceful action to close an expectations/achievements gap is blocked by the employer. Ordinarily, an expectations/achievements gap is necessary for an employee to pursue these outcomes with sufficient intensity to lead to readiness for aggressive action.

Even if an employee is blocked in a peaceful attempt to close an expectations/achievements gap, readiness for aggressive action against the employer may not result. If the employee does not identify the employer as the agent responsible for the blocking, readiness for aggression against the employer is unlikely. If the employee is overwhelmed with fear of the employer, this fear will be the predominant reaction. If the individual has a personality predisposed to resignation or withdrawal, readiness for aggressive action may not come about.

Given a readiness for aggressive action by an individual employee, there still remains the question of whether the aggressive action will take collective form. The integrative theory speaks to this problem in the following manner. First, it holds that employees already constitute a "group" organized by the employer for the purposes of work. Second, it states that the phenomenon of collective aggressive action by this group is likely to occur where: (1) a substantial proportion of the group's members are individually ready for aggressive action; (2) conditions inhibiting collective aggressive action are absent; and (3) conditions facilitating collective aggressive action are present. The inhibiting conditions are workers' norms that militate against collective aggressive action and fear of punishment for engaging in it. The facilitating conditions can be subsumed under the headings of *love, hope,* and *saliency.* The *love* condition is a positive affective relationship among members of the group which is believed to facilitate their engaging in collective aggressive action. The *hope* condition is employee perceptions of a reasonable prospect of success. The *saliency* condition requires that collective aggressive action be recognized as a possible, and appealing, avenue of action.

THE MODEL

A more formal statement of the theory is provided in the model in Figure 1. The model has two levels: the first pertains to *individual readiness* for action; the second has to do with the occurrence of *collective aggressive action.* The model begins with very general human predispositions. It ends with the occurrence of industrial conflict in a unit of an industrial relations system. It speaks as much to reasons that industrial conflict does not take place as it does to reasons for it taking place. That is, rather than being simply a predictive model that concerns itself only with industrial conflict as an outcome, it is a more general attempt to explain the dynamics of the processes of both conflict and its absence. Consequently, instances in which movement through the model stops short of industrial conflict are of equal interest with those where the ultimate point of industrial conflict is reached.

The model illustrates the theory's complexity, its stages, and its paths to action or inaction. It begins with general human predispositions to pursue material resources and social dominance. These are moderated by the relation between expectations and achievements with respect to these outcomes. The model shows an employee moving to an individual readiness for aggressive action against the employer by one or more of three paths. The simplest path is that of rational calculation by the individual that such action would have

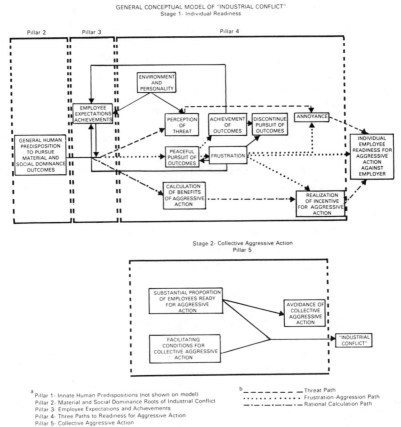

GENERAL CONCEPTUAL MODEL OF "INDUSTRIAL CONFLICT"
Stage 1- Individual Readiness

Stage 2- Collective Aggressive Action
Pillar 5

a Pillar 1- Innate Human Predispositions (not shown on model)
Pillar 2- Material and Social Dominance Roots of Industrial Conflict
Pillar 3- Employee Expectations and Achievements
Pillar 4- Three Paths to Readiness for Aggressive Action
Pillar 5- Collective Aggressive Action

b ――――― Threat Path
············· Frustration-Aggression Path
―·―·―·―·― Rational Calculation Path

Figure 1

more benefits than costs. The other two paths are moderated by the
occurrence of an expectations/achievement gap. This gap derives
from the individual employee's environment, personality, or both. If
the gap is caused by a "threat," the employee may move directly to a
high level of annoyance and become ready for aggressive action
against his or her employer.

The most common effect of the occurrence of an expectations/
achievements gap is to lead the employee to pursue the outcomes
with greater intensity, but still peaceably. This involves the central
path of the model. The first step along this path, peaceful pursuit of
these outcomes, may result in the achievement of expected levels of
these outcomes. If so, the individual is likely to discontinue this pursuit, at least temporarily. If, on the other hand, action by the employer

prevents these achievements from being attained, a frustration will have occurred. This is likely to lead to a readiness for aggressive action against the employer. This may happen directly. It may also come about through the employee feeling a high degree of annoyance or realizing that there is an incentive for aggressive action.

The model shows that frustration can also lead to a discontinuance of the pursuit of these outcomes. The conditions capable of leading to discontinuance, even after frustration, are overwhelming fear of the employer, inability to identify the employer as the frustrator, and an individual propensity for resignation or withdrawal.

The model has a separate stage for collective aggressive action. It depicts industrial conflict as resulting from: (1) a substantial proportion of the group members being individually ready for aggressive action against the employer, and (2) the presence of conditions facilitating aggressive collective action. It can still fail to occur, however, if conditions that inhibit collective aggressive action are present.

The several "pillars" of the integrative theory are superimposed upon the model. Each pillar pertains to the segment of the model indicated in Figure 1. The model both indicates the composition of each pillar and links together the several pillars into a single structure.

THE THEORY'S GUIDING PROPOSITIONS

The integrative theory involves two general propositions regarding the structuring of industrial relations theory. It also has one central substantive proposition.

In structuring industrial conflict theory, every effort should be made to link such theory with the general body of scientific knowledge. There are compelling reasons to believe that much of the weakness of social scientific theorizing can be traced to failure to make such a connection.[10] Fortunately, making this connection has recently been made possible by developments in the fields of biology and ethology, which are the most proximate bodies of scientific knowledge. Biology and ethology have a bedrock theoretical proposition, natural selection, to which members of those disciplines hold with confidence and which can be linked, in turn, to physics and chemistry.[11] The same cannot be said for even what is said to be the most rigorous of the social sciences, economics.[12]

The second structuring proposition is that theory in industrial relations needs to be highly eclectic, at least at the outset. Both the complexity of the phenomena and our experience with unidisciplinary research argue strongly for this conclusion.[13] Furthermore, it becomes rather difficult to justify the existence of an interdisciplinary field called industrial relations unless that field can produce theory that is somehow different from, and more useful than, the theories of the separate traditional disciplines.

The theory contains at least one fundamental substantive proposition that is admittedly rather controversial—that industrial conflict involves aggressive action. By this is meant action that is aimed at harm to another, or his interests or goals.[14] In a sense, this flows naturally from the definition of industrial conflict as involving the action of employees in opposition to their employers. Very importantly, this argument is an assertion that this conflict can be most usefully seen as highly emotional, not merely as an exercise in cool and deliberate decision-making. Although this does not mean that industrial conflict is to be understood as entirely nonrational, it argues for an emotive content quite different from that of a mere market transaction.

THE FIVE PILLARS OF THE INTEGRATIVE THEORY

The integrative theory can be visualized as being founded upon five conceptual pillars (see Figure 1) and linked together by the model. Each of these must be sound in order for the theory to stand. All of the pillars of the integrative theory are somewhat controversial; they have all been subjected to thorough-going attack within the disciplines from which they are derived. One consequence of this is that is is necessary to discuss the pros and cons of each in some detail in order to justify a choice of one, or a blending of several, contending views in a particular discipline. This is a task that requires one to deal in some depth with the disciplines of others and to choose among competing schools of thought. However, it is hoped that so long as one obeys Alfred Adler's injunction not to indulge in "too much presumption and pride" in building theory, and gives each approach its due, a plausible set of ideas can be obtained without too much offense to the denizens of the disciplinary territories.[15]

The five conceptual pillars of the integrative theory are: (1) the existence of innate human predispositions; (2) employee predispositions to pursue material and social dominance outcomes at work (the "roots" of industrial conflict); (3) expectations/achievements as a moderator of the pursuit of material and social dominance outcomes by workers; (4) the three paths to individual readiness for aggressive action against an employer; and, (5) facilitating and inhibiting conditions for collective aggressive action against an employer. This is an attempt to construct a theory of industrial conflict on the basis of these elements drawn from economic, social-psychological, biological, ethological, political, sociological, and industrial relations theory.

The First Pillar—Innate Human Predispositions

All theories involving human social behavior are based on some model of humankind, whether explicit or implicit. The model added by the integrative theory is biological man. This is man as a human animal who has certain enduring capabilities, wants, and needs. These characteristics of human nature are determined by the heavy hand of natural selection. They influence, but do not mechanically determine, his behavior. Among them are propensities to calculate advantage and to learn from experience. They include "whisperings within" which make certain behaviors—such as obtaining material resources, dominating others, and engaging in aggressive activity— naturally "sweet."[16]

The integrative theory requires a biological model of man. Without it, there is no force to propel employees through important paths of the model. Although economic man, who calculates his advantage and pursues it, is sufficient for the rational calculation path to readiness for aggressive action, this is not the case with the other paths. These paths propose both a propensity to pursue certain outcomes, and innate patterns of response to contingencies that arise regarding achievement of those outcomes. This is fundamentally different from a purely utilitarian dynamic. It is not dependent upon any presumed pleasure/pain calculus, but only upon observed regularities of behavior that can be demonstrated to be of evolutionary origin.

The origins of the biological model of humankind lie in the last century with the work of Charles Darwin and Herbert Spencer. Darwin, in a lifetime of patient investigation, provided the scientific foundation. In 1895 his classic *The Origin of Species* rocked the world with its theory of evolution. The heart of this theory is the theory of natural selection. He summarized as follows:

> Owing to this struggle for life any variance, however slight and from whatever cause providing if it be in any degree profitable to an individual of any species, in its infinitely complex relations to other organic beings and to external nature will generally be inherited by its offspring.[17]

This proposition is the basic underpinning of the modern science of biology.

The work of Herbert Spencer, on the other hand, is a prime example of a good idea (natural selection) gone wrong. Spencer's "Social Darwinism," actually preceded Darwin's work. Although its logic is somewhat similar to Darwin's and it adopts a biological view, the conclusions are more ethical than scientific. Spencer believed in the naturalness and "rightness" of systems in which only the fittest survive. From this he concluded that the weeding out of the poor and weak in human societies is a good thing, as it improves the race.[18]

Beginning in the early 1960s the biological concept began to re-emerge from the outer darkness to which it had been consigned because of the misuse by the Social Darwinists, rapacious capitalists, and advocates of racial purity. This was a result of the efforts of a group of scientists and writers, most of whom are biologists, working in the field of ethology, the "naturalistic study of whole patterns of animal behavior."[19]

The ethologists believe that humans are animals and can only be understood when considered as such. They argue that the complete human is one of instinct as well as of rationality. They draw parallels to the behavior of other related animals to throw light on human behavior. This approach has been defended by Desmond Morris in his book, *The Naked Ape*.[20]

Perhaps the most persuasive of the ethologists is Irenaus Eibl-Eibesfeldt. In his book, *Love and Hate*, Eibl maintains that physical structures are the ultimate source of behavior patterns.[21] On the basis of the existence of common behaviors across many human societies, he concludes that many human behaviors are innate. His evidence is impressive.

Edward O. Wilson's recent work on sociobiology has given additional impetus to the biological view.[22] At the core of sociobiology is the same proposition propounded by the ethologists—that human behavior is strongly influenced by inherited predispositions. Wilson's greater scientific rigor gives his argument somewhat more weight than that of the ethologists. He argues persuasively that *there is such a thing as human nature*. Although human nature is uneven and complex, it is "just one hodge-podge out of many conceivable."[23] We share much of this nature with Old World monkeys and apes. It is inconceivable that we would be socialized into the repertoires of behavior of other taxonomic groups such as fishes, birds, antelopes, or rodents. This would "run counter to deep emotional response and have no chance of persisting through as much as a single generation."[24] Whatever one believes about some of Wilson's more heroic conclusions in his highly controversial work on sociobiology, even some of his critics seem to accept this fundamental argument.[25] However, some distinguished critics, such as Ashley Montagu, have challenged the very notion of significant genetic influences on behavior.[26]

In what has been termed the "Sociobiology Debate" the discussions have tended to involve "rival fatalisms" regarding competing social and genetic explanations for human behavior. A British moral philosopher, Mary Midgley, has criticized this debate:

> People have been strangely determined to take genetic and social explanations as alternatives instead of using them to complete each other. Combining them without talking nonsense is therefore by now fearfully hard work. But there is no future in refusing to try.[27]

Midgley sees human behavior as deriving from calculations of instrumentality, social learning, and human nature. She makes the case for the importance of human nature:

> To effect any change, we have to understand the permanent. An obvious instance is the set of currently popular suggestions that marriage, or "the family" in the abstract, is a dispensable institution, a mere passing whim of certain cultures, or that there is really no maternal instinct, just cultural conditioning by the women's magazines. Or that we should behave in exactly the same manner to women and men. Or of course, that it is only bad education which makes us aggressive. All this, I think, is just spitting against the wind. We can vary enormously the forms these things take and our own individual part in them. We can no more get rid of them than we can grow wings and tusks. Nor is there any good reason why we should want to.[28]

Midgley argues that one of the great problems with thought in this area is inadequate conceptualization of the term *instinct*. She argues that instinct is nothing mysterious, but is simply a "disposition, a set of causal properties."[29] She makes the very useful distinction between "closed" and "open" instincts. Those that are closed are behavior patterns gentically determined in every detail. An example of this is the bee's honey dance. Open instincts, on the other hand, are "programs with a gap." In the case of open instincts, "parts of the behavior pattern are innately determined, but others are left to be filled in by experience."[30] It is this latter type of instinct that characterizes the behavior of all higher animals, including humans. Such an instinct influences behavior but does not determine it.

This extensive literature, which is only briefly summarized here, leads one to conclude that there *is* such a thing as human nature and that this nature influences our behavior. We do mind the "whisperings within." We do have certain identifiable predispositions that influence our behavior. Having concluded this, the task of theorizing about human behavior in industrial conflict leads one to next inquire about the indentity of those predispositions relevant to this phenomenon.

The Second Pillar—Material and Social Dominance Roots of Industrial Conflict

The second pillar of the integrative theory is the proposition that there are innate predispositions on the part of employees to pursue social dominance and material resources at work. These are viewed as the "roots" of industrial conflict. This involves two arguments: (1) that such predispositions exist, and (2) that they are pursued at work.

The second of these arguments is based on the view that, when one applies Occam's razor to lay bare the core of the industrial relationship, one finds an exchange of autonomy for pay. According to John R. Commons, when a worker accepts employment, "what he sells when he sells his labor is his *willingness* to use his faculties according to a purpose that has been pointed out to him. He sells his promise to obey commands."[31] The exchange that the employee makes is, then, his agreement to be on the subordinate end of a social dominance relationship in return for a promise of material rewards. This is clearly an accurate description of the legal relation between employer and employee.[32] If social dominance and material outcomes are at the heart of the employment relationship, one would expect predispositions regarding them to be central to conflicts arising from that relationship.

The first argument, that such predispositions exist, is more complicated. Even an introduction to it requires us to consider each of these two potential roots of industrial conflict in some depth.

Material Resources

Viewed from a biological perspective, the predisposition to pursue material resources is one of the easiest predispositions to justify. Animals not inclined to obtain the physical requirements for life are not likely to last long enough to pass on their genes to future generations.

Conventional economic theory, although speaking in different terms, in effect also holds that a predisposition to pursue material resources exists. This takes the form of arguments supporting the notion of "economic man."

"Economic man," and indeed, modern neoclassical economic thought, is based upon theories of utility developed by Jeremy Bentham and his many disciples. Bentham believed that "nature has placed mankind under the governance of two sovereign masters, pain and pleasure."[33] Humans seek to achieve pleasure and avoid pain.[34] This view of human nature has been much criticized and does appear to have its problems when expressed in such general terms.[35]

A more modest, limited, view of economic man says simply, as suggested by Senior's "pure" theory: "Every man desires to obtain additional wealth with as little sacrifice as possible."[36] Alfred Marshall has argued that it is the focus on pay as the "material reward for work" that has allowed economics "far to outrun every other branch of the study of man."[37] Joseph Schumpeter has argued that the utilitarians created "the shallowest of all conceivable philosophies of life."[38] Yet he was of the opinion that, unlike general utility theory, the simple notion that human beings pursue wealth at minimum cost forms a sound basis for economic theory.[39]

The integrative theory adopts the view of Schumpeter and others that people at work seek pay without painful effort. Whether broader statements of utility theory are valid or not, this more limited proposition seems sound and is consistent with natural selection theory.

Social Dominance

Support for the proposition that human beings are predisposed to pursue social dominance in organizations comes from a variety of sources. Its primary justification here is biological/ethological. However, psychology, sociology, and industrial relations all lend some support to it.

Ethologists and sociobiologists make a solid case for the following conclusions: (1) human beings have an innate predisposition to establish hierarchies of social dominance relations; (2) this tendency is one of considerable durability; (3) social dominance relations follow certain recognizable patterns, both in human beings and in our closest animal relatives; and (4) the social dominance relationship is a dynamic one, involving contradictory tendencies toward dominance and subordinance, and "status tension."

Both Nobel laureat Konrad Lorenz and Desmond Morris agree that the establishment of social dominance systems is innate and common among social animals. According to Lorenz, "a principle of organization without which a more advanced social life cannot develop in higher vertebrates is the so-called ranking order."[40]

According to Morris, "in any organized group of mammals, no matter how cooperative there is always a struggle for social dominance. As he pursues this struggle, each adult individual acquires a particular social rank, giving him his position, or status, in the group hierarchy."[41] Morris describes the hierarchy system as something with which human beings are already "loaded" as it is "the basic way of primate life."[42]

George Maclay and Humphry Knipe argue convincingly that hierarchies are not mere cultural inventions of human beings but are, rather, instinctual. Despite the human development of a combination of modifiable instincts and cultural adaptations to the extent of no other animal type, the "instinctive blueprint" nevertheless remains. This "instinctive legacy" includes a predisposition for both dominant and subordinate roles.[43]

According to Maclay and Knipe there are many forms of dominance-signalling that help maintain hierarchies. They believe that there is a "high dominance swagger or strut" that exists in a number of species. An upright aristocratic, or military, bearing also signals dominance. In addition, lower power personalities tend to find it difficult to assume a high power stance. Maclay and Knipe agree with Desmond Morris that relaxed and deliberate body movements are signals of dominance. This is also shown through the display of "face." Dominants tend to be at the center of attention, defining the social situations in which they are involved. This is true of humans as well as of our animal cousins.[44]

As a result of individuals in a social hierarchy struggling for status improvement there is a constant state of what Desmond Morris has called "status tension."[45] As Lorenz notes, the fact that all social animals are "status seekers" leads them into situations of rather high tension, particularly with respect to individuals who hold immediately adjoining positions in the status hierarchy.[46] Although the establishment of a dominance hierarchy may reduce overall aggression, the potential for aggression is still present.[47]

Psychologists have approached the phenomenon of social dominance in several different ways. Freud early recognized a "desire for freedom" springing from the remains of the original personality "untamed by civilization."[48] More recently, Jack W. Brehm has created a "theory of psychological reactance," contending that a person deprived of freedom will aggressively respond to restore it.[49]

The other side of the social dominance coin is the ability to restrict the freedom of others. Alfred Adler spoke convincingly of a "tendency toward domination and superiority," and for a time placed this at the

core of his psychoanalytical theory.[50] Abraham H. Maslow found
that individuals have, and differ with respect to, "dominance-feeling."[51] Similarly, David C. McClelland has concluded that human beings have a need for power (n Power) and have individual differences
as to this need.[52] A predisposition for subordination has also been
documented by psychologists. This is shown most dramatically in
the work of Stanley Milgram, who found his subjects quite willing to
inflict pain on others when ordered to do so.[53] Milgram concluded
that there is a "drive, tendency or inhibition" that leads to obedience.[54]

Sociologists have long studied the pervasiveness and the dynamics of hierarchy in human organizations. Robert A. Dahl and Charles
E. Lindblom, writing in the 1950s, noted that the "vital and ubiquitous role of hierarchial processes" constituted "one of the most striking features of Western society.[55] Amitai Etzoni has argued that
"compliance is universal, existing in all social units. . . . it is a central
element of organizational structure."[56] According to Daniel Katz
and Robert L. Kahn, "there is no more pervasive law of organization
than that the occupants of certain roles shall respond to and obey
certain kinds of requests from the occupants of certain other
roles."[57] David J. Hickson and Arthur F. McCullough have written
that it is hierarchy that makes an organization.[58]

There is rather broad agreement among sociologists as to what
constitutes "authority," which is a central concept in their writings
on organizational hierarchies. Typical is Allen W. Lerner's definition
of authority. According to Lerner authority is a special case of power.
It is present where the subordination of one's own preferences to
those of another is deemed *justified* in situations that are acceptable
under the "organizational social contract."[59] Its exercise involves
the element of command.[60] Authority creates a "zone of indifference"
or an "area of acceptance" within which commands will be obeyed
without question.[61] Outside of this zone, or area, assertions of power
are seen by the subordinate as being illegitimate.

According to Ralf Dahrendorf, every large organization has a
dominant class and a subordinate class. The dominant class is entrusted with the right to utilize coercion in controlling members of
the subordinate class.[62] This right, which is the same thing as "authority," is believed by Dahrendorf to be "a universal element of social structure."[63]

Industrial relations scholars have noted both the stabilizing and
destabilizing effects of social dominance hierarchies within organizations. Reinhard Bendix has argued that hierarchical systems have

operated to justify control by managers.[64] Both Herbert Marcuse and William Gamson have written of the ability of the hierarchical authority system to contain rebellion against domination.[65] On the other hand, Jack Barbash has spoken of the tensions generated by authority that may lead to industrial conflict.[66] A similar argument has been made by William F. Whyte.[67] The jurist Louis Brandeis has attributed industrial conflict to "industrial absolutism."[68]

If one is convinced that innate human predispositions to pursue social dominance exist, that they operate at work, and that they have the potential to be associated with industrial conflict, it still remains to inquire as to the conditions under which it is probable that conflict will occur.

The Third Pillar—Employee Expectations and Achievements

The integrative theory holds that a gap between an employee's expectations and achievements as to social dominance or material resources is highly likely to ready him or her for aggressive action. This condition accelerates the pursuit of those outcomes to a sufficient degree to provoke readiness for conflict either by the frustration-aggression or threat path. Of course, this reasoning does not apply to the rational calculation path of the theory, which requires only a favorable cost-benefit ratio.

Industrial relations scholars writing about industrial conflict have occasionally focused on the phenomenon of employee expectations. Jack Barbash, writing in 1970, cited as one of the major forces underlying the labor unrest in the mid-1960s "the rising expectations of workers stimulated by the long expansion."[69] W. Willard Wirtz also attributed the militancy of the mid-1960s to soaring expectations of workers.[70] It is, however, political scientists who have made the most extensive use of the concept of an expectations/achievements gap to explain social conflict. Although their relative deprivation theory has been used chiefly to explain violent revolution, the genesis of one of its main branches was in the study of an instance of industrial conflict. According to James Chowning Davies, one of the fathers of relative deprivation theory, his well-known "J-curve" theory "popped out of the data, into my head, and onto the pages of notes I was making" as he studied the Pullman strike.[71]

Davies first pronounced his version of relative deprivation theory in 1962.[72] As he later expressed it, his "J-curve" theory says, ". . . when a relatively long period of steady rise in what people want and what people get is followed by a short period of sharp reversal, during which a gap suddenly widens between what people want and what they get, the likelihood of revolution increases sharply."[73]

The work of Ted Robert Gurr, especially his book *Why Men Rebel* (1970), constitutes a major contribution to relative deprivation theory.[74] One of Gurr's earlier writings on this subject states succinctly his basic theoretical proposition: that relative deprivation, a psychological variable, is the "basic precondition" for civil strife. Gurr defines relative deprivation as a discrepancy between "value expectations" and "value capabilities." Value expectations are defined as those goods and conditions of life to which individuals believe themselves to be *justifiably entitled.* Value capabilities are those goods and conditions that they believe they are able to get and keep. Gurr argues that the "underlying causal mechanism" of collective violence is that anger is the innate response when deprivation is perceived. Aggression is "an inherently satisfying response" to that anger.[75] Gurr concludes: "Discontent arising from the perception of relative deprivation is the basic, instigating condition for participants in collective violence."[76]

Relative deprivation has only been moderately successful in testing. Some studies have supported it;[77] others have shown mixed support for its hypotheses.[78] It has been subjected to vigorous attack,[79] to which its proponents have responded rather effectively.[80] Where the measure of expectations has conformed closely to Gurr's definition, that is, those outcomes to which a person believes herself to be *justly entitled,* the results have been more favorable.[81]

A review of the relative deprivation literature reveals two major problems with these studies. The first is poor measures. Almost universally they utilize measures of doubtful construct validity, not convincing as measures of what they claim to reflect.[82] This is especially true in the case of direct measures of perceptions regarding deprivation and participation in collective violence. This was less of a problem in some of the earlier literature, such as the work of Davies in which objective data were plausibly connected to these constructs. The second problem is a failure to follow frustration-aggression theory in an important respect. This involves the mistaken use of the mere existence of an expectations/achievements gap as evidence of frustration. Frustration-aggression theory clearly holds that frustration is the blocking of an ongoing response sequence. This requires, in this setting, that the individual be *acting to close* the gap and experiencing a blocking in that effort. Frustration-aggression theory does not predict aggression under the conditions posited by the relative deprivation theorists.

There is an extensive literature on the sources of expectations. These sources are of two main types: personality-related and environmental. By environmental is meant sources outside the individual personality. These include reference to an individual's perceptions of the experience of others, an individual's perceptions of his or her own experience, and abstract ideals.

A number of scholars argue for the influence of perceptions with respect to the experience of others. This may be framed in terms of reference groups,[83] achievements of ancestors,[84] "reference standards,"[85] comparison persons,[86] other persons,[87] generalized others,[88] or comparable others.[89] Reference to one's own experience has been simply so identified,[90] and given the label of "status inconsistency."[91] Reference to an abstract ideal may come about through the statements of a leader,[92] or tradition.[93]

There is a much more limited body of literature with respect to personality-related sources of expectations. This literature is, however, useful in considering the saliency and level of expectations. As to saliency, one might look to the expectancy theory literature.[94] Those outcomes that are highly "valent," attractive, to an employee would more likely receive his or her attention. There is some evidence in the literature that there may be systematic differences between white-collar workers and blue-collar workers as to which outcomes they see as highly valent.[95] Research testing Abraham Maslow's "need hierarchy" theory can be read as suggesting that needs such as social dominance only come to motivate behavior when economic needs are satisfied.[96]

There may be some personality-related differences with respect to the level of expectations for social dominance. McClelland's work suggests that a person with high n Power would expect a high degree of social dominance.[97] A person high in "dominance-feeling," in Abraham Maslow's terms, would have high social dominance expectations.[98] But a person with an "authoritarian personality" who is placed in a subordinate position may have low social dominance expectations.[99]

Success or failure in achieving expectations may affect future expectations. Frank Parkin has argued that the "disprivileged" in society tend to adjust their expectations to a modest level on the basis of their experience.[100] George Caspar Homans argues that we eventually cease to compare ourselves to others if the comparison remains unfavorable.[101] Peter Blau argues, however, that success may cause an increase in expectations.[102]

Achievements form the other face of the expectations/ achievements gap and can be affected by a number of factors either internal or external to the work organization. They operate through the actions of management as it puts into operation particular terms and conditions of employment. The integrative theory does not speak to the determinants of worker achievements but takes them as given, a limitation on the theory that should be recognized.

Given that an expectations/achievements gap leaves an employee poised on the brink of readiness to take aggressive action against his or her employer, actual readiness depends on following one or more of the paths that constitute the next pillar of the theory.

The Fourth Pillar—The Three Paths to Readiness for Aggressive Action

The integrative theory holds that a readiness for aggressive action can be arrived at through one or more of three paths: frustration-aggression, threat, and rational calculation. Individuals in the same group may move along different paths but nevertheless arrive at a readiness for aggressive action at about the same time. To posit three paths to readiness for aggression rather than one exclusive path is to recognize the legitimacy, but not the claim for exclusiveness, of several possible explanations for industrial conflict. It is reasonably clear from the very extensive literature on aggression that readiness for aggressive action can come about in a number of ways. James T. Tedeschi recognized at least two major classes of aggressive responses: "(a) instrumental aggression, in which the occurrence of harm or injury to another individual is only incidental to the actor's goal of achieving some other goal; and (b) angry aggression, in which the only object of the actor's response is to inflict injury on another person or object."[103]

The frustration-aggression and threat paths of the integrative theory might thus be categorized as "angry aggression" and the rational calculation path as "instrumental aggression." However, it is believed that the frustration-aggression, and perhaps the threat, paths are rather a *blending* of the angry and the instrumental. Frustration-aggression under Leonard Berkowitz's formulation of it involves anger, but anger that is chiefly directed at the frustrator who has blocked the ongoing pursuit of a goal. The motivation to aggress includes that of removing the blockage. This seems to be a mix of both instrumental and noninstrumental aggression. The rational calculation path is simpler. It is purely instrumental.

The frustration-aggression and threat paths are based on the notion that there are innate behavioral structures connected with aggression. This is consistent with some early theories of aggression. Sigmund Freud, for example, argued that *"Homo homini lupus* (Man is a wolf to man)."[104] Konrad Lorenz agrees and believes that the instinct for aggression once served a valuable evolutionary function.[105] More recent statements of the view that aggressive mechanisms are innate have been made by Irenaus Eibl-Eibesfeldt,[106] Edward O. Wilson,[107] and Mary Midgley.[108] Wilson likens the instinct for aggression to "a pre-existing mix of chemicals ready to be transformed by specific catalysts that are added, heated, and stirred at some later time."[109] This view is at odds with the extreme environmentalist position taken by social psychologists such as Albert Bandura. Bandura argues that "except for elementary reflexes, people are not equipped with inborn repertories of behavior."[110]

The Frustration-Aggression Path

It is the frustration-aggression path of the model that is believed to provide the most common and powerful explanation of industrial conflict. The frustration-aggression pattern is the one that, to use James C. Davies' words, seems to pop out of the data. Although frustration-aggression theory is generally highly controversial, it is believed that the manner in which it is used in the integrative theory is not.

The version of frustration-aggression theory utilized by the integrative theory is that which has been stated by Leonard Berkowitz.[111] According to Berkowitz, if a person is instigated to enter into a response sequence aimed at some goal and that response sequence is interfered with, a readiness for aggression is likely to result. The interference, or blocking, is termed a frustration. Anger (readiness for aggression) results, and aggression is likely to occur if certain cues, such as identifying the frustrator, are present. The drive to aggress may be overwhelmed by fear. It may be inhibited by the anticipation of punishment or by the person's belief that the aggressive act will violate his own standards of conduct.

It is hardly a new idea to apply frustration-aggression theory to industrial conflict. Indeed, the original statement of frustration-aggression theory in 1939 by the "Yale group" led by Dollard contained the following statement: "The frustrated worker, doomed to monotony and insecurity, tends to grow more sympathetic to unions, not only in order *to raise his wages and shorten his hours of work, but also as a means of expressing aggression* against the employer."[112] This dual aspect of worker collective aggressive action is what the integrative theory proposes. Dollard and his group also considered strikes an expression of aggression.[113]

A bit later, in 1946, Norman R. F. Maier explained strikes in terms of frustrated persons forming social movements and engaging in nonspecific aggressive activity.[114] Arthur Kornhauser, writing in his classic volume on industrial conflict in 1954, saw the inability of individuals to fulfill their wants as leading to "unrest, dissatisfaction, emotional irritability and a striking about for some way out, for some means to break through or to withdraw from the struggle."[115] According to Kornhauser: "The extent to which these conditions of frustration are prevalent in different groups in present-day industry will go far in determining the occurrence of industrial conflict."[116]

Ross Stagner and Hjalmar Rosen, writing in 1965, proposed a theory of industrial conflict based upon the frustration-aggression hypothesis. They were concerned chiefly with the physical violence involved in industrial conflict. Like those who had gone before them, they spoke in terms of frustrated persons "lashing out" in a general, irrational fashion because they were frustrated.[117]

Although frustration-aggression theory has had only mixed results in the testing, there is a core of it which has performed rather well. Only its most severe critics would argue that frustration never leads to aggression.[118] Furthermore, there is fairly strong evidence that frustration that is perceived by a person to be illegitimate, arbitrary, or unjustified will probably produce aggression.[119] Robert A. Baron and Donn Byrne, who are generally strong critics of frustration-aggression theory, concede that intense frustration perceived as illegitimate or arbitrary is likely to lead to aggression.[120] The frustration-aggression path of the integrative theory deals with *illegitimate* frustration. This is because it posits a blocking of *expected* levels of achievements as leading to aggression and defines expected levels as those to which persons believe themselves *justly entitled.* Therefore, it would seem to be using frustration-aggression theory in a way with which even many of its critics could not reasonably take exception.

Frustration-aggression theory provides for contingencies that may prevent aggressive action from occurring, even where a frustration has occurred. It suggests that frustration will not lead to aggression if the person is overwhelmed by fear. This would make fear rather than anger the predominant response to frustration.[121] It will also fail to lead to a readiness to aggress against the frustrator if the individual is unable to identify the frustrator with the frustration.[122]

The integrative theory adds the further possibility that certain individuals may, as suggested by social learning theorists, simply resign themselves to the frustration.[123] In the work setting there is the further possibility of exit.[124] These reasons for frustration failing to lead to readiness for aggressive action are incorporated into the integrative theory's model in the branch of the model which shows discontinuance of pursuit of outcomes rather than readiness for aggressive action. Frustration-aggression theory also holds that aggressive action may be inhibited by certain conditions. This notion will be discussed in a later section.

The Threat Path

The threat path of the model is relatively uncontroversial. Social psychologists are generally in agreement with the proposition that attack on a person or his interests, or a threat of such an attack, has a high probability of producing aggression.[125] Albert Bandura explains this within a reinforcement framework, arguing that aggression in response to threats in the past has likely been rewarded by a cessation of the threats.[126] Dolf Zillman believes that an evolved "fight-flight" response is involved.[127] Zillman sees "annoyance motivated hostility and aggression" as arising from threat as well as from other causes.[128] Threat can give rise to high levels of annoyance, under which the person strikes out unthinkingly, moving directly from the threat to a readiness for aggression. At this high level of arousal, peaceable means of ending the threat are not considered.

The threat path is included in the integrative theory to deal with open and severe "attacks," or threats of attack, on expected levels of outcomes. When this occurs, as suggested by Zillman, arousal may be so high that an individual does not seek a peaceful solution. Although it may be relatively rare for this extreme situation to exist, it is nevertheless present in important instances of industrial conflict.

The Rational Calculation Path

The rational calculation path is also relatively uncontroversial. It is supported by both economic theory and social-psychological/ social learning theory. Indeed, it is an interesting conjunction between the two.

Neoclassical economic theory argues for action on the basis of rational calculation of advantage.[129] Under this theory humans act, aggressively or otherwise, in such a way as to achieve resources where the costs are not too great. Social psychologists have reached the same conclusion. Baron and Byrne essentially adopt this view.[130]

Albert Bandura, a leading social learning theorist, argues that human beings learn the expected consequences of behavior and perform those acts, including aggressive acts, best calculated to maximize pleasure and minimize pain.[131] This is clearly an instrumental view of aggression.

The threat path posits a readiness for aggression at an exceptionally high level of arousal. The rational calculation path operates at an exceptionally low level of arousal. Indeed, it depends not at all on powerful emotive forces. It, like the threat path, appears to be rare relative to the middle path of frustration-aggression. Nevertheless, it is important in accounting for those few instances of organizing and striking that are entirely calculated. It should be noted that it shares with the threat path the characteristic of going rather directly to a readiness for aggressive action.

Once readiness for aggressive action against the employer is achieved by some workers, the individual action stage of the model has done its work. What remains is the difficult task of identifying the conditions under which this readiness will lead to *collective* aggressive action against the employer.

The Fifth Pillar—Collective Aggressive Action

Industrial conflict, as it is here defined, is a collective phenomenon and, as such, must be explained at the level of collective action. The integrative theory attempts to do so by holding that the probability of industrial conflict is high when: (1) a substantial proportion of the members of a group of employees is ready for aggressive action against their employer; (2) conditions inhibiting collective aggressive action against the employer are absent; and, (3) the special "hothouse" facilitating conditions of love, hope, and saliency are present.

The notion of inhibiting conditions is drawn from frustration-aggression theory. Frustration-aggression theory holds that aggressive action will not take place if the person anticipates punishment as a result of the action or believes that the action will violate his or her accepted norms. Accordingly, the integrative theory states that the presence of a perception that punishment will occur or the holding of norms that would be violated by collective aggressive action against the employer decrease the probability of industrial conflict.

The "hothouse" facilitating conditions that encourage the development of the rare organism known as industrial conflict are drawn from a variety of literatures. These literatures range from the group psychology writings of Sigmund Freud to the modern sociological literature on collective behavior. Freud argues that groups are held together by the *love* of the members for one another. Individuals give up their distinctiveness because of their need for being in harmony with other group members.[132] There are ties between "fellow-workers which prolong and solidify the relation between them, to a point beyond what is merely profitable."[133] According to Freud, "love alone acts as the civilizing factor in the sense that it brings a change from egoism to altruism."[134]

Karl Marx and Friederich Engels, in the manifesto of the Communist party, speak of the mechanisms for collective worker action.[135] One of their most compelling points is the argument that it is the capitalists who, largely by their creation of the factory, bring into being the human group that ultimately destroys them. This is an important way in which the "bourgeoisie . . . produces . . . its own gravediggers."[136] Workers organized for factory production have common interests, work together, and have ready means of communication.

Among writers on industrial relations, Clark Kerr and Abraham Siegel have probably made the greatest contribution to our understanding of collective employee action.[137] In their 1954 study they identified certain industries that were "strike prone." The main characteristic of these industries was that their workers formed an "isolated mass." Their workers were highly cohesive and had the same grievances against the same persons at about the same time.[138] These industries also tended to have "bad" employers who "dominate their employees unduly."[139]

Ralf Dahrendorf has theorized regarding the "conditions of organization."[140] According to him, the *technical* conditions necessary for the formulation of an organized group are "founders" and a "charter," or set of ideas provided either by a leader or an ideology.[141] A *political* condition is the state allowing the group to exist. The necessary *social* condition is communication among group members.[142]

In the early 1960s a body of literature began to develop which came to be known as the collective behavior literature. It has two main branches: the first, in historical terms, is labelled the "classic" approach; the second is "resource mobilization theory."

Neil Smelser is one of the fathers of classic collective behavior thought. Smelser theorizes that collective behavior only takes place when there is a "strain" that disturbs the existing social equilibrium. This strain, at least for a "norm-oriented" movement such as a labor union, involves the occurrence of deprivation. Deprivation becomes and actual social conditions. Indeed, strains are themselves "discrepancies between social conditions and social expectations."[143]

Smelser posits a number of conditions other than strain that are necessary for the occurrence of collective behavior. Several of these he places under the heading of "structural conduciveness." For a norm-oriented movement such as a labor union, the first and most important condition of structural conduciveness "concerns the possibility for demanding modifications of norms *without simultaneously appearing to demand a more fundamental modification of values.*"[144] In addition, structural conduciveness requires that avenues for agitation be open, that there be an unavailability of other channels for expressing dissatisfaction, and that there be a possibility of communication.[145] Another condition for collective behavior is a "generalized belief" in which the "strain" is exaggerated and seen to be of immediate importance. Also required is "mobilization" which can occur either by a dramatic event or the actions of a leader.[146]

Resource mobilization theory holds that conditions of exploitation are ever-present because of established economic relations. This exploitation is held to be itself sufficient to account for any discontent or strain necessary to give rise to collective behavior. Human beings are seen as constantly willing to act to try to relieve conditions of exploitation. Resource mobilization theorists elieve that most instances of collective behavior can be explained by referring to the resources made newly available to exploited groups. It is these resources that permit them to realize long-standing desires to end their exploitation. Although differing fundamentally from the classical view in major respects, research mobilization theory agrees with the usefulness of setting out a number of facilitating conditions that make collective behavior possible.

One of the clearest statements of resource mobilization theory was made by J. Craig Jenkins and Charles Perrow in a study published in 1977.[147] From their analysis of the organizing of farm workers in the 1960s, they concluded: "What increases, and gives rise to insurgency, is the amount of social resources available to unorganized groups, making it possible to launch an organized demand for change."[148] Jenkins and Perrow argue that "discontent is ever-present for deprived groups, but collective action is rarely a viable option because of lack of resources and the threat of repression."[149]

Another important statement of resource mobilization theory appears in an article written by Mayer N. Zald and Michael Berger in

1978.[150] Zald and Berger posit a set of determinants of mass movements in organizations. These determinants pertain to "size, homogeneity, vertical segmentation, exit option, and associational density."[151]

Zald and Berger hypothesize that the larger in *size* the subordinate group the more probable organizational mass movements become,[152] and the greater the *homogeneity* the more likely there will
be collective action.[153] As to *vertical segmentation*, they hypothesize
a blocking of channels for grievances, mobility, and communication
and, apparently, a higher probability for collective action, where segmentation is high.[154] With respect to *exit*, the difficulty or costliness
of exit increases the probability of social movements within the organization.[155] As to *associational density*, Zald and Berger hypothesize that a high proportion of organizational participants being
members of intraorganizational associations facilitates mobilization.[156]

Bruce Fireman and William A. Gamson have created a social
group-oriented utility framework for collective action.[157] Fireman
and Gamson argue that individuals act to obtain benefits for a group
with which they feel solidarity: "Solidarity is rooted in the configuration of relationships linking the members of a group to one another.
People may be linked together in a number of ways that generate a
sense of common identity, shared fate, and general commitment to
defend the group."[158] They suggest five factors that form a basis for
an individual having solidarity with a group: ties of friendship and
blood relationship to members of the group; participation with
group members in other associations; support among group members for the general conduct of one another's lives; sharing of the
same set of superordinate and subordinate relations with persons
outside the group; and difficulty of exit from the group.[159]

To our thinking on facilitating conditions should be added one idea
that comes from a separate literature. This is the notion of "instrumentality" used to some effect in the psychologically-based literature on union organizing. DeCotiis and LeLouran and others have
found that one of the determinants of an employee's decision to join
a union is the perception of its instrumentality in removing personal
dissatisfaction.[160] Positive instrumentality estimates can be an important aspect of whether employees hope for a favorable result
from collective action.

It should be noted that the integrative theory does not utilize one
rather well-known theory of collective behavior, the individual ra-

tionality theory of Mancur Olson.[161] Olson is apparently unable to speak helpfully to some of the phenomena with which we are here concerned. His theory logically would result in there being no large labor unions, an obviously inaccurate conclusion.[162]

Drawing upon the above literature, the integrative theory holds that the facilitating conditions for industrial conflict can be conceptualized as *love, hope,* and *saliency.* Although these terms may seem unusually informal for theorizing, they most accurately denote the concepts involved. From the perspective of these conditions, the heart of the matter seems to be having strong positive affects among group members, hope of success, and saliency of collective action as an avenue for this success. These, then, are the "hothouse" conditions for the occurrence of collective aggressive action by employees against their employers.

PLAN OF THE BOOK

The remainder of the book will review the existing literature on industrial conflict, set out the integrative theory, and then apply the theory. Chapter 2 will summarize and critique the literature. Chapters 3 through 7 will discuss in some detail the five pillars of the integrative theory. Chapters 8 and 9 will apply the theory and consider its significance. The material presented in Chapters 1 through 7 has been briefly summarized above.

Chapter 8 consists of an application of the theory to instances of industrial conflict. Hypotheses are generated. A beginning is made at the testing of these hypotheses by viewing them in relation to: (1) the Pullman Strike; (2) a West Virginia mine war; (3) the organization of workers at the Marinette Knitting Mill in Wisconsin; (4) the Memphis sanitation strike; (5) the Charleston (South Carolina) hospital strike; and, (6) the Minnesota Community College strike.

Chapter 9 aims at "making sense" out of industrial conflict in terms of the integrative theory. It involves discussions of both the internal plausibility of the theory and its usefulness in external application. The great upsurges of unionization of the 1930's and 1960's–1970's are considered in the light of the theory. Finally, some unanswered questions about industrial conflict are addressed. These questions relate to the rarity of industrial conflict, differences in union proneness, the occurrence of "irrational" strikes, the intensity of managerial anti-union feelings and the structuring of collective bargaining.

NOTES

[1] John R. Commons, *Legal Foundations of Capitalism* (Madison: University of Wisconsin Press, 1968).

[2] Selig Perlman, *The Theory of the Labor Movement* (New York: Augustus M. Kelly, 1970).

[3] Thorstein Veblen, *The Theory of the Leisure Class: An Economic Study of Institutions* (New York: Modern Library, 1899).

[4] Andre Gorz, *Strategy For Labor* (Boston: Beacon Press, 1967).

[5] Konrad Lorenz, *On Aggression* (New York: Harcourt, Brace & World, 1966).

[6] Robert Ardrey, *African Genesis* (New York: Atheneum Publishers, 1961).

[7] Edward O. Wilson, *Sociobiology* (Cambridge: The Belknap Press, 1980).

[8] Jack Barbash, "The Work Society," mimeographed (Madison: University of Wisconsin, 1971), p. 1.

[9] Alan Fox, "Management's Frame of Reference," in *Collective Bargaining*, ed. Allan Flanders (Baltimore: Penguin Books, 1969), pp. 399–400.

[10] Alexander Rosenberg, *Sociobiology and the Preemption of Social Science* (Baltimore: The Johns Hopkins University Press, 1980), pp. 1–6.

[11] Ibid., pp. 7, 151.

[12] Ibid., p. 129.

[13] Thomas A. Kochan, *Collective Bargaining and Industrial Relations* (Homewood, Ill.: Richard D. Irwin, 1980), pp. 1–2, 507.

[14] Elliot Aronson, *The Social Animal*, 2nd ed. (San Francisco: W.A. Freeman and Co., 1976), p. 146.

[15] Alfred Adler, *Understanding Human Nature* (Greenwich, Conn.: Fawcett Publications, 1927), p. 15.

[16] David Barash, *The Whisperings Within* (New York: Harper & Row, 1979), p. 39.

[17] Charles Darwin, *The Origin of Species* (Baltimore: Penguin Books, 1979), p. 115.

[18] Herbert Spencer, *Social Statics* (London: Chapman & Sons, 1859), pp. 321, 416.

[19] Edward O. Wilson, *Sociobiology*, abgd. ed. (Cambridge: The Belknap Press, 1980), p. 5.

[20] Desmond Morris, *The Naked Ape* (New York: Dell Publishing Co., 1967).

[21] Irenaus Eibl-Eibesfeldt, *Love and Hate*, trans. Geoffrey Strachan (New York: Holt, Rinehart & Winston, 1972), p. 112.

[22] Wilson, *Sociobiology*.

[23] Edward O. Wilson, *On Human Nature* (Cambridge: Harvard University Press, 1978), p. 23.

[24] Ibid., p. 21.

[25] Stephen Jay Gould, "Biological Potential vs. Biological Determinism," in *The Sociobiology Debate*, ed. Arthur S. Caplan (New York: Harper & Row, 1978), p. 344.

[26] Ashley Montagu, *The Nature of Human Aggression* (Oxford: Oxford University Press, 1976), pp. 3–4.

[27] Mary Midgley, *Beast and Man* (New York: The New American Library, 1978), p. 183.

[28] Ibid., p. 326.

[29] Ibid., p. xviii.

[30] Ibid., p. 53.

[31] John R. Commons, *Legal Foundations of Capitalism* (Madison: University of Wisconsin Press, 1968), p. 284.

[32] 66 *CJS, Master and Servant*, 1 (1948); 53 *Am Jur 2d, Master and Servant*, 1 (1970).

[33] Jeremy Bentham, *A Fragment on Government and An Introduction to the Principles of Morals and Legislation*, ed. Wilfred Harrison (Oxford: Basil Blackwell, 1967), p. 125.

[34] Frederick Copleston, *A History of Philosophy*, vol. 8. (New York: Doubleday Co., 1966), p. 45; George A. Wilson, *Classics of Economic Theory* (Bloomington: Indiana University Press, 1954), p. 545.

[35]David Hamilton, *Evolutionary Economics* (Albuquerque: University of New Mexico Press, 1970), p. 29; Joseph A. Schumpeter, *History of Economic Analysis* (New York: Oxford University Press, 1954), pp. 131–133.

[36]Schumpeter, *History of Economic Analysis,* p. 576.

[37]Wilson, *Classics of Economic Theory,* pp. 570–571.

[38]Schumpeter, *History of Economic Analysis,* p. 131.

[39]Ibid., p. 577.

[40]Konrad Lorenz, *On Aggression,* trans. Marjorie Kerr Wilson (New York: Harcourt, Brace & World, 1966), p. 40.

[41]Desmond Morris, *The Human Zoo* (New York: McGraw-Hill Book Co., 1969), p. 41.

[42]Desmond Morris, *The Naked Ape* (New York: Dell Publishing Co., 1967), p. 120.

[43]George Maclay and Humphry Knipe, *The Dominant Man* (New York: Dell Publishing Co., 1972), pp. 13–15.

[44]Ibid., p. 67.

[45]Morris, *The Human Zoo,* p. 41.

[46]Lorenz, *On Aggression,* p. 41.

[47]R. A. Hinde, *Biological Bases of Human Social Behavior* (New York: McGraw-Hill Book Co., 1974), p. 343.

[48]Sigmund Freud, *Civilization and Its Discontents,* ed. and trans. James Strachey (New York: W.W. Norton Company, 1961), p. 43.

[49]Jack W. Brehm, *A Theory of Psychological Reactance* (New York: Academic Press, 1966).

[50]Adler, *Understanding Human Nature,* p. 32.

[51]A. H. Maslow, "Dominance-Feeling, Behavior, and Status," *Psychological Review* 44 (1937): 404–429.

[52]David C. McClelland and David H. Burnham, "Power is the Great Motivator," *Harvard Business Review* 54, no. 2 (March–April 1966): 101.

[53]Stanley Milgram, "Some Conditions of Obedience and Disobedience to Authority," *Human Relations* 18 (1965), p. 74.

[54]Ibid., p. 69.

[55]Robert A. Dahl and Charles E. Lindblom, *Politics, Economics and Welfare* (New York: Harper & Row Publishers, 1953), p. 230.

[56]Amitai Etzioni, *A Comparative Analysis of Complex Organizations,* rev. and enl. ed. (New York: The Free Press, 1975), p. 3.

[57]Daniel Katz and Robert L. Kahn, *The Social Psychology of Organizations* (New York: John Wiley & Sons, 1966), p. 204.

[58]David J. Hickson and Arthur F. McCullough, "Power in Organizations," in *Control and Ideology in Organizations,* ed. Graeme Salaman and Kenneth Thompson (Cambridge: MIT Press, 1980), p. 30.

[59]Allan W. Lerner, "On Ambiguity and Organizations," *Administration and Society* 10, no. 1 (May 1978), p. 12.

[60]Ibid.

[61]Chester I. Barnard, *The Functions of the Executive* (Cambridge: Harvard University Press, 1962), p. 165; James A. F. Stoner, *Management,* 2nd ed. (Englewood Cliffs, N.J.: Prentice-Hall, 1982), p. 304.

[62]Ralf Dahrendorf, *Class and Class Conflict in Industrial Society* (Stanford: Stanford University Press, 1959), p. 165.

[63]Ibid., p. 618.

[64]Reinhard Bendix, *Work and Authority in Industry* (New York: John Wiley & Sons, 1956), pp. 2–3.

[65]Herbert Marcuse, *Eros and Civilization* (New York: Vintage Books, 1962), p. 82; William A. Gamson, *Power and Discontent* (Homewood, Ill.: The Dorsey Press, 1968), p. 8.

[66]Jack Barbash, "The Work Society," p. 1.

[67]William F. Whyte, *Money and Motivation* (New York: Harper & Row Publishers, 1955), p. 234.

[68]Louis D. Brandeis, "The Fundamental Cause of Industrial Unrest," in *Unions, Management and the Public,* ed. E. Wight Bakke, Clark Kerr, and Charles W. Anrod (New York: Harcourt, Brace & World, 1967), p. 244.

[69]Jack Barbash, "The Causes of Rank-and-File Unrest," in *Trade Union Government and Collective Bargaining,* ed. Joel Seidman (New York: Praeger Publishers, 1970), p. 53.

[70]W. Willard Wirtz, "Labor Unrest and Social Unrest," in *Trade Union Government and Collective Bargaining,* ed. Seidman, p. 4.

[71]James Chowning Davies, "Communication," *American Political Science Review* 73, no. 3 (September 1979), p. 825.

[72]James C. Davies, "Toward a Theory of Revolution," *American Sociological Review* 27, no. 1 (February 1962), p. 5–19.

[73]Davies, "Communications," p. 825.

[74]Ted Robert Gurr, *Why Men Rebel* (Princeton: Princeton University Press, 1970).

[75]Ted Gurr, "A Causal Model of Civil Strife: A Comparative Analysis Using New Indices," *American Political Science Review* 62, no. 4 (December 1968), p. 1104.

[76]Gurr, *Why Men Rebel,* pp. 12–13.

[77]Davies, "Toward a Theory of Revolution," pp. 8–19; Gurr, "A Causal Model of Civil Strife: A Comparative Analysis Using New Indices."

[78]Edward N. Muller, "The Psychology of Political Protest and Violence," in *Handbook of Political Conflict,* ed. Ted Robert Gurr (New York: The Free Press, 1980), p. 701; Edward N. Muller, "A Test of a Partial Theory of Potential for Political Violence," *American Political Science Review* 77, no. 3 (September 1972), pp. 928–959; Bernard N. Grofman and Edward N. Muller, "The Strange Case of Relative Gratification and Potential for Political Violence: The V-Curve Hypothesis," *American Political Science Review* 67, no. 2 (June 1973), pp. 514–539; Douglas A. Hibbs, Jr., "Industrial Conflict in Advanced Industrial Societies," *American Political Science Review* 70, no. 4 (December 1976), p. 1043.

[79]Abraham H. Miller, Louis H. Bolce, and Mark Halligan, "The J-Curve Theory and the Black Urban Riots: An Empirical Test of Progressive Relative Deprivation Theory," *American Political Science Review* 71, no. 3 (September 1977), pp. 964–982.

[80]James Chowning Davies, "Communications," *American Political Science Review* 72, no. 4 (December 1978), pp. 1357–1358; Faye Crosby, "Relative Deprivation Revisited: A Response to Miller, Bolce and Halligan," *American Political Science Review* 73, no. 1 (March 1979), pp. 103–111.

[81]Edward N. Muller, *Aggressive Political Participation* (Princeton: Princeton University Press, 1979), pp. 157–159.

[82]Thomas D. Cook and Donald T. Campbell, "The Design and Conduct of Quasi-Experiments and True Experiments in Field Settings," in *Handbook of Industrial and Organizational Psychology,* ed. Marvin D. Dunnette (Chicago: Rand McNally Publishing Co., 1976), pp. 238–245.

[83]Gurr, *Why Men Rebel,* pp. 24–25.

[84]Ibid., p. 27.

[85]Peter M. Blau, "Exchange Theory," in *The Sociology of Organizations,* ed. Oscar Grusky and George A. Miller (New York: The Free Press, 1970), p. 143.

[86]George Caspar Homans, *Social Behavior: Its Elementary Forms* (New York: Harcourt, Brace Jovanovich, 1974), p. 241.

[87]Martin Patchen, *The Choice of Wage Comparisons* (Englewood Cliffs, N.J.: Prentice-Hall, 1961), p. 11.

[88]Morris Zelditch, Jr., Joseph Berger, Bo Anderson, and Bernard P. Cohen, "Equitable Comparisons," *Pacific Sociological Review* 13, no. 1 (Winter 1970), pp. 19–26.

[89]J. Stacy Adams, "Toward an Understanding of Inequity," *Journal of Abnormal and Social Psychology* 67, no. 5 (1963), pp. 422–424.

[90]Gurr, *Why Men Rebel,* pp. 24–25; Davies, "Toward a Theory of Revolution," 8–19; Blau, "Exchange Theory," p. 143.

[91]Emile Benoit-Smullyan, "Status, Status Types, and Status Interrelations," *American Sociological Review* 9, no. 1 (February 1944), pp. 160–161; Elton F. Jackson, "Status Consistency and Symptoms of Stress," *American Sociological Review* 27, no. 4 (August 1962), p. 469; Irwin W. Goffman, "Status Consistency and Preference for Change in Power Distribution," *American Sociological Review* 22, no. 3 (Winter 1957), p. 275.

[92]Gurr, *Why Men Rebel,* pp. 24–25.

[93]Ibid., p. 27.

[94]Victor H. Vroom, *Work and Motivation* (New York: Wiley & Sons, 1964), pp. 15–17.

[95]Robert P. Quinn and Graham L. Staines, *The 1977 Quality of Employment Survey* (Ann Arbor: Survey Research Center Institute for Social Research, 1979).

[96]Wendell L. French, *The Personnel Management Process,* 5th ed. (Boston: Houghton Mifflin Co., 1982), p. 82.

[97]McClelland and Burnham, "Power is the Great Motivator," pp. 100–110.

[98]A. H. Maslow, "Dominance-Feeling Behavior and Status," pp. 406–408.

[99]T. W. Adorno, Else Frenkel-Brunswik, Daniel J. Levinson, and R. Nevett Sanford, *The Authoritarian Personality* (New York: Harper & Row, 1950), pp. 759–762.

[100]Frank Parkin, *Class Inequality and Political Order* (New York: Praeger Publishers, 1971), p. 70.

[101]Homans, *Social Behavior: Its Elementary Forms,* p. 253.

[102]Peter M. Blau, *Exchange and Power in Social Life* (New York: Wiley & Sons, 1964), p. 149.

[103]James T. Tedeschi, R. Bob Smith, III, and Robert C. Brown, Jr., "A Reinterpretation of Research on Aggression," *Psychological Bulletin* 81, no. 9 (1974), p. 548.

[104]Freud, *Civilization and Its Discontents,* pp. 58–61.

[105]Lorenz, *On Aggression,* pp. 20–45.

[106]Eibl-Eibesfeldt, *Love and Hate,* pp. 72–84.

[107]Wilson, *On Human Nature,* p. 106.

[108]Midgley, *Beast and Man,* p. 48.

[109]Wilson, *On Human Nature,* p. 106.

[110]Albert Bandura, *Social Learning Theory* (Englewood Cliffs, N.J.: Prentice-Hall, 1977), p. 161.

[111]Leonard Berkowitz, "Aggression: Psychological Aspects," in *International Encyclopedia of the Social Sciences,* ed. David L. Sills, vol. 1 (New York: Crowell Collier and MacMillan Inc., 1968), pp. 168–174; Leonard Berkowitz, *Aggression: A Social Psychological Analysis* (New York: McGraw-Hill Book Co., 1962).

[112]John Dollard, Leonard W. Doob, Neal E. Miller, O. H. Mowerer, and Robert R. Sears, *Frustration and Aggression* (New Haven: Yale University Press, 1939), p. 160.

[113]Ibid., p. 10.

[114]N. R. F. Maier, *Psychology in Industry* (Boston: Houghton-Mifflin Co., 1946), pp. 70–79.

[115]Arthur Kornhauser, "Human Motivations Underlying Industrial Conflict," in *Industrial Conflict,* ed. Arthur Kornhauser, Robert Dubin, and Arthur M. Ross (New York: McGraw-Hill Book Co., 1954), p. 73.

[116]Ibid.

[117]Ross Stagner and Hjalmar Rosen, *Psychology of Union-Management Relations* (Belmont, Cal.: Wadsworth Publishing Co., 1965), pp. 42–54.

[118]Albert Bandura, *Aggression: A Social Learning Analysis* (Englewood Cliffs, N.J.: Prentice-Hall, 1973), pp. 133–134, 170, 174.

[119]Tedeschi, Smith, and Brown, "A Reinterpretation of Research on Aggression," pp. 543–544; James. A. Kulik and Roger Brown, "Frustration, Attribution of Blame, and Aggression," *Journal of Experimental Social Psychology* 15, no. 2 (March 1979),

34 • Introduction

pp. 190-193; Stephen Worchel, "The Effect of Three Types of Arbitrary Thwarting on the Instigation to Aggression," *Journal of Personality* 42, no. 2 (June 1974), pp. 314-317.

[120] Robert A. Baron and Donn Byrne, *Social Psychology: Understanding Human Interaction* 3rd ed. (Boston: Allyn and Bacon, 1981), p. 326.

[121] Berkowitz, *Aggression: A Social Psychological Analysis*, p. 45.

[122] Berkowitz, "Aggression: Psychological Aspects," p. 171.

[123] Bandura, *Aggression, A Social Learning Analysis*, p. 170.

[124] Albert O. Hirschman, *Exit, Voice and Loyalty* (Cambridge, Harvard University Press, 1970).

[125] Robert A. Baron, *Human Aggression* (New York: Plenum Press, 1977), p. 93; Baron and Byrne, *Social Psychology: Understanding Human Interaction*, p. 328; H. A. Dengerink, "Personality Variables as Mediators of Attack-Instigated Aggression," in *Perspectives on Aggression*, ed. Russell G. Geen and Edgar C. O'Neal (New York: Academic Press, 1976), p. 62; Bandura, *Aggression: A Social Learning Analysis*, p. 155.

[126] Bandura, *Aggression: A Social Learning Analysis*, p. 163.

[127] Dolf Zillman, *Hostility and Aggression* (Hillsdale, N.J.: Lawrence Erlbaum Associates, 1979), p. 307.

[128] Ibid., pp. 275-276.

[129] Milton H. Spencer, *Contemporary Economics* (New York: Worth Publishing, 1971), p. 31; Arnold S. Tannenbaum, *Social Psychology of the Work Organizations* (Belmont, Cal.: Brooks/Cole Publishing Co., 1966), pp. 30-31.

[130] Baron and Byrne, *Social Psychology: Understanding Human Interaction*, p. 321.

[131] Bandura, *Social Learning Theory*, pp. 28, 161, 173, 209.

[132] Sigmund Freud, *Group Psychology and the Analysis of the Ego*, trans. J. Strachey (New York: Harper & Row, 1970), p. 24.

[133] Ibid., p. 35.

[134] Ibid.

[135] Karl Marx and Friederich Engels, "Manifesto of the Communist Party," in *Marx and Engels Basic Writings on Politics and Philosophy*, ed. Lewis S. Feuer (Garden City, N.Y.: Doubleday & Co., 1959), pp. 6-41.

[136] Ibid., pp. 12-14.

[137] Clark Kerr and Abraham Siegel, "The Interindustry Propensity to Strike—An International Comparison," in *Industrial Conflict*, ed. Arthur Kornhauser, Robert Dubin, and Arthur M. Ross (New York: McGraw-Hill Book Co., 1954), pp. 189-212.

[138] Ibid., pp. 191-192.

[139] Ibid., p. 193.

[140] Dahrendorf, *Class and Class Conflict in Industrial Society*, p. 184.

[141] Ibid., pp. 185-186.

[142] Ibid., pp. 186-187.

[143] Neil J. Smelser, *Theory of Collective Behavior* (New York: The Free Press, 1962), p. 290.

[144] Ibid., p. 278.

[145] Ibid., p. 284.

[146] Neil J. Smelser, "Theoretical Issues of Scope and Problems," in *Collective Behavior*, ed. Meredith David Pugh (St. Paul, Minn.: West Publishing Co., 1980), pp. 9-10.

[147] J. Craig Jenkins and Charles Perrow, "Insurgency of the Powerless: Farm Worker Movements (1946-1972)," *American Sociological Review* 42 (April 1977), pp. 249-268.

[148] Ibid., p. 250.

[149] Ibid., p. 251.

[150] Mayer N. Zald and Michael A. Berger, "Social Movements in Organizations: Coup d'Etat, Insurgency and Mass Movements," *American Journal of Sociology* 83, no. 4, (January 1978), pp. 823-861.

[151]Ibid., p. 843.
[152]Ibid.
[153]Ibid., pp. 843-844.
[154]Ibid., pp. 844-845.
[155]Ibid.
[156]Ibid., pp. 845-846.
[157]Bruce Fireman and William A. Gamson, "Utilitarian Logic in the Resource Mobilization Perspective," in *The Dynamics of Social Movements,* ed. Mayer N. Zald and John D. McCarthy (Cambridge: Winthrop Publishers, 1979), pp. 3-44.
[158]Ibid., p. 21.
[159]Ibid., p. 22.
[160]Thomas A. DeCotiis and Jean-Yves LeLouran, "A Predictive Study of Voting Behavior in a Representation Election Using Union Instrumentality and Work Perceptions," *Organizational Behavior and Human Performance* 27 (1981): 103-118.
[161]Mancur Olson, *The Logic of Collective Action* (Cambridge: Harvard University Press, 1971).
[162]Ibid., p. 68.

CHAPTER 2

The Industrial
Conflict Literature

The strike has been a classic feature of industrial relations since the early days of the labor movement. Just as political history is chiefly built around wars, a large part of labor history is a recounting of major strikes.

Arthur M. Ross and Paul T. Hartman,
Changing Patterns of Industrial Conflict.

It is no new thing to attempt to understand and predict industrial conflict. Many efforts have preceded this one. Before embarking on our journey through the integrative theory, it is of some use to review at least part of what has gone before.

Industrial conflict, as it is defined in this book, consists principally of strikes and union organizing. Both of these phenomena have been the subjects of extensive and relatively cohesive sets of scholarly inquiries. In consequence, the main body of industrial conflict literature, which is reviewed in this chapter, consists of studies of strikes and union organizing.

Other, generally less extensive, literatures relating to industrial conflict will be considered as the theory is developed. While a departure from the more common strategy of reviewing and critiquing all the relevant literature at the outset, the peculiar nature of the integrative theory, constructed out of numerous parts of the existing literature, requires that each area of literature be discussed, and sometimes modified, at the point at which it is added.

The strike studies have been conducted mainly by economists. Studies of union organizing have been conducted from an applied psychological perspective. The strike studies are the most numerous, and have been around for more than fifty years. Organizing studies reflect the relatively recent interest of psychologists in the phenomenon of unionization. Both of these lines of research occupy significant amounts of space in the more prestigious scholarly journals. They represent the two disciplines whose attention has most often been brought to bear upon industrial conflict—economics and psychology. They also demonstrate both the strengths and weaknesses of the use of these disciplines to analyze this phenomenon.

STRIKE STUDIES

Strike studies exist in bewildering variety. Among other things, studies have been conducted of national strike rates, wildcat strikes in particular industries, particular cases of strikes, intercity and interunion differences in strike propensity, and the effects of particular leaders on strikes. The effects on strikes of various measures of economic, political, and other variables have been estimated in many ways. It is possible to bring some order to this diversity by classifying these studies into two general categories—macrolevel and microlevel. Within these categories the studies vary mainly with respect to whether they focus on economic or political variables.

Macrolevel Strike Studies

There have been a number of waves of macrolevel strike studies. The earliest of these utilized economic variables. Then came a number of studies using political variables. In recent years we have seen a blending of economic and political approaches, with many studies utilizing both economic and political variables. What has remained constant in a substantial body of this literature is the use of macrolevel variables to predict national strike rates. It is interesting to note that Arthur Kornhauser, one of the first psychologists to take an interest in the strike issue, agreed with the economists that the appropriate level of analysis is society as a whole. His reason for supporting research at this level was that this is where workers' expectations originate.[1]

Economic Studies

Strike studies focusing upon economic variables have been with us for a long time. One of the earliest of these, by Alvin Hansen, found that strike activity increased in times of prosperity. According to Hansen, strikes increase when the business cycle is in a favorable phase.[2] This relationship has been variously explained as reflecting "increased sense of grievance by workers during the period where prices and living costs rise more than wage levels" or a period during which unions have a tactical advantage because they are able to impose substantial costs of disagreement on employers without suffering greatly themselves.[3]

In 1952, Albert Rees performed a study that provided the theoretical underpinnings for many subsequent studies.[4] In considering why strike rates appear to be linked to the business cycle, Rees arrived at a number of conclusions. First, he argued that union behavior is principally influenced by the state of the labor market, that is, the amount of employment available. As employment is highly correlated with the business cycle, Rees argues that, in effect, the business cycle is a measure of the employment situation. Increases in employment and improving business conditions offer the unions certain strategic advantages. In good times the employer is reluctant to lose his market share through an interruption of production. The employer's observation that wages are rising elsewhere lowers his resistance to union wage demands, thereby increasing the probability of agreement. He is also less able to replace strikers with nonstrikers, and striking workers have a better opportunity to obtain employment elsewhere if they are replaced. Furthermore, if the cost of living rises, workers whose wages fall behind feel a need to protest. On the other hand, when employment is falling there would be expected to be a drop in strikes arising out of organization attempts as employees are susceptible to being victimized if they attempt to organize. Already organized employees will fear striking because they can observe that the employer's bargaining power is great. The employer may also be strengthened by his ability to continue making sales from his inventory or make up for lost production at the end of the strike. The union may also fear damaging the competitive position of the employer by a strike or by obtaining economic concessions, thus imperiling workers' jobs.

Rees makes the important point that unions and employers may focus their attention on different things. Unions are likely to be chiefly concerned with employment. Employers are more likely to focus on general business conditions, such as business failures. According to Rees, this incongruity of focus produces a gap between the perceptions of labor and management at the peak of a cycle, thereby making strikes more likely to occur.[5]

Subsequent to the Rees study, a large number of scholars have attempted to explain national strike rates either on the basis of the general business cycle or particular economic variables. Kochan has summarized this literature by describing its main conclusions as a positive relationship between the business cycle and strikes, ordinarily explained on the basis of increased union bargaining power during prosperous times and a negative relationship between real wage growth and strikes, ordinarily explained by presumed connections between real wage decreases and worker deprivation.[6] In 1965, O'Brien published the earliest of the post-Rees studies. He found a positive relationship between the business cycle and strike rates, as earlier found by Rees.[7] However, O'Brien criticized the rationale proposed by Rees, arguing that the point at which the unions are strongest and most willing to strike is when employers are weakest and most anxious to avoid a strike.

In a study published the following year, Weintraub found a significant relationship between downturns in the economy and downturns in strikes, when viewed on a monthly basis. He found fewer strikes when the economy was declining.[8] Mulvey, analyzing Irish data, found an inverse relationship between unemployment rate and strike rate.[9] He argued that this was because union leaders value strikes more highly when unemployment is low and there is a difference in the bases for union and employer preferences regarding strikes. Specifically, Mulvey argues that unions base their policy preferences on the labor market, while employers base theirs on the product market. Mulvey goes on to argue that these conclusions relate not to the *reasons for* workers striking but rather to the *timing* of strikes, which is a matter of "industrial tactics of trade unions." Mulvey also argues that in times of rising demand for goods the wages of some workers rise, while others remain the same. Those workers whose wages do not rise would be expected to become increasingly dissatisfied, and therefore more prone to strike.

A study by Scully, published in 1971, found that strike activity was not clearly related to business cycles in the United States from 1919 to 1969. Interestingly, Scully states that there are clear policy implications of his findings for business, labor, and government.[10] Yet, the policy implications are neither obvious nor specifically named.

The above literature is not explicitly based upon any general theory. In it some allusions are made to bargaining theory, but the theoretical grounds of the argument are not systematically developed. Beginning in the late 1960s and early 1970s scholars began considering economic variables on the basis of economic bargaining theory. Quite often reference was made to the Hicks bargaining model.[11] The Hicks model is relatively simple: it utilizes the wage level demanded and the expected length of the strike as the two variables upon which bargaining focuses. It should be noted that Hicks gives no rationale for focusing on these two variables. They are convenient, perhaps necessary, for the purposes of his analysis, as they allow him to view variables that would appear to be influential in decisions of both labor and management. With clear and persuasive logic, Hicks argues that, given his assumptions, the parties should always reach agreement, and, if they fail to do so, this is "the result of faulty negotiations." It is quite important to note that the Hicks model bears only the faintest resemblance to the phenomenon known as collective bargaining. Indeed, many of the better studies in this area (Rees and Mulvey, for example) expressly state that, contrary to the Hicksian assumptions, labor and management rely upon *different* considerations in deciding upon the desirability of a strike. Unfortunately, this extraordinarily naive model has served as the basis for much of the thinking about collective bargaining, perhaps explaining why scholars have had so much difficulty finding meaningful answers.

The other major theoretical set utilized by recent studies of economic determinants of strike rates is a system developed by Ashenfelter and Johnson in 1969.[12] Ashenfelter and Johnson (hereafter referred to as A & J) developed what they call a "political" model of strikes to rationalize the use of various economic variables. The A & J model is "political" in that it makes reference to dynamics of internal union politics. A & J state that they assume that union leaders have somewhat different interests from the rank and file. These leaders will refuse to sign a collective bargaining agreement they think the rank and file will not accept, regardless of whether or not the leaders believe it is a good contract. They will, rather, lead a strike and then sign a contract when rank-and-file expectations have become low enough. A & J argue that strike length is one of the variables involved in the leaders' estimation of whether a particular wage increase is acceptable to the rank and file. A & J assume that only one party, management, can vary its wage proposal, since union leaders are constrained by rank-and-file desires. In a famous statement, A & J argue that the "basic function of the strike is as an equilibrating mechanism to square up the union memberships wage expectations with what the firm may be prepared to pay."[13] A & J argue that the wage increase a union will accept without a strike depends on the unemployment rate, previous wage increases, and profits. They recognize, however, that at high profit levels the employer may give in and pay what the union wants, avoiding a strike. A & J found that, as they hypothesized, strike rates were: (1) higher when real wages had declined, (2) lower when the unemployment rate was high; (3) higher when price changes were high; and, (4) lower when money wage increases were high. They explain the negative relationship between real wage increases and strikes by arguing that the wage increase that workers will accept at the end of their existing contract is lower if real wages have been increasing. They offer no explanation for the money wage and price change connections with strike rates. They found no effects of profits on strike rates.

The A & J theoretical formulation has been widely used and widely criticized. Perhaps the most compelling criticism is that the theorizing is unnecessary and not of any particular help in understanding or predicting strikes. One can justify A & J's hypotheses on many grounds other than those proposed in their theory. Their theory is also weak in that it: (1) retains the unverified Hicksian notion that anticipated strike *length* is a crucial determinant of negotiator behavior; (2) looks only at the worker side of bargaining; (3) focuses solely upon strikes as a result of bargaining over wages, which neglects nearly half of the American strikes; and, (4) it commits the usual bargaining theory mistake of viewing each strike as an "isolated campaign."[14]

Most of the studies that follow the Ashenfelter and Johnson study, both in time and in theory, view economic variables and political variables together. They tend to base their economic variables upon the A & J theory, and their political variables on other grounds. It is interesting that the last, and perhaps the best, of the studies utilizing economic variables, published by Michael Shalev in 1980, rejects the Ashenfelter and Johnson theory. Shalev poses a devastating criticism of the Ashenfelter and Johnson model, and then goes on to build his own model based upon midrange theories.[15] Shalev argues that there is a certain amount of conflict on either side of the labor-management relationship which is constant or "durable." The question to be asked is under what conditions does this unrest translate into overt conflict. He then focuses upon the question of how aggregate forces, both economic and noneconomic, affect "the interest and opportunities of unions and employers for initiating overt conflict."[16] Shalev maintains that in the United States the labor movement is highly dependent upon market forces, as it is practically without political and other nonmarket resources. This dependence on the market is "reinforced by institutional factors" which include stable union membership, decentralization of collective bargaining, and availability of strike breakers and nonunion labor to employers. The ideologies of both employers and unions legitimate the centrality of market forces in their strategies. Shalev argues that this centrality of economic forces makes it reasonable to look to economic variables as those that determine industrial conflict.[17]

Shalev argues that the set of economic variables he includes in his study is capable of explaining national strike rates. These variables are labor market conditions, product market conditions, changes in workers' economic welfare since the last contract, wage increases received by other unionized workers, factor shares prior to a potential stoppage, opportunities to strike, and seasonal variations. He argues that labor market conditions, such as unemployment, are the primary determinants of workers' bargaining power and, therefore, more likely to affect the behavior of workers than that of employers. Product market conditions are also argued to affect union behavior: unions have greater bargaining power when demand is high and inventories low. Shalev predicts more strikes under this condition. He maintains that higher prices since the last contract will cause workers to try to "catch up" and, therefore, increase their demands. Increasing real wages since the last contract would make the workers less likely to strike. He argues that the greater the wage increases obtained by other unionized employees, the greater the desire will be on the part of a particular group for wage increases. Falling profits are expected to make employers tougher and, therefore, cause a greater likelihood of the occurrence of strikes. Shalev's study confirms significant effects in the predicted directions for all of his variables.[18]

Political Studies

It has long been maintained that strikes have causes that are other than economic. For example, Ross and Hartmann, writing in 1960, argued that the leading influences in relative (between country) strike activity were: (1) organizational ability of the labor movement; (2) leadership conflicts in the labor movement; (3) status of union-management relations; (4) labor political activity; and, (5) role of the state. They argue that labor political action is a deterrent to strikes because strikes are injurious to the political fortunes of labor parties, and because political action channels worker unrest into the political sphere.[19]

In 1972, David Snyder and Charles Tilly concluded, in a study of collective violence in France, that the "principal immediate causes of collective violence are political."[20] This argument was developed at much greater length in a book by Edward Shorter and Tilly, published in 1974.[21] Contrary to Ross and Hartman, Shorter and Tilly argue that "strikes expand as workers organize and as their organizations acquire increasing stakes in the national structure of power."[22] They conclude that economic variables are not particularly helpful in explaining strike activity, except as higher wages lead to greater resources on the part of workers, and, therefore, of unions, thereby increasing their ability to strike.

In a later paper, written in 1975, David Snyder again found that it was political, rather than economic, variables that best explained strike activity over time in several countries.[23] According to Snyder, the economic analysis of strikes rests on assumptions valid only for the post–World War II period in the United States and not for France or Italy during any period. He argues that where the labor movement is not established it fights for power in general terms, not just for better bargaining results. Because of this, bargaining models of strike rates will not work. His results show two economic variables, unemployment and real wage changes, as being significantly associated with strike rates in the United States after World War II. Previous to World War II there is no such association. During this period union membership, the percent of Democrats in Congress, and the party of the president are associated most strongly with strikes. In France, only union membership and the presence of an election year are significantly related to strikes in the period previous to World War II. After World War II only election year is significant, but this is opposite the predicted direction. Economic variables are not significant. In Italy, the only variable significant during any period is union membership. Snyder's argument in support of political variables is essentially that unions tend to strike when they have the resources to do so. This is the case where they have large membership, or support from the political system. This is consistent with "resource mobilization theory," which appears in the collective behavior literature.

Snyder's variables are highly plausible at the conceptual level. However, his measure of union strength in society, union membership, is contaminated by the fact that it represents more than just the opportunity for unions to strike. Union membership may also be jointly determined, along with strikes, by worker militancy or other factors. The political variables also suffer from serious construct validity problems because they use as measures periods of time in which many matters of importance occurred. For example, in the United States the party of the president was Democratic and the Congress was Democratic (the variables used as proxies for union political strength) during two world wars and the Great Depression. It seems rather likely that these concurrent events, as well as the party of the president and the percent of Democrats in Congress, might have had something to do with the strike rates during these periods. In a study published in 1977, Snyder reached similar results analyzing data for the United States and Canada. He found economic variables to be unimportant, while political variables were highly significant.[24]

In an interesting study published in 1979, Walter Korpi and Shalev explain low strike rates in Sweden and some other Western countries on the basis of working class success in politics. According to Korpi and Shalev, a high degree of strength on the part of the labor movement leads to a political strategy that, in turn, means fewer strikes. They agree with Marx that one should look to the relations arising from the sphere of production as a starting point in explaining industrial conflict. When one does this, attention is drawn to the inequality of power in capitalist societies. This inequality is "reflected in the subordination in the realm of work of the sellers of labor power to its buyers. Since this subordination involves the domination of men by men, it is basically of a political character."[25]

Economic and Political Studies

In recent years a number of scholars have utilized both economic and political variables in attempting to explain national strike rates. One study doing this was reported by Jack W. Skeels in 1971.[26] Skeels found that real gross national product was positively associated with strikes, that unemployment was related to some, but not all, strike measures, and that upward changes in hourly earnings had a positive effect on the number of strikes. He further concluded that the political party in power in Congress and the party of the president significantly affected strike rates.

A similar strategy was adopted by P. K. Edwards in a study published in 1978.[27] Edwards found that economic variables were of some importance, but varied greatly in their effects, and worked in different directions in different periods. He concluded that political variables were not important, but his results show that the party of the president was related to strikes during the period prior to 1946 in the U.S. He also concluded that the data supported the proposition that inflation was a major source of rising strike activity in the U.S. in the 1960s.

Two papers combining economic and political variables have been written by Bruce Kaufman.[28] In the later of these, Kaufman's more interesting findings include the significance of union membership, unemployment, and price changes as predictors of strike rates from 1900 to 1948 in the U.S. During the period from 1949 to 1977 unemployment and price changes were found to be significantly related to the number of strikes. Kaufman's arguments regarding the effects of different political and economic constructs upon strike rates are quite well taken. However, his political variables are virtually meaningless. This is mainly because he chooses as political variables periods of time and labels them "welfare capitalism." As argued above, such variables have obvious construct validity problems.

Included in the same issue of *Industrial and Labor Relations Review* with the later Kaufman article are studies by Skeels, and by Martin Paldam and Peder J. Pedersen. [29] The Skeels study finds significant relationships between strike rates and unemployment (−), "trough unemployment" (+), union density (+), and consumer price index change (+). Trough unemployment is the rate of unemployment at the lowest point in the immediately previous recession. The union density variable is an estimate of the proportion of the labor force that is unionized. Paldam and Pedersen, in their study of seventeen countries, found that: (1) nominal wage changes are the most stable predictor (+) of strikes; (2) both real and nominal wage changes are positively related to strikes (contrary to A & J); (3) unemployment rate is an unstable predictor of strike rates; and, (4) conflict is more plentiful under left-wing governments than under right-wing governments. The instability of unemployment rate as an independent variable is contrary to many of the economic studies. Paldam and Pedersen conclude that changes in wage structure are probably the phenomenon that underlies changes in strike rates.

Problems with the Macrolevel Strike Literature

There are several things wrong with the macrolevel strike literature. These lead to some rather radical conclusions with respect to these studies.[30] First, assuming that some agreement could be reached on which of a multitude of variables relate to national strike rates, it has become fairly clear that over a half-century of study on this subject has brought us no closer to understanding *why* they do so. Second, there are no policy implications of any importance to be drawn from these studies. Third, the attempts at theorizing that have been made in this area have been woefully inadequate. Fourth, the plausibility of the measures in so many of these studies has been so weak as to cast doubt on the whole body of literature.

Why have we learned so little about the causes of strike rates after so much study? One of the problems, as Kaufman notes, is "the lack of a satisfactory theory of strike causation."[31] As is argued above, both the Hicks and A & J theories have simply not been adequate to form a foundation for research.

Some scholars utilizing economic variables have abandoned general theories and have instead employed the rational justification of individual variables within a general utility maximization framework. The attempt by Shalev in this direction is probably about as good as can be done.[32] However, even this attempt at theorizing meets with insurmountable difficulties. These difficulties flow from a disjunction between the level of analysis of the theory and that of the variables used. Without question the theories that have the best prospects for explaining strike behavior are microlevel theories. The problem, which has been recognized in the literature, is to relate these theories to macrolevel variables.[33] For example, the commonly used variable of national inventory levels may or may not reflect conditions existing in a firm in which a strike takes place. National inventory levels and strike levels might be influenced in opposite directions by unemployment, general demand, or other factors, producing the negative macrolevel relationship usually observed between inventory and strike levels. This result would be consistent with microlevel theory predicting more strikes if the employer's bargaining power declines as his inventory declines.[34] At the same time, in particular firms experiencing strikes, inventories might be high, allowing employers to be adamant in opposing even minimal union demands—and thus forcing strikes.

Use of the macrolevel measure would wrongly lead one to conclude that there is a negative causal relationship between inventory levels and strikes, and confirm a false microlevel theory. Under these circumstances, microlevel theory is of no use. It is clear, therefore, that, in order to justify the use of macrolevel variables, it is necessary for theory to speak in terms of these variables themselves, not some presumed microlevel equivalent. Yet it is probably impossible to do so, except perhaps in the case of the macrolevel variables of unemployment and inflation. This problem is endemic to this type of research and is, I believe, intractable.

At one time, it appeared as though a breakthrough might be accomplished by scholars utilizing political, rather than economic, variables. It does seem likely that, at least in some countries and for some periods, political variables influence national strike rates. Yet, quite different results have been obtained by scholars using measures of favorableness of political climate and strike rates. On theoretical grounds, and on the basis of empirical studies, one can argue with an equal degree of confidence that unions strike less where government is favorable to them, as strikes are less necessary,[35] and that unions strike more when government is favorable to them, as their power is greater.[36] Perhaps the difficulty here is that all "strikes" are not the same. A strike that has politics as its purpose is unlikely to have the same determinants as one aimed at immediate economic gains. Although some purposes may be served by claiming that a particular set of strikes is fundamentally economic[37] or political,[38] clarity of thought is not aided by broad claims that *all* strikes are related to either economic or political determinants. It may well be, for example, that economic strikes are facilitated by having a friendly government in power, but that political strikes are rendered unnecessary by the policies of such a government.

A more serious problem with studies offering political explanations of strikes lies in the measures that they have utilized.[39] A key variable in these studies is the level of union membership in the society, which is believed to reflect the amount of resources available to unions to conduct strikes.[40] As suggested above, the problem with this measure is that it is equally susceptible to other interpretations. Increases of union membership may, along with strikes, simply reflect increased worker militancy. Increased membership also increases the opportunity for at least some types of strikes.

Other measures used in the political explanation literature have similar problems. As is the case in Kaufman's 1982 article, a period of time is often used to represent one of a variety of potentially relevant phenomena that occurred during the period. As noted above, in the United States during the period 1900–1948 both the percent of Democrats in Congress and the party of the president (Democrat = 1; other = 0), two variables commonly employed, happen to assume high values during wartime and the Great Depression, both of which could arguably affect strike rates. This problem is exacerbated by biases in the design of some strike rate measures. These measures sometimes use strike frequency, strike length, hours lost, number of workers involved, or some combination of these. Measures that exclude the *length* of strikes, which was less during at least one of these periods (the World War II years) certainly facilitate the finding of positive effects for these political variables.[41]

What then, is the value of all the macrolevel strike research? Has it significantly added to our understanding of strikes? To their prediction? To policy-making? Clearly, the answer to the last three of these questions is no. The failure to develop even midrange theory leaves us without knowledge of the *reasons* for relations between certain variables and strike rates. Therefore, our understanding is not aided. As to prediction, the high statistical significance of the results assist prediction in only a blind, mechanical sense. It is logically fallacious to extrapolate these curves into the future. This argument, of course, runs counter to at least the vulgar version of the old bromide that it doesn't matter whether one variable causes another, so long as they behave as though it does. Although this statement is true in a sense, it is, of course, incorrect to use it to justify conclusions from correlations not theoretically justified.

Even if these studies do not help us to better understand or predict strike rates, they might still be useful if they serve policy-making purposes. That is, an observed correlation accompanied by *some* explanation might be an improvement over the information that policymakers have available, and could assist in the making of policy. However, there are no such possibilities for findings of these studies, as they relate to outcomes not likely to be manipulated in order to control the variable of interest, strikes. One is hard-pressed to imagine circumstances under which policymakers would increase unemployment or adjust inflation in order to influence the national strike rate, or vice versa. In addition, national strike rates have not been a burning policy issue, at least in the United States, for about thirty-five years.

Microlevel Strike Studies

A large number of studies have been constructed at other than the macrolevel. Some of these studies have produced interesting results, and appear to be more fruitful than the macro studies. Upon reviewing these studies, Kochan concludes that studies of strike rates at the level of the industry support a union power hypothesis regarding strikes, finding strikes are more frequent in industries with: (1) lower levels of unemployment; (2) greater proportions of male workers; and (3) a higher proportion of the workforce unionized.[42] The union power hypothesis is supported by the Britt and Galle study, which found that the degree of unionization and average size of unions were positively related to strike levels across industries.[43]

A very interesting study at the *level of the firm* by Mauro is supported by one of the clearest rationalizations of variables that can be found in this literature.[44] Similar to Rees and others, Mauro argues that anything that has a differential impact upon the concession preferences of the parties will lead to more strikes. That is, if the union is basing its willingness to concede on one factor, and the employer is basing its concessions on another factor, there will be no agreement. Mauro maintains that the union focuses on the consumer price index, income taxes, real wage changes, and wage changes compared to those occurring in other industries. Management focuses on the firm's product prices, profits, and labor productivity. Under conditions of imperfect information, changes in these variables will create diverse expectations.[45] Mauro found effects on strike rates across firms of pattern-following (–), unemployment (–), profits (–), productivity (–), and relative wages (–).

The strategy of viewing strikes on an industry-by-industry basis, or a firm-by-firm basis, is supported by the earlier work of Arthur Ross, who argues that a large proportion of strikes in the United States has been in certain "centers of conflict."[46] Ross predicts a decline in strike activity, largely because of an institutionalization of collective bargaining, the reduction of the ability to strike in many industries because of automation, and sustained overcapacity that allows stockpiling and reduces the union's ability to strike. The other short-run influence alluded to by Ross is that of a management bargaining offensive, which, when it occurs, causes unions to struggle to defend themselves against attack.

Three recent studies, although difficult to classify, are worthy of mention. David B. Lipsky and Henry S. Farber studied strikes in the construction industry. They found significant relationships between strikes and unemployment with respect to strike composition, that is, time lost, but not strike *frequency*. Wage controls were found to be negatively related to strikes over economic issues in that industry.[47] Robert N. Stern performed an interesting study of strikes across metropolitan areas.[48] In high conflict cities, he found a significant relationship between strikes and city population (–), unionization (+), plant size (+), and "economic vulnerability" (+). The economic vulnerability variable was a measure of how high wages were in the metropolitan area. Presumably employers in high wage areas are more likely to be faced with strong demands for higher wages. In low conflict cities a large number of variables was associated with strike rates. Stern identified a "syndrome" of low conflict involving cities of small size in the South, with right-to-work laws, low wages, and high property tax rates (the rationale for this last variable is unclear). He found unemployment rates insignificant as a strike determinant for both high and low conflict cities. Myron Roomkin, in a study of the impact of union structure on strikes, found that the size of the national union and the frequency of union conventions were both negatively related to strikes. Building trades unions were more likely to strike. Among local product market oriented unions such as the building trades unions, the requirement for national approval before a strike could occur was negatively related to strikes.[49]

A Miscellany of Strike Studies

In addition to the literature reviewed above, there is virtually an endless miscellany of interesting writings and studies on the subject of strikes. One of the earlier and better known studies was reported in 1951 by Arthur M. Ross and Donald Irwin.[50] They concluded that strikes were caused by employer resistance to unions, communist unionism, single firm bargaining, and the absence of a labor party. The absence of a labor party is presumably a measure of a lack of political avenues to pursue labor's goals. Thomas A. Kochan, after a review of much of this literature in his book, concludes that strikes are positively affected by a political climate favorable to unions, laws protecting the right to strike, efforts to change the bargaining structure, pattern leading, negotiators having inadequate decision-making power, intraorganizational conflict that spills over into bargaining, management policies, union policies (decentralization leading to more strikes), interpersonal and personal hostility, procedural sources of conflict (incompetent negotiators), and a history of strikes.[51] Robert Dubin, looking at long-run trends in strikes, concluded that the adversaries being evenly matched leads to more strikes.[52] Blum and Horel, in a study of Israeli strikes, conclude that strikes have the following "internal" causes: (1) unions becoming more democratic, making leaders more militant; (2) local union segmentation into small units; (3) mistakes in bargaining; (4) improper bargaining practices; (5) ease of making comparisons, giving rise to feelings of inequity; and (6) unsatisfactory labor legislation. As an "external" cause, they identified economic conditions that created rising expectations.[53]

Several studies have focused on the personalities of individuals involved as causing strikes. The work of James and James suggests a "great man" theory of strikes, describing how Jimmy Hoffa controlled teamster strikes on the basis of his own calculations, with little or no consultation with the membership.[54] Walter Uphoff makes much the same argument with respect to the Kohler strike.[55] In a recent study, Kochan and Baderschneider concluded that interpersonal hostility between negotiators was significantly related to impasses in negotiations.[56]

There is an interesting literature on causes of particular strikes or waves of strikes. David Montgomery argues that the imposition of scientific management caused theories of "New Unionism," "bread and butter" unionism, worker sabotage, and passive resistance.[57] Amsten and Brier similarly argue that strikes in the coal industry in the 1880s and 1890s in the United States were caused by miners responding to aggressive action by employers by trying to create and extend a "permanent institution of self defense."[58] Strikes among skilled workers in the late nineteenth century and early twentieth century have been explained as a response to employer pressure that threatened their unions.[59] Strikes in the auto and rubber industries in the 1930s have been explained by the great problems of worker insecurity in those industries.[60]

A considerably different approach to strike causes has been adopted by James E. Cronin. He explains strikes in Britain in terms of strike waves. He theorizes that it is the uneven character of economic growth that causes unevenness in industrial conflict. He views economic growth as going through a variety of stages, each qualitatively distinct and imposing new strains upon all of the actors in an industrial relations system.[61] The workers, being in an unequal power position, are in a position of simply reacting to actions initiated by the employers.

In addition to the literature on strikes in general, there is a small body of literature having to do with union "pressure tactics" and "wildcat" strikes. Slichter, Healy, and Livernash attribute wildcat strikes and other pressure tactics to generalized hostility, and to workers' perceptions that such tactics will be instrumental in achieving desired goals.[62] They maintain that these tactics are used most often in the earlier stages of bargaining relationships. In a study of wildcat strikes in coal mining, Brett and Goldberg concluded that low strike mines were characterized by the ability to solve problems at the local level, and that this was the most important difference between low strike mines and high strike mines.[63] They also found that there were more strikes where workers believed that striking would be instrumental, and was necessary, to get management to talk to workers about their problems.

Conclusions from the Strike Literature

The macrolevel strike literature helps us very little, given the amount of effort that has been devoted to it. However, the general body of strike literature does have some important lessons to teach, both with respect to substantive knowledge about the strike and for the development of improved theory.

With regard to substantive knowledge about the strike, even the macrolevel strike literature makes some contribution. It does direct our attention to the importance of economic variables, particularly the state of the labor market, in understanding and predicting worker behavior. Some of the earlier work by Rees and Mulvey, and the later work by Mauro, argue for the necessity of considering that different factors may influence labor and management in their calculations of advantage in negotiations over the contents of a new collective bargaining agreement. The macrolevel political strike literature has produced results consistent with resource mobilization theory, useful in building a theory of industrial conflict. This suggests that an important determinant of industrial conflict is the ability of workers to engage in it and the importance to that ability of resources from outside the work unit. Findings with respect to the effects of unemployment rate (a variable generally well known to workers) in the macrolevel studies, as well as the results found by Mauro in one of the stronger microlevel studies, direct our attention to the potential explanatory power of worker expectations.

For purposes of constructing theory, the clearest lesson one can draw from this literature is the importance of developing useful theory. The lack of useful theory seems to be the fatal flaw in much of the strike literature. Carefully performed empirical work that utilizes sophisticated techniques is of little use without good theory to guide it. It is also relatively clear that the theory must be capable of operating both at the individual level and the collective level. Because it is human beings who act, it is necessary to base a theory of their action on a comprehensive and valid theory of human behavior. Because a collective phenomenon is the subject of analysis, it is necessary to build a sound bridge between the individual level and the collective level.

STUDIES OF UNION ORGANIZING

Of considerably less extent, but perhaps of greater significance, than the strike literature, is the literature on union organizing developed within the last decade. Psychologists and others who have probed for the reasons that workers take the aggressive collective action of organizing into unions have been rather successful in casting some light on this phenomenon.

These studies have taken the form of attempts to determine the individual and contextual characteristics that influence workers to favor, or vote for, representation by a union. This has usually involved asking workers whether they favor, or have in fact voted for, union representation, eliciting other attitudes from them, perhaps obtaining some demographic information, and then correlating the union-related attitudes or actions with the other data. Some studies have simply compared demographic characteristics of unionized and non-unionized workers.

The chief result of this research has been the identification of a fairly wide range of variables that have an impact on worker preference for unions. The most important of these are job satisfaction (economic or noneconomic), perceived instrumentality of the union for achieving the worker's goals, attitudes toward unions in general, and demographic characteristics. Perceived degree of worker influence, though used in only a few studies, is also of interest.

One of the clearest findings of many studies is that there is a negative relationship between a prounion decision by a worker and job satisfaction.[64] Some of these studies find satisfaction with economic concerns to be most important.[65] One major study finds that satisfaction with a noneconomic matter, supervision, is of primary importance.[66]

A major finding of several studies is that workers are more likely to make a prounion decision if they perceive the union as being instrumental for the achievement of outcomes they desire.[67] Some find significant effects on a prounion decision of interaction between dissatisfaction and instrumentality.[68] Worker attitudes toward unions in general have also often been found to be associated with a prounion decision.[69]

Although there have been some interesting and significant findings with respect to demographics, these are somewhat difficult to interpret. In several studies it has been found that younger workers are more union prone than their older colleagues.[70] Blacks and other minority group members have been found to be more union prone.[71] Some differences in the determinants of union proneness have been found between blue-collar and white-collar workers, principally that blue-collar workers are more strongly influenced by economic and white-collar workers by noneconomic factors.[72] Perhaps blacks and other minority group members are more accustomed to social action in general and therefore are more union prone. It may also be that they are generally more deprived and therefore have more reason to be dissatisfied. It has been suggested that younger workers are simply more likely to join new groups. There may also be personality differences between those workers who choose to be white-collar workers and those who choose to be blue-collar workers.

There is quite a long list of other factors that have, in one study or another, been found to be related to a prounion decision. A study by DeCotiis and LeLouarn found positive effects of job-related psychological stress, role ambiguity, degree of worker influence, perceptions of unfair treatment, and lack of support by supervisors.[73] Degree of influence is an item that deserves special note because it is similar in an interesting way to findings in two other studies. In one of these, by William J. Bigoness, it was found that externals (those perceiving their lives to be controlled by outside forces) were more union prone.[74] In the other, by Allen and Keaveny, it was found that worker perceptions that performance had not led to pay increases in the past were related to a prounion decision.[75] Both these studies agree that a perception of outcomes being beyond the control of the worker leads toward a prounion decision. What is unclear is whether, as suggested by Bigoness, this is a personality variable, or, as suggested by Allen and Keaveny, it is a reflection of the reality of the work place.[76]

In addition to its empirical findings, this literature includes some interesting discussions helpful in the development of theory. One is that workers tend to pursue their goals by means other than aggressive collective action so long as this is successful and will only take the avenue of industrial conflict when other means have failed. This is very strongly suggested by Kochan and by DeCotiis and LeLouarn.[77] It also follows from the findings of Allen and Keaveny, who find that, at least for some workers, it is only after they conclude that high performance fails to produce the desired results that they will favorably consider unionization.

A good deal can be learned from the literature on union organizing. First, it indicates rather clearly that there is a strong link between job-related dissatisfactions and willingness to organize. Although it is not entirely clear what "satisfaction" or "dissatisfaction" meant to the subjects of these studies, it is at least in some way connected to a difference between a state of affairs they desire and one they have. Second, the importance of instrumentality of the union to workers found in these studies indicates the necessity of recognizing the intelligent, calculative component of workers' behavior. Third, the findings regarding worker attitudes toward unions in general give evidence of a normative aspect of human behavior in this context. Fourth, the significance of demographic variables requires that some attention be paid to individual differences among workers, based perhaps upon differences in personality or life experience. Fifth, the association between a feeling of being out of control of one's own destiny and a preference for unionization gives rise to at least a suspicion that matters of autonomy and control are important. The centrality of satisfaction with supervision found in one major study is also supportive of this view. Last, findings that indicate a preference for obtaining one's goals by other means and only turning to unionization when this fails, lead one to believe that a model of union organizing should posit a flow of behavior that involves the more extreme action of unionization only when other strategies have proved unsuccessful.

Perhaps the greatest weakness of this literature is the lack of an adequate general theory to support it. To the extent that it is based upon theory, it relies on a simplified version of utility theory. It is believed that this theoretical framework is not adequate to the task of operating effectively in this area. This is partly because it focuses exclusively upon *individual* behavior, ignoring the *social* dimension of human behavior. While this may be appropriate for dealing with some kinds of behaviors, it is rather clearly inappropriate for dealing with social behavior. Industrial conflict, as it is here defined, is collective behavior. One would expect, therefore, that collective concerns would be at least relevant. Yet, taking an exclusively individualistic perspective ignores the fundamental variable of solidarity, and other variables pertaining to group behavior. In studies of voting behavior, for example, the decision to vote for a union may simply be a consequence of the collective action of organizing that has preceded it and is determined by considerations other than individual rationality.

When one reviews the two major literatures on industrial conflict discussed above, as well as the variety of literatures on this and related subjects, it becomes apparent that considerable progress has been made in achieving partial understandings of some facets of industrial conflict. It is equally apparent, however, that there exists no single theoretical framework capable of providing an integrated general view of industrial conflict. It is to the task of creating such a framework that we now turn.

NOTES

[1]Arthur Kornhauser, "Human Motivations Underlying Industrial Conflict," in *Industrial Conflict*, ed. Arthur Kornhauser, Robert Dubin, and Arthur M. Ross (New York: McGraw-Hill Book Co., 1954), p. 76.

[2]Alvin Hansen, "Cycles of Strikes," *American Economic Review* 11, no. 4 (December 1921), p. 620.

[3]Michael Shalev, "Trade Unionism and Economic Analysis: The Case of Industrial Conflict," *Journal of Labor Research* 1, no. 1 (Spring 1980), pp. 234–235.

[4]Albert Rees, "Industrial Conflict and Business Fluctuations," *Journal of Political Economy* 60, no. 5 (October 1952), pp. 371–382.

[5]Ibid., pp. 380–381.

[6]Thomas A. Kochan, *Collective Bargaining and Industrial Relations* (Homewood, Ill.: Richard D. Irwin, 1980), p. 251.

[7]F. S. O'Brien, "Industrial Conflict and Business Fluctuations," *Journal of Political Economy* 73, no. 6 (December 1965), pp. 653-654.

[8]Andrew R. Weintraub, "Prosperity Versus Strikes: An Empirical Approach," *Industrial and Labor Relations Review* 19, no. 2 (January 1966), p. 238.

[9]C. Mulvey, "Unemployment and the Incidence of Strikes in the Republic of Ireland 1942-1966," *Journal of Economic Studies* 3, no. 2 (July 1968), p. 82.

[10]Gerald W. Scully, "Business Cycles and Industrial Strike Activity," *Journal of Business* 44, no. 4 (October 1971), p. 360.

[11]J. R. Hicks, *The Theory of Wages* (London: MacMillan & Co., 1963).

[12]Orley Ashenfelter and George E. Johnson, "Bargaining Theory, Trade Unions and Industrial Strike Activity," *American Economic Review* 59, no. 1 (March 1969), pp. 35-49.

[12]Orley Ashenfelter and George E. Johnson, "Bargaining Theory, Trade Unions and Industrial Strike Activity," *American Economic Review* 59, no. 1 (March 1969), pp. 35-49.

[13]Ibid., p. 39.

[14]See Michael Shalev, "Trade Unionism and Economic Analysis: The Case of Industrial Conflict," *Journal of Labor Research* 1, no. 1 (Spring 1980), pp. 145-147; P. K. Edwards, "Time Series Regression Models of Strike Activity: A Reconsideration with American Data," *British Journal of Industrial Relations* 16, no. 3 (November 1978), pp. 320-323.

[15]Shalev, "Trade Unionism and Economic Analysis: The Case of Industrial Conflict," pp. 139-153.

[16]Ibid., p. 154.

[17]Ibid., p. 155.

[18]Ibid., p. 156.

[19]Arthur M. Ross and Paul T. Hartmann, *Changing Patterns of Industrial Conflict* (New York: John Wiley & Sons, 1960), pp. 63-64.

[20]David Snyder and Charles Tilly, "Hardship and Collective Violence in France, 1930 to 1960," *American Sociological Review* 37, no. 4 (August 1972), p. 520.

[21]Edward Shorter and Charles Tilly, *Strikes in France, 1930-1960* (London: Cambridge University Press, 1974).

[22]Ibid., p. 8.

[23]David Snyder, "Industrial Setting and Industrial Conflict: Comparative Analyses of France, Italy and the United States," *American Sociological Review* 40, no. 3 (June 1975), pp. 259-278.

[24]David Snyder, "Early North American Strikes: A Reinterpretation," *Industrial and Labor Relations Review* 30, no. 3 (April 1977), pp. 325-341.

[25]Walter Korpi and Michael Shalev, "Strikes, Industrial Relations and Class Conflict in Capitalist Societies," *British Journal of Sociology* 30, no. 2 (July 1979), p. 169.

[26]Jack W. Skeels, "Measures of U.S. Strike Activity," *Industrial and Labor Relations Review* 24, no. 4 (July 1971), pp. 515-525.

[27]P. K. Edwards, "Time Series Regression Models of Strike Activity: A Reconsideration with American Data," *British Journal of Industrial Relations* 16, no. 3 (November 1978), pp. 320-334.

[28]Bruce E. Kaufman, "Bargaining Theory, Inflation, and Cyclical Strike Activity in Manufacturing," *Industrial and Labor Relations Review* 34, no. 3 (April 1981), pp. 333-335; Bruce E. Kaufman, "The Determinants of Strikes in the United States, 1900-1977," *Industrial and Labor Relations Review* 35, no. 4 (July 1982), pp. 473-490.

[29]Jack W. Skeels, "The Economic and Organizational Basis of Early United States Strikes, 1900-1948," *Industrial and Labor Relations Review* 35, no. 4 (July 1982), pp. 491-503; Martin Paldam and Peder J. Pedersen, "The Macroeconomic Strike

Model: A Study of Seventeen Countries, 1948–1975," *Industrial and Labor Relations Review* 35, no. 4 (July 1982), pp. 504–521.

[30]Hoyt N. Wheeler, "Determinants of Strikes: Comment," *Industrial and Labor Relations Review* 37, no. 2 (January 1984), pp. 263–269.

[31]Kaufman, "Bargaining Theory, Inflation, and Cyclical Strike Activity in Manufacturing," p. 333.

[32]Shalev, "Trade Unionism and Economic Analysis: The Case of Industrial Conflict."

[33]Ibid., pp. 166–167; Paldam and Pederson, "The Macroeconomic Strike Model: A Study of Seventeen Countries, 1948–1975," p. 517; P. K. Edwards, *Strikes in the United States, 1881–1974* (New York: St. Martin's Press, 1981), pp. 62–64.

[34]Rees, "Industrial Conflict and Business Fluctuations," p. 381; Shalev, "Trade Unionism and Economic Analysis," p. 164.

[35]Korpi and Shalev, "Strikes, Industrial Relations and Class Conflict in Capitalist Societies," pp. 164–187.

[36]Paldam and Pedersen, "The Macroeconomic Strike Model: A Study of Seventeen Countries, 1948–1975," p. 517.

[37]Shalev, "Trade Unionism and Economic Analysis: The Case of Industrial Conflict," pp. 154–155.

[38]Shorter and Tilly, *Strikes in France, 1930–1968*, p. 16.

[39]Edwards, "Time Series Regression Models of Strike Activity: A Reconsideration with American Data," pp. 323–325.

[40]Snyder, "Institutional Setting and Industrial Conflict: Comparative Analyses of France, Italy and the United States," p. 268.

[41]Ibid., pp. 268–274.

[42]Kochan, *Collective Bargaining and Industrial Relations*, p. 255.

[43]David Britt and Omer R. Galle, "Industrial Conflict and Unionization," *American Sociological Review* 37, no. 1 (February 1972), p. 54.

[44]Martin J. Mauro, "Strikes as a Result of Imperfect Information," *Industrial and Labor Relations Review* 35, no. 4 (July 1982), pp. 522–538.

[45]Ibid., p. 527.

[46]Arthur M. Ross, "The Prospects for Industrial Conflict," *Industrial Relations* 1, no. 1 (October 1961), p. 59.

[47]David B. Lipsky and Henry S. Farber, "The Composition of Strike Activity in the Construction Industry," *Industrial and Labor Relations Review* 29, no. 3 (April 1976), pp. 398–399.

[48]Robert N. Stern, "Intermetropolitan Patterns of Strike Frequency," *Industrial and Labor Relations Review* 29, no. 2 (January 1976), pp. 218–235.

[49]Myron Roomkin, "Union Structure, Internal Control, and Strike Activity," *Industrial and Labor Relations Review* 29, no. 2 (January 1976), pp. 209–213.

[50]Arthur M. Ross and Donald Irwin, "Strike Experience in Five Countries, 1927–1947: An Interpretation," *Industrial and Labor Relations Review* 4, no. 3 (April 1951), pp. 323–342.

[51]Kochan, *Collective Bargaining and Industrial Relations*, p. 257.

[52]Robert Dubin, "Industrial Conflict: The Power of Prediction," *Industrial and Labor Relations Review* 18, no. 3 (April 1965), p. 363.

[53]Albert A. Blum and Gedaliahue Horel, "The Generic Reasons for Strikes: An Interpretative Analysis of the Israeli Case," *Relations Industrielles* 35, no. 1 (1980), pp. 99–112.

[54]Ralph C. James and Estelle Dinerstein James, *Hoffa and the Teamsters* (Princeton, N.J.: D. Van Nostrand Co., 1965), pp. 186–193.

[55]Walter H. Uphoff, *Kohler on Strike* (Boston: Beacon Press, 1966), pp. 400–404.

[56]Thomas A. Kochan and Jean Baderschneider, "Dependence on Impasse Procedures: Police and Firefighters in New York State," *Industrial and Labor Relations Review* 21, no. 4 (July 1978), pp. 443, 446.

[57]David Montgomery, "The 'New Unionism' and the Transformation of Workers' Consciousness in America, 1909–1922," *Journal of Social History* 7, no. 4 (Summer 1974), p. 518.

[58]Jon Amsden and Stephen Brier, "Coal Miners on Strike: The Transformation of Strike Demands and the Formation of a National Union," *Journal of Interdisciplinary History* 7, no. 4 (Spring 1977), p. 616.

[59]Edwards, *Strikes in the United States, 1881–1974*, p. 125.

[60]Ibid., p. 157.

[61]James E. Cronin, "Theories of Strikes: Why Can't They Explain the British Experience?" *Journal of Social History* 12, no. 2 (Winter 1978), pp. 194–220.

[62]Sumner H. Slichter, James J. Healy, and E. Robert Livernash, *The Impact of Collective Bargaining on Management* (Washington, D.C.: The Brookings Institution, 1960), pp. 663–691.

[63]Jeanne M. Brett and Stephen B. Goldberg, "Wildcat Strikes in Bituminous Coal Mining," *Industrial and Labor Relations Review* 32, no. 4 (July 1979), p. 480.

[64]Thomas A. DeCotiis and Jean-Yves LeLouarn, "A Predictive Study of Voting Behavior in a Representation Election Using Union Instrumentality and Work Perceptions," *Organizational Behavior and Human Performance* 27, (1981), pp. 111–112; Henry S. Farber and Daniel H. Saks, "Why Workers Want Unions: The Role of Relative Wages and Job Characteristics," *Journal of Political Economy* 88, no. 2 (April 1980), pp. 362–363; Peter Feuille and James Blandin, "Faculty Job Satisfaction and Bargaining Sentiments: A Case Study," *Academy of Management Journal* 17, no. 4 (December 1974), p. 687; Thomas A. Kochan, "How American Workers View Labor Unions," *Monthly Labor Review* 102 (April 1979), p. 25; Chester A. Schriesheim, "Job Satisfaction, Attitudes toward Unions, and Voting in a Representation Election," *Journal of Applied Psychology* 63, no. 5 (October 1978), p. 550; W. Clay Hamner and Frank J. Smith, "Work Attitudes as Predictors of Unionization Activity," *Journal of Applied Psychology* 63, no. 4 (August 1978), p. 417; Julius G. Getman, Steven B. Goldberg, and Jeanne Brett Herman, *Union Representation Elections: Law and Reality* (New York; Russell Sage Foundation, 1976), pp. 54–55.

[65]Farber and Saks, "Why Workers Want Unions: The Role of Relative Wages and Job Characteristics," pp. 362–363; Schriescheim, "Job Satisfaction, Attitudes toward Unions, and Voting in a Representation Election," p. 550; Getman, Goldberg, and Herman, *Union Representation Elections: Law and Reality*, pp. 56–57; William J. Bigoness, "Correlates of Faculty Attitudes toward Collective Bargaining," *Journal of Applied Psychology* 63, no. 2 (April 1978), p. 232; R. P. Quinn and G. L. Staines, *The 1977 Quality of Employment Survey* (Ann Arbor: Survey Research Center, University of Michigan, 1978).

[66]Hamner and Smith, "Work Attitudes as Predictors of Unionization Activity," pp. 418–419.

[67]DeCotiis and LeLouarn, "A Predictive Study of Voting Behavior in a Representation Election Using Union Instrumentality and Work Perception," pp. 112–113; Farber and Saks, "Why Workers Want Unions: The Role of Relative Wages and Job Characteristics," p. 364; Feuille and Blandin, "Faculty Job Satisfaction and Bargaining Sentiments: A Case Study," p. 687: Kochan, "How American Workers View Unions," p. 25; Stuart A. Youngblood, William H. Mobley, and Angelo S. DeNisi, "Attitudes, Perceptions and Intentions to Vote in a Union Certification Election: An Empirical Investigation," *Proceedings of the Industrial Relations Research Association* (Madison, Wisc.: Industrial Relations Research Association, 1981), pp. 250–251.

[68]Farber and Saks, "Why Workers Want Unions: The Role of Relative Wages and Job Characteristics," p. 364; Kochan, "How American Workers View Labor Unions," p. 25; Youngblood, Mobley, and DeNisi, "Attitudes, Perceptions and Intentions to Vote in a Union Certification Election: An Empirical Investigation," pp. 250–251.

[69]Youngblood, Mobley, and DeNisi, "Attitudes, Perceptions and Intentions to Vote in a Union Certification Election: An Empirical Investigation," pp. 250–251; Schriesheim,

"Job Satisfaction, Attitudes toward Unions, and Voting in Representation Elections, p. 550; Getman, Goldberg, and Herman, *Union Representation Elections: Law and Reality*, p. 550; Jeanne Brett Herman, "Are Situational Contingencies Limiting Job Attitude—Job Performance Relationship?" *Organizational Behavior and Human Performance* 10, no. 2 (October 1973), pp. 218–219.

[70]Farber and Saks, "Why Workers Want Unions: The Role of Relative Wages and Job Characteristics," p. 365; Bigoness, "Correlates of Faculty Attitudes toward Collective Bargaining," p. 230; Feuille and Blandin, "Faculty Job Satisfaction and Bargaining Sentiments: A Case Study," p. 688.

[71]Farber and Saks, "Why Workers Want Unions: The Role of Relative Wages and Job Characteristics," p. 365; Kochan, "How American Workers View Labor Unions," pp. 302–303; Herman, "Are Situational Contingencies Limiting Job Attitude—Job Performance Relationship?"; Quinn and Staines, *The 1977 Quality of Employment Survey*.

[72]Quinn and Staines, *The 1977 Quality of Employment Survey;* Youngblood, Mobley, and DeNisi, "Attitudes, Perceptions and Intentions to Vote in a Union Certification Election: An Empirical Investigation," pp. 250–251.

[73]DeCotiis and LeLouarn, "A Predictive Study of Voting Behavior in a Representation Election Using Union Instrumentality and Work Perceptions," pp. 111–112.

[74]Bigoness, "Correlates of Faculty Attitudes toward Collective Bargaining," p. 232; Laurie A. Broedling, "Relationship of Internal—External Control to Work Motivation and Performance in an Expectancy Model," *Journal of Applied Psychology* 60, no. 1 (February 1975), p. 68.

[75]Robert E. Allen and Timothy J. Keaveny, "Correlates of University Faculty Interest in Unionization: A Replication and Extension," *Journal of Applied Psychology* 66 (1981), p. 585.

[76]Ibid.

[77]Kochan, "How American Workers View Unions," p. 302; DeCotiis and LeLouarn, "A Predictive Study of Voting Behavior in a Representation Election Using Union Instrumentality and Work Perceptions," p. 116.

CHAPTER 3

The Theory's First Pillar— Innate Predispositions

You ask me how thought and wish are formed in us. I answer you that I have not the remotest idea. I do not know how ideas are made any more than how the world was made. All we can do is grope in the darkness for the springs of our incomprehensible machine. Voltaire,

Philosophical Dictionary.

Sound theory must rest on a solid foundation. Theories pertaining to human social behavior must somehow manage to establish a foundation in a comprehensive view of the grounds and dynamics of human action. What is needed is a model of the human person sufficiently accurate and broad to help support a weighty theoretical edifice. Neglect of this precondition can only lead to theory that is incapable of useful explanation. Accordingly, this chapter sets out a model that, it is believed, meets this precondition and forms the first pillar of the integrative theory.

One might argue that it is an expendable luxury for a theory of industrial conflict to have an explicitly constructed foundation of fundamental statements regarding human behavior. Indeed, existing theories of industrial conflict make only passing nods in this direction. It is fashionable to suppose that the careful and systematic observation of relations among variables, combined with sufficiently sophisticated statistical analysis, represents the highest possible degree of scientific rigor in the social sciences. If this were only true it would certainly save a great deal of trouble. The problem is that such analyses inevitably fail to answer the question of *why* observed relationships exist, at least at a level of generality that renders the answer of any use. And it is the "whyness" that is of prime importance. As William Beebe once said: "The isness of things is well worth studying; but it is their whyness that makes life worth living."[1] Without the "whyness," predictions into the future are little more than the commission of the classical logical fallacy of extrapolating a curve. Observed relations give us little information about what we could expect if the context shifted, or about the direction of the causal flow. Work that is badly flawed by failures to handle the "whyness" problem is dramatically exemplified by the macrolevel strike literature reviewed in the last chapter.

It is reasonably clear that any inquiry into the whyness of even *collective* human behavior, such as industrial conflict, must begin with a consideration of the *individual human being*. Leonard Berkowitz has argued:

> ... the present writer is still inclined to emphasize the importance of individualistic considerations in the field of group relations. Dealings between groups ultimately become problems for the psychology of the individual. Individuals decide to go to war; battles are fought by individuals, and peace is established by individuals. Theoretical principles can be formulated referring to the group as a unit and these can be very helpful in understanding hostility between groups. But such abstractions refer to collections of people and are made possible by interindividual uniformities in behavior.[2]

Although this writer disagrees with Berkowitz's statement that collective behavior is most usefully viewed as *mere* "interindividual uniformities in behavior," his point regarding the fundamental importance of the behavior of the individual human being seems unexceptionable. After all, it is the individual who is the ingredient of the mass. One can hardly expect to have a firm understanding of the mass without understanding its constituents. It is necessary, therefore, to grasp "the springs" of the individual human machine.

Of course, as is argued by the model, a general understanding of individual human behavior is not in itself sufficient to provide a theory of industrial conflict. It is additionally necessary to decide what particular behaviors are the subject of one's interest. For industrial conflict theory this requires some notion of the industrial relationship. In addition, one must arrive at an understanding of how the basic human tendencies translate into the kind of action in which we are interested. This requires theory that operates at the level of collective, as well as individual, behavior. The best foundation for a theory of industrial conflict lies in combining biological and ethological efforts to identify enduring characteristics of individual human nature with existing economic and behavioral models. There is, I believe, overwhelming evidence that fundamental, enduring characteristics exist. The discoveries of sociobiologists and ethologists hold glittering promises of a wealth of scientifically respectable ideas that can be beneficial in theorizing about industrial conflict. A model using them is believed to be superior to the solitary use of either well-worn utility theory or behaviorist notions.

A foundation is necessary for sound theorizing, and, as most of us in the field of industrial relations are unfamiliar with much of this literature, a somewhat extensive explanation is called for. Integrative theory requires the development of a set of ideas firmly grounded in general theories of human behavior and the drawing of these theories into the study of industrial relations. This can only be done if these are explicated in some detail. Furthermore, the significance of the conclusions reached in this chapter being generally accepted in the field could be considerable. What these conclusions propose is a fundamental shift in the way the field sees its phenomena of interest. At present, the neoclassical economists' "economic man" and what has been called the "blank paper" view of the behaviorists are the only models of humankind available. Here a new model is proposed.

MAN FROM A BIOLOGICAL PERSPECTIVE

Man as a human animal, or "biological man," is a being with certain rather enduring capabilities, wants, and needs. His fundamental capacities and inclinations have been determined, like those of all other animals, by the heavy hand of evolution. He is, of course, like economic man, characteristically intelligent and rational. He is also, however, prone to certain feelings and native inclinations without which he would have long ago become an extinct species.

If biological man has one most important advantage over his principal competitor for social scientific recognition, economic man, it is that he really does exist. Economic man has always suffered from the disability of being an admitted abstraction from reality. While abstraction often serves theoretical purposes, and economic man has served some purposes rather well, it is reasonably clear that in important areas of social scientific research this particular abstraction has created severe practical difficulties. Furthermore, economic man has always had a credibility problem stemming from the fact that so few persons would seriously maintain that humans act *in all cases* on the basis of actual, deliberate calculations. Indeed, economists have long since abandoned this notion. They have retreated to the rather mysterious explanation that human beings simply *act as though* they were rationally calculating entities. What has been missing is a rationale for human beings behaving in this fashion unless they were in fact engaging in these calculations. It must, however, be said for the discipline of economics that it has at least chosen a distinctive model of humankind that captures an obviously important aspect of human behavior. That the model is limited is of less importance than the fact that it captures a substantial portion of the reality. The considerable explanatory power of economics has in large part derived from the fact that it has adopted a clear, coherent view of man. What would seem to be needed to progress beyond the point to which economic theory has carried us is a concept of man that is similarly clear and coherent, but more complete.

Biological man is a necessary complement to economic man because he feels as well as thinks. He acts innovatively and creatively to explore and create new realities. He reflects, in ways he does not really understand, his evolutionary heritage. Indeed, how can it be otherwise? If one subscribes to evolutionary theory, and one must reject the whole of biological science in order to do otherwise, it seems absolutely clear that man must in part behave as he does because doing otherwise would have caused him not to survive. Behavioral patterns that do not favor the reproduction and the passing on of genes of a group of human beings will, under evolutionary theory, be eliminated over the generations. If behaving in a calculated fashion were in conflict with evolutionary success, man would not so behave. If erecting dominance orders were contrary to evolutionary success, man would not erect dominance orders.

When human behavior is viewed from the perspective of biological science, the scales fall from our eyes. Otherwise inexplicable patterns of action become understandable because, in the biological sense, we understand their *functions* as well as their origin. Human nature becomes a meaningful construct that can be used to understand and predict human behavior.

The chief argument against biological man is that the biological perspective necessarily involves "biological determinism." This misperception flows from the great confusion that has historically accompanied attempts to discuss things called "instincts," a term even the great Darwin was loath to attempt to define. What must be understood from the outset in considering the biological perspective is that no one seriously contends that, because of instincts, human beings are mere automata. For that matter, such a characterization of any higher animal would be ludicrous. Furthermore, showing that a predisposition exists, and that it has at some point in human history had a species-preserving function, does not indicate that human beings will inevitably continue to engage in this behavior through all eternity. Even from a purely evolutionary standpoint, behaviors that have at one time been adaptive can become maladaptive. It can, for example, be argued that this is the case with respect to human inclinations toward aggressive activity.

Resistance to biological man has also stemmed from confusion between scientific truth and moral judgment. Contrary to the views of biological man's critics, the existence of a predisposition for a behavior has nothing to do with whether such a behavior is "good." Merely because a behavior has favored the survival of the species during evolutionary history does not indicate that human beings should favor such behavior. We are free to choose behaviors on many grounds; fitness for natural selection purposes is only one of these. It would hardly be argued in American society, for example, that it would be "good" to destroy at birth all seriously malformed infants, whatever the advantages for survival of the species.

Perhaps one of the reasons that biologically oriented scholars have been accused of determinism is that this forms a symmetrical contrast with the extreme behavioral view that man is totally malleable. This view, labelled by Robert Ardrey as the "romantic fallacy," holds that man's capability of becoming whatever he wishes to become is unconstrained and uninfluenced by natural inclinations. If man wishes to form a perfectly cooperative society all that is required is for him to so decide and act accordingly. Rousseau's argument that, "man is born free, yet everywhere he is in chains," assumes that man is naturally able to do anything he wishes to do and that it is only society that has constrained him. What is extraordinary about this point of view is that it fails to recognize that it is man who composes and creates society. This wonderfully pure being has somehow created brutally oppressive societies that shock our more compassionate sensitivities. Those who take this point of view also have the serious difficulty of explaining the consistent failure of the many efforts at cooperative societies. If man is entirely free to choose his direction, and cooperation is desirable, why does he fail when he moves in that direction? Might it not be the case that human nature makes it difficult for us to establish cooperative societies? This is not to say that such a goal is impossible, only difficult. Man is not bound to behave forever in accordance with past patterns of behavior. However, when he attempts to swim against the tide of fundamental human impulses, he must expect it to be difficult. Recognizing that these difficulties exist would seem to be useful for the purpose of overcoming them. Ignoring them may be what has doomed many human efforts to failure.

THE ORIGINS OF BIOLOGICAL MAN

Biological man has been around for a long time. The origins of the notion lie with Charles Darwin and Herbert Spencer. Although Darwin and Spencer were contemporaries, and their ideas are commonly associated with one another, their theories are really quite different. Indeed, Darwinism and the "Social Darwinism" of Spencer are founded on highly divergent views of natural selection, the dynamic at the heart of both theories.

Darwinism

From the results of a lifetime of careful study, Charles Darwin produced, in 1859, his classic, *The Origin of Species*.[3] Darwin's theories offended against the biblical story of creation and the views of the scientific establishment of the day. It provoked vigorous popular responses, of which the comment of the wife of the Bishop of Worcester is perhaps typical: "Descended from the apes! My dear, let us hope that it is not true but if it is, let us pray that it will not become generally known."[4]

At the heart of Darwin's work is his theory of natural selection. He stated it rather simply:

> Owing to this struggle for life any variance, however slight and from whatever cause providing if it be in any degree profitable to an individual of any species, in its infinitely complex relations to other organic beings and to external nature, will tend to the preservation of that individual, and will generally be inherited by its offspring. The offspring also, will thus have a better chance of surviving, for, of the many individuals of any species which are periodically born, but a small number can survive. I have called this principle by which each slight variation, if useful, is preserved, by the term of Natural Selection, in order to mark its relation to man's power of selection.[5]

Darwin maintained that "the struggle almost invariably will be most severe between individuals of the same species," because they compete for the same food sources and other necessities of life.[6]

Interestingly, Darwin's thought showed the heavy influence of classical economic theory, particularly the ideas of Malthus. He argued that more individuals are produced than can possibly survive and that there must, therefore, in every case, be a struggle for existence. According to Darwin:

> It is the doctrine of Malthus applied with manifold force to the whole animal and vegetable kingdoms; for in this case there can be no artificial increase of food, and no prudential restraint from marriage. Al-

though some species may be now increasing, more or less rapidly, in numbers, all cannot do so, for the world would not hold them.[7]

It is quite important to recognize that Darwin was not speaking primarily of the length of life of particular individual members of a species. It is success in passing on one's traits to offspring that is of prime importance. In a little noticed passage, Darwin says, "I should premise that I use the term Struggle for Existence in a large and metaphorical sense, including dependence of one being on another, and including (which is more important) not only the life of the individual, but success in leaving progeny."[8] This distinction becomes particularly important when Darwin comes to the point of attempting to explain the prevalence in nature of behavioral and physical characteristics not in the survival interests of the individual possessing them. For example, the sting of the bee, which injures an enemy, at the same time causes the death of the bee. Yet the use of the sting does protect the community that includes the bee's progeny. A similar problem exists with respect to sterile castes of ants. Darwin's explanation of the survival of this trait is that, even though the passing on of genes of the sterile invididual is impossible, the gene-passing ability of the entire community is enhanced because of the unique and necessary functions the sterile individuals serve.

These last arguments are crucial to Darwin's theory of evolution. Without them, the theory of natural selection would not be plausible, for it would fail to account for the survival of many common traits. These arguments also make it clear that it may be in the survival interest of groups to have some individuals who are "altruistic" with respect to passing on their own genes. Communities that do not contain some "altruistic" individuals may be at a severe competitive disadvantage with other communities. This constitutes an early statement of the theory of group selection, which has been much discussed by later biologists.

Social Darwinism

Social Darwinism is a good idea gone wrong. Even its name is misleading—it is *not Darwinist*. Herbert Spencer's original statement of this theory in his work *Social Statics* actually preceded the publication of Darwin's work. Spencer's essentially ethical arguments are based on the presumed "naturalness" and "rightness" of systems in which only the fittest survive. This view was understandably appealing to the rapacious capitalists of the nineteenth century. It also drew considerable support from popular misunderstandings of Darwinian theory. As a consequence, it terribly confused the application of Darwin's theories to human beings. It also gave Darwinism, as applied to human beings, an extraordinarily unsavory reputation. Spencer's essential argument is that the misery and suffering of the poor and their resulting higher mortality rate serve a beneficial purpose for society. It is through these selective mechanisms that the weak are weeded out and the human race strengthened.[10] Mechanisms for the relief of public suffering, public health, and relief for the poor were viewed as antisocial since they interfered with the beneficial workings of natural processes for the improvement of the race. Unfortunately, one of the chief proponents of Darwin's theories, Thomas Huxley, known as "Darwin's bulldog," did make some statements that were compatible with Spencer's views. According to Huxley:

> As among these, so among primitive men, the weakest and stupidest went to the wall, while the toughest and shrewdest, those best fitted to cope with their circumstances, but not the best in any other sense, survived. Life was a continual free fight and beyond the limited and temporary relations of the family, the Hobbesian war of each against all was the normal state of existence.[11]

There are two things wrong with the Spencer's views. First, they are incompatible with Darwinian theory. As noted above, Darwin recognized that selection was in many respects a group phenomenon. His treatment of "altruistic" behavior in *The Origin of Species* makes it clear that he viewed the viciously selfish behaviors approved by Spencer to be maladaptive. Social groups whose members behaved in the ruthlessly competitive manner described by Spencer would clearly have a hard time surviving in competition with other groups.[12]

The second problem with Spencer's views is that they lead to a very unpleasant society. A society organized along Spencerian lines would violate deep-seated human tendencies toward love, mutual aid, and affection which are just as "natural" as competitiveness. Few would wish to live in such a society. The Nazis used similar theories to support their confused and reprehensible theories of racial purity.

Perhaps one of the more unfortunate consequences of Spencer's theory is that it gave such a bad reputation to biologically based views of man. Spencer's work showed the potential of such views for the justification of brutally oppressive and selfish societies. This unpleasant taint stems in part from the long-standing confusion between "isness and oughtness" which has plagued this area of thought. Spencer believed that man *is* naturally selfish. From this he concluded that man *ought to be selfish.* For those without any other moral rudder, it is easy to slip into the notion that whatever is "natural" is also "good." There are, however, some fundamental difficulties with this view. One of the problems is that this view becomes terribly unworkable when confronted with the complexities of reality. That is, such a theory of natural ethics has difficulty dealing with contradictory human impulses, such as those toward aggression and mutual aid. If what is "natural" is also good, how can it be that contradictory impulses are natural? Is good's negation also good?

The predicament into which Spencer's ideas place us can be easily escaped by separating the empirical and moral questions. Humans are as we are. What we ought to be is an entirely different matter. As one might expect, the world's great religions have dealt with questions of oughtness much more effectively than has science. It seems that science should worry about the *is* without concerning itself about the *ought.* Such a separation allows scientific theories to be judged empirically, not on the basis of their possible moral consequences.

Although Spencer's views appear to be patently without scientific merit, their weakness should have no effect upon the credibility of Darwinism. Spencer and the other Social Darwinists were not Darwinists. Yet their use of Darwinist trappings for their theory made biological man something of a pariah in the social sciences. Certainly anyone who judged biological man according to the uses to which he had been put would consider him to be highly suspect. Indeed, some might argue that biological man should not be used for theorizing about industrial conflict because of the danger of his leading us to Spencerian conclusions.

ETHOLOGY: A NEW LIFE FOR BIOLOGICAL MAN

Beginning in the early 1960s, biological man began to reemerge from the shadows accoutred in new garb. This was the result of the efforts of a group of scientists and writers, mainly biologists, working in the field of ethology, the "naturalistic study of whole patterns of animal behavior."[13] Ethological studies had proceeded quietly enough until they began applying their techniques to the study of the behavior of the animal called *homo sapiens.* Simply put, they studied man as an animal. By doing so, they gave biological man a new lease on life. He had badly sullied his reputation by lending support to predatory capitalism and Nazi theories of racial purity. Yet here he was in new clothing, still burdened by his past, but offering once again to furnish some aid in the understanding of human behavior.

The ethologists forthrightly assert that man is an animal and can only be so understood. They argue that the complete man is a man of instinct and of rationality. They draw analogies to the behavior of other related animals in order to understand human behavior. In general, they apply the same methods to human behavior that they apply to the behavior of other animals. This approach is argued for by Desmond Morris in his book, *The Naked Ape*:

> I am a zoologist and the naked ape is an animal. He is therefore fair game for my pen and I refuse to avoid him any longer simply because some of his behavior patterns are rather complex and impressive. My excuse is that, in becoming so erudite, *Homo Sapiens* has remained a naked ape nevertheless. . . . there is no hope of quickly shrugging off the accumulative genetic legacy of his whole evolutionary past. He would be a far less worried and more fulfilled animal if only he would face up to this fact.[14]

The most eloquent, if not the most scientific, of the ethologists is Robert Ardrey. A playwright turned scientist, Ardrey has furnished ethology with many a well-turned phrase. As Ardrey is eminently quotable, perhaps we should listen to his words for a moment. In *African Genesis*, Ardrey maintains:

> Man is a fraction of the animal world. Our history is an afterthought, no more, tacked to an infinite calendar. We are not so unique as we should like to believe. And if man in a time of need seeks deeper knowledge concerning himself, then he must explore those animal horizons from which we have made our quick little match.[15]

He further argues:

> Within a species every member is born in the essential image of the first of its kind. No child of ours, born in the middle twentieth century, can differ at birth in significant measure from the earliest of Homo sapiens. No instinct, whether physiological or cultural, that constituted a part of the original human bundle can ever in the history of the species be permanently suppressed or abandoned.[16]

"Man's nature, like his body, is the product of evolution. . . Man's nature must be regarded like his body, as the sum total of all that has come before plus those modifications which are the hallmark of his kind."[17] "Allied to an instinct, judgment may act. In conflict with instinct, human thought becomes a wish."[18]

Perhaps the most persuasive of the ethologists is Irenaus Eibl-Eibesfeldt. Unfortunately for Eibl, the clarity of his thought and the impressive evidence produced by his work has been somewhat obscured in the United States by the difficulty of pronouncing and spelling his name. In his book, *Love and Hate*, Eibl argues that physical structures are the ultimate source of behavior patterns.[19] His study of behavioral patterns of humans has been extraordinarily broad in scope. His conclusions are supported by a large number of photographs that graphically depict behavioral similarities across many different civilizations. Eibl's chief conclusion is that the existence of many common behaviors across societies provides strong evidence of their innateness, particularly in light of the human inclination toward variety. Eibl argues that aggressive behavior has never been found entirely lacking in any human group and that it finds essentially the same expressions throughout the world. Everything from threat displays, attempts to make ourselves taller or to exaggerate the width of our shoulders, assuming an aura of calm or a haughty expression, a facial expression of threat and rage, and the stamping of feet and clenching of fists to express anger are constant throughout all societies. This consistency of behavior in many different social circumstances and settings leads one to suspect, as Eibl concludes, that it is based on something more than random learning or mechanical rationality.

One of the better known ethologists is Niko Tinbergen. Tinbergen sees man as a social ape who has turned carnivore. He is a social primate, yet has had to develop behaviors similar to those of the hunting carnivores, such as lions and hyenas.[20] Determining the "nature" of man is important, according to Tinbergen, because "we still carry with us a number of behavioral characteristics of our animal ancestors, which cannot be eliminated by different ways of upbringing. . . ."[21] He recognizes that man, because of his unparalleled ability to pass on experience from generation to generation, has changed greatly because of cultural evolution. He argues, however, that such modifiability has its limits, "imposed upon us by our hereditary constitution, a constitution which can only change with the far slower speed of genetic evolution."[22]

In an operational sense, how does biological man behave? He behaves *both* through *reason* and through *instincts*. With respect to instincts, there is no single distinctive behavioral guidance pattern. Konrad Lorenz, perhaps the premier ethologist, has described the constitution of instincts as resembling a "parliament": "[a] more or less complete system of interactions between many independent variables; its true democratic nature has developed through a probationary period in evolution, and it produces, if not always complete harmony, at least tolerable and practical compromises between different interests."[23] Lorenz has described the human mind as a ship commanded by many captains. When there is agreement among these captains, the human being operates in a rather straightforward fashion. When there is disagreement, there is confusion.[24]

With respect to the parliament of instincts, Eibl has argued that both aggressive and altruistic behaviors are "preprogrammed . . . and . . . are therefore preordained norms for ethical behavior."[25] He argues that the innate social tendencies of human beings counterbalance the innate aggressive impulses. There is an innate disposition toward cooperation and mutual aid as well as toward aggression. We are, therefore, "good" and "bad" by inclination as well as by conditioning.

Tinbergen makes an important point with respect to instincts. He argues that thirty years ago it may have been necessary for ethologists to stress the innate roots of behavior in order to contrast with the "almost grotesquely environmentalist bias of psychology."[26] He suggests that this is no longer the case, and that it is possible to talk sensibly about behavior without making a sharp distinction between innate and acquired behavioral patterns. According to Tinbergen, this is because we have learned that many innate patterns are developed at an early stage by interaction with the environment and that learning is limited by internally imposed restrictions. Quite importantly, he argues that learning is not indiscriminate, but is selective on the part of the animal doing the learning.

The economic and behavioral views of man both deny the importance, perhaps even the existence, of instincts. Extreme behaviorists approaching the question with what Tinbergen terms their "grotesquely environmentalist bias," consider human beings to be a "blank slate" upon which any instructions can be written according to largely random occurrences that reinforce some behaviors and not others. The extreme economic view sees man as a completely rational being who, unconstrained by instincts, chooses from a repertoire of behaviors to enhance pleasure and avoid pain. The ethologists challenge the common assumption of "behavioral man" and "economic man" that man has no natural predispositions. Desmond Morris expresses the nub of the ethological argument, saying, "Unfortunately we tend to forget that we are animals with certain specific weaknesses and certain specific strengths. We think of ourselves as blank sheets on which anything can be written. We are not. We come into the world with a set of basic instructions and we ignore or disobey them at our peril."[27]

Why does man insist upon viewing himself as if he had no natural inclinations? Konrad Lorenz believes that this inclination exists because of three obstacles to man's self-knowledge. The first of these obstacles is man's disinclination to view himself as behaving like his nearest relative, the chimpanzee. The second obstacle is that we are reluctant to accept the fact that our own behavior is subject to the laws of natural causation. We wish to belive that we possess free will and do not have our actions determined by outside causes. The third obstacle is "idealistic" philosophy, which dichotomizes the world into the external world of things and the internal world of thought. This division, which appeals to our spiritual pride, attributes values solely to the internal world of human thought and reason. Lorenz argues that the animal roots of human behavior are in fact a glorious heritage. He believes that anyone who understands this will be repulsed neither by Darwin's finding that humans and other animals have a common origin, nor by Freud's discovery that we are driven by the same instincts that drove our prehuman ancestors.[28]

The view of man as possessing completely free will is admittedly appealing, at least at first blush. Freed from instincts, man pursues his own good as he sees fit. This is man as a rational, semidivine being, rather than man as a beast. Yet it appears that many of his more admirable qualities stem from his beastly heritage. We share with many other animals loyalty to friends, sacrificing and tenderness for our young and our community, and a number of other endearing attributes. Indeed, as Lorenz argues, "Man as a purely rational being, divested of his animal heritage of instincts, would certainly not be an angel—quite the opposite."[29] Furthermore, as Lorenz maintains, reason alone cannot determine ends, but only means to ends. Lorenz likens unaided reason to a computer into which no useful information has been fed and without a motor to make it operate. He argues that the motive power of humans stems from distinctively human behavioral mechanisms. These are the sources of love and friendship, warmth of feeling, appreciation of beauty, artistic creativeness and our insatiable curiosity. He maintains that these mechanisms are not essentially different from the instincts of other animals, but that human beings have erected on their basis a unique superstructure of social norms and rites. The function of these norms and rites is not greatly different from that of ritualized instinctive behavior among other animals.

As indicated above, Robert Ardrey describes the view that virtually all human behavior results from causes within the human experience as the "romantic fallacy."[30] This fallacy allows man to be seen as completely controlling his own destiny. If he wills a just society, therefore, he will have it. Ardrey sees this fallacy as particularly dysfunctional for those who wish to effect changes in society, as it misleads them into believing that this task is an easy one.

What distinguishes the ethological view of man from other current views is its assertion that man is linked to the rest of the animal kingdom. Ethology provides a rather compelling apology for biological man. It has, of course, been heavily criticized. It is beyond dispute that, as its critics charge, it has often been characterized by something other than the highest degree of scientific rigor.[31] Its advocates have made some mistakes, such as Lorenz's hydraulic, or "flush toilet," theory of aggression. It also appears that one of its number, Robert Ardrey, has badly confused intraspecific (within species) and interspecific (across species) aggression. Nevertheless, the ethologists must be credited with resurrecting biological man, and, as Edward O. Wilson has said, with "breaking the stifling grip of the extreme behaviorists."[32]

SOCIOBIOLOGY

It is through sociobiology that biological man is making his latest attempt to achieve scientific respectability. Unlike other approaches to biological man, *Sociobiology: A New Syntheses*, by Edward O. Wilson, published in 1975, presents a clearly structured scientific examination of the social behavior of animals, including man.[33] In a later book, *On Human Nature*, Wilson extensively and powerfully argues for the application of a wide range of biological theories to man.[34] It is clear that one cannot reject the core of Wilson's argument without at the same time rejecting the central propositions of biological science. However, in some of his more speculative statements about human nature, he has, as argued by his critics, gone rather far afield from his biological core. It is only this core that is used as a basis for the integrative theory.

The logical place to begin a consideration of Wilson's theory is with the summary statement of Darwinian doctrine with which he opens *Sociobiology*:

> In a Darwinist sense the organism does not live for itself. Its primary function is not even to reproduce other organisms; it reproduces

genes, and it serves as their temporary carrier. Natural selection is the process whereby certain genes gain representation in the following generations superior to that of other genes located at the same chromosome positions.

In the process of natural selection, then, any device that can insert a higher proportion of certain genes into subsequent generations will come to characterize the species. One class of such devices promotes prolonged individual survival. Another promotes superior mating performance and care of the resulting offspring.[35]

At the outset of *Sociobiology*, Wilson takes up what he considers to be the "central theoretical problem of sociobiology," the transmission of genes that lead to "altruistic" behavior. For Wilson, as for biologists generally, an altruistic act is one that decreases the probability of an individual passing on his genes to the next generation. As does Darwin, Wilson resorts to explanations relating to selection of the genes of groups of individuals. For this, Wilson, at least in the early stages of his argument, appears to rely primarily on the notion of "kin selection."[36] It does seem clear that individual acts of self-sacrifice, if they are engaged in on behalf of one's kin, may actually enhance the probability that genes similar to those of the individual will pass on to succeeding generations. As Wilson aruges, the biological function of traits that endure has to do with maximizing the transmission of genes, which may have nothing to do with maximizing happiness and pleasure.

It is the final chapter, "Sociobiology to Sociology," which has generated the most controversy. Wilson attempts to draw together the carefully developed principles of sociobiology as they have been used to study other animals and to apply them to man. Here, Wilson is much concerned with explaining variation among cultures on the basis of genetic differences. He maintains that "although the genes have given away most of their sovereignty" they still do influence behavioral qualities that underlie variations in behavior among human groups.[37] He maintains that hereditability has been documented with respect to introversion-extroversion, personal tempo, certain psychomotor activities, neuroticism, dominance, and several other features of human behavior. Wilson calls for the eventual development of a discipline of "ethological genetics." He argues that, in the meantime, human nature can be explored by two indirect methods. The first method is to construct, on the basis of empirical observation, elementary rules of human behavior. Wilson views the work of Abraham Maslow and George Homans as being aimed in this direction. Homans is seen as having such a perspective because he speaks in terms of "rewards" that *all* human beings want. Maslow has structured a hierarchy of "needs" postulated to represent a single psychological structure for *all* human beings. Wilson suggests that the emotive centers of the human brain have been programmed by genetic influences to serve the interest of survival. If this is so, the discovery of what human beings find rewarding, and the structure of those rewards, will identify some of the enduring human characteristics that have been programmed by means of natural selection.[38]

The second indirect method operates through the mechanism of phylogenetic analysis. This strategy is to "identify basic primate traits that lie beneath the surface and help to determine the configuration of man's higher social behavior."[39] He notes that this has been the strategy of the ethologists, who have done so "with great style and vigor."[40] Wilson applauds their efforts, as "calling attention to man's status as a biological species adapted to a particular environment."[41] As noted above, he credits them with with breaking "the stifling grip of the extreme behaviorists, whose view of the mind of man as a virtually equipotent response machine was neither correct nor heuristic."[42] Wilson criticizes the ethologists, however, for engaging in inefficient and misleading work in that they "selected one plausible hypothesis or another based on a review of a small sample of animal species, then advocated the explanation to the limit."[43]

In contrast to the approach of the ethologists, Wilson suggests that what should be done is to "base a rigorous phylogeny [history of the group] of closely related species on many biological traits."[44] With respect to man, the procedure that Wilson suggests is the observation of the lowest taxonomic level at which various characters, or traits, show significant variations between classifications. According to Wilson, "characters are conservative if they remain constant at the level of taxonomic family as throughout the order Primates, and they are the ones most likely to have persisted in relatively unaltered form into the evolution of *Homo*."[45] Wilson identifies as "conservative" traits aggressive dominance systems in which males are ordinarily dominant over females, variation in the intensity of responses (particularly during aggressive interactions), intensive and prolonged maternal care with pronounced socialization of the young, and matrilineal social organization. It is these traits that Wilson believes have a genetic basis that we share with other primates. These are "homologous" traits.

Some of Wilson's more interesting statements have to do with the future of the study of humans as it is affected by sociobiology. Wilson contends that sociology, which is at present at a premature stage, will eventually merge with cultural anthropology, social psychology, and economics. These disciplines may yield the first real scientific laws of sociology. Indeed, Wilson argues that some basis for these laws already exists in the "most general model of economics."[46] He maintains that the full development of a fundamental theory in sociology, however, must "await a full, neuronal explanation of the human brain."[47]

Sociobiology's role in the growth of sociological knowledge will, according to Wilson, have two aspects. First, it will help to reconstruct the history of behavioral mechanisms and identify how adaptive are many of its functions. For example, activities such as aggression may have become maladaptive. However, the evolutionary history of aggressive machinery may indicate that the tendency toward aggression is extraordinarily difficult to suppress. The second contribution of evolutionary sociobiology would be the monitoring of genetic change. He suggests that the elimination of certain genetic characteristics may lead to unintended elimination of other genetic characteristics. For example, elimination of aggressiveness may lead to the elimination of other, more desirable, traits. He suggests that planned societies may unintentionally produce a dwindling of those behaviors that make us human.

The closing chapter of *Sociobiology: A New Synthesis* is much too brief to give a full exposition of the application of sociobiological theory to man. Wilson attempted to remedy this by writing a second book, *On Human Nature*. At the outset of this later book, Wilson forthrightly declares, "Biology is the key to human nature, and social scientists cannot afford to ignore its rapidly tightening principles."[48] Wilson describes sociobiology as being largely based on systematic comparisons of social species. Each of these is seen as an "evolutionary experiment" that has been produced by interaction between the environment and genes.[49]

Through the examination of many of these experiments, sociobiologists have begun to construct the first general principles of "genetic social evolution."[50] Wilson claims that it is possible to apply this knowledge to the study of human beings as animals. According to Wilson, "Sociobiologists consider man as though seen through the front end of a telescope, at a greater than usual distance and temporarily diminished in size, in order to view him simultaneously with an array of other social experiments."[51]

The role of culture in human behavior is highly problematic for sociobiologists. While conceding that culture is important among humans, Wilson denies that culture has become all-powerful through

the course of evolution. He decries the misconception of "more traditional Marxists, some learning theorists, and a still surprising proportion of anthropologists and sociologists that social behavior can
be shaped into virtually any form."[52] Wilson attacks the view of
what he calls "ultra-environmentalism"—that man is entirely the
creature of his own culture. According to Wilson culture makes man,
but man in turn makes culture. "Each person is molded by an interaction of his environment, especially his cultural environment, with
the genes that affect social behavior."[53] He argues that it is no longer
a matter of serious dispute *whether* genes influence behavior, but
rather only *to what extent* they do so. He defines a genetically determined trait as one that "differs from other traits at least in part as a
result of the pressure of one or more distinctive genes."[54]

What are perhaps Wilson's most compelling arguments have to do
with the notion that *there is such a thing as human nature.* Wilson
argues that, although human nature is uneven and complex, it is
nevertheless "just one hodge-podge out of many conceivable."[55] We
do share certain traits with other members of a taxonomic group
which includes Old World monkeys, apes, and human beings. These
traits include intimate social groupings of certain sizes, males of
greater size than females, young molded by a long period of social
training (first with the mother and then with peers) and social play
as a strongly developed activity which features role practice, mock
aggression, sex practice, and exploration. To Wilson, it is beyond our
conception that human beings could be socialized into performing
the totally different repertories of behavior of other taxonomic
groups such as fishes, birds, antelopes, or rodents. This would "run
counter to deep emotional responses and have no chance of persisting through as much as a single generation."[56] Our civilization and
social practices stem from our nature; any human society exhibits
certain characteristics different from those that would be exhibited
by societies based on different evolutionary backgrounds with different genetic connections. Our civilization is "linked to the anato-
my of bare-skinned, bipedal mammals and the peculiar qualities of
human nature."[57] Wilson summarizes:

> The general traits of human nature appear limited and idiosyncratic
> when placed against the great backdrop of all other living species. Ad-
> ditional evidence suggests that the more stereotyped forms of human
> behavior are mammalian and even more specifically primate in charac-
> ter, as predicted on the basis of general evolutionary theory. Chimpan-
> zees are close enough to ourselves in the details of their social life and
> mental properties to rank as nearly human in certain domains where it

was once considered inappropriate to make comparisons at all. These facts are in accord with the hypothesis that human social behavior rests on genetic foundation—that human behavior is, to be more precise, organized by some genes that are shared with closely related species and others that are unique to the human species. The same facts are unfavorable for the competing hypothesis which has dominated the social sciences for generations, that mankind has escaped its own genes to the extent of being entirely culture-bound.[58]

Given human nature, Wilson argues, quoting Lionel Trilling, there is a "hard, irreducible, stubborn core of biological urgency and biological necessity and biological reason, that culture cannot reach and that reserves the right, which sooner or later it will exercise, to judge the culture and resist and revise it."[59] He argues that attempts to go against this biological core may be doomed to failure.

Wilson recognizes the importance of human learning in producing a highly flexible set of actions and responses. Yet, he argues, even human learning is constrained.

So the human mind is not a tabula rasa, a clean slate on which experience draws intricate pictures with lines and dots. It is more accurately described as an autonomous decision-making instrument, an alert scanner of the environment that approaches certain kinds of choices, and not others in the first place, then innately leans toward one option as opposed to others and urges the body into action according to a flexible schedule that shifts automatically and gradually from infancy into old age. The accumulation of old choices, the memory of them, the reflection on those to come, the re-experiencing of emotions by which they were engendered, all constitute the mind. Particularities in decision making distinguish one human being from another. But the rules followed are tight enough to produce a broad overlap in the decisions taken by all individuals and hence a convergence powerful enough to be labelled human nature.[60]

In Wilson's work we see a number of major assertions. First, that there *is* an identifiable human nature that has genetic roots. Second, that some variations among human societies are partly genetic. Third, he draws a number of conclusions about human societies which are rather speculative. It is this writer's judgment that at least the first assertion is fundamentally sound. We do have a nature. It does constrain us in ways we tend not to notice. The whole experience of human history seems to bear out the difficulties of constructing what men have believed to be more reasonable societies. Yet, within our genetic boundaries we behave very freely. We learn readily. We construct culture, which performs some of the same functions, and behaves in somewhat the same way, as genetic evolution. Nevertheless, genetic influences do endow us with predispositions that influence our behavior in all aspects of our lives, including work.

Wilson's rather speculative, miscellaneous conclusions about human societies are much more dubious. Indeed, it is these that have caused him the greatest difficulties with his critics. But it seems unnecessary to reject all of his approach because of some questionable, speculative, and politically biased conclusions.

In Defense of Sociobiology

Sociobiology has had a number of defenders. These have included moral philosophers, sociobiologists, political scientists, psychologists, and many others. The diversity of the approaches of the supporters of sociobiology has guaranteed the development of a fascinating variety of arguments on the subject.

Speaking to the ethics of sociobiology, Bernard Davis poses some interesting arguments.[61] He argues that sociobiology "provides a naturalistic base for escaping from the shallowness of pure egoistic utilitarianism."[62] Furthermore, he argues that if there is a genetic element to our competitive and cooperative drives, and to the rational and irrational aspects of our behavior, we can never completely escape the necessity for dealing with conflict among these. As Davis argues, this has always been recognized by traditional moralists and theologians, but in recent years has been opposed by "utopians imbued with unlimited confidence in the power of environmental manipulation."[63] The realistic necessity to take into account conflicting aspects of our nature is one that needs to be recognized in order to construct a good society.

One of sociobiology's most eloquent defenders is David Barash. The title of Barash's book, *The Whisperings Within*, itself expresses something important about sociobiology. Indeed, it is Barash's main argument that it is these "whisperings" that control our behavior to certain degree. He maintains that "sociobiology offers dramatic insights into our own behavior."[64] He credits sociobiology with the new insight that fitness for survival, which is mediated by natural selection, "includes complex social behaviors, such as courting, fighting, associating with friends and caring for offspring."[65] Those individuals that function more effectively socially turn out to be more fit and more favored by natural selection. It is not just the possession of a good body that is a guarantee of evolutionary success. The body must *behave adaptively* in order for its favorable characteristics to be useful. He further argues:

> Individuals behave, not genes, but the behaviors reflect strategies that the genes have evolved for replicating themselves: find food, of the right sort and the right amounts; find mates, also of the right sort and the right numbers; care for your children and compete with others, if that suits your interests. Any way you choose to see it, the fact is we tend to do things that maximize our fitness. This is the central principle of sociobiology: insofar as a behavior reflects at least some component of gene action, individuals will tend to behave so as to maximize their fitness.[66]

Similarly, Barash argues: "But we may have to open our minds and admit the possibility that our need to maximize our fitness may be whispering somewhere deep within us and that, know it or not, most of the time we are heeding these whisperings."[67]

Barash addresses these whisperings quite graphically. For example, he poses the question, "Why is sugar sweet?" The why, of course, has to do with the *function* of sugar tasting sweet, not particularly with any intelligent designer. He answers by saying that it is reasonably clear that it was to the advantage of our tree dwelling ancestors, who ate a good deal of fruit, to be able to select ripe fruit. Therefore, tasting ripe fruit, which contains sucrose, as pleasant was a matter of evolutionary advantage. Barash argues that, just as we find sugar sweet, we find certain behaviors to be "sweet." That is, we are inclined to do things because these contribute to our fitness. As do other apologists for sociobiology, Barash argues that he is not talking about genetic *determinism*, but rather genetic *influence*: "This is the difference between shooting a bullet at a target (determinism) and throwing a paper airplane (influence) . . . in a strong wind. Environment is that wind, and certainly for human beings culture, our major environmental fact of life, does a great deal to modify our genetically-influenced predispositions."[68]

Among the more philosophical defenses of sociobiology is the book *Sociobiology: Sense or Nonsense?* by Michael Ruse.[69] Ruse looks first for the evidence of genetic components of social behavior in "natural experiments" which is available. He is referring to the differences between identical and nonidentical twins and the evidence that schizophrenia, manic depression, and perhaps alcoholism all have a genetic component. From the examination of this "direct evidence," Ruse concludes that there is substantial reason for believing that some human behavior is controlled by genes.[70] Ruse also finds supporting evidence in studies of psychologists showing that certain things are innately learned more easily than others.[71] A similar "natural experiment" approach is taken by Rene Dubos, who finds proof of genetic links to behavior in the ease with which primitive people adapt to Western life, ways, and language.[72]

Ruse defends the reasoning by analogy which is a part of ethological and sociobiological thought. He maintains that such reasoning is not bad per se; the question is whether the analogy is a good one or a poor one. In this respect, it is important to inquire whether the properties invoked as analogous are relevant. He describes the general scheme of this strategy of argument in sociobiology as follows:

> Animals and humans share many biological attributes particularly in the way that genes cause morphological [physical] characteristics. Moreover, these attributes are relevant to the causes of behavior. Animals have genetically caused behavior. There are no relevant dissimilarities great enough to rule out an inference to genetic bases for human behavior. Therefore, it is reasonable to conclude by analogy that there are genetic bases for at least some behavior.[73]

Animal and human behavior are similar in many respects and it is clear that some animal behavior is controlled by genes, so there is good reason to believe that human behavior is also controlled by genes.

Certainly the most complex and ambitious apology for sociobiology is that of Alexander Rosenberg.[74] Rosenberg's essential argument is that, in order for the social sciences to be truly scientific, they must adopt biological theory. Rosenberg contends that the well-recognized failure of the social sciences to develop scientific theory is not, as John Stuart Mill argued, the result of the complexity of the phenomena involved. According to Rosenberg this explanation is based mainly upon a desire to preserve the empiricist view that beliefs and desires jointly operate to produce actions rather than on its merits.[75]

This situation involves a "trilemma": (1) "the common assumption" that we are usually correct in attributing actions to beliefs and desires; (2) the failure to find a law of human action to sustain this; (3) "the implicit view that causal claims must be sustained by laws."[76] The fundamental problem is that the concepts "belief" and "desire" are logically incapable of being made into a system of general statements in any scientific theory. This is the case because beliefs and desires are not "natural kinds," that is, causally homogeneous classes of events, states, or conditions. "Natural kinds" exist only where causal links are shared by sets of phenomena. Because they are not natural kinds, beliefs and desires may be involved in true singular statements, but are incapable of being incorporated into a law.[77] One of the difficulties with terms relating these reasons and actions is that they pertain only to human beings. To connect with the general body of scientific knowledge, and operate in the form of general scientific laws, it is necessary to have causal statements that pertain to something broader than a particular species. Rosenberg argues that biology, particularly population biology, contains the narrowest natural kinds into which we can be sure that human behavior falls. It is, therefore, biology to which we should turn for theory. In taking the position that human beliefs and desires are not natural kinds Rosenberg argues:

> But the stupefying complexity, redundancy, and interconnection of brain states finely enough structured to be localized and credited with identity to particular states of belief and desire at particular times, together with the equally myriad bodily movements any one of which could constitute a particular action, make the provision of the specifications required for a mental notion's being a natural kind as unlikely as an empirical possibility can be.[78]

According to Rosenberg, the biological laws that represent the content of the theory of natural selection meet all the requirements for scientific laws. They deal with natural kinds. Additionally, they are ultimately reducible to laws of physics and chemistry, and therefore connectible with the general body of scientific knowledge. Economic theory, which is perhaps the best that social science has produced, fails in part because, "we do not have the same degree of assurance about the assumptions of maximization that plays for the economist the role which natural selection of the fittest plays for the biologist."[79] Rosenberg maintains that "there are no discoverable general laws standing part way in generality between the biochemical laws in which neurophysiological regularities are expressed and the evolutionary laws in which the findings of the ethology and sociobiology are expressed."[80] He concludes that ". . . the prime movers of selection, variation and mutation, provide the most fundamental, the lowest-level systematic causal *explanations* available for individual instances of behavior. . . ."[81]

Rosenberg maintains that sociobiologists are committed to "explanatory biological determinism." This is the notion that scientifically acceptable explanations of the behavior of human beings are available only at the level of dispositions that can be inherited, or the neurological facts underlying those dispositions. This view commits the sociobiologist to remain at a fundamental level of human behavior. It does not allow extrapolation to matters such as intelligence, earning power, and sex roles. Furthermore, biological determinism is not committed to the fixity of inherited dispositions. On this limited ground, Rosenberg believes sociobiology to be reasonably safe. Rejecting these grounds would amount to rejecting the fundamental tenets of biology.[82]

The response of psychologists to sociobiology has been particularly interesting. As one would expect, the more extreme behaviorists have been opposed to it, particularly as it revives the "biologism" of Freud which is anathema to them. On the other hand, some psychologists have found sociobiology to be a source of useful notions. The response to this area of research by psychologists is colored deeply by their notion of the concept of instinct. According to Boice, "The treatment of instinct in American psychology has passed from dispute, to disuse, to, finally, disguise. The power of behaviorism was in making a straw man of instincts and then destroying them. Instincts were defined by behaviorists as concatenated reflexes, different from ordinary reflexes only in degree of complexity."[83] Yet instincts have never really been seen in this way by biologists, but rather as urgent reactions which, although having an invariant core, are *modifiable*. Neither learning nor biological disposition necessarily excludes the other.

According to Boice, American behaviorists have had difficulty accepting ethology and sociobiology because the behaviorists have a *causal* perspective, rather than a *functional* perspective. That is, their method is to manipulate and observe the results, so as to predict which manipulation will lead to a behavior, rather than trying to figure out what *purpose* the behavior serves. Additionally, the behaviorist tends to organize knowledge through consideration of ideal situations rather than organizing knowledge according to the way things are. Additionally, the American behaviorists typically use laboratory experiments, whereas the European ethologists use field studies.

Donald T. Campbell is among the psychologists who believe that some lessons can be drawn from sociobiology.[84] He has argued, for example, that habits, attitudes, and thoughts that are learned must have physiological embodiments just as do inborn behavioral tendencies. Mutations that modify the physiology of the brain or hormonal distributions are just as likely as those affecting other anatomical features. These could have direct behavioral effects, some quite general.[85] Campbell goes on from this reasoning to use natural selection theory to develop his theory of "social cultural evolution."

Biologism has long been present in the Freudian psychological tradition. Erich Fromm has noted that "only a dynamic psychology, the foundations of which have been laid by Freud, can get further than paying lip service to the human factor. Though there is no fixed human nature, we cannot regard human nature as being infinitely malleable and able to adapt itself to any kind of conditions without developing a psychological dynamism of its own."[86] Even members of the highly cognitive social learning theory school would seem to rest their theory upon notions of innate inclinations to imitation, which is somewhat similar to the older notion of "contagion."[87]

Scholars in other social sciences have recognized links between their disciplines and either traditional biology or the new sociobiology. It has even been argued that economics is a biological as well as a social science, as it studies "group relations among the living organisms of the genus *homo sapiens*."[88] As such, it is said that economics must "recognize the general meaning of biological evolution."[89] Political scientists[90] and anthropologists[91] have also found uses for biological or sociobiological theories. Perhaps the best brief argument for a biological approach to social science is contained in an article by Lionel Tiger and Robin Fox entitled "The Zoological Perspective in Social Science."[92] They conclude: "The fact that man is the animal which has relatively recently succeeded in dominating all others does not mean that he is therefore exempt both from being an animal and from being studied as such. Though man's culture is the most evident expression of his biological success over other animals it should not obscure his community with them."[93]

Sociobiology's Critics

Much to the surprise of Edward Wilson, his work on sociobiology produced not only scholarly debate but cries of outrage from a large and vocal group of scientists and political activists. The heat of the response, as well as its rather widespread nature, has made it one of the livelier scientific debates in modern times. Wilson's work has been quoted out of context. He has been attacked personally. His work has been the subject of what can only be characterized as smear tactics. It is necessary to wade through quite a morass of this to ferret out the fundamental, and often sound, criticisms made by sociobiology's opponents.

It appears that the main lines of criticism are three: there is the criticism that sociobiology represents the discredited approach of

"biological determinism"; there is the related argument that sociobiology is highly political in its conclusions; and there have been extensive scientific critiques of sociobiology.

One of the most often heard criticisms of sociobiology is that it is a
revival of "biological determinism." This is one of the chief grounds
for opposition stated by a group of people known as the "Sociobiology Study Group of Science for the People."[94] This prong of the attack on sociobiology attempts to tar it with guilt because of its association with some thoroughly reprehensible and discredited theories
and even such plain silliness as the classic statement by John D.
Rockefeller, Sr.: "The growth of a large business is merely a survival
of the fittest. . . . It is merely the working out of a law of nature and a
law of God."[95] It is accused of being consistent with the genocidal
policies of the Nazis.

It is clearly the case that those urging a biological view of man
must be aware of the pitfalls revealed by the use of biological man by
both Nazis and predatory capitalists to justify their abuses. He
should not be so used again. Adopting a contrary, extreme behavioral
view is, however, no guarantee of the absence of brutal oppression in
society. After all, Stalin's Russia was based on the proposition that
man is highly malleable.

The argument that sociobiology is just one more version of biological determinism is one which is of precious little value to serious
intellectual discourse. Its sole constructive purpose is to alert us to
the fact that there may be dangers in drawing from biological reasoning political conclusions that are too facile. However, it also
serves the destructive purpose of introducing into the debate the
sorts of emotions that come about when the smear is used as a substitute for reason. The argument is fundamentally irrelevant. In addition, it is positively harmful in that it calls for a judgment of sociobiology on the basis of passion rather than cool deliberation.

The related argument that suggests the political nature of sociobiology is perhaps more useful. Again, it is members of the Sociobiology Study Group of Science for the People who make the argument.[96] Although they may or may not be misguided insofar as they
attribute political motives to Wilson, they are on the mark in calling
out the normative political content of sociobiology. As they argue, if
one is not careful it is easy to draw unsupported and speculative political conclusions from sociobiological theory. Indeed, Wilson perhaps innocently does on occasion show a discomforting inclination
to do this—the by now familiar problem of the confusion of isness

with oughtness. Male dominance in human societies is not necessarily right just because it has been common in the past. While it is useful to note, as Wilson does, that a genetic component may be involved, it is patently wrong and undesirable to conclude from this, as Wilson seems to, that political systems must or should reflect this.

The most serious attack mounted on sociobiology has been the one that takes issue with its scientific merits. Several of its critics, including some of the more prominent members of the Sociobiology Study Group, have adopted this strategy. What is perhaps the best of these arguments has been put together by one of the more distinguished members of the group, Steven Jay Gould.[97] Gould describes the difference between his views and those of Wilson as being the difference between biological *potentiality* and biological *determinism*. Gould agrees with Wilson that the patterns of human social behavior are subject to "genetic control" in that they "represent a restricted subset of possible patterns that are very different from the patterns of termites, chimpanzees and other animal species."[98] Gould disagrees with Wilson's speculations with respect to genetic origins of specific traits of human behavior such as spite, aggression, homosexuality, and male-female differences. Gould goes on to argue that there is no direct evidence for genetic control of specific human social behaviors.

Gould makes an extensive argument regarding what he believes are Wilson's three major strategies of presenting indirect proof of genetic control of human social behavior. These strategies are *universality, continuity,* and *adaptiveness.* The *universality* argument, according to Gould, is that behaviors invariably found both in our closest primate relatives and among humans are likely to have a common inherited base. As Gould argues, mere similarities do not necessarily indicate common genetic origins. This is recognized by biologists in their distinction between homologous structures, which have genetic roots, and analogous, which have similar appearances but not common genetic roots. It should be said in Wilson's defense that he does not rely upon the mere fact that behaviors are similar. Instead, he offers the more conservative approach of looking for traits (characteristics) common within groups that we know are closely related in evolutionary terms.

The Wilson argument regarding *continuity,* according to Gould, has to do with explaining the passing on of traits such as altruism. Wilson's *adaptiveness* argument hangs on the relentless operation of natural selection to cull disadvantageous social structures. Gould argues that both of these last two arguments can be explained by social and cultural adaptation as well as by genetic action:

> Why imagine that specific genes for aggression, dominance, or spite have any importance when we know that the brain's enormous flexibility permits us to be aggressive or peaceful, dominant or submissive, spiteful or generous? Violence, sexism, and general nastiness are biological since they represent one subset of a possible range of behaviors. But peacefulness, equality, and kindness are just as biological and we may see their influence increase if we can create social structures that permit them to flourish. Thus, my criticism of Wilson does not invoke a nonbiological "environmentalism"; it merely pits the concept of biological potentiality, with a brain capable of the full range of human behaviors and predisposed toward none, against the idea of biological determinism, with specific genes for specific behavioral traits.[99]

Gould concludes his arguments by stating that social reform is not impeded by biological nature, because humans are, as Simone de Beauvoir said, "the being whose essence lies in having no essence."[100]

In many respects Gould's arguments are sound and well taken. They are not quite as extreme as some of the other criticisms of sociobiology; indeed, Gould accepts the influence of biological parameters on human social behavior. Where he differs with Wilson is with respect to the specificity of human behaviors that can usefully be analyzed in genetic terms. He disagrees with Wilson that such human behaviors as aggression have important genetic components. Yet many of the behavioral characteristics to which Wilson alludes exist universally in human societies. It seems to this writer that it is upon this rock that Gould's argument founders. There are some human behaviors that are universal. From whence do they come? Given a great variety of environments and cultures, it is hardly plausible to argue that they are derived from culture or environment. As does Eibl, this writer is inclined to believe that there is no plausible explanation other than the genetic one.[101] Gould's declaration that man is a being who has no essence and is therefore free is of comfort only to existentialists. If man has no nature, what meaning does his freedom have? If he is free to be human, his freedom has some meaning. If being a human being means nothing except being flexible, the freedom to be human is not very appealing.

Others have attacked the general field of sociobiological and ethological research. James Chowning Davies, in his search for theories relating to social conflict, has concluded that ethology and sociobiology are of little value. He characterizes the work of ethologists as "chronically fuzzy." He argues that sociobiologists work at a distance very far removed from behavior. He generally accuses ethologists and sociobiologists of a lack of rigor and maintains that the work of physiologists is much more promising than that of ethologists and sociobiologists.[102]

Perhaps the best known critic of this field of research is Ashley Montagu.[103] Montagu argues that: (1) no specific human behavior is genetically determined; (2) "human beings are capable of any kind of behavior"; and (3) "the kind of behavior that human beings display in any circumstance is determined not by the genes, although there is of course some genetic contribution, but largely by the experience he has undergone during his life in interaction with those genes."[104] Montagu, like Gould, argues that there are genetic potentialities in human beings, but that the explanation for human behavior lies almost entirely in their experience, rather than in their genetic makeup. It is the arguments for the effects of "instincts" to which Montagu is opposed. Montagu (wrongly) defines the term instinct as it is used by the ethologists in the following terms: "To a specific stimulus, the creature will always react in a specific predetermined manner. . . ."[105] Montagu maintains that "humans as such lost virtually all remnants of any instincts which they may have once had."[106] Specifically with respect to sociobiology, Montagu accuses Wilson of "biologism," the "conviction that since humans are animals who have evolved in much the same way as other animals they must be explicable in much the same way."[107] Montagu sees human beings as operating in an entirely different fashion than other animals: "What sociobiologists do not fully understand is that as a consequence of the unique history of human evolution humankind has moved into a completely new zone of adaptation, namely, culture, the human-made part of the environment; that it is through the learned part of the environment that humans respond to the challenges of their environments, and not through the determinative or decisive action of genes."[108]

The critics of sociobiology and ethology have been lively and stimulating in their criticism. Their enthusiasm leaves little doubt that they have engaged in heroic efforts to refute sociobiology's conclusions. As adversaries of sociobiological notions, they have effectively pointed out all the conceivable limitations upon, and difficulties with, sociobiological reasoning. Additionally, they have prompted Wilson and his fellow sociobiologists to clarify and refine their thoughts, and even to pull back from their less defensible positions. All of this has been useful. However, there comes a time in an intellectual discourse when the limits of adversarial arguments have been reached. Synthesis of conflicting approaches becomes necessary where, as here, it appears that both sides have something to be said for them. Fortunately, in the writings of the British moral philosopher Mary Midgley, one finds such a synthesis.

THE NEWER SYNTHESIS: A BALANCED VIEW

Mary Midgley has introduced the welcome voice of sweet reason into the sociobiology debate. As one of the chief protaganists, Ashley Montagu, has said, Midgley's work should cause the debators "furiously to think."[109] One of Midgley's prime points, and the one that apparently engendered Montagu's remarks about furious thinking, is that the tone and approach of the debate has been fundamentally misguided. She terms the extreme views on both sides "rival fatalisms." Furthermore, she notes that the proponents of these fatalisms speak largely in terms of military metaphors, such as "attack" and "defense." She suggests that it is more appropriate to speak of a journey toward the solution to problems, or to speak in terms of "complementary tools or crafts in building the conceptual scheme that we need."[110] Yet, as she notes, instead of viewing social and genetic explanations as *complementing* one another, writers have tended to place them *in opposition* to one another, as if a contest were involved. According to Midgley, "people have been strangely determined to take genetic and social explanations as alternatives instead of using them to complete each other. Combining them without talking nonsense is therefore by now fearfully hard work. But there is no future in refusing to try."[111] In her very sensible book she accomplishes this to an extraordinary degree.

The burden of Midgley's argument is that: (1) human beings have natures that we would do well to understand; (2) the "blank paper" view that denies the existence of a fundamental human nature is wrong in many respects; (3) human nature is quite complex, and cannot be reduced to a simple principle such as rational egoism. Midgley does not deny the importance of learning or culture. In fact, she propounds highly persuasive arguments for their importance. Similarly, she is not opposed to the notion of human rationality. She does attempt, however, to place it in the context of other human characteristics.

To begin with, Midgley maintains that human beings are animals with our own nature, and "not that of any other species."[112] Because this is so, "our basic repertoire of wants is given."[113] If we want certain things, it is because we have been "programmed" to do so. Human beings "all have to have a conceptual frame within which wants are related."[114] The set of wants human beings have are not "random impulses." Instead "they are articulated recognizable aspects of life; they are the deepest structural constituents of our characters."[115] In support of the innateness of certain structures of behavior, Midgley cites rather impressive evidence collected by Eibl and others regarding the universality of certain behaviors. For example, many human gestures are not only universal among human beings, but also among primates.[116] Not only are the gestures themselves universal, but so is the ability to read them. These gestures include smiling, frowning, laughing and crying, growling, stamping, snorting, and spitting.[117] Midgley summarizes:

> We take these things for granted just because they are constant. And in a way our business is always with the mutable, with what we can change. This makes some people think it a waste of time to attend to innate factors. But not trying to do anything about innate factors is a quite different thing from denying that they exist. And in fact, if we want to change anything we obviously must attend to innate factors, since they include the possible mechanism for change. To effect any change, we have to understand the permanent. An obvious instance is the set of currently popular suggestions that marriage, or "the family" in the abstract, is a dispensable institution, a mere passing whim of certain cultures, or that there is really no maternal instinct, just cultural conditioning by the women's magazines. Or that we should behave in exactly the same manner to women and men. Or of course, that it is only bad education which makes us aggressive. All this, I think, is just spitting against the wind. We can vary enormously the forms these things take and our own individual part in them. We can no more get rid of them than we can grow wings and tusks. Nor is there any good reason why we should want to.[118]

Midgley argues strongly and persuasively that the notion that human beings have a nature is in derogation neither of human freedom nor of the possibility of societal reform. Indeed, she argues that the concept of a nature is absolutely essential to the concept of freedom. As she reasons, "if we were genuinely plastic and indeterminate at birth, there could be no reason why society should not stamp us into any shape that might suit it."[119] Granting that notions of inborn tendencies have been used by conservative theorists to justify the status quo, Midgley argues that fundamental assumptions about human nature also underlie all of the liberating creeds, including those of Rousseau, Kant, Mill, and Marx. As she suggests, one could hardly imagine a more useful bit of knowledge for reformers than a sound understanding of our genetic constitution. She accurately characterizes the notion that reformers can do without this as "a bizzare tactical aberration."[120] Indeed, it seems obvious that knowing one's inclinations creates the possibility of being able to change them.

Midgley argues that one of the great problems in this area is an inadequate conceptualization of the term *instinct*. She argues that instinct is nothing mysterious, but is simply a "disposition, a set of causal properties."[121] She makes the very useful distinction between "closed" and "open" instincts. Closed instincts are behavior patterns that are genetically determined in every detail. An example of this is the bee's honey dance. Open instincts, on the other hand, are "programs with a gap." In the case of open instincts, "parts of the behavior pattern are innately determined, but others are left to be filled in by experience."[122] She gives as an example the general locomotive predisposition to "come home" which many animals share. The animal has this as a "general ruling motive." It does not just wander around aimlessly until it finds something that reinforces its movement. For one thing, a pattern of random behavior would surely be the path to an early death. Each animal has a range of behaviors that it must find rather quickly in order to survive. Therefore, its programming includes a considerable number of *general* tendencies such as getting home, seeking water, hiding by day, and avoiding open spaces. The more complex the behaviors, and the more intelligent the creatures become, the more their programming is general. Many activities of higher animals are *both* innate and learned. That is, a creature may be born with the ability to perform certain actions and a strong wish to do so. It may, however, require time, practice, or the observation of others before its powers in this regard can be used. As a limitation on its behaviors, there are other inclinations and powers it does not have and would find extremely hard to acquire. Midgley gives the example of swimming as being outside the usual range of behaviors for cats and apes. Such a behavior is not part of the character of their species.[123]

Midgley on What Is Human Nature

Human nature, in the first place, is highly complex. The needs of human beings are multiple. "We get nowhere by ignoring their complexities or by pretending to reduce them to one."[124]

> We want incompatible things, and want them badly. We are fairly aggressive, yet we want company and depend on longterm enterprises. We love those around us and need their love, yet we want independence and need to wander. We are restlessly curious and meddling, yet

long for permanence. Unlike many primates, we do have a tendency to pair-formation, but it is an incomplete one, and gives us a lot of trouble. We cannot live without a culture, but it never quite satisfies us. All this is the commonplace of literature. It is also, to a degree, the problem of the other intelligent species too. In each, a group of counteracting needs and tendencies holds life in a rough but tolerable equilibrium. In each there are endemic conflicts. Yet an individual depends for his satisfaction on the repertory of tastes native to his species; he cannot jump off his feet. What is special about people is their power of understanding what is going on, and using that understanding to regulate it. Imagination and conceptual thought intensify all the conflicts by multiplying the options, by letting us form all manner of incompatible schemes and allowing us to know what we are missing, and also by greatly increasing our powers of self-knowledge, which is our strongest card in the attempt to sort conflicts out.[125]

Given this complexity, what can be said in general about human nature? First, like all higher animals we have a structure of deep and lasting preferences.[126] One of these is a preference for *culture*. It is essential to us because of our innate needs; culture is not something foreign or optional to human beings.[127]

It is important to recognize that our "animal" nature cannot be understood without inquiring to which animals we are making reference. We have much in common with other primates, but we also share many characteristics with the hunting carnivores. Like them, but unlike primates, we have large corporate enterprises and the loyalty and developed skills that go with such enterprises. Also like the hunting carnivores, we have homes and families. We cooperate with one another, like the hunting carnivores, because we, like they, have a deep preference for doing so.[128] We are loving animals. This characteristic appears to be based on the need for nurturing and caring for our young for an expanded period of time. Midgley makes the interesting argument that this cherishing of the young, rather than sex, is the root of human lovingness. She agrees with Eibl that Freud had it backwards about love and sex, with nurture and care for the young being primary and sex being secondary.[129]

Although Midgley views human nature as being highly diverse and complex, she argues for the existence of a unifying principle. This she considers to be "a reflective facility at the center of ourselves, by which we can think about our various actions and desires, stamping some with approval and rejecting others."[130] This might be called "conscience" or, as Aristotle called it, "the man himself." This governor of our behavior is our own center, "our own sense of how nature works."[131] This center involves both understanding and feelings. It can produce feelings of shame, which are a fundamental aspect of human nature.[132] It is this center and the pursuit of the deep need for unity and integration of personality that allows one to handle the great complexity of human wishes, needs, and desires.[133]

Tearing Up the "Blank Paper"

Midgley vigorously attacks what she considers to be the "unintelligible notion" that human beings are born as blank paper upon which any instructions can be written. She attributes this view to John B. Watson, the founding father of behaviorism. She acknowledges that this view has a firm grip upon the minds of many social scientists in the English-speaking countries.[134]

The blank paper view has been greatly encouraged by the work of B. F. Skinner. Skinner, while acknowledging that there are certain innate influences on human behavior, has concluded that since they cannot be manipulated, they are of little value to experimentalists. Skinner prefers to explain behavior as a response to reinforcement. As Midgley notes, this works only for behaviors that are performed in the first place.[135]

Midgley admits that the behaviorist creed of Watson and Skinner is useful because of its emphasis on facts and its opposition to dogmatic theoretical principles that block our recognition of plain facts. If it could only "complete its metamorphosis from a dogmatic, fighting, metaphysical creed," it might recognize that it is possible to study *both* predispositions and outward behaviors.[136] Unfortunately, this recognition is hampered by the "tantalizing notion of a single cause."[137] This yearning for a single explanation is understandable, but fundamentally misguided. It gets in the way of acquiring knowledge.

Midgley argues that the "blank paper" theorists really have no basis for claiming that their theory is exclusive.

> When people such as Watson say that man has no instincts, they always mean closed instincts. They point to his failure to make standard webs or do standard honey dances, and ignore his persistent patterns of motivation. Why do people form families? Why do they take care of their homes and quarrel over boundaries? Why do they own property? Why do they talk so much, and dance, and sing? Why do children play, and for that matter adults too? Why is nobody living in the Republic of Plato?
>
> According to Blank Paper theory, because of cultural conditioning. But this is like explaining gravitation by saying that whenever something falls, something else pushed it; even if it were true, it wouldn't

help. Who started it? Nor does it tell us why people ever resist their families, why they do what everybody is culturally conditioning them not to do. I have never seen a proper answer to that on the Blank Paper assumption, but I gather it would be expressed in terms of subcultures and cultural ambivalences, of society's need for a scapegoat, and the like. It is a pleasing picture; how do all the children of eighteen months pass the news along the grapevine that now is the time to join the subculture, to start climbing furniture, toddling out of the house, playing with fire, breaking windows, taking things to pieces, messing with mud, and chasing the ducks? For these are perfectly specific things which all healthy children can be depended on to do, not only unconditioned but in the face of all deterrents. Just so, Chomsky asks Skinner how it comes about that small children introduce their own grammatical mistakes into speech, talking in a way that they have never heard and that will be noticed only to be corrected. In dealing with such questions, the Blank Paper theorist's hands are tied by his a priori assumption.[138]

Ultimately, the argument against the blank paper view is that such behavior must necessarily be maladaptive. For human beings, as well as for other animals, the blank paper view would certainly make it highly likely that the randomly behaving young of the species would end up in the belly of a predator.[139] As Robert Ardrey argues, natural selection is "shrewd as a cat" in pouncing on such weakness for the purposes of natural selection.[140]

Midgley on the Disutility of Utility Theory

Midgley very perceptively explores the basic notions of utility theory. Like "blank paper" theory, she believes utility theory to have disutility because it posits a single cause. While not disagreeing that human beings do sometimes calculate advantage, she does not believe that this is a complete explanation of human behavior. While recognizing that deeply discontented animals have little chance of breeding and doing the other things necessary for survival, she maintains that a totally pleasure-seeking, egoistic, species would have small chance for survival.[141] As Midgley argues, one of the things that Wilson convincingly demonstrates is that such egoism pays off very badly genetically. She argues: "If you richly fulfill yourself at the cost of destroying all your siblings and offspring, your genes will perish and your magnificent qualities will be lost to posterity. A consistently egoistic species would be either solitary or extinct."[142]

The question of utilitarianism is closely tied to what Wilson describes as sociobiology's "central theoretical problem," the undeniable prevalence of "altruistic" behaviors. Midgley approaches this in terms of the question, "Can a conscious agent deliberately choose to do things that he thinks will not pay him?"[143] As she argues, in the widest sense, the answer to this question must be "no." But at this level the point is trivial. While it is true that what we deliberately choose to do must somehow please us and attract us, "it need not in any normal sense pay us."[144] Such a use stretches the word *pay* beyond its normal use. To use the word *pay* in the manner in which people making cost-benefit analysis use it would be to define it as, "delivering a competitive, outward advantage."[145] The question then becomes the empirical question of whether people "deliberately do things that they believe will shorten their lives, lessen their income, damage their health, or diminish their power?"[146] We know that people in fact do sometimes commit suicide or pursue vengeance or amusement when it is sure to injure them. They smoke, gamble against hopeless odds, and engage in futile competitions. No person is prudent at all times. The mere existence of imprudence, by itself, destroys the position of "philosophic Egoism."

According to Midgley, in addition to our imprudence, we are considerably lazy minded. We often do not bother to calculate, but instead do what we feel like doing. We often act on the basis of direct desire, not calculation. We do things because we have a taste for them. We admittedly have a taste for future security and benefits, and do calculate in an attempt to achieve these at times. Midgley's argument is not that we never calculate, but rather that this is not all that we do.

Midgley recognizes that there are many good things about utilitarian thought. It has the virtue of cutting through much of the hypocrisy about motives that exists when altruistic statements are used to mask egoistic purposes. Certainly the political message in the utilitarian theory of the nineteenth century as expressed by Hobbes and others had a valid point. Hobbes believed that if people looked after their own interests instead of merely "showing off," they would avoid doing many of the terrible things to which human beings appear to be prone, such as engaging in religious wars. It was the "humbug of chivalry" that was Hobbes' prime target.[147] Certainly enlightened self-interest is often a good motive in politics. Self-preservation is a strong motive of human beings. Midgley argues, however, that it cannot be the only duty or motive we have.[148]

Midgley maintains that we do many things for their own sakes, rather than for the sake of payoffs we expect to gain. Payoffs are an important part of our lives, but not as important as they may appear. One of the problems with payoffs is that there is no moment at which they can be declared. John Stuart Mill's search for payoff points appears to have been one cause of his mental breakdown.[149] As Midgley argues, a person who wants only his own advantage and has no interest in anyone else's is a psychopath, and usually one who ends up being disappointed. He is like a person who wishes to win a race, but has not the least interest in the process of engaging in the physical activity of running. Such a runner is not very likely to succeed. Utilitarianism may be useful as a fighting political doctrine, but not in giving one a prescription for a good life.

As Darwin recognized in dealing with altruistic behavior, it is at the level of the group that natural selection chiefly takes place. The great mistake of the social Darwinists was to suppose that selection works entirely by cutthroat competition between individuals. As Midgley argues, they confused the fact of competition with the motive of competitiveness.[150] The kind of selfishness that would be appropriate for natural selection purposes would be the successful planning for those behaviors that would best profit the individual's genes.[151] This is indeed an odd kind of "selfishness" from the standpoint of utility theory. It seems patently true that a group of animals that fails to contain individuals willing to sacrifice for the good of the group is less likely to survive than groups with individuals willing to make such sacrifices. To again use a phrase of Ardrey's, natural selection "lays the long finger of survival" on groups that contain altruistic members.[152]

As Midgley argues, it is not necessary to have a single gene for altruism in order for altruistic behavior to be selected. All that is necessary is for altruistic acts, such as rescuing, to be inextricably linked to more general patterns of social behavior. If we are bound to a group by ties of sociality and must have feelings of this nature in order to behave in many important ways, these ties will produce many results. One of these results may be altruistic acts.[153]

SUMMARY

The concept of biological man is absolutely essential for general theorizing in the social sciences. Economic man, alone, is at worst a poor, twisted psychopath; at best, he is simply so self-limited as to be unable to perform the task of providing a broad theoretical base for a science of human behavior. Behaviorist, or "blank paper" man, standing alone, is similarly unappealing and useless. Such a randomly behaving creature is not only intuitively implausible, but is so likely to have ended up in the belly of a predatory beast as to be unacceptable to anyone who accepts the central theoretical propositions of modern biology. Biological man, although lacking somewhat in dignity because he reeks with the residue of his animal past, appears at least to be a necessary complement to economic man and blank paper man. It is his very links with the rest of the animal kingdom that tie him to a general and respectable body of scientific knowledge. He provides us with the opportunity to understand some of the fundamental roots of human behavior.

The integrative thoery of industrial conflict is grounded in a concept of man that includes biological man, economic man, and blank paper man. It is biological man that makes the third leg of the stool to form a stable platform for a theory of human behavior in this complex and difficult area. We can understand the phenomenon of industrial conflict only if we see man as having a nature that gives him certain predispositions and tastes, who (sometimes) rationally calculates his advantage, and who is highly capable of learning. As Midgley argues, it is not necessary to view these three models of man as being in opposition to one another. Instead, it appears that the only sensible thing to do is to consider them as complements. This is what the integrative theory does.

It is of some importance to recognize the significance of a biological perspective for the discipline of industrial relations. This field has been a battleground for neoclassical economists and institutionalists for many years. In this intellectual fray, the neoclassicists have had one very substantial advantage. They have had a coherent theory base from which to operate. Although those of a Wisconsin institutional persuasion, such as this author, have been unimpressed with the explanations provided by utility theory, we have had nothing better to put in its place. We do now. By drawing on biological theory we go to a foundation, unlike utility theory, tied to the general body of scientific knowledge. It is also more plausible.

If one accepts the view that man has innate predispositions that influence his behavior in important ways, the next inquiry logically should be the identity of those predispositions that might pertain to industrial conflict. The next chapter analyzes the industrial relationship and uncovers the root causes of collective aggressive action against the employer arising from that relationship.

NOTES

[1]Konrad Lorenz, *On Aggression*, trans. Marjorie Kerr Wilson (New York: Harcourt, Brace & World, 1966), p. 17.

[2]Leonard Berkowitz, *Aggression: A Social Psychological Analysis* (New York: McGraw-Hill Book Co., 1962), p. 167.

[3]Charles Darwin, *The Origin of Species* (Baltimore: Penguin Books, 1979).

[4]Ibid., p. v.

[5]Ibid., p. 115.

[6]Ibid., p. 126.

[7]Ibid., p. 117.

[8]Ibid., p. 116.

[9]Herbert Spencer, *Social Statics*, (London: Chapman & Sons, 1851).

[10]Irenaus Eibl-Eibesfeldt, *Love and Hate*, trans. Geofrrey Strachan (New York: Holt, Rinehart, & Winston, 1972), p. 112; Nicholas Wade, "Sociobiology: Troubled Birth for New Discipline," in *The Sociobiology Debate*, ed. Arthur S. Caplan, (New York: Harper & Row, 1978) pp. 325-332. Anthony Quinton, "Ethics and the Theory of Evolution," in Caplan, *The Sociobiology Debate*, pp. 117-141.

[11]W. C. Allee, "Where Angels Fear to Tread: A Contribution from General Sociobiology to Human Ethics," in Caplan, *The Sociobiology Debate*, p. 52.

[12]Anthony Quinton, "Ethics and the Theory of Evolution," in Caplan, *The Sociobiology Debate*, p. 127; Anthony Few, "From Is to Ought," in Caplan, *The Sociobiology Debate*, p. 153.

[13]Edward O. Wilson, *Sociobiology*, abgd. ed. (Cambridge: The Belknap Press, 1980) p. 5.

[14]Desmond Morris, *The Naked Ape*, (New York: Dell Publishing Co., 1967), p. 9.

[15]Robert Ardrey, *African Genesis*, (New York: Atheneum Publishers, 1961) p. 11.

[16]Ibid., p. 14.

[17]Ibid., p. 155.

[18]Ibid., p. 345.

[19]Eibl-Eibesfeldt, *Love and Hate*, p. 44.

[20]Niko Tinbergen, "On War and Peace in Animals and Man," in Caplan, *The Sociobiology Debate*, p. 86.

[21]Ibid., p. 86.

[22]Ibid., p. 89.

[23]Lorenz, *On Aggression*, pp. 81-82.

[24]Ibid., p. 84.

[25]Eibl-Eibesfeldt, *Love and Hate*, p. 5.

[26]Tinbergen, "On War and Peace in Animals and Man," p. 91.

[27]Desmond Morris, *The Human Zoo*, (New York: Dell Publishing Co., 1969), pp. 197-198.

[28]Lorenz, *On Aggression*, pp. 213-214.

[29]Ibid., p. 239.

[30]Ardrey, *African Genesis*, p. 148.

[31]Wilson, *Sociobiology*, p. 275.

[32]Ibid., p. 275.

[33]Edward O. Wilson, *Sociobiology: The New Synthesis* (Cambridge: The Belknap Press, 1975).

[34]Edward O. Wilson, *On Human Nature*, (Cambridge: Harvard University Press, 1978).

[35]Wilson, *Sociobiology*, p. 3.

[36]Ibid.

[37]Ibid., p. 274.

[38]Ibid., pp. 274-275.

[39]Ibid., p. 275.

[40]Ibid.

[41] Ibid.
[42] Ibid.
[43] Ibid.
[44] Ibid.
[45] Ibid.
[46] Ibid., p. 300.
[47] Ibid.
[48] Wilson, *On Human Nature*, p. 13.
[49] Ibid., p. 17.
[50] Ibid.
[51] Ibid.
[52] Ibid., p. 18.
[53] Ibid.
[54] Ibid.
[55] Ibid., p. 23.
[56] Ibid., p. 21.
[57] Ibid.
[58] Ibid., p. 32.
[59] Ibid., p. 80.
[60] Ibid., p. 67.
[61] Bernard D. Davis, "A Middle Course Between Irrelevance and Scientism," in Caplan, *The Sociobiology Debate*, p. 315.
[62] Ibid., p. 317.
[63] Ibid.
[64] David Barash, *The Whisperings Within* (New York: Harper & Row, 1979), p. 1.
[65] Ibid., p. 22.
[66] Ibid., p. 29.
[67] Ibid., p. 31.
[68] Ibid., p. 39.
[69] Michael Ruse, *Sociobiology: Sense or Nonsense?* (Boston: Reidel Publishing Co., 1979).
[70] Ibid., pp. 31–32.
[71] Ibid., pp. 184–185.
[72] Rene Dubos, *Beast or Angel? Choices that Make Us Human* (New York: Charles Scribner's Sons, 1974), p. 14.
[73] Ruse, *Sociobiology: Sense or Nonsense?*, pp. 142–143.
[74] Alexander Rosenberg, *Sociobiology and the Preemption of Social Science* (Baltimore: The Johns Hopkins University Press, 1980).
[75] Ibid., pp. 1–4.
[76] Ibid., pp. 5–6.
[77] Ibid.
[78] Ibid., p. 112.
[79] Ibid., p. 129.
[80] Ibid., p. 157.
[81] Ibid.
[82] Ibid., pp. 159–160.
[83] Robert Boice, "In the Shadow of Darwin," in *Perspectives on Aggression*, ed. Russell G. Geen and Edgar C. O'Neal. (New York: Academic Press, 1976), p. 16.
[84] Donald T. Campbell, "On the Conflicts Between Biological and Social Evolution and Between Psychology and Moral Tradition," *American Psychologist* 30, no. 12 (December 1975), pp. 1103–1126.
[85] Ibid., p. 1110.
[86] Erich Fromm, *Escape From Freedom* (New York: Holt, Rinehart and Winston, 1941), pp. 14–15.
[87] Kurt Lang and Gladys Lang, *Collective Dynamics* (New York: Crowell, 1961), pp. 212–231.

[88]David Hamilton, *Evolutionary Economics* (Albuquerque: University of New Mexico Press, 1970), p. 13.

[89]Ibid.

[90]Fred H. Willhoite, Jr., "Primates and Political Authority: A Biobehavioral Perspective," *American Political Science Review* 70, no. 4 (December 1976), pp. 1110-1126; Steven A. Peterson and Albert Somit, "Sociobiology and Politics," in Caplan, *The Sociobiology Debate*, pp. 449-461.

[91]Lionel Tiger and Robin Fox, *The Imperial Animal* (New York: Holt, Rinehart and Winston, 1971); Richard D. Alexander, "Evolution, Culture, and Human Behavior: Some General Considerations," in *Natural Selection Behavior: Recent Research and Theory*, ed. Richard D. Alexander and D. W. Timble (New York: Chiron Press, 1981), pp. 509-520.

[92]Lionel Tiger and Robin Fox, "The Zoological Perspective in Social Science," *Man*, New Series 1 (1966), pp. 75-81.

[93]Ibid., p. 80.

[94]Elizabeth Allen et al., "Against 'Sociobiology'," in Caplan, *The Sociobiology Debate*, pp. 280-290.

[95]Ibid., p. 260.

[96]Joseph Alper, Jon Beckwith, and Lawrence G. Miller, "Sociobiology is a Political Issue," in Caplan, *The Sociobiology Debate*, pp. 476-488.

[97]Stephen Jay Gould, "Biological Potential vs. Biological Determinism," in Caplan, *The Sociobiology Debate*, pp. 343-351.

[98]Ibid., p. 344.

[99]Ibid., p. 349.

[100]Ibid., p. 351.

[101]Eibl-Eibesfeldt, *Love and Hate*, pp. 8-32.

[102]James Chowning Davies, "Review of *The Biology of Peace and War: Men, Animals and Aggression*, by Iraneus Eibl-Eibesfeldt," *American Political Science Review* 74, no. 3 (September 1980), pp. 796-797.

[103]Ashley Montagu, *The Nature of Human Aggression* (Oxford: Oxford University Press, 1976).

[104]Ibid., pp. 3-4.

[105]Ibid., p. 56.

[106]Ibid., p. 63.

[107]Ashley Montagu, "Introduction" in *Sociobiology Examined*, ed. Ashley Montagu (Oxford: Oxford University Press, 1980), p. 5.

[108]Ibid., p. 9.

[109]Ibid., p. 13.

[110]Mary Midgley, "Rival Fatalisms: The Hollowness of the Sociobiology Debate," in Montagu, *Sociobiology Examined*, p. 18.

[111]Mary Midgley, *Beast and Man* (New York: The New American Library, 1978), p. xviii.

[112]Ibid.

[113]Ibid., p. 182.

[114]Ibid., p. 183.

[115]Ibid.

[116]Ibid., p.246.

[117]Ibid., p. 312.

[118]Ibid., p. 326.

[119]Ibid., p. xviii.

[120]Ibid., p. xix.

[121]Ibid., p. 51.

[122]Ibid., p. 53.

[123]Ibid., pp. 53-54.

[124]Ibid., p. 190.

[125]Ibid., pp. 282-283.

126 Ibid., p. 259.
127 Ibid., pp. 286–287.
128 Ibid., pp. 335–336, 338.
129 Ibid., pp. 338–342.
130 Ibid., p. 267.
131 Ibid.
132 Ibid., pp. 270–272.
133 Ibid., p. 190.
134 Ibid., p. 19.
135 Ibid., pp. 20–21.
136 Ibid., pp. 21–22.
137 Ibid., p. 22.
138 Ibid., pp. 56–57.
139 Ibid., p. 307.
140 Ardrey, *African Genesis*, p. 60.
141 Midgley, *Beast and Man*, p. 92.
142 Ibid., p. 94.
143 Ibid., p. 118.
144 Ibid.
145 Ibid., p. 119.
146 Ibid.
147 Ibid., p. 123.
148 Ibid.
149 Ibid., p. 125.
150 Ibid., p. 132.
151 Ibid., p. 129.
152 Ardrey, *African Genesis*, p. 60.
153 Midgley, *Beast and Man*, pp. 132–134.

CHAPTER 4

The Theory's Second Pillar—The Roots of Industrial Conflict

I'm, goin' to stop. Everybody will,
'Cause you can't make a livin' in a cotton mill.
David McCarney, "Cotton Mill Colic"

Ay, every inch a king:
When I do stare, see how the subject quakes.
William Shakespeare, *King Lear*

One of the more intriguing questions about industrial conflict is the identity and nature of its root causes. The answer to this complex question is the second pillar of the integrative theory, and involves two steps. First, it is necessary to uncover the roots of the phenomenon, that is, to identify them. Second, they must be painstakingly examined and analyzed.

Identifying the root causes of industrial conflict requires deciding upon the fundamental nature of the employment relationship. This enables one to determine what is important and central to the relationship, and what is not. Once this has been done, it is possible to determine which general areas of human behavior ought to be explored for their possible effects upon industrial conflict. While such a strategy may neglect sources of industrial conflict that are related to matters peripheral to the industrial relationship, it is reasonable to at least start with those aspects of the relationship believed to be most important. This permits a clarity of focus that would otherwise be impossible.

The industrial relationship is, in essence, the exchange of autonomy for pay. It is, therefore, in the areas of the loss of autonomy and the pay received for it that we should look for the roots of important industrial relations phenomena, including industrial conflict. The roots thereby identified are material resources and social dominance. Both of these roots are grounded in biological and social scientific theory. Together they form a major component of the integrative theory of industrial conflict.

THE INDUSTRIAL RELATIONSHIP

When Occam's razor lays bare the core of the industrial relationship from which industrial conflict arises, it reveals an exchange of autonomy for pay. According to John R. Commons, when an employee accepts employment, "what he sells when he sells his labor is his *willingness* to use his faculties according to a purpose that has been pointed out to him. He sells his promise to obey commands."[1] The exchange that the employee makes is, then, his agreement to be on the subordinate end of political, or social dominance, relationship in return for a promise of economic, or material, rewards.

This is a legally accurate description of the relationship. The authoritative legal encyclopedia, *Corpus Juris Secundum*, defines this relation as follows: "Generally speaking a 'servant' or 'employee' is a person who renders service to another, usually for wages, salary, or other financial consideration, and who in the performance of such service is entirely subject to the direction and control of the other, such other being respectively the 'master' or 'employer'."[2]

The other major legal encyclopedia, *American Jurisprudence*, agrees, adding that the older terms, "master" and "servant," denote a more personal relationship than the more modern terms, "employer" and "employee." The substitution of terms is explained by the American aversion to the word "servant."[3]

Pay and subordination are the two pillars of the modern contract of employment. The effort that the employee expends is expended at the direction of the employer. Indeed, the term "employed" itself means that the worker is *used* as someone else wishes to use him. Erich Fromm has captured the essence of the relationship: "The relationship between employer and employee is permeated by the same spirit of indifference. The word 'employer' contains the whole story: The owner of capital employs another freeman being as he 'employs' a machine."[4]

Under modern compensation practices pay takes many forms. Whatever its form, it is nevertheless the primary inducement for the worker to work. She is "compensated" for accepting and acting in a subordinate work relationship. Although an employee receives many other benefits from working, financial compensation is the one universal consequence of the sort of activity in which we are interested.

It cannot be gainsaid that there are other aspects of the employment relationship. It seems reasonably clear, however, that the material and social dominance characteristics of the relationship noted above constitute its core. It therefore seems reasonable to focus upon them when investigating work-related phenomena, such as industrial conflict. This conclusion is supported by Delbert C. Miller and William A. Form in their classic text on industrial sociology. They state: "Many of the battles between organized employers and employees can only be understood as battles for income and status."[5]

MATERIAL ROOTS OF INDUSTRIAL CONFLICT

That human beings generally pursue material goods is patently true. What is debatable is the cause of this behavior. Behaviorists would maintain that this behavior, like all other human behavior, occurs because it is reinforced. Proponents of a biological man view might argue that the pursuit of physical resources is a tendency that any organism must have to survive. Curiously, this omnipresent behavioral tendency is one that has received relatively little notice from ethologists and sociobiologists. It has, quite understandably, fallen to the lot of the economists to produce the most extensive theorizing with respect to material resources. They have produced arguments, based largely on notions that can roughly be described as relating to "economic man," which are highly interesting.

Although economic man had his origins in earlier thinking, he first came to be of fundamental importance to economic thought with the birth of the classical school of economics in the eighteenth and nineteenth centuries. Jeremy Bentham and his intellectual progeny used the concept of economic man, and the utility theory upon which he stood, for economic theorizing. They also used them to develop a moral system and a political creed. Then, as now, proponents of utility theory used it as a justification for liberal, democratic, capitalism.

The fundamental principles of utility theory, as expressed by Bentham and his great successor, John Stuart Mill, are rather straightforward. The following quotations from Bentham's *Principles of Morals* summarize reasonably well the essence of his views:

> Nature has placed mankind under the governance of two sovereign masters, *pain* and *pleasure*. It is for them alone to point out what we ought to do, as well as to determine what we should do. On the one hand the standard of right and wrong, on the other the chain of causes and effects, are fastened to their throne. They govern us in all we do, in

all we say, in all we think: every effort we can make to throw off our subjection, will serve but to demonstrate and confirm it. In words a man may pretend to abjure their empire; but, in reality he will remain subject to it all the while. The *principle of utility* recognizes this subjection and assumes it for the foundation of that system, the object of which is to rear the fabric of felicity by the hands of reason and law, systems which attempt to question it, deal in sounds instead of senses, in caprice instead of light.[6]

By the principle of utility is meant that principle which approves or disapproves of every action whatsoever, according to the tendency which it appears to have to augment or diminish the happiness of the party whose interest is in question; or, what is the same thing in other words, to promote or to oppose that happiness.[7]

A thing is said to promote the interest, or be for the interest, of an individual, when it tends to add to the sum total of his pleasures; or, what comes to the same thing, to diminish the sum total of his pains.[8]

Bentham's chief concern was to provide a criterion by which institutions and commonly received ideas could be judged, with a view to their being reformed. Bentham's utilitarianism, although obviously oversimple as a moral philosophy, has nevertheless, partly by reason of its clarity, been effective in securing social and political reforms.[9] Bentham's follower, James Mill, the father of John Stuart Mill, believed that the destructive selfishness inherent in this view could be avoided through education, which had the power to make people recognize that their true interests were bound up with the interests of others.[10]

John Stuart Mill was Bentham's most famous disciple, yet he had some reservations about utilitarianism and propounded several modifications of Bentham's ideas. Similar to Bentham, Mill viewed utilitarianism as "the creed which accepts as the foundation of morals, Utility or the Greatest Happiness Principle, holds that actions are right in proportion as they tend to promote happiness, wrong as they tend to produce the reverse of happiness. By happiness is intended pleasure, and the absence of pain; by unhappiness, pain, and the privation of pleasure."[11]

Mill saw happiness as the one goal every person seeks. As did Bentham, Mill concluded that the pursuit of one's own interests was not only *expected* behavior, it was also *good*. Mill believed that the principle of utility demanded that every man should be free to develop his own powers according to his own will and judgment so long as he did not harm others. To act in a way that increases pleasure is to act rationally. To act rationally is commendable.[12]

Following a nervous breakdown caused in part by Mill's disillusionment with utilitarianism, he began to express reservations about, and propose modifications of, Bentham's theories.[13] Mill believed that man might pursue spiritual perfection as an end. He also argued that utilitarian morality had to be based in the "social feelings of mankind." Man had a desire to be in unity with other men. According to Mill, "the social state is at once so natural, so necessary, and so habitual to man, that, except in some unusual circumstances, or by an effort of voluntary abstraction, he never conceives himself other than as a member of a body."[14] It was this social feeling that Mill believed would cause individuals seeking their own pleasure to act in a way that benefited their fellows and make it possible for society to function. He believed that simple hedonism was not sufficient to explain human behavior. He saw, as did Aristotle before him, that human behavior cannot be seen solely as a means to the end of happiness. Instead, the actions themselves are constituent parts of happiness.[15]

Since Bentham's day, many economists in the West have enthusiastically adopted a theoretical structure based on Bentham's utilitarianism. A prime example of this sort of work is the late nineteenth-century theoretical writing of W. Stanley Jevons. Jevons states that his theory is "entirely based upon a calculus of pleasure and pain."[16] According to Jevons, the problem of economics is: "To satisfy our wants to the utmost with the least effort—to procure the greatest amount of what is desirable at the expense of the least that is undesirable—in other words, to maximize pleasure."[17] Jevons defines a "commodity," that central concept of economics, as being "any object, substance, action or service, which can afford pleasure or ward off pain."[18] Labor, on the other hand, is "any painful exertion of mind or body undergone partly or wholly with a view to future good."[19] Jevons recognizes that labor may be pleasant up to a point, but that "most men are compelled by their wants to exert themselves longer and more severely than they would otherwise do."[20] Indeed, according to Jevons, we "measure labour by the amount of pain which attaches to it."[21]

Support for this view comes from an interesting source. Sigmund Freud noted that work offers the possibility of considerable pleasure, and yet is not highly prized as a means of happiness. According to the great psychologist: "They do not strive after it as they do after other possibilities of satisfaction. The great majority of people only work under the stress of necessity, and this natural human aversion to work raises most difficult social problems."[22]

Some economists writing in the utilitarian tradition have focused more narrowly upon wealth, rather than upon general notions of utility. One of the postulates of Senior's "pure" theory is "that every man desires to obtain additional wealth with as little sacrifice as possible."[23] Similarly, Alfred Marshall theorizes that "the steadiest motive to ordinary business work is the desire for pay which is the material reward of work."[24] Marshall argues that man's character is molded primarily by the work he does and the material resources he acquires from work. Marshall sees economics as the study of men as they operate in the ordinary business of life. It focuses chiefly on those motives that affect with the greatest force and steadiness the conduct of man in the business part of his life. Marshall suggests that the motive for work is supplied by a definite amount of money, and that it is the definiteness and the precision of measurement of this steadiest of motives which has made it possible for economics "far to outrun every other branch of the study of man."[25] According to Marshall, this does not involve the study of some abstract "economic man" but of man as he is, and as he operates in those aspects of life in which the action of the economic motive can be predicted and verified. This enables economics to operate on a scientific basis.[26] As Joseph Schumpeter has argued, this general postulate, that man desires to obtain wealth, or pay, with as little sacrifice as possible, is quite plausible when "divested of unnecessary utilitarian association."[27]

In spite of the obvious appeal of the simple postulates suggested by Senior and Marshall, many economists have preferred to work in the more elevated realm of general utility theory. The marginalist economists (Jevon, Walras, and Menger) propounded theories involving the notion of *cardinal* utility. They believed that they could attach some value to different choices, and that this could be expressed in terms of some quantity of utility. As it became clear that there were major empirical problems with applying this theory, economists such as Edgeworth and Pareto came to the fore. They believed that it was possible to deal with utility in *ordinal* terms. That is, although it was not possible to quantify the amount of utility that any particular alternative had for an individual, it was possible to rank different alternatives with respect to the degree to which they were preferred. However, even this newer version of utility theory was found to be virtually impossible to apply. Accordingly, modern economists have turned to "revealed preference theory" which abandons many of the earlier arguments for individual rationality, but is still grounded in utility theory.[28]

One of the difficulties from which utility theory has suffered for these many years has been the absence of empirical support for its psychological claims. To be at all intelligible, it seems that utility theory must claim that human beings do in fact make conscious choices between alternatives on the basis of the anticipated consequences with respect to the happiness, or lack of happiness, which they calculate will result from the choices.

Although there is still no clear support for this view, there has been some work by social psychologists which does at least lend a bit more credibility to it. As we shall see in Chapter 6, social learning theorists have adopted a model of man which is quite similar to that suggested by neoclassical economists.

One of these social psychologists, Dolf Zillman, has spoken rather directly to the issue of economic roots to human calculative behavior.[29] Zillman argues that at an early stage of historical development human beings came to bring together objects of value, such as livestock, which formed the subject matter of calculations. Because man is able to anticipate outcomes, largely because of his linguistic ability, he is able to calculate consequences and to plan for them. He is able to consider alternatives concerning his own behavior and choose the one that best suits his needs, while at the same time avoiding undersirable consequences. It is his capacities for language and conceptualization that allow man to become an efficient optimizer, according to Zillman. This set of capabilities and historical experiences gives man a unique potential for violence, as he is able to engage intelligently in incentive-motivated aggression. He needs resources and has the intelligence and cognitive ability to pursue them in a calculated fashion.[30] Zillman's arguments provide some basis for positing mechanisms through which man can act intelligently to obtain the economic resources he desires.

As one would expect, utility theory has been savaged by the attacks of many critics. The attacks on utility theory and the attempts of its acolytes to defend it have followed an interesting path over the years. It seems reasonably obvious that the claims for a mechanical hedonism, which is represented by the most extreme views of utility theory, are patently indefensible. Perhaps the clearest recognition of this is the presence in the literature of such petulant comments as the following by the economist Lionel Robbins:

> The borderlands of Economics are the happy hunting-ground of minds averse to the effect of exact thought, and, in these ambiguous regions, in recent years, endless time has been devoted to attacks on the alleged psychological assumptions of Economic Science. . . . Professional

economists, absorbed in the exciting task of discovering new truth, have usually disclaimed to reply. . . .[31]

Some of the more thoroughgoing criticisms of utility theory have come from the natural enemies of the neoclassicists, the institutional economists. David Hamilton, in his monograph *Evolutionary Economics*, has produced one of the more extensive statements of the institutional critique.[32] According to Hamilton, classical economics is based on Newtonian theories of a mechanical universe governed by fixed and immutable laws. Under this eighteenth-century theoretical mindset, the appropriate scientific activity is to discover these immutable laws and then apply them. Nature is viewed as orderly and rational, as designed by an omniscient creator. Society, similarly to the physical universe, is seen as made up of individually suspended bodies between which an orderly relationship is assured by natural forces.[33] According to Hamilton, both classical political economy and modern "dynamic economics" are products of these eighteenth-century habits of thought.

In Hamilton's view, the immutable law upon which both classical and modern economics rests is hedonism. The discrediting of hedonism as a valid psychology has led contemporary classical economists to deny it. They have retreated from pleasure and pain, to utility, and then to "indifference." According to Hamilton, the new classical economists now have even resorted to denying the necessity of building economic theory upon psychological foundations.[34]

Hamilton maintains that the attempt of classical economists to abandon assumptions about the nature of man are doomed to failure. This is because economics is, and must be, a science of human behavior. As such, it necessarily entails implicit assumptions with respect to the nature of man. Hamilton argues that both classical and neoclassical economics have contained a rather consistent concept of human nature over the years. Adam Smith's economic man was "a shrewd calculator of pecuniary advantage."[35] The entire classical analysis of the concept of supply is stated in hedonistic terms. Goods are produced by painful labor. It is this pain that gives products their value under the labor theory of value. The implicit psychological assumption is that labor is painful and irksome. As a corollary, consumption is viewed as pleasant. Therefore, painful work is undertaken in order to satisfy the pleasant end of consumption. Rational men will exchange commodities only for other commodities that represent an equivalent in pain.[36].

Later classical economists dropped the labor theory of value, but not its accompanying hedonism. Instead, they shifted from emphasizing pain to emphasizing pleasure. Marginal utility theory stresses the pleasure aspect of hedonism. According to Hamilton, "general demand is simply a reflection of the theories of graded sensations experienced by each member of the entire population."[37] According to Hamilton, Alfred Marshall continued the use of hedonism by synthesizing the hedonism of pain with that of pleasure. Hamilton maintains that classical economics is still where Marshall left it, except for mathematical analysis and the notion of monopolistic competition.[38]

As a contrast to neoclassical thought Hamilton poses the ideas of the institutionalists. According to Hamilton, institutional economists do not see human beings as "inert organisms" that respond mechanically to pleasure and pain seeking opportunities. They are seen instead as active entities guided by an evolving society. Rather than being Newtonian, they are Darwinian.[39]

The work of utility theorists has often been criticized because it is so thoroughly deductive in nature. Undoubtedly, purely deductive theory does have its dangers. This has been recognized by that figure in literature most commonly (if incorrectly) associated with the deductive process, Sherlock Holmes. Speaking to his sidekick, Dr. Watson, Holmes says: "It is a capital mistake to theorise before one has data. Insensibly one begins to twist facts to suit theories, instead of theories to suit facts."[40]

The same point has been made by James Gibson Hume:

> This method seems to have a natural tendency to become dogmatic and over-confident; a tendency to look upon all its assumed or accepted principles as fixed, stable, and final; a tendency, therefore, to entirely neglect any critical examination of the principles with which it is all the time dealing; and, lastly, a tendency to underrate or entirely neglect the importance of the observation, statistics and history of economic phenomena.[41]

Rare indeed is the noneconomist social scientist who has not had reason to ponder the dogmatic inclinations of the neoclassical economists.

The criticisms of Joseph Schumpeter are perhaps the most useful. Schumpeter's critique is well documented, balanced, and constructive. He traces the concept of economic man back to the scholastic philosophers and their notion of "prudent economic reason." This notion implies "the intention of gaining in every legitimate way."[42] According to Schumpeter, around the middle of the eighteenth century "Self-Interest" and the "Common Good" were supposed to

be the underlying principles of all the social sciences. This idea of individual self-interest was "oriented on rational expectation of individual pleasure and pain, which must, in turn, be defined in a narrow
hedonistic sense."[43] It could only be defined in such a sense because
using it in any other way, going beyond the "grossest gratifications
of the simplest appetites," comes "dangerously near to identifying
'pleasure' with all possible motives whatsoever, even with the intentional suffering of pain."[44] If this is done, the doctrine then becomes
"an empty tautology."[45] According to Schumpeter, this makes human behavior "turn on beefsteaks," which is a theory of behavior "at
variance with the most obvious facts."[46]

Schumpeter argues that many scholars with excellent minds
adopted utility theory because they were practical reformers. The
simplicity and triteness of the idea was perhaps the reformers' best
answer to the prevailing system of "supermundanely sanctified
rights and duties."[47] Schumpeter credits the utilitarians for having
created "the shallowest of all conceivable philosphies of life that
stands indeed in a position of irreconcilable antagonism to the rest of
them."[48] He goes on, however, to make the important point that, although many economists, such as Jevons, have stated unhesitat-
ingly that utilitarian ideas are fundamental to economic theory, this
is not so. The importance and usefulness of these ideas are greatly
exaggerated, according to Schumpeter. He argues strongly that
much of economic analysis is valid without regard to reference to
utilitarian notions. As noted above, he believes that the simple idea
that human beings pursue wealth at minimum cost forms a sound
basis for much of economic theory. It is this fundamental behavioral
proposition that can be salvaged from classical economic theory.

It is important to note that the fundamental behavioral proposition of human pursuit of wealth at minimum cost has an effort component as well as a pay component. That is, the question is not simply how much am I to be paid. It is also how much effort must I
expend for the pay. This involves the *quantity* of effort, both in
terms of intensity and length of time during which it must be expended.

This writer must admit to some mixed feelings about the utility of
utility theory. Conceptually, it is implausible and shallow. In its most
appealing conceptual forms, cardinal and ordinal utility, it appears
to be untestable.[49] Yet modern work by adherents to utility theory,
such as Gary Becker and his followers, have produced some rather
impressive results.[50] Its translation into expectancy theory in the

area of industrial psychology has also been successful in many respects.[51] Yet, it has never been satisfactorily applied to industrial conflict.

What does appear quite clear is that, as argued by Schumpeter, the argument for economic motivation of behavior is very powerful. As Daniel Katz stated a number of years ago, "the type of dissatisfaction most relevant to [industrial] conflict has to do with wages, since earnings sum up so many of the motivations of human beings in our society."[52] This conclusion is strongly supported by the obvious ties to natural selection theory. Surely beings who do not have strong tendency to acquire physical resources and goods, and to secure them for their future, are not as likely to reproduce as those who have such tendencies. Whether one views humans as primarily economic or biological, it would appear that it is reasonable to conclude that human beings have strong propensities for seeking material goods.

On the effort side of the equation, it seems reasonable to conclude that, as suggested by Jevons, work often requries people to exert themselves more than they would prefer. At the extreme, excessive exertion can be life-threatening. Back-breaking work is not high on the preference schedules of many workers. Exertion that is too intense is, therefore, something we would expect human beings to resist in the work setting. The length of time during which the work effort is to be exerted is also something we would expect workers to be concerned about. As work requries overly intense exertion, it also often requires these to last longer than workers would like. Hours worked in a day, week, month, or year as a part of one's labors are an integral part of the economic relationship referred to as the wage-effort bargain.

Even if we are convinced that the material outcome of pay is at the heart of the employment relationship, and that there is reason to believe that human beings will predictably seek it, it is still not necessarily the case that this will lead to readiness for industrial conflict. If the work organization operates in such a way that the employee's material needs are routinely met by managerial action, there is no ground for linking the pursuit of material outcomes with an individual's readiness to engage in aggressive action. Most managers would argue that this is normally the case, at least where managers are performing their duties properly. How, then, can these propensities lead to conflict?

The pursuit by the individual employee of material interests within a work organization is likely to lead to conflict because it necessarily leads to conflict with other competing interests. To use Alan Fox's terminology, a pluralistic, rather than a unitary, view of the work organization is most appropriate.[53] From a pluralist perspective, rank and file workers and managers have divergent interests.[54]

Borrowing from Jevons, as well as others, we conclude that the employee has an interest in obtaining the maximum pay that can be obtained without exerting a degree of effort that is irksome or painful. The role of a manager is to extract an adequate amount of effort from workers to perform the required work, and to achieve those results in a cost-efficient manner.[55] In order to maximize their own incomes, particularly in the long run, managers must fulfill the requirements of their role. Job security, as well as future income, may be vitally dependent upon the ability to extract production from workers at minimum cost—to serve the "bottom line." In the chain of command that characterizes Western industrial organizations, managers are "responsible" to superiors for the efficient production of those workers who are subordinate to them.[56]

It is, of course, true that rank-and-file employees as well as managers must be concerned about efficiency. However, their position differs from that of management in two important respects. First, the role of manager, unlike that of other employee, includes a special responsibility for efficiency. Second, managers, by definition, direct the work of others and may obtain greater efficiency without greater effort of their own. That is, managers can increase their benefits by imposing costs on others. The result is that one would expect managers to be more intensely concerned about efficiency than other employees, and other employees to be more intensely concerned with their own pay than managers. This creates a natural, and perhaps inevitable, conflict of economic interests between employees and managers.

Economic concerns are at the very foundation of human behavior at work. By the nature of the roles assumed by employee and manager there is inevitably the potential for the employees' and managers' actions in pursuit of their respective preferred economic outcomes to clash. It seems apparent, therefore, that one would expect to find material roots of industrial conflict.

SOCIAL DOMINANCE ROOTS OF INDUSTRIAL CONFLICT

The political, power related outcomes of the industrial relationship have to do with what sociobiologists and ethologists call social dominance. Human work organizations have hierarchies. Both explicit and implicit in these hierarchies are patterns of social dominance relationships. Although these relationships create order to a degree, they also contain within them the seeds of disorder. It is a fundamental part of human behavior both to form hierarchies and to struggle for dominance in them. These basic human predispostions form the integrative theory's second root cause of industrial conflict.

Social dominance has been studied from a number of perspectives. The most fundamental, and perhaps the most enlightening, of these perspectives flows most directly from biological science. This involves the work of sociobiologists and ethologists. In addition, psychologists from a number of intellectual traditions have studied the phenomenon of social dominance relations. Sociologists studying organizations have written extensively about the phenomena of "authority" and "hierarchy." Finally, scholars studying industrial relations have occasionaly focused on social dominance relations as an explainer of industrial conflict.

Social Dominance among Homo Sapiens:
A Biological Perspective

Ethologists and sociobiologists argue that human beings have an innate predisposition to establish hierarchies of social dominance relations; that this tendency is one of considerable durability; that social dominance relations follow certain recognizable patterns in human beings and in our closest animal relatives; and that the social dominance relationship is a dynamic one, involving contradictory tendencies toward dominance and subordinance and "status tension."

When one reads the ethological and sociobiological literatures on social dominance and its patterns, it is impossible not to be impressed by the richness of the penetrating insights these literatures supply. Their arguments "make sense" in an appealing way. Perhaps this is because of the inherent advantages of comparisons in assisting us to understand. Understanding is relating. When human beings are viewed in isolation, common patterns of human behavior cannot be readily understood because they cannot be related to anything. Our proud tendency to view humans as unique may be helpful for some purposes, but not for the purpose of understanding the behavior of the creature with respect to the broadest, and therefore most important, characteristics of human behavior. Perhaps the powerfulness of the human/other animal comparison is the reason for the appeal of the tales of fabulists since Aesop's time. At the very

least, the ethologists and sociobiologists may have managed to remove from social dominance its "magical, science-proof, cloak" and
"demystify" the subject.[57]

The sociobiologist Edward O. Wilson has defined "dominance order," sometimes labelled "dominance hierarchy" or "social hierarchy," as "the set of sustained aggressive-submissive relations"
among "members of an aggressively organized group of animals"
that live together within a single territory.[58] One of the earliest
known and most exhaustively studied of these orders is the so-called
pecking order among chickens.[59] There are, however, many other
varieties of dominance orders. For example, some hierarchies are
"absolute" in that they apply to all locations and circumstances.
Others are "relative" in that they do not operate at all, or operate differently, where a subordinate individual is in the neighborhood of its
personal sleeping place (an animal's sleeping place is his castle).[60]

The ethological argument as to the innate character of social dominance hierarchies, and their essential characteristics, has been summarized by George Maclay and Humphrey Knipe in their book, *The
Dominant Man.* According to this argument, man and his primate
ancestors have been social animals for at least 20 million years. He
has inherited special psychological qualities and capacities that
characterize all species which have hierarchical forms of organization. Three specific character traits with respect to hierarchy are enduring human social characteristics. The first of these is that "every
individual of the species inherits a drive to climb the dominance ladder. All social vertebrates are status-seekers, and *Homo sapiens* is
no exception to the rule." The second characteristic is a "well developed capacity for deference" with which members of the community
must be equipped in order to accept something less than the highest
position in the hierarchy. The third characteristic is a resulting "society of unequals." It is these characteristics, and the relations among
them, which produce the dynamics of the social dominance order.[61]

Social Dominance: A Fundamental Engine of Behavior

Social dominance is seen by ethologists as constituting an ever-
present and central phenomenon in the behavior of social species.
They make a strong case for this proposition both with respect to social animals in general and with respect to man in particular.

With his characteristic eloquence, Robert Ardrey describes the
significance of social dominance among animals:

> In the halls of science there are many doors, and the one with the sign
> that reads *Animal Dominance* is one that we have scarcely opened. We

have learned much: that it is a force at least as old and as deep as territory; that like territory it benefits sex but stands independent of it; that among social animals it is universal, and among our primate family the source of society's most mysterious subtleties; and that among all animal sources of human behavior, the instinct for status may in the end prove the most important.[62]

Ardrey maintains that it is no longer a matter of controversy that "dominance in social animals is a universal instinct."[63] He maintains that "every primate society so far observed maintains within its ranks a system of dominance."[64]

Konrad Lorenz and Desmond Morris are in agreement that the establishment of social dominance systems is both innate and common among social animals. Lorenz argues, "A principle of organization without which a more advanced social life cannot develop in higher vertebrates is the so-called ranking order."[65] According to Morris, "In any organized group of mammals, no matter how cooperative, there is always a struggle for social dominance. As he pursues this struggle, each adult individual acquires a particular social rank, giving him his position, or status, in the group hierarchy."[66] Morris also maintains that the hierarchy system is something with which we are already "loaded." It is "the basic way of primate life."[67]

Although it is interesting to know that social animals generally have dominance hierarchies, the crucial question, as Morris suggests, is whether man shares this disposition. It would seem, however, that one would only have to look around him to be persuaded that human beings have well-established tendencies to form dominance orders. As the anthropologists Tiger and Fox have argued: "No matter how hard and how often we rail against them, the affections for difference in status are also part of our primate structure, part of our 'primate' reflex to be higher rather than lower. We refine this reflex endlessly; we humiliate others; we are rank-makers and flag-planters."[68] According to Maclay and Knipe, "Man is a born status-seeker."[69] They maintain: "History and anthropology demonstrate that all human societies are organized around some kind of dominance hierarchy."[70]

Even if one is convinced that human beings almost universally adopt dominance hierarchies, this does not resolve the problem of identifying the source of that behavior and, accordingly, how enduring one might expect it to be. Ardrey believes that it is a part of the "romantic fallacy" of "special creation" of the human animal to believe that the "human obsession with the acquisition of social status" is not related to basic animal instincts for dominance.[71] Maclay and Knipe argue that hierarchies are instinctual, not mere cultural inventions. They use the term "instinctual" as referring to unmechanical "modifiable instincts." Man has developed an inborn capacity to learn certain behaviors more easily than others. Man has developed modifiable instincts and cultural adaptations to a greater extent than any other animal type. Nevertheless, the "instinctive blueprint" remains. A predisposition for either dominant or subordinate roles is a part of this "instinctive legacy."[72] They conclude:

> Human society is traditionally thought of as the product of man's unique rationality. Perhaps he did not invent the social order, but he is led to believe that he depends on this rational faculty for understanding and obeying it. The discovery of surprisingly sophisticated social systems in apparently irrational animal types forces us to reconsider.
>
> Modern research has shown that we are linked to our remote primate ancestors by an unbroken continuum of cooperative social life. Far from being deliberately designed, we now know that human social structures have evolved through gradual amendments to the pattern that our scarcely rational simian ancestors developed millions of years ago. How has human society coped with our deeply ingrained commitment to the hierarchy system? To what extent does man remain a dominance order animal? To what extent do the age-old laws of hierarchical living continue to govern the growth of each unique human personality? In the process of answering these questions, we will need to look closely at some of the more glamorous aspects of human dominance that have until recently been regarded as beyond the scope of scientific investigation.[73]

Edward O. Wilson's taxonomic analysis of social behaviors of human and other ancestral species supports the proposition that the formation of social dominance orders is an innate human characteristic. His analysis identifies aggressive dominance systems as a "conservative primate trait."[74] This classification argues for this trait being included under those which are inherited from our primate ancestors.

Nature and Operation of Dominance Systems

Ethologists and sociobiologists have written extensively about what constitutes social dominance. One approach that they have taken has been to compare human dominance behavior to that of baboons. They have also pursued other analytical strategies.

Desmond Morris considers the baboon-human comparison to be particularly valuable. According to Morris, its value "lies in the way it reveals the very basic nature of human dominance patterns. The striking parallels that exist enable us to view the human power game with a fresh eye and see it for what it is: a fundamental piece of animal behavior."[75] Morris derives from this comparison ten "golden rules" for dominance. One of the more interesting of these rules is the one that requires the display of the trappings and behaviors of dominance. For this, the baboon needs a "sleek, beautifully groomed, luxuriant coat of hair; a calm relaxed posture, a deliberate and purposeful gait," and the absence of "signs of anxiety, indecision or hesitancy."[76] In place of a luxuriant coat of fur for the baboon comes the elaborate costume of the human ruler. Like the dominant baboon, he must maintain a relaxed and composed posture. When in action he must appear more impressive than his followers. This can be accomplished by humans through artificial aids such as magnifying size by wearing a large cloak or tall headgear, or by mounting a throne, being carried aloft, or simply requiring crouching, bowing, or prostrating by subordinates. The dominant human being must also be dignified and regal in posture and movement. Like Shakespeare's Lear, he "uses his eyes like weapons" staring at subordinates until they divert their gaze. The human leader does not "twitch, fidget, or falter."[77] Leaders who choose not to assume those behaviors consistent with high rank, perhaps such as ex-President Jimmy Carter, risk losing respect.

Maclay and Knipe compare human dominance behavior to that of baboons, as well as to that of Asian macaques. They also describe dominance behavior in more general terms. According to them, large body size has commonly been associated with dominance. To be a "big man," or to be "looked up to" is associated with dominance.[79] Threats of physical contact and actual physical contact ("pushing around") are also associated with dominance.[80] Dominants also have "eye power," or the ability to stare down others.[81] When a dominance contest takes place, there is a strong innate emotional response of elation on the part of the winner ("We're Number One") and of depression and withdrawal on the part of the loser.[82]

The many forms of dominance signalling are discussed at length by Maclay and Knipe. They, like Morris, believe that there is a "high-dominance swagger or strut" that a number of species have.[83] Dominance is also signalled by an upright aristocratic, or military, bearing. Military "enthusiasm" straightens out a human being's bearing. It tilts the head back and signals high self-esteem. A chimpanzee defending his band or family often strikes a similar pose.[84] Furthermore, lower power personalities find it difficult to assume a high power stance. Relaxed and deliberate body movements are also signals of dominance. It is also shown by the display of "face."[85] In addition, dominants tend to be the center of attention. They define the social situations in which they are involved. This is true both of man and of his animal relatives.[86]

The class ranking systems of hereditary aristocracies are rich with dominance signals. As Maclay and Knipe note, aristocrats believe themselves to be "born better" than the lower orders, and reflect this by their relaxed movements, aloofness, self-confidence, and pride.[87] This is often signalled by speaking a language that is different from that spoken by the lower classes. It is also indicated by the language with which the aristocrats are addressed, which shows special respect.[88] Articles of clothing, such as tall hats, the wearing of epaulettes and padded shoulders, and the use of a stiffly starched collar to give its wearer an air of authority by forcing him to hold his head in a dignified way, are all indications of dominance status.[89] Aristocratic rules of behavior make it clear that dominants behave as they wish.[90]

The Pleasures of Being Dominant

Observation of many social species, including mankind, readily reveals that it is indeed a pleasant thing to be a dominant animal. As Tiger and Fox have said, "A dominant animal moves more freely, eats better, gets more attention, lives longer, is healthier and less anxious, and generally has a better time than a lowly and peripheral animal."[91]

Edward O. Wilson describes in some detail the advantages that are the lot of dominant animals. This includes secure access to food and to breeding opportunities.[92] Dominant animals are under less stress. They also receive the benevolent attentions of other animals.[93]

Although there are all sorts of special responsibilities and dangers that go along with dominance, it is clearly a good thing to be a dominant animal. One might even place the striving for dominance in the category of simple pursuit of pleasure. It appears that dominance in and of itself, as well as the external benefits of that status, gives pleasure. From a natural selection perspective, one might argue that human beings are programmed in such a way as to find pleasure in dominance, and that this in turn gives an advantage in fitness to those who are dominant.

The Compensations of Being Subordinate

Crucial to the establishment of a ranking order of social dominance is the ability and willingness of most members of the group to accept a subordinate position. Not everyone can be number one. A social species whose members are unable to cope with being subordinate, and are steadily engaged in constant warfare for position, has little chance of surviving. As Maclay and Knipe state: "The result of many millions of years' development in a social direction is that every hierarchical animal now possesses the ability to abandon his competitive feelings in the presence of an acknowledged superior—a special arrangement of psychological equipment which allows a weaker animal to accept the domination of a worthy leader."[94] They describe the capacity to behave and to feel in a subordinate manner as being among the most important "psychological adaptations" that individuals have to undergo in order to operate in a rank order environment.[95] These authors tend to explain this adaptation in terms of the ability of individuals to adjust their dominance feelings so that they are in harmony with their dominance status. This was clearly the case, accordng to McClay and Knipe, in the old aristocratic hereditary class ranking systems of human society.[96]

Subordinate social animals generally receive some compensation for being subordinate. According to Wilson, the losers in status struggles often have a second chance, or they emigrate to form their own social groups.[97] The subordinate shares in the feeding opportunities of the group. In some species it has some breeding opportunities. It shares in the protection from predators furnished by the group. There may even be some inherent pleasure in being subordinate. If this last statement is true, however, it would have some confusing implications for the application pleasure-pain principle to human social behavior with respect to dominance ordering.

Of course, one advantage to the subordinate is that by assuming the subordinate position he escapes the punishment he might receive if he attempted to improve his position. As Eibl-Eibesfeldt has argued, "the disposition to subordination is based on fear of the high-ranking individual."[98] As Tiger and Fox put it, there is always an underlying threat of force, "the primeval canine tooth," which maintains the dominance order.[99]

Status Tension in Dominance Orders

Individuals in a social hierarchy struggling for status improvement produce a constant state of "status tension."[100] Lorenz argues that the fact that all social animals are "status seekers" constantly leads them into situations of high status tension. This is particularly true with respect to individuals who hold immediately adjoining positions in a status hierarchy.[101] The establishment of a dominance hierarchy may reduce overall aggression. Nevertheless, the potential for aggression is still ever-present.[102] The impetus behind this tension is dramatically described by Robert Ardrey:

> We may say with equal certainty, based on innumerable observations, that dominance brings many an unpleasantness to a society of animals. Punishment tends to be handed down, since pecking goes not to the deserving but to the next creature down the line. To be high in rank is to be privileged in all things, and to be low in rank to possess but one satisfaction, that there is probably someone worse off than yourself.[103]

The predisposition to seek status, the unpleasantness associated with low status, the opportunity for turnover provided by the aging and incapacitation of high status members of the group, and other factors, combine to produce a state of status tension in which there is always some dynamism in the hierarchy. With respect to many human groups, it may be the competition for status that provides much of the challenge and spice to organizational life.

Sex and Status

It is in connection with symbolic sexual behavior that social dominance provides some especially revealing insights. This is the world of "status sex" which Desmond Morris says "is full of unexpected developments and ramifications."[104] As Morris argues, "status Sex is concerned with dominance, not with reproduction."[105]

Although a number of writers have analyzed the phenomenon of status sex, it is Morris, in *The Human Zoo*, who has explored the subject most extensively.[106] Because of the mechanics of the mammalian body, which require it to be the male who penetrates the body of the female animal, Morris sees the sex act as essentially one of submissiveness for the female and dominance, or aggressiveness, for the male. The important thing for our purposes is that actions resembling reproductive activities, and language referring to these activities, have been "borrowed" for use in the context of nonsexual dominance.

This borrowing of symbols from reproduction to dominance occurs in many lower species. Monkeys wishing to signal submissiveness, whether male or female, "present" themselves as if they were ready to assume the female role in the sex act. On the other hand, phallic display has, among men and monkeys, long served as a dominance sign. This translates also into the so-called phallic hand, or "fig" with which dominance aggressiveness is signaled. Verbal insults in phallic form are another example. Seen as an act of dominance and degradation of its object, rape is clearly an expression of status sex. It is an act of aggression and dominance rather than an act of reproductive sex.

Other writers have spoken to the dominance aspects of sexual behavior. Lorenz discusses the use of sexually submissive behaviors by baboons to signal subordinance.[107] Maclay and Knipe note the same behaviors among monkeys.[108] Konner notes that not only among mammals, but among birds, "male gestures of courtship and sexual invitation are similar or identical to those of agonistic threat and dominance."[109]

The use of phallic language pointed out by Carl Sagan is of special interest with respect to theorizing about industrial conflict. Sagan notes that it is necessary to understand the social dominance aspects of sex in order to make sense out of the fact that "most common two-word verbal aggression in English, and in many other languages, refers to an act of surpassing physical pleasure."[110] The English form of this word, according to Sagan, probably derives from a Germanic and Middle Dutch word *fokken*, which means "to strike."[111] With the word "I" added in front of the expression, it is a statement of dominance much the same as the symbolic mounting behavior of monkeys. That this is rooted in a word that means "strike" has some interesting implications for industrial conflict.

Psychology and Social Dominance

There is a substantial body of psychological literature on the phenomenon of social dominance, although it does not usually so label it. The psychologists provide a highly useful set of ideas and findings substantially similar to those of the sociobiologists and ethologists.

At least since Freud's day psychologists have recognized the contradictory predispositions, or needs, of human beings for, on the one hand, personal freedom or dominance, and, on the other hand, subordinance and obedience.[112] As Erich Fromm has said, man has both a desire for freedom and a need to be connected with the external world. Seeking escape from isolation, he can relate to the world constructively by love or productive work. Failing this, he may turn to submission. Submission has its costs, but is preferred to isolation and loneliness.[113] There is, then, a predisposition to seek power, freedom, or social dominance. There is also a predisposition to seek powerlessness, an escape from freedom, and social subordination.

The Psychological Predisposition for Social Dominance

The need for social dominance is seen both as a need to be free from the domination of others and as an inclination to dominate others. It is *both freedom from domination and the ability to dominate* that constitute the single construct of "social dominance." As in the rest of the animal kingdom, the dominant individual is both free to behave as he chooses and able to influence the behavior of others.

Writers in the psychoanalytic tradition have long recognized the predisposition for what we have termed social dominance. Freud early identified a human "desire for freedom." He believed that this derived from the remains of the original personality "untamed by civilization."[114] It was, however, Alfred Adler who fully developed the notion of a "tendency toward domination and superiority."[115] According to Adler, the human child desires security. This consists not of mere safety from danger but of a "further coefficient of safety which guarantees the continued existence of the human organism under optimum circumstances."[116] This "goal of superiority" was, at least in Adler's early writings, accorded the same kind of primacy that Freud accorded to the sex drive.[117]

A number of other writers have followed Adler in emphasizing the need for, or predisposition to pursue, power. Adolph A. Berle maintains that the instinct for power is very fundamental. Berle argues that "the power instinct in men carries forward inherited attributes that must have appeared long before the evolution of man in his present form."[118] Rollo May maintains that in order to understand aggression and violence, power must be seen as "basic to the problem."[119] According to May, human beings need power for self-esteem. Powerlessness is intolerable. May sees aggression as a moving into a position of power.[120] David C. McClelland argues that there exists a need for power (n Power). He distinguishes between two kinds of power: personal dominance over active adversaries and the more socialized power exercised for the benefit of others.[121] He maintains that social scientists have been too much concerned with personal dominance because of having observed dominance hierarchies that were "established by brute force among the lower animals."[122]

One of the more interesting theories about the freedom side of social dominance is the "theory of psychological reactance" of Jack W. Brehm.[123] Brehm's theory holds that if a person's behavioral freedom is reduced, or even threatened with reduction, he will become aroused motivationally. This arousal will be directed both against any further loss of freedom and toward the reestablishment of freedoms already lost or threatened. As this motivational state is a *response*, or a counter force, Brehm labels it "psychological reactance."[124] Brehm argues that the magnitude of the reactance is a function of: "(1) the importance of the free behaviors which are eliminated or threatened, (2) the proportion of free behaviors eliminated or threatened, and (3) where there is only a threat of elimination of free behaviors, the magnitude of that threat."[125] Brehm theorizes that an unjustified interference with freedom poses a threat that *other* freedoms will also be arbitrarily interfered with. A justified interference does not have this threatened generalizability.[126] Reactance is "a motivational state with a specific direction, namely, the recovery of freedom."[127]

It appears that there are ample grounds for concluding that the psychological literature strongly supports the notion that there is an inclination for social dominance among human beings. This is particularly true if we strip away any normative implications. Social dominance includes the freedom from domination of others, as well as the ability to dominate others. A human need for powerfulness and for influencing and controlling the behavior of others is hardly surprising, and not necessarily evil.

The Psychological Predisposition for Subordination

There is also an extensive psychological literature that argues for a human need to be subordinate. Obedience, deference, and subordination are common human characteristics, often identified and studied. This tendency has been described as one of the engines for the destruction of a "brother society"operating in consensual groups, and for the predominance of the authoritarian "father society."[128] It has been expressed more simply as the "need" to "grant or accord deference."[129]

Perhaps the most striking proof of the inclination of human beings to be subordinate and obedient has been provided by the work of Stanley Milgram. Milgram's experiments involved directing people to inflict pain upon others. Milgram found that "with numbing regularity good people were seen to knuckle under the demands of authority and perform actions that were callous and severe."[130] A considerable proportion of his subjects did what they were told to do without being constrained by their conscience, so long as they perceived that the command came from a legitimate authority.[131] He concluded that there must be a "drive, tendency, or inhibition" leading to an obedient response.[132] Milgram further found that there was "some form of dominance-subordination, or hierarchical element" in the experimental situation.[133] According to Milgram:

> Obedience is as basic an element in the structure of social life as one can point to. Some system of authority is a requirement of all communal living, and it is only the man dwelling in isolation who is not forced to respond, through defiance or submission, to the commands of others.
>
> * * *
>
> Obedience is . . . the dispositional cement that binds men to systems of authority.[134]

In one of his rare writings on the subject of group psychology, Freud recognized that "thirst for obedience" exists among human beings.[135] Freud described this as the wish of the group to be "governed by unrestricted force," and as having "an extreme passion for authority."[136] Freud described man as "a horde animal, an individual creature in a horde led by a chief."[137] The chief, or leader, is the primal father to whom the individual is tied by unconscious obedience.[138]

Erich Fromm and Adorno, et al., have seen the "thirst for obedience" as a symptom of the authoritarian personality. According to Fromm, "authoritarian character" refers to the sadomasochistic tendency to admire authority and also to submit to it.[139] Fromm believes that it is the aim of both sadism and masochism to lose one's self in the self of another. This accomplishes the loss of the aloneness the sado-masochist feels.[140] This is supported by the authoritarian notion that man is, after all, not controlled by his own wishes. Happiness can lie only in the submission to outside forces.[141] In their classic work on the authoritarian personality, Adorno et al., argue that authoritarian personalities are not only inclined to exert authority, but are also highly submissive to authority.[142]

There are a number of psychological perspectives from which one could conclude that there is an inclination, predisposition, or need for subordination or deference. It is this need that is in tension with a competing need for dominance within individuals.

Individual Differences in Subordinance and Domination

Although it appears that all individuals have within their makeup inclinations toward dominance or subordination, it is also clear from the psychological literature that there are differences in "dominance-feeling," or need for power, among individuals. Certain roles may be attractive to individuals who have a predominance of either low or high dominance feeling, or low or high need for power.

In 1937, A. H. Maslow published his findings of a major study of "dominance-feeling."[143] Maslow defined a feeling of dominance as involving:

> (1) self-confidence, (2) self-esteem, (3) high self-respect and evaluation of self, (4) consciousness of feeling of 'superiority' in a very general sense, (5) forcefulness of personality, (6) strength of character, (7) a feeling of sureness with respect to other people, (8) a feeling of being able to handle other people, (9) a feeling of masterfulness and of mastery, (10) a feeling that others do and ought to admire and respect one, (11) a feeling of general capability, (12) an absence of shyness, timidity, self-conciousness, or embarrassment, (13) a feeling of pride.[144]

According to Maslow, dominance-feeling is "chiefly the evaluation of, or confidence in, the personality (self-confidence)."[145]

Maslow notes an interesting dynamic of dominance-feeling: persons who are high in dominance-feeling are "apt to be very restive in subordinate status, especially if the person in dominant status is arrogant, tyrannical, silly, bullying, or if in general he is felt not to be worthy of dominance status."[146]

Human dominance behaviors, as described by Maslow, are quite similar to signs of dominance displayed by other animals. In this he agrees with Maclay and Knipe. A dominant person is more likely to stand erect, have a firm handshake, steadily meet the eye of the person to whom he is speaking, walk "with a freer swing of they body," and is "less likely to be hesitant when speaking."[147] Maslow also notes that there are several universal ways of expressing subordinance and dominance. Maslow's studies showed no group in any part of the world where kneeling, bowing, or prostrating oneself before another was an expression of dominance. Maslow notes the similarity between other primates and human beings in the "expression of dominance by sexual aggression." The time honored practice of male soldiers raping the females of a conquered city is such an expression.[148]

David Winter, in his book entitled *The Power Motive*, describes this "motive" as a general disposition or tendency.[149] It is the "disposition to strive for" power as a goal, or "be affected by" certain incentives that have to do with power. This involves wanting to feel more powerful than others.[150] Winter argues that a high need for power (n Power) is, in the terms of Neil Smelser's analysis, directed at norm-oriented activity, not value-oriented activity. That is, it has to do with social rules of behavior that are more narrow than the broadest, most fundamental, rules held by the society. As we shall see in Chapter 7, it is norm-oriented activity in which Smelser considers labor unions to be involved.[151]

David McClelland sees the effective manager as one who has a high need for power and a relatively low need for affiliation.[152] Interestingly, the popular writings of Vance Packard, although not "psychological," are consistent with McClelland's argument, as well as with some of the other arguments advanced above. For example, Packard describes the "born executive" as one who has a "compulsion to be a father-chieftain."[153] Packard states that the "pure type of business master currently in power is predisposed to dominate."[154] Packard notes that recruiters and appraisers of executive talent say that one thing that they look for is "executive bearing."[155] According to Packard, a survey showed that nearly all of the business offices surveyed had an "office caste system" in which there was a certain amount of deference, within a hierarchy, required toward those in authority.[156] Packard has described this phenomenon as "Pecking Orders in Corporate Barnyards."[157]

The Sociology of Social Dominance in Organizations

There is a large body of literature in the area of organization theory, which is mainly sociological, pertaining to social dominance and the phenomenon of hierarchy in organizations. This literature has pointed out the universality of dominance structures. It has described the nature of authority in human social groups, and the various sources of authority. It has also spoken briefly to authority relations in society in general.

This literature, like the sociobiological and ethological literatures, argues for the ubiquity of hierarchy. In the 1950s Dahl and Lindblom observed that the "vital and ubiquitous role of hierarchical processes" was "one of the most striking features of Western society."[158] The distinguished sociologist Amitai Etzioni has stated that: "Compliance is universal existing in all social units. . . . it is a central element of organizational structure."[159] Daniel Katz and Robert L. Kahn maintain that "there is no more pervasive law of organization than that the occupants of certain roles shall respond to and obey certain kinds of requests from the occupants of certain other roles."[160] To achieve reliable performance of roles organizations promulgate and enforce, from above, rules of conduct.[161] According to David Hickson and Arthur McCullough, it is hierarchy that makes an organization. Hierarchy ensures tht the various jobs in the organiation are coordinated.[162]

Yet, for all the emphasis on hierachy and its functions, Katz and Kahn opine that "the advantages of hierarchy have been overstated."[163] Although hierarchy is sometimes efficient, it is sometimes inefficient. They contrast with the usual "military model" democratic forms of organization. Democratic forms involve the functioning of organizational members as a legislative body, the possession of veto power by the assembled membership or its representatives, and the selection of officers from the bottom up.[164] Dahl and Lindblom recognize that the pervasive nature of hierarchical structures runs "flatly counter to some of the ideology, and much of the ethos, of democracy."[165] As they note, one reason for the bureaucractic nature of social organizations is that it provides status and control for members of the top echelons of those organizations.[166] Indeed, Dahrendorf argues that it is authority, not ownership of the means of production, which provides the basis for the formation of entire social classes.[167]

The Nature of Authority

There appears to be broad agreement upon what constitutes "authority." Allan W. Lerner defines "authority" as a special case of power that is present where the subordination of one's own preferences to those of another is deemed justified in situations acceptable under the "organizational social contract."[168] The exercise of authority is seen by Lerner as involving the element of command.[169] Most other definitions of authority in the sociological literature are little more than elaborations of these statements.

Herbert Simon, in his classic work *Administrative Behavior*, discusses the concept of authority at length.[170] Simon believes that authority is the mode of influence that distinguishes the behavior of individuals as participants in organizations from their behavior outside these organizations. It is authority that gives formal structure to organizations.[171] According to Simon, authority involves "a general rule which permits the communicated decision of another to guide [a subordinate's] own choices . . . without deliberation on his own part on the expediency. . . ."[172] The superior in the authority relationship expects that his decisions will be accepted by his subordinate. The subordinate determines his conduct according to the superior's decisions, and expects this to be so. The behavior pattern of the superior is that of command. He makes an imperative statement.[173] The subordinate affects an attitude of obedience that is "an abdication of choice."[174] As Simon succinctly puts it, authority is the "right to the last word."[175]

David V. J. Bell, in his book *Power, Influence and Authority: An Essay in Political Linguistics,* has spoken at length about authority in organizations.[176] According to Bell, authority surrounds itself with "miranda" or things calculated to fill others with admiration and awe. Bell agrees with Simon that authority expresses itself imperatively—it *commands.*

Bell attacks, but does not really solve, the central dilemma of authority. This dilemma is posed by the fact that authority ordinarily possesses both "legitimacy" and punitive power. That is, it has to do with "oughtness," involving the moral obligation to obey. Yet, it usually also involves the superior's ability to inflict punishment. It is indeed difficult to tell whether obedience takes place because of fear of punishment or because of voluntary recognition of legitimacy. Bell argues that an authority crisis can occur when the subordinates recognize that the attempt at exercising authority exceeds the boundaries of legitimacy. If the subordinates are highly sophisticated and educated, they are more likely to have information that will give them a basis for challenging authority and causing a crisis of authority.

A number of other writers have spoken to the nature of authority. Samuel B. Bacharach and Edward J. Lawler write that authority stems from an office or a structural position.[177] Peter Blau defines authority as resting "on the common norms in a collectivity of subordinates."[178] It is the social norms and values of the subordinates that transfrom a superior's power into authority. Yet, authority also "entails imperative control, in contrast to persuasion and personal influence."[179] Michael Bannester defines authority quite broadly as "a form of sociomotive power."[180] According to him, authority has three "idiosyncrasies": (1) it derives only from the sanction of another, (2) it may be both coercive and noncoercive; and (3) it exhibits complimentarity as it may be purchased or bargained for."[181]

French and Raven, in their well-known work on power, specify a number of kinds of power. These have varying degrees of *legitimacy.*[182] Legitimate power is present where an individual "sees certain regions toward which he should locomote, some regions toward which he should not locomote, and some regions toward which he may locomote if they are generally attractive to him."[183] There is a feeling of "oughtness" involved. This feeling may have been internalized as a result of influence of parents, teachers, or religion or developed logically from some system of ethics. Power that is legitimate stems from those internalized values. They convince a person that another has a legitimate right to influence her and that she has an obligation to accept the influence.[184]

Etzioni distinguishes among various kinds of power.[185] Power can be coercive, remunerative, or normative. Different responses are elicited from different kinds of power. Coercive power tends to elicit an alienative, or intensely negative, response. Remunerative power tends to elicit a calculative response. Normative power tends to elicit a moral response that is "a positive orientation or high intensity."[186] Etzioni believes that industry mainly utilizes remunerative power, leading to calculative behavior on the part of workers.[187]

Reeves and Woodward have argued that the use of authority in a mandatory, pyramidal, fashion is strongly entrenched in the industrial system. This usage derives from the simplest form of managerial control. This is the individual owner-employer deciding what he wants done and seeing that it is accomplished. The man at the top gives orders, and the men at the bottom obey them.[188] This pyramid can, of course, be made effective with the exercise of punitive measures. Yet, managers have never been satisfied with this. Perhaps this is because, as Rousseau noted:

> The strongest man is never strong enough to be always master, unless he transforms his power into right, and obedience into duty. Hence the right of the strongest—a right apparently assumed in irony, and really established in principle. But will this phase never be explained to us? Force is a physical power. I do not see what morality can result from its effects. To yield to force is an act of necessity, not of will; it is at most an act of prudence. In what sense can it be a duty?[189]

The legitimacy of power—authority—is a matter of importance to managers as well as to other powerholders, but elusive because of the inevitable mixing of force with moral obligation.

Sources of Authority

There are two major views of the sources of formal authority in an organization, labelled "classical" and "acceptance."[190] Under the classical view, authority is seen as originating at some high level of society and then passing down from level to level. At the top may be God, a king, or the people. Under the acceptance view, the basis of authority is seen as lying in the "influencee" rather than in the "influencer." It is the receiver of a command who decides whether or not to comply, and, therefore, determines whether authority exists.

The classical view has been stated by Cyril O'Donnell as holding that the authority of management comes from property rights which, in turn, come from the Constitution.[191] O'Donnell sees the proximate source of a manager's authority as lying in the "well established law of contract." The employer-employee relationship is one of "right-duty" in which the *manager* possesses the *right* to command and the managed has the *duty* to obey. The *employee* has the *power* to disobey. If he does so, however, penalties may be levied upon him.[192] According to O'Donnell, "since corporations are legal persons created by law, their managers exercise authority which has reached them through the chain of delegation from the people to their constitution and then through government to its creature."[193]

The acceptance view of authority originated with Chester I. Barnard. In his classic book, *The Functions of the Executive*, Barnard defines authority in terms of the person on the receiving end. A communication has authority if, among other things, the receiver believes it to be "compatible with his personal interests." Enduring cooperation exists because the decisions of individuals occur under conditions where: (1) the receiver understands the communication; (2) he believes it is not inconsistent with the purposes of the organization; (3) he believes it is compatible with his interests: (4) he is able to comply. Barnard argues that a "zone of indifference" exists within which orders are acceptable without conscious questioning of their authority.[194] Herbert Simon calls this "zone of indifference" an "area of acceptance" where most individuals will accept orders given by formal superiors.[195]

A number of other writers have taken the acceptance view of authority. Kenneth Thompson believes authority exists where obedience is rested on a belief in the legitimacy of the command. "This is present where the subordinate believes that the orders were justified and that it was right to obey."[196] In bureaucracy obedience is to the impersonal status granted to a *position*. A person obeys *only* as a member of the organization. Lower order members of the organization are personally free.[197] Thompson makes the interesting point that "the pursuit of efficiency is accompanied by an increase in insidious control. It is all the more dangerous because it is often not identified as power, and the individual may not experience it in terms of feeling oppressed."[198]

French and Raven see the acceptance of the social structure as a basis for legitimate power. A person may accept a social structure involving a hierarchy and thereby accept the obligation to obey commands to his office from another office.[199] Peter Blau argues that, although the ultimate source of the obligation to comply lies in the ability of the organization to make its members dependent upon it for their livelihood, this cannot be effective until a social consensus develops among the subordinates in the organization to the effect that they should discharge their obligations to their superiors.[200]

The Class Theory of Ralf Dahrendorf

In his book *Class and Class Conflict in Industrial Society*, Dahrendorf has systematically and carefully developed a view of authority relations, dominance, and subordinance which is highly useful as an aid to understanding these phenomena.[201] Dahrendorf's work is particularly important for our purposes because it utilizes the "class angle" used so effectively by Marxists, but applies it to *authority relations* rather than ownership of the means of production. This allows Dahrendorf's theory to apply cross-culturally more readily than other theoretical attempts to use the notion of class.

Dahrendorf's theory is, essentially, that every large organization has both a dominant class and a subordinate class. The dominant group forms a power elite; its power is based upon the use of organizational resources. The power elite may own the capital under capitalism, control party membership under communism, or have special skills, as suggested by Michels in his "iron law of oligarchy."[202]

Let us examine Dahrendorf's argument. At the outset, Dahrendorf accepts the Marxist assumption of "the ubiquity of change and conflict as well as domination and subjection."[203] For the purpose of his theory, Dahrendorf adopts the "coercion theory of society" that social structures are held together by force.[204] Dahrendorf maintains that, under the coercion theory view, "in every social organization some positions are entrusted with a right to exercise control over other positions in order to insure effective coercion."[205] The differential distribution of power and authority which results "invariably becomes the determining factor of systematic social conflicts of a type that is germane to class conflicts in the traditional (Marxian) sense of this term. The structural origin of such group conflict must be sought in the arrangement of social roles endowed with expectations of domination or subjection. Wherever there are such roles, group conflicts of the type in question are to be expected."[206]

Dahrendorf believes authority to be "a universal element of social structure."[207] It is more fundamental and general than property and status. Dahrendorf writes:

> (1) Authority relations are always relations of super-and-subordination.
> (2) Where there are authority relations, the superordinate element is socially expected to control, by orders and commands, warnings and prohibitions, the behavior of the subordinate element. (3) Such expectations attach to relatively permanent social positions rather than to the character of individuals; they are in this sense legitimate. (4) By virtue of this fact, they always involve specification of the persons subject to control and of the spheres within which control is permissi-

ble. Authority, as distinct from power, is never a relation of generalized control over others. (5) Authority being a legitimate authority."[208]

From his analysis of authority relations, Dahrendorf concludes that those persons who occupy positions of domination and those who occupy positions of subjection hold, by reason of their positions, certain interests that contradict one another both in "substance and direction."[209] He then assumes certain structurally generated orientations of the actions of incumbents of positions.[210] Those in positions of authority have an interest in maintaining the structure that conveys the authority. Those in a position of subjection have an interest in changing social conditions in order to deprive the incumbents of their authority. The conflict can be seen as being "about the legitimacy of relations of authority."[211]

In explaining the differences of interest between subordinates and dominants, Dahrendorf rejects the traditional economic pleasure/pain explanations as being misleading. He prefers a more sociological, role-oriented, explanation. "Role interests," as he defines them, are "expected orientations of behavior associated with authority roles in imperatively coordinated associations."[212] These interests may merely be *latent*. That is, they may constitute "undercurrents" of the person's behavior that are "predetermined" for him while he is an incumbent of the role, but "independent of his conscious orientations."[213] However, these can also become *patent* conscious goals or "manifest interests."[214]

Dahrendorf applies his theory across national boundaries. He argues that in all capitalist and postcapitalist societies the industrial enterprise is "an imperatively coordinated association."[215] Wherever one finds imperatively coordinated associations, one finds the conditions of social structure that give rise to social conflict.[216] According to Dahrendorf, this derives in large part from the division of labor necessary for mechanized factory production. It is a system of supervision and subordination which guarantees the necessary operations for production. Dahrendorf holds that, "For the industrial worker, the labor contract implies acceptance of a role which is, *inter alia*, defined by the obligation to comply with commands of given persons."[217] This industrial authority does not involve subordination of the total person, but rather is limited to a range of activities that encompass work.[218] Dahrendorf chooses to interpret the capitalist interest in income in terms of social status and domination, not in "economic" terms.[219]

Dahrendorf argues that the historical development of industrial association causes the conditions or characteristic organizations to gradually emerge. This, in turn, causes both capital and labor to form organizations to defend their "articulate manifest interests." At this point, "industrial class conflict enters a manifest phase of which strikes and lockouts are the most telling symptons."[220] However, Frank Parkin, following Dahrendorf's arguments, sees work organizations as being basically "accommodative" to the dominant system.[221]

Social Dominance and Industrial Conflict

A number of writers have called out the contradictory effects of an hierarchial dominance system upon industrial peace. On the one hand, it serves to justify the power of those in positions of authority, thereby stabilizing the system. On the other hand, it has given rise to tensions and stresses that have been a source of instability.

The usefulness of a social dominance hierarchy for purposes of maintaining stability and social control has been extensively argued. As Reinhard Bendix notes, industrialization in the West has been supported by rhetorical arguments that justify the exercise of authority by managers. Qualities of excellence have been attributed to managers to make them appear worthy of their positions.[222] According to Bendix:

> The exercise of authority would also be justified in terms of the 'naturally' subordinate position of the many who obey. To this a further reference to the social order was usually added, holding out a promise to the many who with proper exertion might better themselves or even advance to positions of authority.[223]

Ideology has been used to shore up the support for hierarchical forms during times of rapid change.

Herbert Marcuse agrees with Bendix, writing: "The development of a hierarchical system of social labor not only rationalizes domination but also 'contains' the rebellion against domination."[224] William Gamson similarly argues:

> "the instruments of authority are most important scarce resources over which groups with conflicting goals grapple. Legitimate power is the grand prize because it makes it possible to reconcile the losers to their disadvantaged position. Authority is preferable to any other kind of power because it has a built-in 'cooling mechanism;' a device for allowing those who fail in a power struggle to accept the consequences with good grace."[225]

Kenneth Thompson has pointed out the strong class character of British industries and the elitist nature of the industrial system reflected in its ideology of paternalism. The ideology of business has been "modernized" so that leadership can be represented as "a social scientific concept, having to do with motivational techniques—nothing so crude as social dominance."[226] Social dominance is thereby made more palatable—and stable.

Frank Parkin makes an interesting argument with respect to the usefulness to those in power of the "prestige order" involved in organizational hierarchies. Parkin maintains that the "social honour" attached to higher levels of organizational hierarchy helps to justify the large differences in material rewards between those at the top of the hierarchy and those at the bottom.[227] This, too, aids in the maintenance of the dominance order.

The other side of the social dominance coin is the instability created by hierarchical systems. Jack Barbash has written that authority-generated "tensions" are capable of leading to industrial conflict.[228] Robert Wood Johnson, speaking from the management perspective, has recognized that "the root of labor-management trouble is destruction of human dignity."[229] In their classic textbook on industrial sociology, Robert C. Miller and William H. Form argue that the demands of organized labor are in major part "motivated by the desire for greater recognition."[230] They see labor as being strongly motivated to be accepted as a social equal of management. This view involves a concept of the dignity of labor that includes labor as a co-partner with management. According to these sociologists, "to be master of one's destiny has been an endless source of gratification in America."[231]

William F. Whyte sees the worker's position at the bottom of the industrial pyramid as producing an inclination to organize for self-defense. According to Whyte:

> For all the attention some managements may give them today, workers are still at the bottom of the industrial pyramid. They are the only people in the production organization who receive orders and who have no one below them to whom they can give orders. Management is constantly originating activity for them. In many cases they have little opportunity to originate back to management. In or outside of industry, when this one-sided origination situation exists, we find the people in the bottom position developing some resentment against the people who are always originating for them. Consciously or unconsciously they build up a self-defense organization to resist the changes that management is imposing.[232]

Some writers have maintained that it is the struggle for control, status, or dominance that has always been at the heart of American industrial conflict. P. K. Edwards attributes the tendency to have long strikes in the United States to the "continuing vigorous struggle for control of the work place which is being waged between labor and management."[233] According to Edwards, American managers had to build their own feudal traditions in the absence of native feudal conditions. Their ability to do this has been their "genius." In making themselves the focus of loyalty, they provided a solid basis for capitalism. It would have otherwise rested on the very unstable basis of a pure "cash nexus." In many cases recognition of unions would not have challenged financial profitability. What it often consisted of, instead, was a fundamental challenge to management control and therefore to the fundamental feudal relationship between labor and management. A feudal type of loyalty could include only ties to the employer. It could not include ties to an outside organization such as a labor union.[234]

Charles Perrow argues that: ". . . labor history appears conclusive on the point that the discontent of workers is a phenomenon which grows naturally out of the master-servant relationship and that the organization of this discontent owes more to the factory system than to the labor union."[235] Erich Fromm maintains that worker action through trade unions has had the "important psychological effect of giving [workers] a feeling of strength and significance" in dealing with the giant modern organization.[236]

Perhaps the most eloquent argument regarding the tensions caused by authoritarian work structures in a democractic society has been made by the U.S. Supreme Court Justice Louis Brandeis. Brandeis declares that the one fundamental cause of industrial unrest is "the necessary conflict—the contrast between our political liberty and our industrial absolutism."[237] Brandeis believed that unrest can never be eliminated by merely improving the physical and material conditions of workers. If this were to occur, "we should run great risk of improving their material condition and reducing their manhood."[238] According to him: "We Americans are committed not only to social justice in the sense of avoiding things which bring suffering and harm, like unjust distribution of wealth, but we are committed primarily to democracy. . . . And therefore the end for which we must strive is the attainment of rule by the people, and that involves industrial democracy as well as political democracy."[239]

Conclusions on Social Dominance Roots

The variegated literature reviewed above serves two purposes in the construction of a theory of industrial conflict. First, it helps us to "understand" the phenomenon of social dominance. Second, it makes it clear that social dominance can lead to industrial conflict, and gives us some indications as to how and why this might take place.

"Understanding" Social Dominance

Social dominance is a fundamental animal behavior that we share with our animal ancestors and relatives.[240] Hierarchies of power and authority are not purely rational inventions of the human mind. Predispositions, or "whisperings within," to use David Barash's phrase, exist which incline us to construct these hierarchies. These predispositions form an enduring part of the human psyche. These conclusions are supported by psychological, as well as sociobiological and ethological, theory and evidence.

One of the advantages to becoming modern Aesops and comparing our behavior to that of other animals is that it permits us to better "understand" human social dominance behavior. That is, it helps us to identify the causes of the behavior, recognize its nature, and form intelligent expectations as to its concommitants and consequences. As to causes, we now know that this behavior is at least in part caused by innate predispositions. As to its nature, and its concommitants and consequences, ethology and sociobiology provide a treasure trove of ideas.

Recognizing when dominance striving is taking place is greatly assisted by referring to the work of Morris and of Maclay and Knipe. What they point out is that the assumption of certain clothing, posture, demeanor, physical position, bearing, and attempts at using "eye power" are claims for dominance. The use of terminology and signs "borrowed" from the sex act can also be recognized as assertions of dominance. Indeed, these can only be understood when considered as such. The comedian, Lenny Bruce, once inquired why a word for the sex act should be used as a term of abuse. The ethologists appear to have the answer.

The concommitants and consequences of social dominance include priority as to resources, authority, and breeding priority. One can readily draw parallels between a dominant baboon's access to food and the high pay of corporate executives; the order-giving abilities of a silver-backed ape and a corporation executive in his fine attire and impressive office; a lead macaque's access to breeding and the *droit de seigneur* or the "sexual harassment" by powerful executives of female employees. This is not to say that social dominance must be accompanied by these facts, just that we should expect this to be the case rather commonly. Both social order and social turmoil may also be consequences of social dominance.

The sociological literature on the use of "authority" in organizations enlightens us as to the *functions* of social dominance in this setting. We are shown both the rationale for, and the consequences of, social dominance structures in modern associative human groups. We must be careful, however, not to confuse one of the usual functions of authoritative structures in organizations, efficiency, with an exclusive cause of these structures. Indeed, as Katz and Kahn suggest, the benefits of command structures have been greatly exaggerated. That they are retained even when they are not the most efficient forms would seem to indicate that they have their roots elsewhere. Perhaps their source lies in the calculated self-interest of those who control the organizations or their innate inclinations to pursue dominance, or both.

Comments on Social Dominance and Industrial Conflict

The human predisposition for social dominance leads us to establish, and strive for status in, social hierarchies. Individuals who are members of an organization with an hierarchical structure would be expected to have a tendency to attempt to improve their positions in the hierarchy. By definition, since status is determined relative to that of others, the attempt of one individual, or a group of them, to improve their status is an assault of the status of other individuals. Employee attempts to achieve higher status challenge at the very least the distance between employees and managers on the organizational hierarchy.

The tendency of individuals to seek dominance is moderated by a conflicting predisposition for deference. A "thirst for obedience" is a necessary inclination for a social animal who lives in a hierarchical society. It is chiefly this tendency that provides some stability to hierarchical organizations.

The result of these conflicting tendencies is hierarchically organized associations of humans that are relatively stable but inevitably include some "status tension." Each individual has a different mix of dominance and subordinance tendencies. Each organization has a different mix of persons who are either mainly dominant or mainly subordinate in their inclinations. Perhaps the most stable of organizations is that which includes persons who are *both* highly inclined toward controlling the behavior of others *and* toward subordination (authoritarian personalities). A group of individuals whose predispositions for both of these behaviors were very weak might be inclined to form a more democratic organization, a "society of brothers."

Social dominance, as we have herein defined the construct, includes both control over others and the freedom to control one's own behavior. Of course, a predisposition to social dominance, in the form of control over others, on the part of some organization members is likely to conflict with a predisposition for freedom on the part of other organization members. This creates especially difficult problems because a person of an authoritarian disposition who desires both authority and subordinance is unlikely to understand, or sympathize with, the freedom-seeker.

The notion of status tension has been expressed in a number of different ways. Morris speaks of it as arising when social animals struggle for hierarchical position. Maslow, McClelland, and Vance Packard argue that persons with high "dominance feeling" or "n Power" are likely to be restive in positions of subordinance. Dahrendorf speaks of conflicting "interests" of persons in different positions on the status ladder. Simon and other organization theorists predict refusal to obey, which is a status challenge, where legitimacy is not present. Industrial relations scholars and others have recognized that hierarchical forms are often used to justify the power and self-interest of the incumbents of positions of authority. A recognition of this on the part of lower members of organizations might be expected to produce tension and conflict. Brandeis' call for industrial rule by the people is perhaps the ultimate challenge to the dominance of power-holders in organizations. It implies not a narrowing of status differentials but destruction of the system of power so highly beneficial to the dominants. It calls for a levelling of the hierarchy. What makes this call particularly dangerous is its reference to the democratic aspirations of Americans in their political system. There, at least, the ideology is one that calls for a society of brothers. This is anathema to industrial autocracy.

In sum, the following conclusions are reached regarding social dominance:

1. Human beings are innately inclined to form social dominance hierarchies and struggle for position on them.
2. Social dominance hierarchies involve some degree of status tension.
3. The innate predisposition for social dominance causes human beings to act to achieve it in work organizations.
4. Action to achieve social dominance in work organizations can lead to industrial conflict.

CONCLUSIONS ON THE ROOTS OF INDUSTRIAL CONFLICT

Because of their centrality to the industrial relationship, we look to material rewards and social dominance as the roots of conflict in that relationship. We find that there are innate predispositions to pursue both. We further find that it is reasonable to argue that they are rather persistently pursued at work. Given the amount of scholarly attention these two roots of industrial conflict have received, it is possible to extensively explicate them in a manner that is useful for the development of a theory of industrial conflict.

It is hoped that this chapter has accomplished two things: (1) established the plausiblity of innate predispositions to pursue material resources and social dominance as root causes of industrial conflict; and, (2) discussed these roots in such a way that they can be sufficiently understood and used in the development and application of the integrative theory. The first pillar is the existence of innate predispositions; the second pillar is the identification and explication of the particular predispositions relevant for theorizing about industrial conflict. The next pillar is the moderating concept of relative deprivation. It is relative deprivation that is ordinarily required to accelerate the pursuit of material resources and social dominance. When so accelerated they may rise to the level necessary to lead toward industrial conflict.

NOTES

[1] John R. Commons, *Legal Foundations of Capitalism* (Madison: University of Wisconsin Press, 1968), p. 284.

[2] 56 *CJS, Master and Servant*, §1 (1948).

[3] 53 *Am Jur 2d, Master and Servant*, §1 (1970).

[4] Erich Fromm, *Escape From Freedom* (New York: Holt, Rinehart and Winston, 1941), p. 118.

[5] Delbert C. Miller and William H. Form, *Industrial Sociology* (New York: Harper & Brothers, 1951), pp. 377–378.

[6] Jeremy Bentham, *A Fragment on Government and An Introduction to the Principles of Morals and Legislation,* ed. Wilfrid Harrison (Oxford: Basil Blackwell, 1967), p. 125.

[7] Ibid., p. 126.

[8] Ibid., p. 127.

[9] Frederick Copleston, *A History of Philosophy,* Vol. 8: *Modern Philosophy: Bentham to Russell* (New York: Doubleday & Co. 1966), p. 19.

[10] Ibid., p. 35.

[11] Ibid., p. 45.

[12] Ibid., pp. 52–54.

[13] Ibid., p. 54.

[14] Ibid.

[15] Ibid., p. 49.

¹⁶George W. Wilson, *Classics of Economic Theory* (Bloomington: Indiana University Press, 1954), p. 542.
¹⁷Ibid., p. 545.
¹⁸Ibid.
¹⁹Ibid., p. 557.
²⁰Ibid.
²¹Ibid.
²²Sigmund Freud, *Civilization and Its Discontents*, trans. and ed. James Strachey (New York: W.W. Norton Co., 1961), p. 27.
²³Joseph A. Schumpeter, *History of Economic Analysis* (New York: Oxford University Press, 1954), p. 576.
²⁴Wilson, *Classics of Economic Theory*, p. 570.
²⁵Ibid., p. 571.
²⁶Ibid., p. 573.
²⁷Schumpeter, *History of Economic Analysis*, p. 577.
²⁸Alexander Rosenberg, *Sociobiology and the Preemption of Social Science* (Baltimore: The Johns Hopkins University Press, 1980), pp. 34–37.
²⁹Dolf Zillman, *Hostility and Aggression* (Hillsdale, N.J.: Lawrence Erlbaum Associates, 1979), pp. 102–105.
³⁰Ibid.
³¹David Hamilton, *Evolutionary Economics* (Albuquerque: University of New Mexico Press, 1970), p. 29.
³²Ibid.
³³Ibid., pp. 18–22.
³⁴Ibid., p. 29.
³⁵Ibid., p. 30.
³⁶Ibid., pp. 32–33.
³⁷Ibid., p. 34.
³⁸Ibid.
³⁹Ibid., pp. 43–56.
⁴⁰A. Conan Doyle, "A Scandal in Bohemia," in *The Original Illustrated Sherlock Holmes* (Secaucus, N.J.: Castle Books, 1979), p. 13.
⁴¹James Gibson Hume, *Political Economy and Ethics* (Toronto: J.E. Bryant Co., 1792), p. 19.
⁴²Schumpeter, *History of Economic Analysis*, p. 99.
⁴³Ibid., pp. 130–131.
⁴⁴Ibid.
⁴⁵Ibid., p. 131.
⁴⁶Ibid.
⁴⁷Ibid.
⁴⁸Ibid., p. 133.
⁴⁹Rosenberg, *Scoiobiology and the Preemption of Social Science*, pp. 34–67.
⁵⁰Gary S. Becker, *The Economic Approach to Human Behavior* (Chicago: University of Chicago Press, 1976).
⁵¹Victor H. Vroom, *Work and Motivation* (New York: John Wiley & Sons, 1964).
⁵²Daniel Katz, "Satisfactions and Deprivations of Industrial Life," in *Industrial Conflict*, ed. Arthur Kornhauser, Robert Dubin, and Arthur M. Ross (New York: McGraw-Hill Book Co., 1954), p. 88.
⁵³A. Fox, "Management Frame of Reference," in *Collective Bargaining*, ed. Allan Flanders (Baltimore: Penguin Books, 1969), pp. 399–400.
⁵⁴Jack Barbash, "The Elements of Industrial Relations," *The British Journal of Industrial Relations*, 2 (1964), pp. 66–78; Peter Feuille and Hoyt N. Wheeler, "Will the Real Industrial Conflict Stand Up?" in *U.S. Industrial Relations, 1950–1980: A Critical Assessment*, ed. Jack Stieber, Robert B. McKersie, and D. Quinn Mills, (Madison, Wis.: Industrial Relations Research Association, 1981), pp. 256–259.

[55]Neil W. Chamberlain and Donald E. Cullen, *The Labor Sector*, 2nd ed. (New York: McGraw-Hill Book Co. 1971), pp. 223–332.

[56]29 *U.S.C.* §152(11) (1971) [Section 2(11), National Labor Relations Act.]

[57]George Maclay and Humphry Knipe, *The Dominant Man* (New York: Dell Publishing Co., 1972), p. 4.

[58]Edward O. Wilson, *Sociobiology*, abgd ed. (Cambridge: The Belknap Press, 1980), p. 137.

[59]Ibid., pp. 138–139.

[60]Ibid., p. 137.

[61]Maclay and Knipe, *The Dominant Man*, pp. 31–32; Irenaus Eibl-Eibesfeldt, *Love and Hate*, trans. Geoffrey Strachen (New York: Schocken Books, 1974), pp. 88–89.

[62]Robert Ardrey, *African Genesis* (New York: Atheneum, 1977), p.92.

[63]Ibid., p. 13.

[64]Ibid., p. 164.

[65]Konrad Lorenz, *On Aggression*, trans. Marjorie Kerr Wilson (New York: Harcourt, Brace & World, 1966), p. 40.

[66]Desmond Morris, *The Human Zoo* (New York: McGraw-Hill Book Co. 1969), p. 41.

[67]Desmond Morris, *The Naked Ape* (New York: Dell Publishing Co., 1967), p. 120.

[68]Lionel Tiger and Robin Fox, *The Imperial Animal* (New York: Holt, Rinehart and Winston, 1971), p. 33.

[69]Maclay and Knipe, *The Dominant Man*, p. 17.

[70]Ibid., p. 2.

[71]Ardrey, *African Genesis*, p. 149.

[72]Maclay and Knipe, *The Dominant Man*, pp. 13–15.

[73]Ibid., p. 16.

[74]Wilson, *Sociobiology*, p. 276.

[75]Morris, *The Human Zoo*, p. 54.

[76]Ibid., pp. 42–43.

[77]Ibid., pp. 42–45.

[78]Maclay and Knipe, *The Dominant Man*, pp. 8–10, 25.

[79]Ibid., pp. 42–46; Ralph M. Stogdill, "Personal Factors Associated with Leadership: A Survey of the Literature," *The Journal of Psychology* 25 (1948), pp. 40–41.

[80]Maclay and Knipe, *The Dominant Man*, pp. 46–54.

[81]Ibid., pp. 55–60.

[82]Ibid., pp. 60–64.

[83]Ibid., p. 67.

[84]Ibid., p. 70.

[85]Ibid., pp. 75–81.

[86]Ibid., pp. 83–97.

[87]Ibid., p. 103.

[88]Ibid., p. 116.

[89]Ibid., pp. 122–123.

[90]Ibid., pp. 125–127.

[91]Tiger and Fox, *The Imperial Animal*, p. 19; W. C. Allee, "Where Angels Fear to Tread: A Contribution from General Sociology to Human Ethics," in *The Sociobiology Debate*, ed. Arthur L. Caplan (New York: Harper & Row, Publishers, 1978), p. 42.

[92]Wilson, *Sociobiology*, p. 141.

[93]Ibid., pp. 141–142.

[94]Maclay and Knipe, *The Dominant Man*, p. 21.

[95]Ibid., p. 33.

[96]Ibid., p. 137.

[97]Wilson, *Sociobiology*, p. 142.

[98]Eibl-Eibesfeldt, *Love and Hate*, p. 89.

[99]Tiger and Fox, *The Imperial Animal*, p. 39.

[100]Morris, *The Human Zoo*, p. 41.

[101]Lorenz, *On Aggression,* p. 41.

[102]R. A. Hinde, *Biological Bases of Human Social Behavior* (New York: McGraw-Hill Book Co., 1974), p. 343.

[103]Ardrey, *African Genesis,* pp. 110–111.

[104]Morris, *The Human Zoo,* p. 100.

[105]Ibid.

[106]Ibid., pp. 100–120.

[107]Lorenz, *On Aggression,* pp. 130–131.

[108]Maclay and Knipe, *The Dominant Man,* p. 9.

[109]Melvin Konner, *The Tangled Wing* (New York: Holt, Rinehart and Winston, 1982), p. 289.

[110]Carl Sagan, *The Dragons of Eden* (New York: Ballantine Books, 1977), p. 56.

[111]Ibid.

[112]Freud, *Civilization and Its Discontents,* p. 43; Sigmund Freud, *Group Psychology and the Analysis of the Ego,* trans. and ed. James Strachey (New York: W.W. Norton & Co., 1959), p. 59.

[113]Fromm, *Escape From Freedom,* pp. 1–32.

[114]Freud, *Civilization and Its Discontents,* p. 43.

[115]Alfred Adler, *Understanding Human Nature* (Greenwich, Conn.: Fawcett Publications, 1927), p. 32.

[116]Ibid.

[117]Alfred Adler, *The Practice and Theory of Individual Psychology* (New York: Harcourt, Brace & Co., 1927), p. 7; Zillman, *Hostility and Aggression,* p. 115.

[118]Adolph A. Berle, *Power* (New York: Harcourt, Brace & World, 1969), p. 62.

[119]Rollo May, *Power and Innocence* (New York: W.W. Norton & Co., 1972), p. 39.

[120]Ibid., p. 42.

[121]David C. McClelland, "The Two Faces of Power," *Journal of International Affairs* 24, no. 1 (1970), pp. 35–36.

[122]Ibid., p. 38.

[123]Jack W. Brehm, *A Theory of Psychological Reactance* (New York: Academic Press, 1966).

[124]Ibid., p. 2.

[125]Ibid., p. 4.

[126]Ibid., p. 7.

[127]Ibid., p. 11.

[128]Russell Jacoby, *Social Amnesia* (Boston: Beacon Press, 1975), pp. 84–85.

[129]Edward A. Shils, "Deference," in *The Logic of Social Hierarchies,* ed. Edward O. Laumann, Paul M. Siegel, and Robert W. Hodge (Chicago: Markham Publishing Co., 1970), p. 421.

[130]Stanley Milgram, "Some Conditions of Obedience and Disobedience to Authority," *Human Relations* 18 (1965), p. 74.

[131]Ibid., p. 74.

[132]Ibid., p. 69.

[133]Ibid., pp. 58–59.

[134]Stanley Milgram, "Behavioral Study of Obedience," *Journal of Abnormal and Social Psychology* 67, no. 4 (1963), p. 371.

[135]Freud, *Group Psychology and the Analysis of the Ego,* pp. 13, 59.

[136]Ibid., p. 59.

[137]Ibid., p. 53.

[138]Ibid., pp. 54–55.

[139]Fromm, *Escape From Freedom,* p. 164.

[140]Ibid., p. 158.

[141]Ibid., p. 171.

[142]T. W. Adorno, Else Frenkel Brunswick, Daniel J. Levinson, and R. Nevitt Sanford, *The Authoritarian Personality* (New York: Harper and Row, 1950), pp. 182, 192, 228.

[143]A. H. Maslow, "Dominance-Feeling, Behavior, and Status," *Psychological Review* 44 (1937), pp. 404–429.

[144]Ibid., p. 407.

[145]Ibid.

[146]Ibid., p. 413.

[147]Ibid., p. 417.

[148]Ibid., pp. 427–428.

[149]David G. Winter, *The Power Motive* (New York: The Free Press, 1973), p. 21.

[150]Ibid., pp. 17–18.

[151]Ibid., pp. 210–211.

[152]David C. McClelland and David H. Burnham, "Power is the Great Motivator," *Harvard Business Review* 54, no. 2 (March-April 1966), p. 101.

[153]Vance Packard, *The Pyramid Climbers* (New York: McGraw-Hill Book Co., 1962), p. 172.

[154]Ibid., p. 173.

[155]Ibid., p. 96.

[156]Ibid., p. 117.

[157]Vance Packard, *The Status Seekers* (New York: David McKay Co. 1959), p. 114.

[158]Robert A. Dahl and Charles E. Lindblom, *Politics, Economics and Welfare* (New York: Harper & Row Publishers, 1953), p. 230.

[159]Amitai Etzioni, *A Comparative Analysis of Complex Organizations*, rev. and enl. ed. (New York: The Free Press, 1975), p. 3.

[160]Daniel Katz and Robert L. Kahn, *The Social Psychology of Organizations* (New York: John Wiley & Sons, 1966), p. 204.

[161]Ibid., pp. 200–201.

[162]David J. Hickson and Arthur F. McCullough, "Power in Organizations," in *Control and Ideology in Organizations*, ed. Graeme Salaman and Kenneth Thompson (Cambridge: MIT Press, 1980), p. 30.

[163]Katz and Kahn, *The Social Psychology of Organizations*, p. 214.

[164]Ibid., pp. 211–214.

[165]Dahl and Lindblom, *Politics, Economics and Welfare*, p. 230.

[166]Ibid., p. 243.

[167]Ralf Dahrendorf, *Class and Class Conflict in Industrial Society* (Stanford: Stanford University Press, 1959), p. 136.

[168]Allan W. Lerner, "On Ambiguity and Organizations," *Administration and Society* 10, no. 1 (May 1978), p. 12.

[169]Ibid.

[170]Herbert Simon, *Administrative Behavior*, 3rd ed. (New York: The Free Press, 1976), pp. 123–153.

[171]Ibid., p. 124.

[172]Ibid., p. 125.

[173]Ibid., pp. 125–126.

[174]Ibid., p. 127.

[175]Ibid., p. 128.

[176]David V. J. Bell, *Power, Influence and Authority: An Essay in Political Linguistics* (New York: Oxford University Press, 1975), pp. 35–69.

[177]Samuel B. Bacharach and Edward J. Lawler, *Power and Politics in Organizations* (San Francisco: Jossey-Bass Publishers, 1980), pp. 35–36.

[178]Peter M. Blau, "Exchange Theory," in *The Sociology of Organizations*, ed. Oscar Grusky and George A. Miller (New York: The Free Press, 1970), p. 139.

[179]Ibid.

[180]Michael Bannester, "Sociodynamics: An Integrative Theorem of Power, Authority, Interfluence and Love," *American Sociological Review* 34, no. 3 (June 1969), p. 384.

[181]Ibid., pp. 384–386.

[182]John R. P. French and Bertram Raven, "The Bases of Social Power," in *Studies in Social Power,* ed. Darwin Cartwright (Ann Arbor: Institute for Social Research, University of Michigan, 1959), pp. 155–156.

[183]Ibid., pp. 158–159.

[184]Ibid.

[185]Etzioni, *A Comparative Analysis of Complex Organizations,* p. 5.

[186]Ibid., p. 10; Hickson and McCullough, "Power in Organizations," p. 49.

[187]Etzioni, *A Comparative Analysis of Complex Organizations,* p. 31.

[188]Tom Kynaston Reeves and Joan Woodward, "The Study of Managerial Control," in *Industrial Organization: Behaviour and Control,* ed. Joan Woodward (London: Oxford University Press, 1970), p. 44.

[189]Jean Jacques Rousseau, *The Social Contract* (New York: Hofner Publishing Co., 1951), p. 106.

[190]James A. F. Stoner, *Management,* 2nd ed. (Englewood Cliffs, N.J.: Prentice-Hall, 1982), p. 304.

[191]Cyril O'Donnell," The Source of Managerial Authority," *Political Science Quarterly* 67, no. 4 (December 1952), p. 574.

[192]Ibid., p. 584.

[193]Ibid., p. 587.

[194]Chester I. Barnard, *The Functions of the Executive* (Cambridge: Harvard University Press, 1962), p. 165.

[195]Stoner, *Management,* p. 304.

[196]Kenneth Thompson, "The Organizational Society," in *Control and Ideology in Organizations,* ed. Salaman and Thompson, p. 8.

[197]Ibid., p. 9

[198]Ibid., p. 15.

[199]French and Raven, "The Bases of Social Power," p. 160.

[200]Blau, "Exchange Theory," pp. 137–138.

[201]Dahrendorf, *Class and Class Conflict in Industrial Society,* p. 158.

[202]Hickson and McCullough, "Power in Organizations," p. 54.

[203]Dahrendorf, *Class and Class Conflict in Industrial Society,* p. 158.

[204]Ibid., p. 159.

[205]Ibid., p. 165.

[206]Ibid.

[207]Ibid., p. 618.

[208]Ibid., pp. 166–167.

[209]Ibid., p. 174.

[210]Ibid., p. 175.

[211]Ibid., p. 176.

[212]Ibid., pp. 176–178.

[213]Ibid., p. 178.

[214]Ibid.

[215]Ibid., p. 248.

[216]Ibid.

[217]Ibid., p. 249.

[218]Ibid.

[219]Ibid., pp. 242–243.

[220]Ibid., p. 243.

[221]Frank Parkin, *Class Inequality and Political Order* (New York: Praeger Publishers, 1971), p. 91.

[222]Reinhard Bendix, *Work and Authority in Industry* (New York: John Wiley & Sons, 1956), pp. 2–3.

[223]Ibid., p. 3.

[224]Herbert Marcuse, *Eros and Civilization* (New York: Vintage Books, 1962), p. 82.

[225]William A. Gamson, *Power and Discontent* (Homewood Ill.: The Dorsey Press, 1968), p. 8.

[226]Kenneth Thompson, "Organizations as Constructors of Social Reality" in *Control and Ideology in Organizations*, ed. Salaman and Thompson, p. 229.

[227]Parkin, *Class Inequality and Political Order*, pp. 41–42, 44.

[228]Jack Barbash, "The Work Society" (unpublished manuscript, University of Wisconsin, 1971), p. 1.

[229]Robert Wood Johnson, "An Employer Looks at Labor-Management Relations," *Industrial and Labor Relations Review* 1, no. 3 (April 1948), p. 489.

[230]Miller and Form, *Industrial Sociology*, pp. 377–378.

[231]Ibid., p. 378.

[232]William F. Whyte, *Money and Motivation* (New York: Harper & Row Publishers, 1955), p. 234.

[233]P. K. Edwards, *Strikes in the United States, 1881–1974* (New York: St. Martin's Press, 1981), p. 237.

[234]Ibid., pp. 243–244.

[235]Charles Perrow, "The Sixties Observed," in *The Dynamics of Social Movements*, ed. by Mayer N. Zald and John D. McCarthy (Cambridge: Winthrop Publishers, 1979), p. 36.

[236]Fromm, *Escape From Freedom*, p. 126.

[237]Louis D. Brandeis, "The Fundamental Cause of Industrial Unrest," in *Unions, Management and the Public*, ed. E. Wight Bakke, Clark Kerr, and Charles W. Anrod (New York: Harcourt, Brace & World, 1967), p. 244.

[238]Ibid., p. 245.

[239]Ibid.

[240]Morris, *The Human Zoo*, p. 54.

CHAPTER 5

The Theory's Third Pillar— Expectations and Achievements

"[M]ankind are more disposed to suffer, while evils are sufferable, than to right themselves by abolishing the forms to which they are accustomed. But when a long train of abuses and usurpations . . . evinces a design to reduce them under absolute Despotism, it is their right, it is their duty, to throw off such Government. . . ."

Declaration of Independence, 1776

The relationship between employee expectations and achievements constitutes a crucial pillar of the integrative theory. It is an expectations/achievements gap that accelerates our modelled man into intensive motion. It is this gap that provides a good deal of the dynamism and explanatory power of the model. It is theorizing with respect to the relation between expectations and their achievement which provides a base in the social scientific literature for some of the major forces in the model.

At this point in the development of the integrative theory we move from general theories of economics and social dominance to more narrow theories of social conflict. These theories arise from political science and other disciplines concerned with phenomena closely akin to industrial conflict, and even industrial conflict itself.

It has been argued in previous chapters that human beings are predisposed to pursue social dominance and material resources. They constantly pursue both, in great ways and small, with greater or lesser degrees of intensity. Employees engage in their pursuit at their places of work. What is crucial for our purposes is to identify the conditions under which the level of intensity of their pursuit by an employee is sufficient to instigate a feeling of frustration when particular levels of these outcomes are not achieved, or of threat when they are taken away or placed in jeopardy.

It would seem that a crucial condition influencing the intensity of a worker's pursuit of material and social dominance outcomes would be the degree that either material or social dominance outcomes are perceived to be presently achieved. Presumably, workers achieve different levels of these at different times. When a worker perceives that his achievements as to material resources or social dominance are quite low, one would expect him to pursue them with a significant degree of intensity. On the other hand, there must be some point at which his achievements on these outcomes are sufficient to cause him to cease pursuing them with much intensity. The problem is to locate this point so that one can determine when a worker is below it.

One possible candidate for such a point is the rather extreme one at which the person perceives that no greater achievements are possible. An absolute monarch with control of all a dominion's wealth might be in such a position. A somewhat less extreme candidate might be the point at which the individual achieves the degree of social dominance and economic resources that he *wishes,* or to which he aspires. A blue-collar worker might wish to be president of his company with a six-figure income. Yet, one would expect the intense pursuit of social dominance and material resources to stop considerably short of this point for most workers.

Simply on a common-sense basis, it would seem that a prime candidate for the point of interest is the point at which a worker achieves that level of social dominance and material resources he *expects* as his due. It seems highly improbable that a worker would act with much intensity to achieve outcomes he feels he does not deserve. On the other hand, the existence of the cognitive condition of injustice, or inequity, which would arise from believing that one was not receiving one's just deserts, or a threat to them, should provide compelling force to the pursuit of these outcomes. One might suspect, therefore, that a gap between those outcomes a worker *expects* and those he achieves would be a precondition to movement through either the threat or frustration-aggression paths of the model.

This reasoning does not, of course, apply to the purely calculative path of the model. There it is assumed that a favorable cost-benefit calculation is by itself sufficient to produce a readiness for aggressive action.

There is some precedent in the industrial conflict literature for focusing on the phenomenon of worker expectations. Jack Barbash has identified as one of the forces underlying the rank-and-file unrest in the mid-1960s "the rising expectations of workers stimulated by the long expansion."[1] Willard Wirtz also concluded that the labor militancy of that period was attributable to the soaring expectations of workers.[2]

Political scientists have been the chief developers of the concept of an expectations/achievements gap as an explainer of social conflict. Their "relative deprivation theory" has been used mainly to explain violent revolution, although its early development was closely connected with the study of strikes.[3] It is not maintained here that political revolution is identical to industrial conflict—only that the theory of one can be used to assist in understanding the other.

RELATIVE DEPRIVATION THEORY

Relative deprivation theory was developed, beginning in the early 1960s, to explain revolutionary violence. Among its earlier proponents were James Chowning Davies[4] and Ivo K. Feierabend and Rosalind L. Feierabend.[5] A major systemization of relative deprivation theory was produced in 1970 by Ted Robert Gurr.[6] Through the mid-1960s and the 1970s there developed a fairly large body of writing on this subject.

As fully developed, relative deprivation theory involves several related propositions. First, it holds that there are certain basic needs which human beings seek to fulfill. Persons have certain expectations with respect to fulfillment of these needs. These expectations are the levels of need fulfillment to which they believe themselves *justly entitled.* A gap between expected need fulfillment and actual need fulfillment generates a tension. In frustration-aggression theory terms, the individual becomes frustrated. This produces anger, or readiness for aggression. Aggression is seen as an innately satisfying response to this anger. If certain conditions are present, the individual will lash out at society. The collective nature of the phenomenon derives from a number of people feeling deprivation at the same time.

Early Relative Deprivation Theory

James Chowning Davies first propounded his version of relative deprivation theory in 1962.[7] His "J-curve" theory says simply that ". . . when a relatively long period of steady rise in what people want and what people get is followed by a short period of sharp reversal, during which a gap suddenly widens between what people want and what they get, the likelihood of revolution increases sharply."[8] When the gap between expectations and need fulfillment becomes intolerable, revolution occurs.

According to Davies, frustration is produced in a J-curve situation. This frustration creates a state of mind of high tension and generalized hostility. This hostility is at first directed generally outward, but eventually begins to turn toward the government. There are four steps in the sequence of events leading to violent action. The first step is the activation of some "innately rooted demand" within the person, resulting in a state of tension that calls for release. The second step is the frustration of the person's demands. The third step is the mental process of the person deciding how to overcome the frustration—whether by avoidance, substitution, or destruction of the blockage. The fourth step is aggressive, violent, action by the individual.[9]

Davies has applied his J-curve theory to a number of incidents of revolution.[10] These occurrences range from the Pullman strike to the French Revolution. In all these cases Davies finds support for his theory. However, Davies' work, particularly his application of the J-curve to the black protests of the 1960s, has given rise to sharp debate. In a major attack on the J-curve, Abraham Miller, Louis Bolce, and Mark Halligan question the research strategies of relative deprivation theories generally.[11] They also argue from their own analysis of the black protests that no J-curve can be found. They criticize relative deprivation theorists because these theorists "use the language and theoretical foundations of individual data then perform their empirical testing with aggregate social and economic indicators."[12] They argue that economic indicators that measure objective decisions can *never* be read as reflecting individual perceptions. Using perceptual measures, Miller and his colleagues failed to find a J-curve for the period in question. They contend that, to conform to J-curve theory, the perceptual measures should show an increasing proportion of northern blacks perceiving the trend of their finances to be improving prior to 1964 and declining after 1964. Their data show that this is not the case. Although Miller et al., are critical of the use of objective indicators to reflect perceptual data "on a point-by-point basis," they, somewhat confusingly, concede that this may be justified with respect to "the overall trend of the data."[13]

Both Davies[14] and Faye Crosby[15] have responded to this critique of J-curve theory. Davies argues that Miller et al., have failed to take into account that factors other than economic must be taken into consideration. He also argues that the relevant period of time with respect to black protest is longer than that examined by Miller et al. Miller et al., respond to Davies' reference to other than economic factors by arguing that this makes the theory too general and imprecise to be useful.[16] Crosby attacks the Miller, et al., study for misrepresenting the current literature on relative deprivation and for using inadequate measures of felt deprivation. She argues that the critics have really not tested relative deprivation theory at all, and have only tested J-curve theory in a weak manner.

The early Feierabend and Feierabend statement of relative deprivation theory is relatively simple.[17] These authors consider political instability to be aggressive behavior (much like the integrative theory considers industrial conflict to be aggressive behavior). Based on the frustration-aggression hypothesis they suggest that this behavior results when there are "situations of unrelieved, socially experienced frustration."[18] These are situations where "levels of social expectations, aspirations, and needs are raised for many people for significant periods of time, yet remain unmatched by equivalent levels of satisfaction."[19] "Systematic frustration" is seen as occurring where social want satisfaction is out of balance with social want formation. The Feierabends recognize that frustration does not *always* lead to aggression. The existence of systematic frustration does, however, substantially increase the likelihood of political instability.

Gurr's Version of Relative Deprivation Theory

Ted Robert Gurr, in his book *Why Men Rebel* (1970), made a major contribution to the development of relative deprivation theory.[20] One of Gurr's earlier writings on this subject sets out the core of his theory.[21] His primary theoretical proposition is that relative deprivation is the "basic precondition" for civil strife. According to Gurr, the more widespread and intense the deprivation among members of a population, the greater the magnitude of the strife. Relative deprivation is defined as a discrepancy between "value expectations" and "value capabilities." Value expectations are those goods and conditions of life to which persons believe they are justifiably entitled. Value capabilities are the goods and conditions that they believe that they are able to get and keep. According to Gurr, the "underlying causal mechanism" is the innate response of anger where there is a perception of deprivation. Aggression is seen by Gurr as "an inherently satisfying response" to such anger.

In *Why Men Rebel* Gurr sets out his theory at length. There he argues: "The primary causal sequence in political violence is first the development of discontent, second the politicization of that discontent and finally its actualization in violent action against political objects and political actors. Discontent arising from the perception of relative deprivation is the basic, instigating condition for participants in collective violence."[22] Gurr identifies deprivation-induced discontent as a general spur to action. The intensity of the action is a function of the intensity of the discontent. Its specificity is determined by beliefs about the sources of the deprivation, and the normality and utilitarian justifiability of violent action directed at those responsible for the deprivation. Gurr emphasizes that he is not speaking of deprivation as it would appear to an objective observer, but rather of the condition of being "subjectively deprived."[23] What might appear to be abject poverty or terrible deprivation in the eyes of an outsider may not be considered "unjust or irremediable" by those subjected to it. If people do not have reason to expect or hope for more than they have or can readily achieve, they may not be discontented. They may instead be grateful to simply hold onto what they have.

It is "values" to which both expectations and achievements relate. Values, according to Gurr, are the "desired events, objects and conditions for which men strive."[24] Gurr classifies these as welfare values, power values and interpersonal values. Welfare values are defined as "those that contribute directly to physical well-being and self-realization."[25] In the term *welfare values* Gurr includes both economic and self-actualization values. Power values are defined (similarly to the integrative theory's definition of "social dominance") as "those that determine the extent to which man can influence the actions of others and avoid unwanted interference by others in their own actions."[26] This includes participation in decision making and being secure from "oppressive political regulation" and "disorder."[27] Interpersonal values are defined as the "psychological satisfactions we seek in nonauthoritative interactions with other individuals and groups."[28] This includes a desire for status and participation in stable and supportive groups that provide companionship and affection.

It is a gap between value expectations and achievements that creates relative deprivation and discontent. Value *expectations* are an important aspect of Gurr's theory. These he defines as those values to which people believe they are *justly entitled*. There is a sense of rightness about these value expectations. Quite importantly, they are to be distinguished from *aspirations*, which represent what individuals would merely *like to have*.

The potential for collective violence, a variable of focal interest to Gurr, is chiefly a function of the scope and intensity of relative deprivation among members of a group. He argues that this variable can be effectively measured through interviews in which individuals are asked whether they intend to participate in actions of collective violence.

The mechanism upon which Gurr relies to translate relative deprivation into violent political action is frustration-aggression. He argues that ". . . the primary source of human capacity for violence appears to be the frustration-aggression mechanism. Frustration does not necessarily lead to violence, and violence for some men is motivated by expectations of gain. The anger induced by frustration, however, is a motivating force that disposes men to aggression, irrespective of its instrumentalities. If frustrations are sufficiently prolonged or sharply felt, aggression is quite likely, if not certain, to occur."[29] He recognizes that other variables influence the behavior of men, but argues that frustration-aggression theory is the fundamental rule of political violence.

Gurr's discussion of the determinants of the *intensity* of relative deprivation is quite interesting. He hypothesizes that the degree of perceived discrepancies between value expectations and value capabilities will strongly influence the intensity of relative deprivation. An increase in the discrepancy can occur either through an increase in expectations without an increase in capabilities, or a decrease in capabilities without a decrease in expectations. This is consistent with, but considerably broader than, Davies "J-curve" theory.

Gurr hypothesizes that the intensity of relative deprivation varies with the salience of the values with respect to which deprivation is experienced. He also proposes a moderate relationship between the intensity of relative deprivation and the proportion of things with respect to which deprivation is experienced. He describes this last hypothesis as involving the "last straw" phenomenon. Where a large proportion of what men value has been taken from them, the taking of an additional small value may become highly salient and cause intense feelings of relative deprivation. Gurr argues that, in general, economic values are most salient. Autonomy and power values are also recognized as being highly salient. Gurr also argues that the proximity of a goal increases its salience.

Given the centrality of expectations to Gurr's theory, his arguments regarding the sources of increasing expectations are important. He lists as sources of rising expectations: (1) the demonstration effect; (2) articulation of new beliefs that justify heightened expectations; and, (3) the effect of past improvements. With respect to the demonstration effect, Gurr argues that there must be some preexisting relative deprivation before it can be powerful. He sees "conversion" to rising expectations as occurring at some point. This conversion is facilitated by objective circumstances that provide the chance to realize the expectations. One social group's upward mobility may raise the expectations of other similar groups. A group that is high on one set of values but not on another will be in a situation of disequilibrium. As suggested by Davies, past improvements create expectations of future improvements.

As Gurr recognizes, all of the preceding discussion only refers to an individual's or a group's *potential* for collective violence. Whether the violence in fact occurs is also dependent upon underlying attitudes toward violence in politics, particularly with respect to its acceptability and utility. Quite importantly, the occurrence of political violence also depends on the strength and coercive potential of the regime.

Gurr contends that men are likely to have views about the propriety of political violence, and violence generally, which will influence their behavior in this respect. They are also likely to have expectations about the utility of violence as a means of value attainment. Gurr clearly recognizes utilitarian and nonutilitarian motivations for political violence. He argues that they are ordinarily both present in any instance of political violence.

Tests of Relative Deprivation Theory

There has been a great deal of research testing relative deprivation theory. Some of this research is supportive of the theory; some is in conflict with it. Much of it is irrelevant to a genuine test of this theory.[30]

Some of the more interesting tests have been performed by Edward N. Muller. The first of his studies was of the potential for political violence in a midwestern city.[31] In this study Muller found that increased relative deprivation of individuals was not related in a straightforward way to their "potential for political violence." "Potential for political violence" was operationalized as the degree to which a person would *admit to willingness to engage in political violence.* Relative deprivation was measured by a "ladder scale," developed by Hadley Cantril, which asked individuals to compare their perceived achievement to their optimum achievement on several values. This study also produced for Muller and a coauthor the conclusion that a "V-curve" existed with respect to relative deprivation. This meant that the potential for political violence increased among those persons who had experienced the *greatest change* in status relative to aspirations, whether this change was *positive or negative.*[32]

In a later study, Muller tested what he called "expectancy-value-norm" theory.[33] His dependent variable was the degree of participation of individuals in aggressive political activity. In applying this measure, Muller asked respondents whether they had engaged in a variety of behaviors, including a wildcat strike. Several of his independent variables were found to have significant effects. According to Muller, the most important of these was a variable reflecting "the expectation that the action will have beneficial or rewarding consequences, weighted by the value of performing that action as compared with alternative actions."[34] In terms of the integrative theory, this would provide support for the calculative path. The other significant variables were: (1) "personal normative beliefs," which reflected support for, or alienation from, the system; (3) social norms, "facilitative social norms regarding participation in political aggression;" and, (3) availability for collective action.[35] Muller concluded that deprivation did not play a significant role in the explanation of his dependent variable. However, his data seem to lead to the opposite result with respect to *just deserts frustration*. Frustration based upon failure to achieve what respondents felt that they *ought* to have was highly correlated ($r = .40$) with participation in aggressive political action. This relationship remained significant when tested for in multiple regression equations. It was especially strong among respondents who believed government to be responsible for the conditions giving rise to their frustrations.[36] These results furnish clear support for a relationship between just deserts frustration (which is what Gurr is talking about) and aggressive political action against the state when the state is perceived to be the frustrator. This is precisely what we would expect to find with respect to action against an employer in a test of the integrative theory.

One of the most biting of the early attacks on relative deprivation theory was written by Clark McPhail.[37] McPhail reviewed a number of relative deprivation studies and concluded that they had simply not found any significant results. As has been noted by Muller, however, few of the measures that McPhail describes as dealing with relative deprivation theory have any reasonable relation to that theory. In almost all cases they are tests of *objective* deprivation, not *relative* deprivation.[38] McPhail's criticism does, however, underscore the great difficulty that relative deprivation theorists have had in devising measures of those constructs most central to their theory.

Walter Korpi argues that the great failing of relative deprivation theory is that it does not take into account the actual possibilities of achieving change. Korpi emphasizes the power balance as being of crucial importance for this, and argues for a more rational, utilitarian, view of political conflict.[39] Hibbs found no support for his measure of an "expectation-achievement" gap as a short-run predictor of industrial conflict,[40] although he did find that in the *long run* there was some relationship between his measure of an expectations-achievement gap (real wage changes) and the volume of strikes some time thereafter. He found that the unemployment rate had a substantial effect upon the strike rate. The level of Hibbs' study may explain his results to a certain degree. That is, real wage changes may have effects that vary greatly from industry to industry. Accordingly, they may not have an impact on strike rates at the level of society in general (the level of his study). On the other hand, unemployment rates may have effects upon perceptions on a very broad basis and be observable at the societal level.

Perhaps the most penetrating criticisms of relative deprivation theory have been made by Charles Tilly.[41] First, he questions how *regularly* deprivation produces individual discontent, which produces collective discontent and anger, which, in turn, lead to collective violence. This question pertains not to the validity, but rather to the importance, of relative deprivation theory. If one believes that most political violence takes place on other grounds (such as those of utility), relative deprivation theory is not invalid, but merely trivial. Second, Tilly argues that Gurr's theory gives no explanation of violence by agents of the state. Tilly argues that this is more common than violence by the people and is performed by those with a greater ability to inflict harm. If, as Tilly suggests, the most important explanations for political violence are those that predict violence by agents of the state, or, in the case of violence by members of the general population, are considerations of utility or availability of resources, relative deprivation theory is indeed trivial. Of course, it could be trivial for the purposes of explaining political violence and still be highly useful for dealing with the phenomenon of industrial conflict.

In support of relative deprivation theory it should be noted that similar notions have been utilized by scholars other than those who have been labelled as relative deprivation theorists. In constructing his theory of distributive justice, George Caspar Homans makes extensive use of the idea of relative deprivation.[42] He argues that a person who merely fails to receive a reward that he needs will not necessarily be angry. It is only when he does not get what he *expects*, "and what he expected is always becoming what he deserved," that he is likely to find rewarding aggression against either his frustrator or the beneficiary of the frustration.[43] Hubert M. Blalock and Paul H. Wilken, in developing their theory of equity and distributive justice, speak of the need of an individual to fulfill the goal of equity. Failure to accomplish this may lead to anger.[44] Frank Parkin has used arguments relating to expectations to explain why the "disprivileged" do not rebel more often.[45] According to Parkin: "Those who are aware that they occupy a humble place in the hierarchy of rewards are often inclined to tailor their expectations of life to a correspondingly modest level."[46]

Conclusions on Relative Deprivation Theory

Gurr's theory appears to this writer to be rich in insights, analytical rigor and practical potential. Starting from a proposed set of human needs, it posits a discrepancy between expectations and achievements with regard to these needs. This gives rise to discontent—a readiness to aggress (anger). Aggressive action is the innately satisfying response to this anger. The potential for political violence will go unrealized, however, if the ideological or practical climate is unreceptive. Quite importantly, the political authorities simply may be too strong to permit political violence. In general, this seems a plausible formulation. The integrative theory follows it in major respects.

Given its complexity, Gurr's theory has surprisingly few weaknesses. However, some do exist. For example, the treatment of human needs is not nearly as rigorous as one might develop. His concept of needs is rather fuzzy, as it is in much of the relative deprivation literature. We are told *what* the relevant needs are, but not *why* they are. Neither are we told any reason why they should compel action.

The second major failing of Gurr's theory lies in his treatment of the frustration-aggression hypothesis. Under the frustration-aggression hypothesis, frustration arises when an ongoing response sequence is blocked. Yet the theory of Gurr and other relative deprivation theorists does not posit the blocking of a response sequence. Instead, a discrepancy is posited. Gurr's assumption that frustration results from the mere existence of a discrepancy is inconsistent with frustration-aggression theory.

Another weakness of Gurr's theory is that it posits a feeling of *generalized* hostility arising from frustration. Davies is also quite clear on this point. Later articulations of frustration-aggression theory make it clear that it deals not with a generally frustrated man, but rather with a man who is frustrated because he is blocked in a particular response sequence. Such an individual is not hostile in general. He is, instead, hostile toward the frustrator.[47] The usefulness of Gurr's general notions of hostility is highly problematic. Furthermore, they are incompatible with both the fully developed theory of frustration-aggression and the empirical research testing it.

Relative deprivation theory is of considerable interest to anyone concerned about the causes of industrial conflict. It is a rich source of ideas. It provides many guides to the pitfalls that can be encountered in testing such theories. The basic problem with studies testing relative deprivation theory seems to relate to the validity of the measures used. Tests of relative deprivation theory are certainly shot through with such problems. Yet, the idea of an expectations/achievements gap is a powerful one for theorizing about social conflict. Its problems, although of considerable extent, appear to be manageable, at least for the purposes of broad application to historical materials. The main conceptual problems are believed to be solved by the model proposed in this book.

Having decided that worker expectations are important to the occurrence of industrial conflict, it becomes necessary to consider the determinants of these expectations. These are believed to be of two main types: (1) environmental; and (2) personality-related.

DETERMINANTS OF EMPLOYEE EXPECTATIONS

Employee expectations derive from both external and internal sources. Those that are external to the worker are here dubbed "environmental." Those arising from a general internal state that varies among workers are labelled "personality-related." There is a considerable literature on environmental influences. The literature on personality-related influences is quite fragmentary.

Environmental Influences on Expectations

It is fairly clear from the relative deprivation literature that employees can derive expectations from a variety of sources. Chief among these sources are comparisons of one kind or another. Indeed, the whole notion of *relative* deprivation implies that deprivation be determined by judging one's position relative to some outside criterion. It is through comparing one's circumstances, including one's achievements, with some criterion that expectations are formed. Employees form expectations relative to something. The crucial question, then, is, "Relative to what?" Fortunately, this question has been explored at some length in several bodies of literature.

Multiple Determinants of Expectations

A number of scholars believe that persons make reference to multiple criteria, both interpersonal and intrapersonal, in determining their expectations. As noted above, Gurr is of this persuasion. He argues that expectations may arise from perceptions of the achievements of relevant others, a "reference group," the individual's own past condition, an abstract ideal, or the statements of a leader.[48] Gurr refers to an earlier study by Hoselitz and Willner as stating that expectations are, "a manifestation of the prevailing norms set by the immediate social and cultural environment."[49] The source of the expectations, under the Hoselitz and Willner formulation, "may be what his ancestors have enjoyed, what he has had in the past, what tradition ascribes to him, and his position in relation to that of others in the society."[50]

Other social scientists have also posited multiple sources of expectations. Peter Blau has argued that "expectations of social rewards" may be based upon the "past social experience of individuals" and "reference standards they have acquired." These reference standards derive both from "benefits they themselves have obtained in the past" and from what they have learned that others in comparable situations have obtained. From these data common norms develop in societies as to fair rates of exchange between investments and social benefits. A fair exchange is expected. Inequitable treatment, and especially abuse of power, violates this norm.[51]

Interpersonal Determinants of Expectations

Some scholars have focused solely upon interpersonal comparisons as determinants of expectations. George Caspar Homans does this in his theory of distributive justice.[52] He sees the problem of distributive justice as having to do with the distribution of rewards among individuals and groups. He goes to the classical roots of the concept of distributive justice, quoting both Juvenal and Aristotle for the notion that justice involves a proportionality of shares to persons. That is, differences in persons should be reflected in differences in their shares of social goods. Homans argues that this represents "what many men in fact find fair."[53] Men decide whether they are fairly treated by reference to the achievements of "comparison persons." With respect to these, "the general rule seems to be that people are more apt to compare themselves with others they are to some degree close or similar to than with others that are distant or dissimilar."[54]

In an early study, Martin Patchen found that social comparisons were a basis for satisfaction, or lack of satisfaction, with wages. He concluded that, "The comparer's perception that he is, compared to the other person, earning less than he legitimately 'should,' is likely to make him angry or ashamed."[55]

Morris Zelditch, Jr., et al., maintain that it is a perceived inequity between a person and a "general reference group" which creates a "strain."[56] Action is seen as being motivated by perceptions regarding *generalized* others, not by "local" comparisons to a single other person. According to them, what is observed generally is crucial to expectations, and becomes an "ought" when applied to the individual's local situation.[57]

Perhaps the best known of those theories that posit interpersonal comparisons as a source of expectations is J. Stacy Adams' equity theory.[58] Building on the work of Homans, Patchen, and others, Adams has framed a theory stating that inequity exists for a person whenever he perceives the ratio between his job inputs and outcomes is different from the ratio of a comparable other. If, for example, he feels either relatively overpaid or underpaid, he will feel inequity. Adams predicts that a person who perceives the existence of inequity will act to end it, even if it is in his favor.

Both Patchen and Adams rest their work in large part upon the concept of cognitive dissonance developed by Leon Festinger.[59] Festinger theorized that individuals strive for internal consistency. Dissonance, or "nonfitting relations among cognitions" motivates a person to act to reduce it. Therefore, a comparison with others that is inconsistent produces the motivation to act to end the dissonance.

Intrapersonal Determinants of Expectations

Some scholars have identified intrapersonal factors as the crucial determinants of expectations. These can be either past experiences of the individual on the dimension in question or his current situation on other social dimensions. Because they are not entirely reflective of a generalized internal state, and are importantly affected by outside forces, they are considered to be "environmental" in nature, even though they are "internal" in the sense that they refer only to the individual's own experience.

James Chowning Davies' J-curve theory is founded on the proposition that it is the immediate past experience of the individual that provides the datum for the expectations side of the expectations/achievements ratio.[60] Inconsistency of present achievements with expectations based upon past achievements moves the individual toward rebellion.

Status inconsistency is the label given to dissonance between levels of achievement on different social status dimensions. A number of years ago Emile Benoit-Smullyan identified economic status, political status, and prestige status as the three important status types.[61] Status is seen by Benoit-Smullyan as relative position on a hierarchy. According to Elton F. Jackson, one who has a high position on the hierarchy of one type of status expects a similarly high position on other hierarchies.[62] A person in a position of status inconsistency may feel blocked and frustrated. A number of studies, including one by Irwin W. Goffman, have found some evidence of a relationship between status inconsistency and a desire for social change.[63]

It has been suggested that Festinger's cognitive dissonance theory provides an underlying structure that unifies the literature on interpersonal and intrapersonal comparisons.[64] It would certainly be consistent with Festinger's theory to view dissonance as arising from either of these two types of sources. One might arguably view this position of the integrative model as being motivated by a version of dissonance theory, although it is not believed necessary to do so.

Effects of Expectation Success or Failure

Given that individuals form certain expectations, what is the effect upon future expectations of success or failure in achieving past expectations? The formation of *new* expectations, either through one of the feedback loops of the integrative model, or otherwise, creates another layer of complexity.

It has been argued that failure to achieve expectations will lead to a lowering of expectations. As noted above, Parkin believes that the "disprivileged" adjust their expectations to a realistically modest level. According to Parkin, revolutionary movements recognize this and work to "heighten the expectations of the underclass."[65] Homans argues that a man will eventually cease to compare himself to another if the comparison remains unfavorable over a long period. Most of us, according to Homans, are unable to "nurse a grudge" indefinitely.[66]

On the other hand, if we achieve our expectations, they may rise. Blau so argues, taking issue with the usefulness of the declining marginal utility notions of economists. He argues that, although the utility of achieving existing expectations may decline with their achievement, people are prone to *raise* their expectations if they have been successful. This may hold constant, or even increase, their demand for, say, higher pay.[67]

From the above literature on sources of expectations, it appears that the process of expectations-formation involves reference to: (1) the individual's perceptions of others; (2) the individual's perceptions of his own experience; and (3) abstract ideals. A number of scholars argue for the influence of perceptions with respect to the experience of others. This may be framed in terms of a reference group (Gurr), achievements of ancestors (Holselitz and Willner), reference standards (Blau), comparison persons (Homans), other persons (Patchen), generalized others (Zelditch et al.) or comparable others (Adams). Reference to one's own experience has been simply so identified (Gurr, Davies, Blau, Parkin) and also given the label of status inconsistency (Benoit-Smullyan, Jackson, Goffman). Reference to an abstract ideal may come about through the statements of a leader (Gurr) or tradition (Hoselitz and Willner). The process of expectations-formation includes a broad range of expectation sources. Both intrapersonal and interpersonal sources appear to provide expectations. Logically either or both types could provide the source of worker expectations in a particular case of industrial conflict. Accordingly, the model assumes a number of possible sources of expectations. Furthermore, it is believed that present expectations become lower if past expectations are not met, and rise when they are met.

We have considered the process of expectations-formation insofar as it involves identifying sources of comparisons. It remains for us to examine the manner in which these influences operate. The following section does this, in effect speaking to the action of the forces of expectations-formation identified above.

Operation of Environmental Influences

The employee's environment operates to affect his expectations in a rich variety of ways. This complexity is best handled by organizing it according to whether the source of the influence is: (1) interpersonal comparisons; (2) intrapersonal comparisons; or, (3) abstract ideals.

Achievements of Relevant Others

An individual employee lives in a network of social relations. His personal social relations, as well as formal media of communication, provide him with information regarding the achievements of others in his society. What information he receives depends upon: (1) the reality existing in the society; (2) the availability of information with respect to the reality; and (3) the individual's ability and willingness to obtain and understand the available information.

The objective social conditions with respect to achievements of others are relatively easy to identify and analyze. These social facts may also, at least in the long run, be the most important. An individual living in a society in which poverty is widespread may well not expect to be an exception to this general social rule. If he lives in a society which operates in a thoroughgoing authoritarian mode, and shares a position at the bottom of the authority structure along with most others in the society, he may not expect autonomy or opportunities for social dominance on his own part. What this suggests, of course, is that a worker who lives in an impoverished area of, say, the American rural South, observes that those around him have nothing by way of economic resources. He accordingly concludes that he also should expect to have nothing. Additionally, if in this same region there is a powerful authoritarian social structure and he observes that all those to whom he would compare himself are in a very subordinate position, he may not expect either autonomy or a high degree of dominance on his own part. The same arguments also apply, of course, with respect to the worker's narrower social environment composed of his particular community, family, or circle of friends.

The degree of communication within the employee's social network is also highly relevant. In a society that suppresses information, the employee will have little basis for forming expectations stemming from the experiences of others. If he does not know of the experience of others, this particular process of expectations-formation simply cannot take place. Of course, all employees have some geographical or social area within which information is available. This may be limited to friends, family, or a particular isolated community. The more isolated the community, and the more limited the area from which the employee's communications derive, the less probable it is that he will have information regarding the achievements of others to cause his expectations to rise.

Ability and willingness to receive available communications may vary greatly among employees. Workers who are illiterate or semiliterate have much more limited access to information than their better educated counterparts. Those who are not willing to inform themselves through print or other media with respect to conditions outside their narrow personal area of experience are also unlikely to form these expectations.

It is concluded from the above that: (1) if an employee's achievements are in fact reasonably comparable to those of others, he is unlikely to have expectations in excess of those achievements; (2) an employee having only limited knowledge of the achievements of others, either because the information is not available, or because he is unable or unwilling to obtain it, is unlikely to have expectations that are greater than his achievements.

The achievements of others to whom an employee might compare himself is reasonably susceptible of measurement. Data on economic resources of various groups of workers is often obtainable. As indicated by the above discussion, however, one cannot always have a great deal of confidence that the worker's perception matches the objective reality. In addition, this perception is relevant only if it pertains to others to whom the worker in fact compares himself.

Perceptions of Employee's Experience

With respect to the employee's own experience, the objective reality of his situation is particularly salient. If a worker is in fact less well off than he was in the past he is likely to know it. If his status on one social dimension is lower than on another, he is also likely to know this. It is true that his perceptions may be inaccurate. However, the individual's ability to accurately perceive his own circumstances relative to his previous condition, or in comparison with present circumstances on other dimensions, would ordinarily be rather high.

If an employee's environment dictates that she has less money, is required to work harder for it, or is less secure economically, than was the case in the past, it seems reasonably clear that an expectations/ achievements gap is likely to come about. If an employee is deprived of autonomy which she has previously enjoyed, or of past opportunities for dominance, it is not difficult to accept the proposition that an expectations/achievements gap will come into existence. The same can be said for the development of an incongruence between her social dominance position and her economic position.

Intrapersonal sources may be highly susceptible to measurement. Davies' work on the "J-curve" utilizes readily available data on economic resources. If these decline sharply, this can be observed. In addition, one is ordinarily warranted in assuming that workers are perceptive enough to know that this has occurred. Under these conditions, it seems that Miller et al., are off the mark when they argue that it is inappropriate to reach individual perception conclusions from general economic data. Indeed, it is the combination of availability of data and plausibility of it as a measure of expectations and achievements that makes the Davies work more powerful than some of the later studies of Gurr and others.

The Abstract Ideal

The abstract ideal is an important, if elusive, basis for expectations. The ideal comes from the statements of a leader, tradition, or other sources in the worker's environment. It is capable of operating because of the powerful cognitive and imaginative abilities of the human animal. As social learning theorists maintain, we are readily able to imagine states of being that we have never directly experienced. We may become convinced that we are entitled to higher levels of achievements purely on the basis of arguments that we should be able to grasp some glittering vision.

It has been a strategy of revolutionary leaders from time immemorial to attempt to persuade the "disprivileged" that their circumstances ought to approximate some ideal state. The "outside agitator" may refer to the traditions of the "folk." He may rely on his own charismatic authority. Whatever form it takes, it may be a necessary strategy for instigators of collective action where neither interpersonal or intrapersonal grounds are available.

It is relatively easy to determine whether leaders have attempted to appeal to ideal states. It is not so easy to determine whether this actually influenced expectations.

Of the influences on worker expectations, those that derive from the worker's environment are the clearest, and perhaps the most powerful. The accumulated knowledge on this subject is quite useful in constructing a theory of industrial conflict. One finds plausible and measureable environmental variables aplenty. Perhaps of equal importance, but certainly much less studied, are the personality-related influences on expectations.

The Influence of Personality on Expectations

Personality differences among individual workers influence their expectations as to social dominance and material outcomes. Individual differences, based upon personality differences, exist with respect to the *level* of expectations with reference to a particular type of outcome. These also exist with regard to the *importance* attached to meeting expectations on a type of outcome. Although it is difficult to identify which characteristics affect the level and saliency of expectations, there is a limited body of literature that does furnish us with some guidance in these regards. It should be recognized that no attempt is made here to identify the sources of these personality differences.

As to the *saliency* of material or social dominance outcomes, personnel research on "expectancy theory" is of some assistance.[68] This theory, an early statement of which was provided by Victor Vroom, holds that individual workers attach different "valences," or degrees of desirability, to different work outcomes.[69] Those outcomes that have a high valence for a worker are viewed as having the potential for motivating performance. It would also seem that the highly valent outcomes would be those with respect to which expectations would be most important for purposes of producing a significant degree of relative deprivation. If, for example, pay has a high valence for a worker, it seems more likely that he would feel a reasonably high degree of deprivation if he were deprived of his expected level of it.

With respect to the question of which particular outcomes will be salient for different workers, expectancy theory is of little help. Indeed, one finds little in the literature that bears on this question. However, Quinn and Staines, in their extensive survey on worker satisfaction, do find some evidence that blue-collar workers attach more importance to economic aspects of the job. White-collar workers, on the other hand, were found to give greater weight to noneconomic aspects.[70] This might lead one to hypothesize that expectations for material resources would be more important to blue-collar workers, and those for social dominance to white-collar workers.

Research testing Maslow's "need hierarchy" theory indicates that needs for self-esteem and the esteem of others generally become more salient when material needs have been satisfied.[71] One might conclude from these findings that individual employees whose material needs are satisfied are those who would feel a significant degree of deprivation if they did not achieve their expected level of social dominance.

There is some literature identifying a few personality characteristics that might affect the level of individual worker expectations for social dominance and economic outcomes. With respect to *social dominance*, McClelland's work suggests that a person with high n Power would expect a high degree of social dominance.[72] A person high in "dominance feeling," in Maslow's terms, would be likely to have higher social dominance expectations than one who is low in this feeling.[73] A person with an "authoritarian personality" as described by Adorno, et al., might have very low social dominance expectations, as he would find submission pleasurable.[74] This last notion is particularly useful, as one would expect to find regional differences with respect to the proportion of workers having authoritarian personalities. Where, as in the American South, one finds low literacy levels, an authoritarian social structure, and religious and other cultural influences that encourage authoritarian modes of thought, one would speculate that authoritarian personalities are likely to be more common than in other parts of the United States. These workers would have lower social dominance expectations and, therefore, be less prone to active pursuit of an improved social dominance position.

As to individual personality differences leading to different expectations with respect to *material* outcomes, not much is known. Economists have generally assumed that everyone likes economic outcomes (this is a highly plausible assumption). Psychologists have not directly explored the dimensions of personality that lead some individuals to have higher material expectations than others.

In sum, dimensions of the personality of the individual worker would seem to be important in determining expectations. Yet, it is in only a few respects that we can tie personality to expectations with much confidence. Nevertheless, these instances are sufficiently significant to warrant some attention to personality as a determinant of expectations.

CONCLUSIONS ON EXPECTATIONS

A gap between worker expectations and achievements is seen as a necessary condition to those instances of industrial conflict that follow either the threat or frustration-aggression paths to readiness for aggressive action. It is the presence of this gap that produces the required intensity of action to engender a significant frustration. A taking away of achievements to create this gap, or a threat to do so, moves a worker along the threat path to readiness. Human beings do constantly act to achieve social dominance and material outcomes. They constantly have *some* propensity to act in response to a threat to, or the taking away of, social dominance and material outcomes. However, it is only where the person fails to attain, or has threatened or taken away, *expected levels* of social dominance or material resources, that he will respond with a sufficient degree of intensity to lead toward industrial conflict.

Relative deprivation theory is highly controversial. It is a plausible theoretical statement that has had some considerable problems in the testing. It has appeal for use in the development of a theory of industrial conflict because of its plausibility. The methodology problems are manageable. They are probably best solved by pursuing a strategy similar to that of James C. Davies in his earlier studies. His use of historical materials to measure objective conditions that plausibly give rise to relative deprivation is believed to be a superior technique to later attempts to directly measure perceptions.

Employee expectations, or perceptions of what achievements *ought* to be, are determined both by environment and by personality. Employees may observe comparable others with greater achievements. They may also have experienced greater achievements in their own past or on other social dimensions. They may form expectations on the basis of ideals. Expectations may change as they are either met or not met. They may vary according to several dimensions of the individual personality, such as n Power, authoritarianism, dominance feeling, and others. One would expect that factors increasing employee perceptions as to expectations, or decreasing employee perceptions as to achievements, would tend to move them toward industrial conflict.

Having stated and discussed the moderating (accelerating) condition of a gap between expectations and achievements, we arrive at the paths to readiness for aggressive action.

NOTES

[1]Jack Barbash, "The Causes of Rank-and-File Unrest," in *Trade Union Government and Collective Bargaining*, ed. Joel Seidman (New York: Praeger Publishers, 1970), p. 53.

[2]W. Willard Wirtz, "Labor Unrest and Social Unrest," in *Trade Union Government and Collective Bargaining*, ed. Seidman, p. 4.

[3]James Chowning Davies, "Communications," *American Political Science Review* 73, no. 3 (September 1979), p. 825.

[4]James C. Davies, "Toward a Theory of Revolution," *American Sociological Review* 27, no. 1 (February 1962), pp. 5–6.

[5]Ivo K. Feierabend and Rosalind L. Feierabend, "Aggressive Behaviors within Politics, 1948–1962: A Cross National Study," *Journal of Conflict Resolution* 10, no. 2 (June 1966), pp. 249–271.

[6]Ted Robert Gurr, *Why Men Rebel* (Princeton: Princeton University Press, 1970).

[7]Davies, "Toward a Theory of Revolution."

[8]Davies, "Communications," p. 825.

[9]James Chowning Davies, "Aggression, Violence, Revolution and War," in *Handbook of Political Psychology*, ed. Jeanne M. Knutson (San Francisco: Jossey-Bass, 1973), pp. 253–254.

[10]Davies, "Toward a Theory of Revolution"; James C. Davies, "The J-Curve of Rising and Declining Satisfactions as a Cause of Some Great Revolutions and a Contained Rebellion," in *The History of Violence in America*, ed. Hugh Davis Graham and Ted Robert Gurr (New York: Frederick A. Praeger, 1969), pp. 690–730.

[11] Abraham H. Miller, Louis H. Bolce, and Mark Halligan, "The J-Curve Theory and the Black Urban Riots: An Empirical Test of Progressive Relative Deprivation Theory," *American Political Science Review* 71, no. 3 (September 1977), pp. 964–982.

[12] Ibid., p. 968.

[13] Ibid.

[14] James Chowning Davies, "Communications," *American Political Science Review* 72, no. 4 (December 1978), pp. 1357–1358.

[15] Faye Crosby, "Relative Deprivation Revisited: A Response to Miller, Bolce and Halligan," *American Political Science Review* 73, no. 1 (March 1979), pp. 103–111.

[16] Abraham H. Miller, Louis H. Bolce, and Mark Halligan, "Communications," *American Political Science Review* 72, no. 4 (December 1978), pp. 1357–1359.

[17] Feierabend and Feierabend, "Aggressive Behaviors within Politics, 1948–1962: A Cross-National Study."

[18] Ibid., p. 250.

[19] Ibid.

[20] Gurr, *Why Men Rebel*. Gurr's theory is presented more formally in Ted Robert Gurr and Raymond D. Duvall, "Introduction to a Formal Theory of Political Conflict," in *The Uses of Controversy in Sociology*, ed. Lewis A Coser and Otto N. Larsen (New York: The Free Press, 1976), pp. 134–154.

[21] Ted Gurr, "A Causal Model of Civil Strife: A Comparative Analysis Using New Indices," *American Political Science Review* 62, no. 4 (December 1968), pp. 1104–1124.

[22] Gurr, *Why Men Rebel*, pp. 12–13.

[23] Ibid., p. 24.

[24] Ibid., p. 25.

[25] Ibid.

[26] Ibid.

[27] Ibid., p. 26.

[28] Ibid.

[29] Ibid.

[30] Edward N. Muller, "The Psychology of Political Protest and Violence," in *Handbook of Political Conflict*, ed. Ted Robert Gurr (New York: The Free Press, 1980), p. 70.

[31] Edward N. Muller, "A Test of a Partial Theory of Potential for Political Violence," *American Political Science Review* 66, no. 3 (September 1972), pp. 928–959.

[32] Bernard N. Grofman and Edward N. Muller, "The Strange Case of Relative Gratification and Potential for Political Violence: The V-Curve Hypothesis,"*American Political Science Review* 67, no. 2 (June 1973), pp. 514–539.

[33] Edward N. Muller, *Aggressive Political Participation* (Princeton: Princeton University Press, 1979).

[34] Ibid., pp. 38–39.

[35] Ibid., p. 95.

[36] Ibid., pp. 157–159.

[37] Clark McPhail, "Civil Disorder Participation: A Critical Examination of Recent Research," *American Sociological Review* 36, no. 6 (December 1971), pp. 1058–1073.

[38] Muller, "The Psychology of Political Protest and Violence," p. 73.

[39] Walter Korpi, "Conflict, Power and Relative Deprivation," *American Political Science Review* 68, no. 4 (December 1974), pp. 1569–1570.

[40] Douglas A. Hibbs, Jr., "Industrial Conflict in Advanced Industrial Societies," *American Political Science Review* 70, no. 4 (December 1976), p. 1043.

[41] Charles Tilly, "Review of *Why Men Rebel*, by Ted Robert Gurr," *Journal of Social History* 4, no. 4 (Summer 1971), pp. 416–419.

[42] George Caspar Homans, *Social Behavior: Its Elementary Forms* (New York: Harcourt, Brace Jovanovich, 1974), p. 241.

[43] Ibid.

[44] Hubert M. Blalock, Jr., and Paul H. Wilken, *Intergroup Processes* (New York: The Free Press, 1979), p. 253.

[45]Frank Parkin, *Class Inequality and Political Order* (New York: Praeger Publishers, 1971), p. 48.

[46]Ibid., p. 61.

[47]Leonard Berkowitz, "Aggression: Psychological Aspects," in *International Encyclopedia of the Social Sciences*, ed. David L. Sills (New York: Crowell, Collier and Macmillan, 1968), p. 171; Leonard Berkowitz, *Aggression: A Social Psychological Analysis* (New York: McGraw-Hill Book Co., 1962), pp. 28, 117–120.

[48]Gurr, *Why Men Rebel*, pp. 24–25.

[49]Ibid., p. 27.

[50]Ibid.

[51]Peter M. Blau, "Exchange Theory," in *The Sociology of Organizations*, ed. Oscar Grusky and George A. Miller (New York: The Free Press, 1970), p. 143.

[52]Homans, *Social Behavior: Its Elementary Forms*.

[53]Ibid., p. 249.

[54]Ibid., p. 252.

[55]Martin Patchen, *The Choice of Wage Comparisons* (Englewood Cliffs, N.J.: Prentice-Hall, 1961), p. 11.

[56]Morris Zelditch, Jr., Joseph Berger, Bo Anderson, and Bernard P. Cohen, "Equitable Comparisons," *Pacific Sociological Review* 13, no. 1 (Winter 1970), pp. 19–26.

[57]Ibid.

[58]J. Stacy Adams, "Toward an Understanding of Inequity," *Journal of Abnormal and Social Psychology* 67, no. 5 (1963), pp. 422–424.

[59]Leon Festinger, *A Theory of Cognitive Dissonance* (Stanford: Stanford University Press, 1957), pp. 1, 3, 6, 18.

[60]Davies, "Toward a Theory of Revolution."

[61]Emile Benoit-Smullyan, "Status, Status Types, and Status Interrelations," *American Sociological Review* 9, no. 1 (February 1944), pp. 160–161.

[62]Elton F. Jackson, "Status Consistency and Symptoms of Stress," *American Sociological Review* 27, no. 4 (August 1962), p. 469.

[63]Irwin W. Goffman, "Status Consistency and Preference for Change in Power Distribution," *American Sociological Review* 22, no. 3 (Winter 1957), p. 275.

[64]James A. Geschwender, "Continuities in Theories of Status Consistency and Cognitive Dissonance," *Social Forces* 46, no. 2 (December 1967), pp. 160–171.

[65]Parkin, *Class Inequality and Political Order*, p. 70.

[66]Homans, *Social Behavior: Its Elementary Forms*, p. 253.

[67]Peter M. Blau, *Exchange and Power in Social Life* (New York: Wiley & Sons, 1964), p. 149.

[68]Wendell L. French, *The Personnel Management Process*, 5th ed. (Boston: Houghton-Mifflin Co., 1982), pp. 86–90.

[69]Victor H. Vroom, *Work and Motivation* (New York: Wiley & Sons, 1964), pp. 15–17.

[70]Robert P. Quinn and Graham L. Staines, *The 1977 Quality of Employment Survey* (Ann Arbor: Survey Research Center Institute for Social Research, 1979).

[71]French, The *Personnel Management Process*, p. 82.

[72]David C. McClelland and David H. Burnham, "Power is the Great Motivator," *Harvard Business Review* 54, no. 2 (March-April 1966), pp. 100–110.

[73]A. H. Maslow, "Dominance-Feeling Behavior and Status," *Psychological Review* 44 (1937), pp. 407–408.

[74]T. W. Adorno, Else Frenkel-Brunswik, Daniel J. Levinson, and R. Nevett Sanford, *The Authoritarian Personality* (New York: Harper & Row, 1950), pp. 759–762.

CHAPTER 6

The Theory's Fourth Pillar: The Paths to Readiness for Aggressive Action

---

... a "strike" is ... an open expression of aggression. ... If strikes took place without aggression, it is doubtful if anyone's applecart would be upset.

Alvin W. Gouldner, *Wildcat Strike.*

The fourth pillar of the integrative theory's model of industrial conflict consists of the paths to *readiness for aggressive action*. This readiness must be achieved before industrial conflict becomes possible. It is a matter of the individual force to act being a precondition to collective action.

The argument of the model is that predispositions to pursue certain outcomes, usually moderated by expectations and achievements, can ready workers to act aggressively in pursuit of these outcomes. It is only when this has occurred that collective aggressive action is likely to take place. Furthermore, the model posits three distinct paths to readiness for aggressive action.

INDUSTRIAL CONFLICT AS "AGGRESSION"

The aggressive nature of industrial conflict is one of its crucial aspects. Industrial conflict is not a phenomenon that simply involves a coldly calculated market transaction. Organizing, striking, and other instances of industrial conflict are a type of fighting behavior. The term *strike* itself is quite revealing of the flavor of industrial conflict. While industrial conflict is a means to determine the price of labor, it is also a variegated complex of emotions, songs, and martyrs. It is, as shown in the old Industrial Workers of the World pamphlet, the raised fists of individual workers uniting to form a giant striking force on behalf of their hopes and aspirations. It is the red flag of rebellion and the red blood spilled at the Memorial Day Massacre. It is men and women standing together in the name of solidarity and brotherhood, striking out at an oppressor. Theories that ignore this reality of industrial conflict run great risk of incompleteness and irrelevance. Theory should capture the essence of the phenomenon to which it relates. At the very heart of industry conflict is aggression against an oppressor.

Aggression has been defined in a number of ways. It is most commonly described as action aimed at doing harm.[1] Some writers make a distinction between *aggression* and *hostility*. The social psychologist Dolf Zillman, for example, defines *aggression* as involving the infliction of physical injury, and *hostility* as having to do with the infliction of harm other than physical injury.[2] Ethologists define aggression more broadly. They consider it to be present in "every act which leads to a spacing or subordination."[3]

The integrative theory adopts the most common definition of *aggression*, considering it to include all actions intentionally contrary to the interests and goals of others. Industrial conflict, defined as collective aggressive action by workers in opposition to their employers, fits within this definition. The use of the term *aggression* to cover industrial conflict is consistent with the ethological use of the term, as industrial conflict has to do both with subordination and an equivalent of spacing, or territory, that is, possession of material resources. In our context, Zillman's distinction between actions aimed at physical harm and those aimed at other kinds does not add any precision to our analysis.[4] To make this distinction would be inconsistent with terminology used in many disciplines, and could create unnecessary confusion in applying theories drawn from these disciplines. All things considered, it is believed to be both legitimate and analytically useful to attach the label *aggressive* to industrial conflict.

THE PATHS TO READINESS

The integrative theory states that a readiness for aggressive action can be arrived at through one, or more, of three paths. These paths are frustration-aggression, threat, and rational calculation. An individual may be led to a readiness for aggressive action by more than one of these paths at the same time. Persons in the same social group may move along different paths but arrive at a readiness for aggressive action at the same time.

To set out three paths to readiness for aggression, rather than only one path, is to accept several complementary explanations for industrial conflict. It is clear from the aggression literature that a readiness for aggressive action can be arrived at in a number of ways. As James T. Tedeschi et al. have concluded, at least two major classes of aggressive responses have become generally recognized: "(a) instrumental aggression, in which the occurrence of harm or injury to another individual is only incidental to the actor's goal of achieving some other goal; and (b) angry aggression, in which the only object of the actor's response is to inflict injury on another person or object."[5]

Robert A. Baron and Donn Byrne, in their text on social psychology, identify three categories of theories of aggressive action. These attribute aggressive action to: "(1) innate urges or tendencies, (2) externally elicited drives, (3) existing social conditions coupled with previous social learning."[6]

The frustration-aggression and threat paths of the integrative theory might be considered by Tedeschi et al. as "angry aggression." Baron and Byrne might class them as "innate" or "externally elicited." Tedeschi et al. would see the rational calculation path as "instrumental aggression." For Baron and Byrne, the rational calculation path would reflect existing social conditions and previous social learning. Instead, it is believed that the frustration-aggression and threat paths are clearly a *blending* of the angry and the instrumental. Frustration-aggression (under the Berkowitz formulation) does involve anger. However, the anger is directed mainly at the frustrator who has blocked the ongoing pursuit of a goal. Removal of the blockage is involved in motivation to aggress. This is a mix of both instrumental and noninstrumental aggression. Only the rational calculation path is simple—it is clearly instrumental.

Roots of Human Aggression

Earlier in this book, in Chapter 3, it was argued that innate predispositions exist which influence human behavior. In Chapter 4 it was maintained that predispositions toward seeking material resources and social dominance were involved in moving human beings toward industrial conflict. Here it will be considered whether aggression is rooted in such predispositions. As the reader might suspect, it is concluded that there are innate roots of aggression.

The older theories of aggression were largely innatist. They have been called "instinct" theories. Sigmund Freud, in a 1932 letter to

Albert Einstein, expressed the view that aggression was innately and fundamentally linked to the death wish, a basic human instinct. According to Freud, human beings seek a lessening, and eventually a complete absence, of stimulation. This is balanced by the erotic, or life, instinct. Freud believed that aggressive instincts build up and must find release, either against the self, or against others.[7] According to Freud:

> The element of truth behind all this, which people are so ready to disavow, is that men are not gentle creatures who want to be loved, and who at the most can defend themselves if they are attacked; they are, on the contrary, creatures among whose instinctual endowments is to be reckoned a powerful share of aggressiveness. As a result, their neighbor is for them not only a potential helper or sexual object, but also someone who tempts them to satifsy their aggressiveness on him, to exploit his capacity for work without compensation, to use him sexually without his consent, to seize his possessions, to humiliate him, to cause him pain, to torture and to kill him. Homo homini lupus. [Man is a wolf to man.].[8]

Ethologists and sociobiologists have also argued for an innate tendency to aggress. Konrad Lorenz, the Nobel prize-winning biologist and ethologist, argues that an instinct for aggression has served a useful function for the survival of the human species. Although it has become dysfunctional in modern society, it is an evolved instinct that served natural selection purposes during the evolution of the species *Homo sapiens.*[9] As did Freud, Lorenz believes that the need to aggress is something that builds up in man and requires release. This has been termed "hydraulic" or, less respectfully, a "flush-toilet," view of aggression.

Other ethologists have argued for innate engines of aggression. Irenaus Eibl-Eibesfeldt concluded from his studies of humans and other animals that there is an innate drive to be aggressive.[10] This drive tends to produce aggressive behavior when appropriate releaser stimuli are present.[11] The occurrence of aggressive behaviors across many diverse societies, even among the socially inexperienced young, is his chief reason for believing that this behavior is innate.[12] As does Lorenz, Eibl-Eibesfeldt believes that aggressive behavior has been adaptive for the survival of many animals because it is functional. Its functions include spacing to avoid exhausting food supplies, the establishment of territory, and, in the case of fights between rival males for mating, the passing along of the genes of the strongest males.[13] This does not mean that aggression among humans is either inevitable or good, however. Furthermore, it can be controlled by conditioning, particularly through use of the strong innate human tendencies for love and caring for others, which stem from parental care for the young.[14] Aggression can become maladaptive as conditions change, as it may in fact have already done.[15] Eibl-Eibesfeldt's work provides a particularly strong empirical base for theories that posit an innate, but avoidable, tendency for human aggression.

The clearest and best of the writing in this area, as in others discussed above, is by Mary Midgley. Midgley contends that aggression is part of the nature of human beings, but that this does not mean that we must inevitably shed blood.[16] We have the highly adaptive mechanism of intelligence that allows us to "play chess or sue each other" when fighting is not convenient.[17] In social animals, generally, attack is not typically aimed at killing, but rather at "other motives connected with space and dominance."[18] Ordinarily an attack ends when submission is shown. She characterizes the notion that human beings would not be aggressive in the absence of learning as "spitting against the wind." Midgley argues that we can no more eliminate the tendency to be aggressive "than we can grow wings and tusks."[19] She does strongly contend, however, that aggression is only one of many human tendencies and can be countered by other tendencies and moral choices.

The sociobiologist Edward O. Wilson also believes that there is an innate human tendency to aggress. He argues that aggression can be "compared to a pre-existing mix of chemicals ready to be transformed by specific catalysts that are added, heated, and stirred at some later time."[20] Wilson sees aggression as being subject to cultural evolution, which is guided by the "genetic predisposition for learning aggression, environmental conditions and the history of the group."[21] Wilson argues that the "learning rules" of aggression evolved over hundreds of thousands of years of human evolution and "confer a biological advantage on those who conform to them with the greatest fidelity."[22] Although the evolutionary advantage of aggression has disappeared, to merely state that it is obsolete is not to "banish" it.[23]

From the arguments and evidence of the instinct theorists, the author is persuaded that there is indeed an innate human predisposition to aggress. Its near universality among human beings and the plausibility of the arguments for its functions argue for its genetic derivation. It would appear that the predisposition is to aggress when certain conditions exist. Eibl-Eibesfeldt and Lorenz refer to these as "releasers." Even in the presence of "releasers," they recognize that the tendency to aggress can be countered by contrary tendencies, such as those for love, affection, and mutual aid, all of which have equal evolutionary status. Therefore, human beings do not automatically aggress in all circumstances, or even when releasers are present.

There are, of course, those who challenge the proposition that innate engines of aggression exist. Dolf Zillman has argued that it is based upon invalid generalizations from animal behavior. According to Zillman, in this area one can generalize from the behavior of animals to the behavior of humans "only under the assumption that all factors attributing to the occurrence and the particular manifestation of aggression are present and equally salient in the animal species involved and in man."[24] Yet, Zillman does not explain why this assumption is necessary. Nor is its necessity readily apparent. Biologists attempting to determine whether behavioral similarities among different animals are homologous, genetically based, do not impose this requirement.

Albert Bandura has taken a rather extreme environmentalist view, claiming that "except for elementary reflexes, people are not equipped with inborn repertories of behavior."[25] According to Bandura, the kind of innate programming that works for lower animals is not advantageous for humans.[26] If this is so, any attempt to base theory on innate predispositions is doomed to failure. Yet, Bandura does admit that it "is now widely acknowledged that experiential and physiological influences interact in subtle ways to determine behavior and therefore are not easily separable."[27]

In order to maintain his position, Bandura is faced with the seemingly impossible burden of explaining why all human beings happen to learn to behave in an aggressive way. His task is further complicated by the fact that this tendency is shared with our closest relatives in the animal world and by plausible arguments pertaining to the functions of aggressiveness during our evolutionary history. An extreme environmentalist view seems to be contrary to the best evidence and to common sense.

All things considered, it appears that there are grounds for believing that human beings have a predisposition to aggress. What is truly interesting is the discovery of the conditions under which this predisposition is translated into action. It is this question that is attacked by the integrative theory of industrial conflict. The several paths of the integrative theory are aimed at explicating those conditions under which an employee would become ready to take aggressive action against his or her employer.

Frustration-Aggression—the Central Path to Readiness

The integrative theory's most powerful explanation for industrial conflict is furnished by the central path of theory. This path utilizes frustration-aggression theory. It is a frustration-aggression pattern that most commonly fits the behaviors involved in industrial conflict. Frustration-aggression theory is highly controversial and has been much attacked over the years. Nevertheless, there remains a core of theory and evidence regarding frustration-based aggression which can be used to undergird a theory of industrial conflict.

The integrative theory makes use of the version of frustration-aggression theory that was stated by Leonard Berkowitz.[28] Under this formulation, if a person is instigated to enter into a response sequence that is aimed at some goal, and the response sequence is interfered with, a readiness for aggression is likely to be the result. The interference (blocking) is termed "frustration." Anger (readiness for aggression) results. Aggression is likely to follow if the appropriate cues are present. The force to aggress may be overcome by fear or may be inhibited either by anticipation of punishment or by a belief that the aggressive act will be contrary to the persons's own standards of conduct.

In 1939, the original statement of frustration-aggression theory by the "Yale group" led by Dollard contained the following statement: "The frustrated worker, doomed to monotony and insecurity, tends to grow more sympathetic to unions, not only in order to raise his wages and shorten his hours of work, but also as a means of expressing aggression against the employer."[29] Those who formulated this theory believed strikes to be expressions of aggression.[30]

In 1946, N. R. F. Maier explained strikes in terms of frustrated persons engaging in nonspecific aggressive activity.[31] Arthur Kornhauser, writing in his classic volume on industrial conflict in 1954, viewed the inability of individuals to fulfill their wants as leading to "unrest, dissatisfaction, emotional irritability and a striking about for some way out, for some means to break through or to withdraw from the struggle."[32] Kornhuaser stated: "The extent to which these conditions of frustration are prevalent in different groups in present-day industry will go far in determining the occurrence of industrial conflict."[33]

In 1965, Ross Stagner and Hjalmar Rosen propounded a theory of industrial conflict that was based upon the frustration-aggression hypothesis. They focused mainly on the physical violence often involved in industrial conflict. Like those who had gone before, they spoke of frustrated persons "lashing out" in a general, irrational, fashion.[34]

George Strauss has described the Stagner and Rosen work as a "brave effort which failed."[35] Understandably, Stagner took umbrage at this characterization of his work.[36] Yet the Strauss criticism seems valid not only for Stagner's work but also for that of the scholars who attempted to apply frustration-aggression theory to industrial conflict in earlier years. The problem is that they utilized a weak, and what came to be a dated, version of frustration-aggression theory. The best, most modern, statements of it by Berkowitz and others posited a more specific, rational, response to frustration than did the earlier version. Instead of predicting a generalized lashing out, modern frustration-aggression theory speaks in terms of a lashing out *at the frustrator*. Among other things, this could conceivably have the effect of removing the blockage, which would be instrumental in achieving a resumption of the response sequence. Whereas the earlier version was entirely nonrational, the newer version is an interesting mixture of the rational and the nonrational. It captures both the emotional flavor of industrial conflict and its rationality. It is perhaps the most integrative facet of the integrative theory.

The Development of Frustration-Aggression Theory

Frustration-aggression theory received its first full explication at the hands of Dollard's Yale group in 1939,[37] although the main ideas had been anticipated by Sigmund Freud.[38] Dollard et al. state that their hypothesis is that "aggression is always a consequence of frustration."[39] Frustration comes into existence if "the organism could have been expected to perform certain acts," and "these acts have been prevented from occurring."[40] They define "frustration" as the condition that exists when a goal-response suffers interference."[41] The strength of the instigation to aggress is determined by: "(1) the strength of the instigation to the frustrated response, (2) the degree of interference with the frustrated response, and (3) the number of frustrated response-sequences."[42] The aggressive response can be inhibited. The strength of an inhibition is principally determined by "the amount of punishment to be a consequence of that act."[43]

In the 1960s, after there had been much discussion and testing of the frustration-aggression hypothesis, Leonard Berkowitz revised it into a more plausible form. Berkowitz began by adopting the essentials of the Yale group's formulation of frustration-aggression theory. He posited frustration as a major cause of aggression. Aggression was defined as "any behavior whose goal is the injury of some person or thing."[44] A frustration is defined as "an interference with the occurrence of an instigated goal-response at its proper time in the behavior sequence."[45] He distinguishes "instigated response sequences" from "drives" on the basis that the former "more clearly implies any ongoing activity."[46] Yet, somewhat confusingly, he uses the terms *drive* and *response sequence* interchangeably in his work. It is clear, however, that when Berkowitz talks about either instigated response sequences or drives he is talking about a "response tendency that has been set into operation."[47] The important distinction is between this kind of drive, or response sequence, and those drives that are not "active." Frustration occurs when an *active, ongoing,* instigated response sequence suffers interference.

In order to illustrate the occurrence of frustration, Berkowitz uses an example that originated with the Yale group. A boy hears an ice cream vendor's bell and decides that he wants an ice cream cone. He is said to be "instigated" to get an ice cream cone. He enters into a response sequence that involves going to his mother, thinking of ice cream, asking for the ice cream, and pulling her toward the door. If she refuses, the series of responses leading to the consumption of the ice cream cone is interrupted. The instigated goal-response is interfered with and the boy cannot eat the ice cream. Frustration occurs.[48]

Berkowitz distinguishes between *frustration*, which arises from interference with a continuing goal-response sequence, and mere deprivation. Interestingly, he uses one of the few work-related examples in this literature to make this point. Berkowitz argues that a person who is engrossed in his work does not become frustrated merely because he is deprived of food for a long period of time. His failure to eat at his regular meal time will not produce an aggressive reaction. If, however, the same person is prepared to eat at a certain time, is thinking of food that he plans to enjoy, and the employer unexpectedly gives him additional work that causes him to miss a meal, this will produce frustration. It is when the worker expects and mentally anticipates the meal, and the employer blocks him from obtaining it, that he becomes frustrated. This distinction between deprivation and frustration is especially important when one considers the problems of the relative deprivation literature discussed in the previous chapter. As indicated there, relative deprivation theorists have concentrated on *deprivation*, rather than frustration. This truly does depart from frustration-aggression theory in a fundamental way.[49]

Berkowitz argues that frustration is likely to produce the emotional state of *anger*, which is a readiness for aggressive acts.[50] Anger, an emotional state, "serves as a drive heightening the likelihood of aggressive behavior."[51] A person who is angry is "primed" to take aggressive action if appropriate cues are present.[52]

The requirement of an appropriate cue has led one social psychologist to label Berkowitz's theory as the "aggressive-cue theory."[53] These cues are "stimuli associated with the present or previous anger instigators."[54] The cue may be the physical presence of the frustrator or merely his presence in the mind of the potential aggressor. In some manner, it is necessary for the person to associate the frustration with the frustrator in order for an aggressive response toward the frustrator to occur.

Berkowitz believes that the strength of the aggressive reaction "is a joint function of the intensity of the anger (readiness for aggression) and the degree of identification of the frustration with the frustrator."[55] It is also influenced by the strength of the drive that is frustrated and the degree to which it is frustrated.

Frustration will not produce a readiness for aggression against the frustrator if the dominant reaction is fear rather than anger. That is, the readiness for aggressive action that is anger may be swamped and overcome by fear. According to Berkowitz, this may occur when the potential aggressor perceives that the frustrator's power to hurt or control him is much greater than his power to control or harm the frustrator.[56]

Avoidance or submission may also overcome anger as a response under some circumstances. Although the general bodily reaction to frustration is rage or anger, and this is the "innately dominant response to frustration," it may be modified by later learning.[57] This may operate through the effects of learning upon the individual's definition of the situation in deciding whether his actions have in fact been blocked. It may determine whether other response tendencies are aroused that are stronger than the tendency toward aggression. It may also affect the exact nature and intensity of aggressive acts.[58] Particularly where the frustration has occurred in an "associative" organization such as an employing organization, a preference for exit may overcome the inclination to aggress. The importance of this option has been argued for extensively by Albert O. Hirschman.[59]

Even if a person becomes ready to aggress, an aggressive action will not take place if it is prevented by inhibition. Inhibition will occur where the individual anticipates punishment for the aggressive behavior or believes that this aggressive act will violate standards of conduct, or norms, which he wishes to uphold.[60] Inhibition, of course, may vary with the type of aggressive act being considered. That is, individual aggressive action might be available where collective aggressive action were inhibited, in which case, one would expect individual, not collective, action.

Berkowitz's formulation of frustration-aggression theory, unlike that of the Yale group, recognizes the existence of causes of aggression other than frustation. Berkowitz agrees with Bandura and others that aggression may be *instrumental* as well as frustration-based.[61] According to Berkowitz, the Yale group, quite legitimately, decided to limit its concern to those types of aggression that have as their sole object the injury of the object of the aggression.[62] Berkowitz's formulation of the frustration-aggression hypothesis is broader than that of the Yale group in this respect. He not only recognizes instrumental motivation as an independent cause of aggression. He also projects some rationality into frustration-based aggression itself.

The Debate over Frustration-Aggression Theory

Frustration-aggression theory, both in its earlier formulations and as posited by Berkowitz, has had both its supporters and its detractors. Among its supporters are relative deprivation theorists such as Ted Robert Gurr. Indeed, Gurr uses the Berkowitz formulation of frustration-aggression theory as a central part of his theory.[63] Some psychologists have found evidence that frustration leads to aggression. This finding is particularly strong where the frustration is contrary to expectations, and severe.[64] It is generally agreed that illegitimate, arbitrary, or unjustified frustration leads to anger and aggression.[65]

The opponents of the frustration-aggression hypothesis include within their number some very distinguished social psychologists. Albert Bandura, for example, believes that "severe frustration is generally accompanied by feelings of hopelessness and massive servility," not by aggression.[66] Bandura criticizes frustration-aggression theorists for postulating that anger provocation is necessary for aggressive action to occur. Bandura, under his social learning theory, regards anger provocation as just one type of emotional arousal which "serves as a facilitator rather than a prerequisite for aggressive modeling."[67] According to Bandura, the "aversive events assumed under the term frustration—be they physical assaults, insults, reinforcement withdrawal, or thwarting of goal-directed activities—are, at best, facilitative rather than necessary or sufficient conditions for aggression."[68] It is for individuals who have *learned* to behave aggressively, and for whom acts of aggression have "functional value," that frustration is most likely to bring on aggression.[69]

Robert A. Baron and Donn Byrne argue that frustration will lead to aggression *only* when it is quite intense and is perceived as illegitimate or arbitrary.[70] Dolf Zillman believes that blocking a goal reaction, while it may bring on a reaction of disappointment, annoyance, or anger, will not generate any personal hostility or aggression. He argues that the blocking of a goal reaction will likely evoke behaviors that will remove the blockage so that the initial goal reaction can be executed. If aggressive responses promise this outcome, aggression becomes likely to produce this result. Accordingly, "hostile and aggresive reactions in response to the blockage of a goal response are likely only if the specified instrumental value of such reactions exceeds that of nonhostile and nonaggressive alternatives or if this condition has prevailed in the past with some consistency."[71]

Zillman believes that when frustration of a goal response is coupled with a personal attack, feelings of annoyance and anger are likely to occur. This may increase the likelihood of hostile and aggressive actions. Here the blocking, which is perceived by a frustrated person as being intentional, arbitrary, or unjustified, would be perceived as a personal attack. It appears to this writer that the differences between Zillman's formulation and that of Berkowitz are less than Zillman believes. In both approaches there is a mix of the cognitive and the innate. Although the arguments are phrased somewhat differently, the predicted results are about the same.

After taking into consideration the various criticisms of frustration-aggression theory, it appears that it still remains an appealing explainer of aggressive behavior. This is true for two reasons. First, its central proposition, i.e., that frustrated individuals are likely to aggress, is supported by a large number of rigorous studies. Second, only its most extreme critics claim that frustration is *never* a cause of aggression. The controversy largely rages around whether it is the only, or an important, cause of aggression. The integrative theory adopts the position that *frustration is an important source of aggression*, but not the only one.

Frustration-based readiness for aggression that can lead to industrial conflict comes about in the following manner. An employee who is innately predisposed to pursue economic and social dominance outcomes has less of these than he expects. He engages in a response sequence that involves a nonagressive pursuit.[72] If he achieves these outcomes he temporarily discontinues their pursuit. If he is blocked, he becomes frustrated. The frustration will fail to move him toward a readiness for aggression if: (1) fear is the dominant response; (2) he does not identify the employer as the source of his frustration; (3) he acts pursuant to an individual predisposition for resignation or withdrawal. In the alternative, it can lead to readiness for aggression, or, in frustration-aggression theory terms, anger, by any of three routes. It may do this directly, as suggested by frustration-aggression theorists.[73] It may also, as does a threat, give rise to annoyance, which creates a state of high agitation and arousal, and produces a readiness for aggressive action.[74] As suggested by social learning theorists, it may lead to a search process that causes the individual to discover that there exists an incentive for taking aggressive action.[75]

Threat

Many social psychologists believe that the surest way to provoke aggression from a person is to pose a threat to him, or actually harm him. The literature on this subject, though interesting, is very limited in size. Consequently, the discussion of the literature pertaining to the threat path is more abbreviated than those regarding the other paths.

Robert Baron argues that "the results of several . . . studies provide suggestive evidence that verbal provocation may often serve as a stronger antecedent of overt aggression than several types of frustration."[76] Baron and Byrne believe that direct verbal or physical confrontations can readily produce aggression.[77] H. A. Dengerink is of the opinion that attack is the principal cause of physical aggression.[78] According to Albert Bandura, "if one wished to provoke aggression, the most dependable way to do so would be simply to physically assault another person, who would then be likely to oblige with a vigorous counterattack."[79] Bandura also agrees with Baron and Byrne that verbal threats and insults produce aggression, perhaps because aggression in response to these insults is positively reinforced by making it less likely that threats and insults will be repeated.[80]

Dolf Zillman argues that human nature includes an evolved tendency to have excitatory reactions when threatened. This takes the form of "a burst of energy," or a fight-flight reaction. This occurs when risk is threatened to the individual or "those entities essential to his or her welfare."[81] According to Zillman, annoyance occurs when an excitatory state is attributed to endangerment. The behavioral implications of annoyance can be either an attack on the source of the annoyance or avoidance.[82]

Zillman's treatment of "annoyance motivated hostility and aggression" is quite interesting. He believes that such hostility and aggression is under cognitive control at intermediate levels of excitation. Under that condition the person calculates consequences in such a way as to avoid retribution. At high and low levels of excitation the individual is unable to "interchange complex considerations." At high levels, he is too aroused to think in a complicated way. At low levels, he doesn't bother to do so. At a high level of excitation the response is to unthinkingly terminate the annoyance, or avoid it, immediately. At an intermediate level, the person will take hostile or aggressive action to avoid or terminate an annoyance only if he is confident of success. An individual calculates his chances of success based upon: (1) his hostile or aggressive abilities; (2) the force that is likely to obstruct his efforts and possible retribution against him; and, (3) likelihood of social approval."[83] According to Zillman, the extremely aroused individual readily violates the concept of "rational man."[84] A "transitory cognitive incapacitation" takes place.[85]

Threat, like frustration-aggression, is an appealing explainer of industrial conflict. It is fairly clear from the literature that threat can lead to annoyance, which in turn can lead to a readiness to aggress. Yet, at least at most levels of annoyance, inhibition is possible, as in the case of frustration-aggression.

Threat could lead to individual conflict in the following manner. An employee whose wages are consistent with his expectations either has them cut or has a reduction threatened. This leads to a sufficiently high level of annoyance to cause him to become ready to aggress. He will take aggressive collective action if the appropriate facilitating conditions are present, and he is not inhibited.

Rational Calculation

Rational calculation of advantage as a ground of aggressive action is supported both by economic theory and by social-psychological social learning theory. In fact, this is a highly interesting conjunction of economic and psychological theory.

Neoclassical economic theory posits that human action takes place on the basis of rational calculation of advantage. It essentially holds that economic man acts in such a way as to achieve resources where the costs are not too great.[86] Economic theory would predict that an individual becomes ready to take aggressive action where the costs of such action are exceeded by the benefits.

Social learning theory arrives at the same conclusion as economic theory, but by a different route. It holds that human beings aggress because: "(1) they have learned such response through past experience, (2) they either receive or expect various forms of reward for performing such behaviors, and (3) they are directly encouraged to aggress against others by specific social conditions."[87] Albert Bandura, the chief proponent of this view, argues that human beings are born with only the most rudimentary behavioral repertoires. Everything else, including aggression, must be learned.[88] In his earlier work he subscribes to the extreme behavioral view that virtually all behavior is learned through the reinforcement of random behavior.[89] Social learning theory holds that, contrary to the frustration-aggression hypothesis, frustration does not produce an aggressive drive. Rather, aggression against a person is seen as sharing with other aversive stimuli the ability to generate a general state of emotional arousal. This state of arousal can produce a variety of responses. The particular behavior is dependent on "the types of responses the person has learned for coping with stress and their relative effectiveness."[90]

Under social learning theory, aggressive behavior is learned in the same fashion as other behaviors. This occurs through "observation and direct experience."[91] It occurs not only through reinforcement mechanisms, but also through cognitive processes in which the person makes an intelligent choice of behaviors based upon expectations regarding consequences.[92] In his 1973 book, *Aggression: A Social Learning Analysis,* Bandura speaks of the reinforcers that encourage aggression. He labels these, (1) direct external reinforcement, (2) vicarious reinforcement, and (3) self-reinforcement. Direct reinforcement occurs when valued ends are achieved by aggressive action. Vicarious reinforcement, a concept central to Bandura's theory, is present when a person observes that others are rewarded for aggression, convincing the person that aggression pays. It also has "incentive motivational effects," acting as a motivator. Self-reinforcement occurs when a behavior is consistent with the person's image of the way that he should behave. This is derived chiefly from human models.[93] In his later book, *Social Learning Theory,* Bandura emphasizes the cognitive component, essentially arguing that human beings learn the expected consequences of behavior and perform those acts, including aggressive acts, which are best calculated to maximize pleasure and minimize pain.[94] This is, of course, highly compatible with economic utility theory. Indeed, it may be little more than a psychological restatement of traditional economic theory.

An interesting statement of aggression theory akin to that of Bandura is provided by Dolf Zillman.[95] Zillman argues that aggression is of two types, *incentive-motivated* and *annoyance-motivated*. He maintains that *incentive-motivated* aggression, or aggression "in cold blood," is the most common. Humans most often aggress to obtain valued rewards. As with Bandura, we see a highly "rational" model operating. According to Zillman, "*in the cognitive guidance of hostility and aggression, Man's superior cognitive faculties de facto serve the hedonic principle and . . . they do so primarily through the anticipation of immediate and future consequences.*"[96] In what he describes as a "radical qualification" of this statement, Zillman says that cognitive guidance of hostility and aggression becomes less likely at either high or low levels of excitation. Where the level of excitation is high, aggression is likely to be annoyance-motivated rather than incentive-motivated. *Annoyance-motivated* aggression is aimed at immediate elimination of the annoyance rather than at some other goal. At high levels of annoyance nonimmediate consequences may be altogether ignored.

Economic and social learning arguments for instrumental aggression garner some support from the proponents of frustration-aggression. For example, as noted above, Berkowitz recognizes the existence of instrumental aggression. He argues that "both businessmen and labor unions have employed violence as an economic weapon not only because they were thwarted but because they believed the open hostility was necessary to reach their desired ends."[97] Berkowitz not only recognizes that instrumental aggression takes place, but also concedes that it is very common.[98]

Rational calculation of advantage is, like its brethren, frustration-aggression and threat, an appealing explainer of industrial conflict. There is surely sufficient evidence both from economic and psychological sources to persuade one that purely instrumental motivations may lead a worker to become ready to engage in conflict. For example, workers at a new General Motors Corporation plant, at which there has been neither an attempt by management to suppress organization nor an attempt by a union to organize, might simply decide that it would be to their advantage to organize. The cost of unionization would appear to be quite small, whereas the benefits in terms of higher wages and guaranties of fair treatment might be substantial. This calculation by itself might lead the workers to become ready to engage in industrial conflict. If they were not inhibited, and sufficient facilitating conditions were present, this would likely lead to the aggressive collective action of organizing.

CONCLUSIONS

Given the great diversity of theories relating to human aggression and the claims of some theories to be exclusive, it is a difficult task to fashion a coherent theoretical statement usable for the understanding and prediction of industrial conflict. Nevertheless, it can be done, largely because the various theories have more in common than appears at first glance. This is particularly true with respect to innatist and frustration-aggression theories, both of which posit some kind of drive to aggression. The Eibl-Eibesfeldt version of ethological theory simply holds that there is an innate tendency on the part of human beings to aggress, given the appropriate conditions. Berkowitz is relatively friendly to the notion of innate mechanisms, and indeed recognizes that he is relying upon them. Although he argues that the drive to aggress comes into existence through frustration, and does not preexist it, he recognizes that the ability of frustration to instigate aggression is dependent upon a preexisting tendency to aggress when frustrated. Both theories posit a behavioral predisposition that is translated into action in the presence of the appropriate stimuli. Berkowitz provides the conditions under which the innate tendencies become active.

Integration is more difficult with social learning theory, at least from the point of view of the social learning theorists. They deny the proposition that innate mechanisms exist. They also deny that frustration is, under most circumstances, likely to lead to aggression. This author is of the view that the great weight of the evidence favors the existence of innate mechanisms. He is further of the opinion that there is considerable evidence that frustration causes aggression—even proponents of social learning theory concede that severe, unjustified frustration is likely to lead to aggression. Neither of these conclusions is in conflict with the social learning theory arguments that aggression can be learned, or that it is often engaged in for instrumental purposes. Neither the ethologists nor Berkowitz deny that aggression is often engaged in for instrumental purposes. In addition, the Berkowitz formulation of frustration-aggression theory is itself highly cognitive and rational. It seems, therefore, that it does no violence either to ethological or frustration-aggression theories to include in a model of industrial conflict propositions derived from social learning theory in order to analyze instrumental aggression. Indeed, it would seem highly useful to do so, as it provides theoretical underpinnings for that body of industrial conflict that does not involve frustration.

Threat-based aggression is rather easily integrated into theory that utilizes frustration and instrumental aggression. It is recognized by both frustration-aggression theorists and social learning theorists that a threat can give rise to an aggressive response. While it is possible to translate this into frustration-aggression terms, it seems to add nothing to our understanding of aggression to do so. Threat-based aggression is reasonably well supported by the evidence and is not theoretically inconsistent with either of the other approaches.

The integrative theory posits three alternative paths to readiness for aggressive action. An individual may pursue more than one path at the same time. Within a social group, different individuals may be moving toward a readiness for aggressive action by different paths. All of these paths are believed to be important routes to industrial conflict. The path of rational calculation is perhaps the least common, but does exist in an important number of instances. It, of course, may take on less of a flavor of aggressive action than do the others.

Having made our way to the point in the integrative theory where a readiness for aggressive action has been arrived at by individuals, it is now possible to move on to the collective stage of the model. This is perhaps the most difficult step, and one that has not been satisfactorily taken by theories relating to industrial conflict. Although it is indeed individual human beings who act and whose motivation must be considered in order to understand industrial conflict, it is nevertheless true that the sort of action we are talking about is collective in nature. Building a separate stage of the model for collective action presumes that there is something different about collective action and that is not simply an accumulation of individual motivations. Fortunately, in theorizing about industrial conflict, we are helped along the way by the labors of sociologists and political scientists who have long studied the phenomenon of social conflict.

NOTES

[1]Elliot Aronson, *The Social Animal,* 2nd ed. (San Francisco: W. A. Freeman and Company, 1976), p. 143; Leonard Berkowitz, *Aggression: A Social Psychological Analysis* (New York: McGraw-Hill Book Co. 1962), p. 1.

[2]Dolf Zillman, *Hostility and Aggression* (Hillsdale, N.J.: Lawrence Erlbaum Associates, 1979), p. 32.

[3]Irenaus Eibl-Eibesfeldt, *Love and Hate,* trans. Geoffrey Strachan (New York: Schocken Books, 1974), p. 73.

[4]Zillman, *Hostility and Aggression,* p. vii.

⁵James T. Tedeschi, R. Bob Smith, III, and Robert C. Brown, Jr., "A Reinterpretation of Research on Aggression," *Psychological Bulletin* 81, no. 9 (1974), p. 548.

⁶Robert A. Baron and Donn Byrne, *Social Psychology: Understanding Human Interaction*, 3rd ed. (Boston: Allyn and Bacon, 1981), p. 318.

⁷Sigmund Freud, "Why War," in *The Dynamics of Aggression*, ed. E. L. Megargee and J. E. Hokanson (New York: Harper and Row, 1970), pp. 33–34.

⁸Sigmund Freud, *Civilization and its Discontents*, trans. James Strachey (New York: W. W. Norton Co., 1961) pp. 58–61.

⁹Konrad Lorenz, *On Aggression*, trans. Majorie Kerr Wilson (New York: Harcourt, Brace Jovanovich, 1963), pp. 20–45.

¹⁰Eibl-Eibesfeldt, *Love and Hate*, pp. 72–84.

¹¹Ibid., pp. 20–24.

¹²Ibid., pp. 11–20.

¹³Ibid., pp. 64–65.

¹⁴Ibid., pp. 243–246.

¹⁵Ibid., p. 75.

¹⁶Mary Midgley, *Beast and Man* (Ithaca: Cornell University Press, 1978), p. 48.

¹⁷Ibid.

¹⁸Ibid., p. 55.

¹⁹Ibid., p. 326.

²⁰Edward O. Wilson, *On Human Nature* (Cambridge: Harvard University Press, 1978), p. 106.

²¹Ibid., p. 114.

²²Ibid., p. 119.

²³Ibid.

²⁴Zillman, *Hostility and Aggression*, p. 3.

²⁵Albert Bandura, *Social Learning Theory* (Englewood Cliffs, N.J.: Prentice-Hall, 1977), p. 161.

²⁶Ibid., pp. 73–74.

²⁷Ibid., p. 16.

²⁸Leonard Berkowitz, "Aggression: Psychological Aspects," in *International Encyclopedia of the Social Sciences*, vol. 1, ed. David L. Sills (New York: Crowell Collier and MacMillan, 1968), pp. 168–174; Berkowitz, *Aggression: A Social Psychological Analysis*.

²⁹John Dollard, Leonard W. Doob, Neal E. Miller, O. H. Mowrer, and Robert R. Sears, *Frustration and Aggression* (New Haven: Yale University Press, 1939), p. 160.

³⁰Ibid., p. 10.

³¹N. R. F. Maier, *Psychology in Industry* (Boston: Houghton-Mifflin Co., 1946), pp. 70–79.

³²Arthur Kornhauser, "Human Motivations Underlying Industrial Conflict," in *Industrial Conflict*, ed. Arthur Kornhauser, Robert Dubin, and Arthur M. Ross (New York: McGraw-Hill Book Co., 1954), p. 73.

³³Ibid.

³⁴Ross Stagner and Hjalmar Rosen, *Psychology of Union—Management Relations* (Belmont, Cal.: Wadsworth Publishing Co., 1965), pp. 42–54.

³⁵George Strauss, "Can Social Psychology Contribute to Industrial Relations?" in *Industrial Relations: A Social Psychological Approach*, ed. Geoffrey M. Stephenson and Christopher J. Brotherton (Chicester: John Wiley & Sons, 1979), p. 370.

³⁶Ross Stagner, "Review of *Industrial Relations: A Social Psychological Approach*," *Personnel Psychology*, 33, no. 1 (Spring 1980), pp. 176–177.

³⁷Dollard, Doob, Miller, Mowrer, and Sears, *Frustration and Aggression*.

³⁸Berkowitz, "*Aggression: Psychological Aspects*," p. 169.

³⁹Dollard, Doob, Miller, Mowrer, and Sears, *Frustration and Aggression*, p. 1.

⁴⁰Ibid., p. 7.

⁴¹Ibid., p. 11.

[42]Ibid., p. 28.

[43]Ibid., p. 25.

[44]Berkowitz, "Aggression: Psychological Aspects," p. 168.

[45]Ibid., p. 169.

[46]Berkowitz, *Aggression: A Social Psychological Analysis*, p. 27.

[47]Ibid.

[48]Ibid., pp. 26–27.

[49]Berkowitz, "Aggression: Psychological Aspects," p. 170.

[50]Ibid.

[51]Berkowitz, *Aggression: A Social Psychological Analysis*, p. 32.

[52]Berkowitz, "Aggression: Psychological Aspects," p. 171.

[53]Robert A. Baron, *Human Aggression* (New York: Plenum Press, 1977), p. 28.

[54]Berkowitz, "Aggression: Psychological Aspects," p. 171.

[55]Ibid.

[56]Berkowitz, *Aggression: A Social Psychological Analysis*, p. 45.

[57]Ibid., p. 47.

[58]Ibid.

[59]Albert O. Hirschman, *Exit, Voice and Loyalty* (Cambridge: Harvard University Press, 1970).

[60]Berkowitz, "Aggression: Psychological Aspects," pp. 171–172; Berkowitz, *Aggression: A Social Psychological Analysis*, pp. 90–91, 103.

[61]Berkowitz, *Aggression: A Social Psychological Analysis*, pp. 29–32.

[62]Ibid., p. 31.

[63]Ted Robert Gurr, *Why Men Rebel* (Princeton: Princeton University Press, 1970) pp. 9, 33–37.

[64]Stephen Worchel, "The Effect of Three Types of Arbitrary Thwarting on the Instigation to Aggression," *Journal of Personality*, 42, no. 2 (June, 1974), pp. 314–317.

[65]Tedeschi, Smith, and Brown, "A Reinterpretation of Research on Aggression," pp. 543–544; James A. Kulik and Roger Brown, "Frustration, Attribution of Blame, and Aggression," *Journal of Experimental Social Psychology*, 15, no. 2 (March 1979), pp. 190–193.

[66]Albert Baudura, *Aggression: A Social Learning Analysis* (Englewood Cliffs, N.J.: Prentice-Hall, 1973), p. 170.

[67]Ibid., pp. 133–134.

[68]Ibid., p. 174.

[69]Ibid.

[70]Baron and Byrne, *Social Psychology: Understanding Human Interaction*, p. 326.

[71]Zillman, *Hostility and Aggression*, p. 139.

[72]This is consistent with the findings in Thomas A. Kochan, *Collective Bargaining and Industrial Relations* (Homewood, Ill.: Richard D. Irwin, 1980), pp. 149–150, and Thomas A. De Cotiis and Jean-Yves LeLouarn, "A Predictive Study of Voting Behavior in a Representation Election Using Union Instrumentality and Work Perceptions," *Organizational Behavior and Human Performance*, vol. 27 (1981), p. 116.

[73]Berkowitz, *Aggression: A Social Psychological Analysis*, pp. 32–33.

[74]Zillman, *Hostility and Aggression*, p. 139.

[75]Ibid.

[76]Baron, *Human Aggression*, p. 93.

[77]Baron and Byrne, *Social Psychology: Understanding Human Interaction*, p. 328.

[78]H. A. Dengerink, "Personality Variables as Mediators of Attack—Instigated Aggression," in *Perspectives on Aggression*, ed. Russell G. Geen and Edgar C. O'Neal (New York: Academic Press, 1976), p. 62.

[79]Bandura, *Aggression: A Social Learning Analysis*, p. 155.

[80]Ibid., p. 163.

[81]Zillman, *Hostility and Aggression*, p. 307.

[82]Ibid., p. 312.

[83]Ibid., pp. 275–276.

[84]Ibid., p. 279.

[85]Ibid., p. 280.

[86]Milton H. Spencer, *Contemporary Economics* (New York: Worth Publishing, 1971), p. 31; Arnold S. Tannebaum, *Social Psychology of the Work Organization* (Belmont, Cal.: Brooks/Cole Publishing Co., 1966), pp. 30–31.

[87]Baron and Byrne, *Social Psychology: Understanding Human Interaction*, p. 321.

[88]Bandura, *Social Learning Theory*, p. 16.

[89]Albert Bandura and Richard H. Walters, *Adolescent Aggression* (New York: The Ronald Press Co., 1959), pp. 89–90.

[90]Bandura, *Aggression: A Social Learning Analysis*, p. 54.

[91]Ibid., p. 68.

[92]Bandura, *Social Learning Theory*, p. 161.

[93]Bandura, *Aggression: A Social Learning Analysis*, pp. 183, 184, 205–206, 207.

[94]Bandura, *Social Learning Theory*, pp. 28, 161, 173, 209.

[95]Zillman, *Hostility and Aggression*.

[96]Ibid., p. 262.

[97]Berkowitz, *Aggression: A Social Psychological Analysis*, p. 182.

[98]Ibid., p. 31.

CHAPTER 7

The Theory's Fifth Pillar— Collective Aggressive Action

But with the development of industry the proletariat not only increases in number; it becomes concentrated in greater masses, its strength grows, and it feels that strength more *** the ever expanding union of the workers . . . is created by modern industry.

Karl Marx and Friedrich Engels, *The Communist Manifesto,* 1848

One of industrial conflict's most distinctive features is its collective nature. It is, if nothing else, a phenomenon that involves human beings acting as parts of a collectivity. It is from this that it both derives its greatest strength and generates its most vigorous opposition. Whether it is coldly calculated or a "cri de coeur," whether it is through a permanent organization or a spontaneous informal group, whether it is based upon threat, frustration or calculation, it involves mutual aid, cooperation, and perhaps even brotherhood, among those who engage in it. It is explanation at this level that forms the final pillar of the integrative theory.

One of the prime anomalies of this field is that recent theories pertaining to industrial conflict, while paying lip service to its collective nature, have largely neglected this aspect of the phenomenon analytically. The integrative theory attempts to remedy this situation. Although it begins with individual motivation, it goes on to explicitly deal with the phenomenon at the level of collective action. This would seem to be necessary, as industrial conflict does not involve *either* individual or collective dynamics. It clearly involves *both.* There would appear to be no good reason for ignoring this reality. Eclecticism is not only desirable, but necessary, in constructing an explanation for this complex and multilevel social phenomenon.

The argument of the integrative theory is that individuals must become ready to engage in aggressive action toward their employer before collective action becomes possible. Once they become ready for *some form* of aggressive action, they are likely to move to *collective* aggressive action of industrial conflict only if: (1) a substantial proportion of the group is ready; (2) collective aggressive action is not avoided because of inhibition; and, (3) facilitating conditions are present. The requirement of an absence of inhibitions is borrowed from the social psychologists. The notion of facilitating conditions is based on the work of collective behavior theorists, most of whom are sociologists. Even within the collective stage of the model there is some eclecticism as to sources of ideas.

Although much of the literature that follows deals with violent revolution and political action generally, it is not argued here that industrial conflict and these other types of action are identical. Industrial conflict is aggressive collective action against an employer by a group of employees. It is not a politically motivated general strike or a proletarian revolution. One would not, therefore, expect studies of such phenomena to completely explain industrial conflict. However, as we shall see below, they do furnish a rich body of theory and empirical findings from which the collective action stage of a theory of industrial conflict can be built.

THE AVOIDANCE OF INDUSTRIAL CONFLICT

Even though individuals are ready to engage in aggressive action against their employer, this will not take a collective form if collective aggressive action is avoided because of inhibitions. The absence of inhibitions is a necessary, but not sufficient, condition for industrial conflict.

In frustration-aggression theory terms, the readiness to aggress is akin to anger. This emotional state is highly likely to produce aggressive action. It will not do so, however, if effective inhibition takes place.[1] For our purposes, we are primarily concerned with whether a particular form of aggressive action (industrial conflict) takes place. Therefore, our inquiry is under what circumstances collective aggressive action against the employer will be inhibited.

The Yale group led by Dollard believed that inhibition occurs only where punishment for the aggressive act is anticipated, and furthermore, that the strength of the inhibition varies with the amount of punishment expected.[2] Berkowitz agrees that the anticipation of punishment can inhibit aggressive action.[3] However, he takes a much broader view of inhibition. He argues that the social status of the object of the intended aggression, such as that of one's employer, can inhibit aggressive behavior.[4] Disapproval of others can also inhibit.[5] A belief that aggressive behavior is ethically improper or morally wrong can inhibit the behavior.[6] In sum, Berkowitz concludes: "Aggressive actions are inhibited when the individual anticipates punishment for such behavior and/or believes that these hostile acts will violate the standards of conduct he wants to uphold."[7]

From these frustration-aggression arguments is derived the proposition that aggressive action will be inhibited where: (1) severe punishment is anticipated as a consequence of the aggressive act; or, (2) to engage in the aggressive act would violate strongly held norms of conduct the potential aggressor wishes to uphold. Applying this to industrial conflict as a form of aggressive action means that employees are unlikely to engage in industrial conflict in either of these conditions. Of course, they might engage in other forms of aggressive action that are not inhibited, such as individual acts of violence or sabotage, but not the inhibited act of collective action.

If industrial conflict is inhibited, it will be avoided. However, in the absence of effective inhibition it may occur if the appropriate facilitating conditions are present.

FACILITATING CONDITIONS FOR COLLECTIVE ACTION

Collective aggressive action does not come about easily. As human behaviors go it is relatively rare, a rather exotic social organism that can grow and flourish only in a very special environment. Even given the presence of all of the conditions discussed up to this point, it is still unlikely to occur unless further facilitated. The final necessary "hothouse" conditions for the development of industrial conflict are those that the integrative theory labels "facilitating conditions."

There is a voluminous literature that may help us ascertain the facilitating conditions. This literature contains a large variety of theories of human collective action. Our task is made more difficult by the fact that these theories were not written for the purpose of providing the reader with a convenient list of facilitating conditions. In addition, the theories are so diverse that they are very difficult to present systematically. However, it is possible to categorize them into two main groups. First, there is the general literature on human *collective action*, ranging from the psychoanalytical to the rational-economic, which has developed over a considerable period. Second, there is the modern literature on *collective behavior* developed by sociologists in recent years. Although it is upon the latter that the integrative theory chiefly draws, the former provides an interesting and fruitful foundation for all the literature on the subject.

Theories of Collective Action

Prior to the development of modern sociological theories of collective behavior there existed only a rich but bewildering cacophony of ideas and philosophies pertaining to human collective action. For the purposes of our discussion, these theories of collective action will be grouped as follows: (1) group psychology theory; (2) convergence theory; (3) individual rationality theory; (4) class theory; and, (5) industrial relations theory.

Group Psychology Theory

The foundation for theories of collective action by human beings was laid by those who considered the human group as having its own special psychology. The "contagion" theory of Gustave LeBon so holds.[8] LeBon believed that human beings in crowds, or groups, possess a "mental unity" that derives from being part of the group.[9] The feelings of each member of the group are contagious to other members of the group. This leads to the development of a group mind. LeBon believed this group mind to be intellectually inferior to that of the isolated individual.[10] The group mind is impulsive, changeable, irritable, and led almost entirely by unconscious impulses. The crowd is always barbaric. The individual is, at least sometimes, civilized.

Based upon LeBon's theory, one would predict that groups of human beings would behave on an emotional, nonrational, basis. If it receives a stimulus that causes it to act, the human collective would be expected to act violently and extremely. The human group is a herd that will trample anything in its way. LeBon also believed that the herd has such a "thirst for obedience" that it will instinctively submit to anyone who appoints himself its master.

Sigmund Freud, in a rare moment of theorizing about *group* psychology, commented extensively on LeBon's theory and added to it.[11] He describes LeBon's theory as a "brilliantly executed picture of the group mind."[12] As one might expect, Freud is highly receptive to LeBon's suggestion of unconscious determinants of behavior. Additionally, he believes that "suggestability," which is similar to LeBon's notion of contagion, "is actually an irreducible, primitive phenomenon, a fundamental fact in the mental life of man."[13]

Freud believed that it is the love of the members for one another that holds a group together. Individuals give up their distinctiveness because of their need for being in harmony with other group members.[14] There are ties between "fellow-workers which prolong and solidify the relation between them to a point beyond what is merely profitable."[15] Freud argues that "love alone acts as the civilizing factor in the sense that it brings a change from egoism to altruism."[16] Such feelings can arise among *persons who work* in common.[17]

Where Freud parts company somewhat from LeBon is in his greater emphasis upon the importance of group leadership. Freud argues that individuals not only identify with fellow members of the group, but particularly with a group leader. As individuals regress to a more primitive stage of mental activity, as suggested by LeBon, they more readily obey the commands of a father figure. A very important feature of a group, therefore, is that it has a leader who commands it. Freud maintains that man is, "a horde animal, an individual creature in a horde lead by a chief."[18]

There is much to be learned from the theories of LeBon and Freud. First, they call out the mutual influences of group members upon one another. They argue rather persuasively that the result of this may be primitive and unconscious behavior. They also speak in very compelling terms of the role of the leader. More directly and more forcefully than later theorists, Freud speaks to the *affective nature of group activity*. If we are to believe Freud, individuals often act in groups because of their affection for other members of the group.

There are some limitations upon the LeBon and Freud theories. Even given the usefulness of their approaches to collective action in some respects, one is hardly tempted to consider them as a full explanation of this phenomenon. As a description of crowd, or mob, behavior they do quite well. As a description of the collective action of large and diverse groups of human beings in an economic context, they seem inadequate. We must go beyond LeBon and Freud to understand such behavior.

Convergence Theory

Of the older theories of collective action, the second main type is "convergence" theory.[19] This view is essentially that human beings in collectivities behave according to their individual predispositions. Their willingness to act is admittedly affected by the facilitation provided by other like-minded persons who reveal responses they had previously suppressed.[20] Nevertheless, "the convergence of a sizeable number of persons with similar predispositions is the explanatory principle. . . ."[21]

Later writers about social conflict have adopted notions similar to convergence theory. This is the case with the relative deprivation theorists. James C. Davies relies upon finding that "large groups of human beings in a society are at approximately the same stage of development and are likely to want to enter the next stage at about the same time."[22] Indeed, Davies has been criticized for not going beyond this to specify how individual deprivations and frustrations are translated into collective action.[23]

Another relative deprivation theorist, Ted Robert Gurr, writing with coauthor Raymond D. Duvall, attempts to deal more specifically with the transition from individual motivation to collective action, but comes out with something very close to convergence theory. Although his general theory is rested on individual motivations, he does recognize that an important condition for collective action is that members of the group share the belief that collective behavior is desirable and has utility.[24] This position towards collective behavior is recognized by Gurr and Duvall to be something other than "a simple aggregation or average of individual dispositions."[25] The group takes on a characteristic disposition, which reflects the fact that the individual's dispositions are modified by those of others in the group.[26] Gurr and Duvall suggest that a necessary condition for collective action is that the workers must commonly wish to take collective action.[27] Even with these qualifications, we are left with little more than a suggestion that individual preferences converge, with no explanation of why, or the conditions under which, they might do so.

If one were to accept convergence theory, all that would be required for collective action would be for members of the group to come together and communicate to one another their mutual desire for action. Assuming some urgency to the situation, one would expect collective action to follow. This would essentially argue that what we have termed "facilitating conditions" are unnecessary. Yet it does not seem that the mere coming together of likeminded persons has ordinarily been adequate to produce the kind of collective aggressive action about which we are concerned.[28] Furthermore, such an approach does not at all consider that collective action is a distinctive type of action that may have its own special requirements. Convergence theory may be an excuse for not having a theory of collective action rather than a theory of such action.

Individual Rationality Theory

Given the long-standing popularity of utility theory, it would be surprising if there were not a theory of collective action based on this bedrock principle of the discipline of economics. In fact, one of the more widely known of these theories is a theory of individually rational collective behavior propounded by the economist Mancur Olson.[29]

Olson sees the willingness to take collective action as resting entirely upon the incentives for individuals to do so. The chief purpose of organizations, according to Olson, is "the furtherance of the interests of their members."[30] Although all members of the group have an interest in sharing in the common goods provided by the group, they do not have a common interest in paying the costs of providing particular collective goods. Each group member would prefer that the others pay the entire cost, particularly as he would often receive the collective benefits regardless of whether he bore any part of the costs.[31]

According to Olson, individuals may be motivated to take collective action by social sanctions and social rewards from other members of the group. These serve as "selective incentives." However, these incentives generally operate only in small groups, where face-to-face contact is possible.[32]

Olson analyzes the historical development of the American labor movement. He argues that one would expect small unions to become organized, but that great difficulties would be expected in the expansion of unions from small units to large units. According to Olson: "By far the most important single factor enabling large unions to survive was that membership in these unions . . . was to a great degree compulsory."[33]

Olson's theory is essentially that individuals make rational decisions to maximize their benefits and minimize their costs. This considers only benefits to the individual, and not those that might accrue to the social group with which the individual feels solidarity. Perhaps the most useful accomplishment of Olson is to call out the importance of individual rationality and offer some explanation of the "free-rider" phenomenon in trade unions. Indeed, why should an individual join a union if he can receive a union wage without paying union dues or incurring the risks of striking?

There are, however, some fundamental weaknesses in Olson's theory. First, he ignores the utility to the individual of benefits to a group with which the person identifies. Even in utility theory terms, his view seems unnecessarily narrow. Second, Olson truly does consider human nature to "turn upon beefsteaks" as Schumpeter accuses utility theorists of believing. As Schumpeter suggests, this is an inherently implausible view of human nature.[34] Third, as he applies it to trade unions, his theory is simply nonsensical. His explanation for small unions becoming large unions is that this was accomplished largely through compulsion. If he means physical compulsion, he is simply at odds with the facts of development of trade unions in the United States. If he means legal compulsion after a union becomes the official representative of employees, he ignores the fact this can only occur *once a majority of employees in a unit has opted for a union*, selecting it as their exclusive representative. Under Olson's theory, there is no way that small unions could have developed into large unions. Having to choose between the fact that large unions do exist and Olson's theory, it seems reasonable to side with the facts rather than his theory. Indeed, for all the attention it has received, Olson's theory seems to be a particularly egregious case of attempting to stretch reality to fit economic utility theory.

A more reasonable utility-oriented view has been expressed by Samuel Bacharach and Edward Lawler.[35] Bacharach and Lawler argue that most workers, because they have invested some costs in the employing organization, have an interest in voicing their opinions about organizational concerns. Yet, unless they are members of the organization's elite it is difficult for them to voice opinions without being victimized. They run the risk of forced exit (dismissal) when they try to assert individual voice. The benefits of asserting voice are attractive, but the costs are simply too great. A way to avoid these costs may be to express grievances through a group, which may be able to protect its members against retaliation. There is strength in numbers, making collective action profitable where individual action would be costly.

The Bacharach and Lawler formulation has some appeal. It calls out the advantages of collective action as opposed to individual action. It suggests that collective action will be appealing where it is possible for the group to protect the individual from victimization for asserting his interests. Although it does not provide us with any facilitating conditions for collective action, it does furnish a plausible rationale for collective action in utility terms.

Class Theory

Although understandably not in vogue in the bastion of capitalism that is the United States, the best grounded of the existing theories of aggressive collective action is the Marxist theory of revolution.

The "class angle" of the Marxists, and others who have utilized some Marxist ideas, can be very powerful in analyzing social action. The basic ideas were formulated quite early by Marx and remain, with some modifications, a "class theory" answer to collective action. A few of the ideas expressed by Marx and Engels in the manifesto of the Communist party summarize these arguments reasonably well.

In the manifesto, Karl Marx and Friederich Engels set out their theory of revolution.[36] The essential argument is rather straightforward. They believed that there is inherent in capitalism the seeds of its own destruction. The capitalist mode of production inevitably brings into existence a self-conscious proletariat. This proletariat has means of communication and solidarity largely because its members work in the factories of the capitalists.[37] In addition, capitalism produces a progressively greater concentration of wealth and a declining rate of profit.[38] Consequently, capitalists are not able to maintain the worker even at subsistence level. As conditions become intolerable, workers realize that their enemy is the capitalist. After "progressive immiserization" they rise up and seize power.[39] In this way, economic exploitation leads to the formation of a working class that buries the capitalists.

Marx's theory is mainly a theory of revolution, not a theory of industrial conflict. It looks primarily toward a rising of the working class to control society as a whole, not merely for improving conditions of work. Therefore, there are some limits on its relevance for our purposes. Nevertheless, we may borrow from Marx some useful ideas. First, the economic exploitation of workers identified by Marx is, as he recognizes, grounds not only for revolution, but also for industrial conflict. Furthermore, it is very clear that the mode of production does affect the relations among workers in important ways. The opportunities for communication and worker feelings of solidarity are powerfully influenced by the social relations of production. Additionally, the recognition of the existence of a working class with economic interests at odds with those of capital is given a convincing and scientific explanation in Marxist theory. Lastly, although the general idea of "progressive immiserization" has not produced an explanation of industrial conflict useful in itself, it has led scholars to focus on the phenomenon of relative deprivation and its effects. Indeed, one can argue that Marx is the originator of the notion of relative deprivation as it applies to worker action.

Industrial Relations Theory

There have been a number of attempts by industrial relations scholars to explain industrial conflict as a collective phenomenon. Perhaps best known is the paper by Clark Kerr and Abraham Siegel published in 1954.[40] Kerr and Siegel attempted to explain the "strike proneness" of various industries. Their basic explanation was the presence of an "isolated mass" of workers in such strike-prone industries as mining, longshore, lumber, and textiles. In these industries groups of workers have their "own codes, myths, heroes, and social standards." There are few neutrals to "dilute the mass."[41] Kerr and Siegel speak directly to the collective nature of the phenomenon. They argue that although all people have grievances, "what is important is that all the members of each of these groups have the same grievances."[42] The totality of grievances, after having been shared among the members of the group, may be greater than the sum of the individual grievances. The employees form a largely homogeneous, undifferentiated, mass. They all do the same work and have the same experiences.[43] The grievances of the employees are the same, they have them at the same time and at the same place. The grievances are against the same people.[44]

Another characteristic of the strike-prone group of workers is that the "mass" is difficult to exit. Specialization of jobs causes the worker to be specialized, making it difficult for a worker to leave the organization or industry. Exit from the working class, by moving up in the organization, is also difficult. Workers are detached both from the employer and from the community.

In addition to the conditions of shared grievances and difficulty of exit, Kerr and Seigel suggest that a third condition is necessary for strike-proneness. This is the "capacity of the group for cohesion." They argue that it is almost always there if the first two conditions are present.[45]

Strike-prone industries contain "bad" employers. These employers "disregard the welfare of their employees because of the casual nature of their connection with them or . . . undertake to dominate their employees unduly . . . because they are the preponderant power of a one-industry community. . . ."[46]

The Kerr and Siegel rationale for the conditions that facilitate strikes still stands as the best that has been produced by industrial relationists. Their analysis makes a convincing case for the importance of solidarity in this type of industrial conflict. It also argues for the importance of numbers of workers moving toward conflict simultaneously. This would lead one to search for conditions that would affect many workers in the same way at the same time. In addition, it points out the extreme *dominance* of the workers by the employer present in strike-prone industries. This, of course, supports the integrative theory's singling out of social dominance as a prime root cause of industrial conflict.

Another industrial relations scholar, Leonard R. Sayles, identifies worker groups that differ, among other things, on their propensity to accept management (or union) action: (1) apathetic; (2) erratic; (3) strategic; or (4) conservative. Each type of group behaves differently with respect to collective action.[47] The apathetic group is the least likely to develop grievances or engage in any sort of collective action. Worker discontent is ordinarily present, but is unfocused. There is low group cohesion.[48] Erratic groups are those in which there seems to be no relation between the seriousness of grievances and the intensity of protest.[49] It is as if an emotional reaction to "deep frustration" has blinded members of the group to their failure to react appropriately to the circumstances.[50]

Sayles found that apathetic and erratic groups are apt to act to preserve customary rights. They tend to engage in actions that involve a high emotional content and "real frustration." They fight savagely, but do not have the cohesiveness for sustained action. They do not ordinarily seek long-run economic gains and prestige.[51]

Strategic groups are at the very center of most important grievances. These groups seem to contain shrewdly calculating persons. They constitute a pressure group that never tires of objecting to unfavorable management decisions. They seek loopholes in management policies and in contract clauses. They constantly compare their benefits with those of other departments in a plant.[52] Strategic groups exert carefully measured pressure. They have highly cohesive leadership, with a small core of active and influential members. They are usually involved in individual operations that require judgment. The behavioral characteristics of strategic groups are: (1) "continuous pressure"; (2) "activity on grievances which are consistent and well planned;" (3) high degree of internal unity; (4) sustained participation in the union; and, (5) ordinarily, good production records.[53]

Conservative groups are the most stable and the least likely to use assertive action without warning. They are also the least likely to participate in union affairs. They have a monopoly on critical scarce skills. It is more common for management to have grievances against them than for them to have grievances against management. They are ordinarily privileged employees and have a good external job market.[54]

Conservative and strategic groups constantly work out the ratio of their contributions and importance to their earnings versus those of other groups in the plant. They are quite apt to act collectively when they believe that their rewards are not as great as they ought to be.[55] There are several distinctive influences on work group goals that can lead such groups to engage in conflict. These are: (1) intra-plant comparisons of benefits; (2) a direct threat to job security; and, (3) successful experience of the group in responding to either of the first two influences. Sayles also found that high degree of activity with respect to collective action is associated with an ambiguous prestige position.[56]

From Sayles' analysis of different types of worker groups and their propensities for industrial conflict it is possible to identify some promising facilitating conditions. For example, the fact that a group has low group cohesion, unfocused discontent, and the absence of clearly defined leadership would lead one to believe that it is an "apathetic" group, and, therefore, is unlikely to engage in industrial conflict. On the other hand, if a group of workers is one in which there is much interaction, similar tasks, worker-paced work, centralized leadership, an inclination to being easily inflamed, and a proneness to the use of both uncontrolled pressure and quick conversion to a good relationship with management, one might expect such a group to be active in organizing, but perhaps not in striking. If a group meets the description of a strategic or conservative group, one would expect a relatively high *ability* to be successful in collective action. Given a readiness for aggressive action, and a lack of cost-related inhibition, it would seem that such groups would be likely to act.

In addition to furnishing predictions about collective action according to the type of the group involved, Sayles also identified some other conditions that might serve as facilitating conditions for industrial conflict. He found, for example, that large groups tend to have a greater tendency to engage in collective action because: (1) they are more likely to be successful; (2) the probability of finding a good leader is higher; and, (3) there is more dissatisfaction in large groups.[57] He also found a greater inclination for collective activity where the function of a group of workers is essential to the operation, as it gives them a greater ability to be successful.[58] He found that workers who do common tasks have more common grounds upon which to grieve, producing greater solidarity.[59] It should be noted that the Sayles research may be somewhat unsystematic and "soft."

Writing nearly twenty years later, Clayton P. Alderfer stated that "one dimension on which nonmanagement work groups vary considerably is their level of protest activities, or their tendency to petition for improved working conditions."[60] Alderfer relies upon the Sayles analysis of types of work groups to predict the tendency of a group to engage in these activities.

Jon Amsten and Stephen Brier make an interesting point when they argue that in modern industrial society the strike is not a mere informal protest, but must be "carried through as a concerted and conscious effort by the workers involved." It is necessarily "coherent and sustained." It is not just an expression of discontent by "the people." Amsten and Brier believe that the strike is a "form of conscious action which emerges with industrialism and which expresses a new complex of class relationships in society."[61] The Amsten and Brier conception of a strike is not as broad as our definition of industrial conflict. However, it does point out that at least some types of industrial conflict require sustained and organized effort. Groups of workers that lack the capacity for this kind of effort may be unable to engage in at least some types of industrial conflict.

Ralf Dahrendorf has addressed himself to the problem of the "technical conditions of organization."[62] These conditions, as their name implies, pertain to organizing rather than to other types of industrial conflict; Dahrendorf speaks in terms of the formation of "organized groups." In order for such a group to emerge from a "quasigroup," a group that has common interests but does not act in common, certain persons have to make organization their business, carry it out as a practical matter, and take the lead.[63] Having such "founders" is a *technical* condition necessary, but not sufficient, for the formation of organized interest groups.[64] In addition, Dahrendorf argues that a "charter" is needed, whereby the common interests of the quasigroup are articulated. For this to take place it is required that there either be a leader or an ideology (a system of ideas).[65]

According to Dahrendorf, *political* conditions of organization also need to exist. This means a state that permits a plurality of conflicting parties.[66] In addition, *social* conditions of organization are necessary. Citing Marx, Dahrendorf maintains that these are mainly conditions having to do with communication. He also argues that an organized interest group can form only if the recruitment into the quasigroup follows a structured pattern, rather than being by chance. Groups formed in "structurally irrelevant ways," often from the lower levels of society, form a mere "lumpen proletariat," and are not capable of being combined into organized interest groups.[67]

Dahrendorf's work suggests several facilitating conditions for organizing. First, a *founder*, or leader, is required. Second, some kind of articulation of the group's common interests is necessary, supplied by an ideology if not by a leader. Third, the state must permit the organizing to take place. Fourth, communication among members of the group must be possible. Fifth, group membership must not be a random, unstructured, matter.

The literature discussed above is a highly diverse miscellany of theories and approaches. A number of ideas about facilitating conditions can be drawn from this literature. It also forms the foundation for what has come to be known as the "collective behavior" literature.

Theories of Collective Behavior

Largely because of the massive outbreaks of civil disorder in the 1960s and early 1970s, a good deal of scholarly attention was directed to the phenomenon of collective human action. This produced a substantial body of literature explaining what was labelled "collective behavior."

There are two main approaches taken in the literature on collective behavior, both sociological. The first approach, chronologically, is labelled "classic" and is a structural one. The second, resource mobilization theory, is drawn from a political sociology tradition. Both of these streams of thought and research are helpful in providing us with facilitating conditions.

Classical Theories

Classical collective behavior theory begins by assuming a social equilibrium. When this equilibrium is disturbed by a "strain," collective behavior becomes possible. It only occurs, however, in the presence of certain conditions. Insofar as its framework goes, then, it is quite similar to the integrative theory. Neil J. Smelser, the originator and chief proponent of the classical view, defines collective behavior as "purposive behavior in which people are trying to reconstitute their social environment."[68] They attempt to reconstitute the environment in accordance with a "generalized belief." Generalized beliefs are similar to "magical beliefs" in which "the world is portrayed in terms of omnipotent forces, conspiracies, and extravagant policies, all of which are imminent."[69] Collective action occurs where there is "uninstitutionalized action taken in the name of such a belief."[70]

Smelser argues that collective behavior will only take place when there is a strain that disturbs the existing social equilibrium. This strain, at least for a "norm-oriented" movement such as a labor union involves the occurrence of deprivation. Unions are "norm-oriented," rather than "value-oriented," because they operate at the level of societal rules which are not the most general and fundamental. Deprivation becomes a strain when there is a disharmony between normative standards and actual social conditions. Indeed, strains are themselves "discrepancies between social conditions and social expectations."[71]

According to Smelser, in order for collective behavior to take place, there must be "structural conduciveness," which includes the pressure of a strain as well as other conditions. He posits the conditions of structural conduciveness using a "value added" approach. Under this approach the determinants of collective behavior are ordered in a scale from general to specific. Each determinant is logically, though not necessarily temporally, prior to the one following it. Each is seen as operating within the scope of the prior, more general, determinant. Each determinant is a necessary, but not sufficient, condition for the occurrence of collective behavior. All the conditions taken together are sufficient for the occurrence of an episode of collective behavior.[72]

For a movement such as a labor union, the first and most important condition of structural conduciveness "concerns the possibility for demanding modifications of norms *without simultaneously appearing to demand a more fundamental modification of values.*"[73] That is, the necessity for challenging the fundamental values of society in order to act is a condition unfavorable to such action taking place. Smelser argues that it is generally possible for norm-oriented movements to operate in this fashion in Western Europe and the United States but not in totalitarian societies. In addition, structural conduciveness requires that avenues for agitation be open, that there be an unavailability of other channels for expressing this dissatisfaction, and that there be a possibility of communication.[74]

The second condition posited by Smelser is some kind of strain. The third condition is a "generalized belief" in which the strain is exaggerated and seen to be of immediate importance. The fourth condition is mobilization, which can occur either by a dramatic event or the actions of a leader. The fifth and last condition is social control, the activation of counter measures by other actors in the society.[75] That is, if society is likely to suppress the collective behavior, this is a condition that renders the behavior less probable.

Ralph Turner is another proponent of a classical approach to collective behavior. Turner labels his approach the "emergent norm" approach. Turner argues that each person has a framework for perceiving socially relevant situations. This framework is derived from a group, and depends upon consensus among group members for "the conviction of reality in the experience."[76] Collective behavior is given its distinctive character by two circumstances: (1) ordinary social norms are replaced by special norms, or special definitions for norms; (2) neither the established social group nor the individual relations of a primary group is able to supply a framework for collective decision-making and action.[77] Turner's focus is quite different from that of other collective behavior theorists in its tight focus upon norms. There is, however, a fuzziness of concept and language involved in the Turner approach that makes it very difficult to apply.

Turner does make some useful comments with respect to collective movements such as labor organizations. He would categorize a trade union as a "respectable-factional organization." Such an organization is "within the acceptable range of conventionality, its members defined as respectable but sometimes misguided, able to recruit responsible citizens, granted full access to legitimate means, but opposed by counter movements and competing movements with similar objectives."[78] This is a reasonably accurate description of the position of unions in American society.

The classical view of collective behavior is an interesting one. Smelser has performed the very useful function of outlining a set of necessary, but not individually sufficient, conditions for collective behavior. His notion of a strain would certainly be appropriate in some instances of collective behavior, although probably not in others. Yet, the arguments regarding strain are not necessary to the validity of Smelser's conditions for collective behavior.

Resource Mobilization Theory

The term *resource mobilization theory* is an umbrella that covers a somewhat diverse set of approaches to collective behavior. In spite of their diversity, however, resource mobilization approaches have two characteristics in common. First, they disagree with the classical assumptions that an equilibrium generally exists and that it requires a strain in order for collective behavior to occur. Secondly, they argue that the crucial determinant of collective behavior is the resources available to exploited groups.

Resource mobilization theory holds that conditions of exploitation are ever-present because of established economic relations. This exploitation is itself sufficient to account for any discontent or strain. Human beings are always willing to act to try to relieve conditions of exploitation. Most instances of collective behavior are believed to be explainable by reference to resources made available to exploited groups. It is new access to resources that permits them to realize their long-standing wishes to end their exploitation. Resource mobilization theory does agree with the classical view in setting out a number of facilitating conditions that make collective behavior possible. These facilitating conditions are quite similar to those suggested by Smelser.

What is perhaps the clearest statement of resource mobilization theory, as well as the one most relevant for our purposes, was by J. Craig Jenkins and Charles Perrow in a study published in 1977.[79] Jenkins and Perrow hypothesize that the farm worker insurgency of the late 1960s can be best explained by changes in the political environment. Jenkins and Perrow criticize the classical model which attributes collective behavior to social changes that produce a strain in social relations and generate discontent. They disagree with the classical notion that it is when discontent increases rapidly enough, and is widely enough shared, that collective action will occur. They maintain that recent research has cast substantial doubt on these classical formulations, showing that disorder arises from a "group organizationally able to defend and advance their interest."[80]

Jenkins and Perrow argue that it is difficult to believe that farm worker discontent was any greater in the 1960s than it was, for example, in the 1950s, when there was no farm workers' movement. Instead "it seems more plausible to assume that farm worker discontentment is relatively constant, a product of established economic relations rather than some social dislocation or disfunction."[81] Although not questioning the *existence* of discontent, Jenkins and Perrow question the *usefulness* of formulations involving discontent for the purpose of explaining or predicting the emergence of social organization. According to them, "what increases, and gives rise to insurgency, is the amount of social resources available to unorganized groups, making it possible to launch an organized demand for change."[82] Jenkins and Perrow conclude that, "discontent is ever-present for deprived groups, but collective action is rarely a viable option because of lack of resources and the threat of repression."[83] When deprived groups mobilize, it is because of the injection of external resources such as money and the support of other groups in society. Their challenges often fail because of a lack of such resources.

From their study of farm worker organizing in the 1960s, Jenkins and Perrow conclude that the "critical factor" differentiating between the earlier, unsuccessful farm worker organizing and the later, successful effort was "the societal response to insurgent demand."[84] As they had hypothesized, it was not an increase in discontent, but rather an increase in resources at their command that provided the impetus for this collective action. They found that the active support of government, and of a powerful, mobilized, liberal community, were highly useful to the development of the farm worker movement of the 1960s.[85]

Another important application of resource mobilization theory appears in a 1978 article written by Mayer N. Zald and Michael Berger.[86] Zald and Berger describe the resource mobilization approach as having two components that make it particularly useful: "First [it] examines the cost of participation in social movement action as well as the distribution of grievances. That is, it examines . . . the risk-reward ratio. Second, it treats mobilization of resources from whatever source as a central topic."[87]

Zald and Berger suggest that the resource mobilization approach is akin to the political sociology tradition. That is because it treats many issues with which social movements deal as being "rooted in the enduring cleavages, status relationships, collective definitions, and traditions of the social system."[88] It also examines the infrastructure of society to identify supports for collective action, as well as hindrances to it. Furthermore, it recognizes the responses of authorities as well as "linkages among authorities, partisans, and reference elites."[89] All of these characteristics of resource mobilization theory link it to Marxist and other approaches which utilize the notion of mobilized social classes and related ideas.

Industrial conflict, as it is here defined, would be considered by Zald and Berger to constitute a "mass movement" within an organization.[90] Mass movements are "collective attempts to express grievances and discontent and/or to promote or resist change."[91] Zald and Berger argue, however, that "strikes need not represent the social movement-like phenomenon of unconventional politics."[92] This is because they have become a fully institutionalized part of the process of collective bargaining. Zald and Berger consider strike action by institutionalized unions as a part of "normal politics." They see some parallels between industrial strikes and organizational mass movements. As they note, both involve mobilization of workers and cost-benefit calculations. They argue, however, that there are differences that prevent a "wholesale" incorporation of the industrial conflict literature into a consideration of mass movements in organizations.[93]

Zald and Berger posit a set of determinants of intraorganizational mass movements. These are highly useful to us in our search for facilitating conditions for industrial conflict. The Zald and Berger determinants are "size, homogeneity, vertical segmentation, exit option, and associational density."[94]

As to *size*, Zald and Berger hypothesize that the larger the subordinate group, the more probable an organizational mass movement. Larger groups are more likely to include members who have grievances. They are more likely to be cut off from their superiors. They can hide dissidents and are generally more impervious to social control. They are "more likely to generate association within them." Accordingly, large establishments are easier to organize than smaller ones.[95]

As to *homogeneity*, they hypothesize that the greater the homogeneity the more likely that collective action will occur. Homogeneity and shared values increase group consciousness. Heterogeneity might, however, make for conflict within the subordinate group. It might also allow for alliances between some groups of subordinates and superordinates. Zald and Berger agree with Kerr and Siegel that a small degree of occupational differentiation facilitates conflict between subordinates and superordinates.[96]

With respect to *vertical segmentation*, Zald and Berger hypothesize that, where segmentation is high, there will be a blocking of channels for grievances, mobility, and communication and, apparently, a higher probability for collective action. This is caused by increased "within group solidarity" and "chances for resentment."[97]

As to *exit*, Zald and Berger hypothesize that the probability of social movements within the organization is increased by costliness or difficulty of exit. They view difficulty of exit as an important determinant of collective action. Quite interestingly, it helps explain why collective action might be taken by free riders. Where exit is impossible or very difficult, the benefits of action are more likely to overcome those of inaction.[98]

As to *associational density*, they hypothesize that mobilization is facilitated by a high proportion of organizational participants being members of intraorganizational associations. Individuals belonging to associations and networks within the organization lessens the cost of information and, therefore, the difficulty of mobilization. They hold that "a dense associational field within a hierarchical organization facilitates internal social movements."[99]

Zald and Berger discuss briefly the relevance of resource mobilization theory to strikes. They argue that strikers are dependent upon several kinds of external resources, particularly money for necessities and the honoring of the strike by others. Access to welfare payments by strikers has been shown to be associated with increased strike length. The individuals in a larger organization may provide resources that contribute to the maintenance of a strike. Political resources provided by police, the military, or the courts may affect worker collective action.[100]

One of the originators of resource mobilization theory is Anthony Oberschall. Oberschall sees negatively privileged groups, or "challengers," as putting forth collective demands because they are unable to "increase their well-being through individual efforts."[101] If the exit option is not available by way of immigration, social mobility, or changing group membership and disadvantage prevails, the only alternative for dealing with this situation is "voice." This involves, however, inducing others to give up something that is valuable, that is, the positively privileged must be persuaded to share with the negatively privileged group. There are two ways of doing this. The first is through exchange, giving the positively privileged group something in exchange for the resources the negatively privileged groups wants. However, exchange is unlikely because the challenger often has no resources to use in the exchange. It is likely, then, that the negatively privileged challenger will "resort partly to nonconventional means of conflict," such as "harassment, obstruction, coercion, and threatening of actual violence which lower the welfare of the target."[102] Overschall includes strikes within his definition of "nonconventional means of conflict." If conciliation fails, the challenger then determines whether to engage in collective action. This is done through a rather complex cost-benefit analysis, according to Overschall.[103] Essentially, the challenger calculates the utility of challenging versus that of not challenging. This is, of course, quite similar to the rational calculation path to readiness for aggressive action set out in the integrative theory.

In contrast to the individual utility orientation of Overschall, and of Mancur Olson as well, Bruce Fireman and William A. Gamson suggest a social group-oriented utility framework.[104] Fireman and

Gamson argue that, instead of calculating individual "collective incentives" as suggested by Olson, individuals look to benefits obtainable for a group with which they feel solidarity. According to Fireman and Gamson, "solidarity is rooted in the configuration of relationships linking the members of a group to one another. People may be linked together in a number of ways that generate a sense of common identify, shared fate, and general commitment to defend the group."[105]

Fireman and Gamson posit five factors that make up a basis for an individual having solidarity with a group. These are as follows:

1. Friends and relatives. To the extent that a person has friends and relatives within the group, and to the extent that he is indirectly related to others in the group through their friendship and kinship with his friends and kin, he has a basis for solidarity with the group.
2. Participation in organizations. To the extent that a person acts collectively with other members of the group in productive organizations, voluntary associations, clubs, and other associations, he has a basis for solidarity with the group.
3. Design for living. Groups frequently offer members as set of techniques for handling the problems they encounter in their daily lives—problems like finding and keeping good jobs and good spouses, making friends, raising children, staying out of trouble, and getting treated with dignity and respect. In trying to implement some design for going through life, a person may rely to a greater or lesser degree on support from other people and organizations in the solidary group. To the extent that a person's design for living is shared and supported by other group members more than by outsiders, he has a basis for solidarity with the group.
4. Subordinate and superordinate relations. To the extent that a person shares with other group members the same set of subordinate and superordinate relations with outsiders, he has a basis for solidarity with the group.
5. No exit. To the extent that a person is readily identified and often treated as a member of the group, so that exit from the group is difficult, he has a basis for solidarity with the group.[106]

Fireman and Gamson's five factors for solidarity constitute potentially useful facilitating conditions for industrial conflict.

In an article published in 1972, David Snyder and Charles Tilly launched a major attack on the classical explanations of political violence, arguing that a resource-mobilization perspective is superior.[107] Snyder and Tilly argue that, although men become angry when their expectations are violated and on occasion hardship can precipitate rebellion, there is not "any general connection between collective violence and hardship such that an observer could predict one from the other."[108] They disagree that such diverse events as "protest, collective behavior, rebellion, and violence have anything more in common than the fact that authorities disapprove of them."[109] They argue that "the principal, immediate causes of collective violence are political: collective violence results from changes in the relations between groups of men and major concentrations of coercive power in that environment."[110] Their study of collective violence in France finds that expectation-achievement arguments do not explain year-to-year fluctuations in this violence. It is political variables, namely the extent of government repression and the degree of national political activity, that are the best explainers. Both a low amount of government repression of their activities and high political activity on their part are believed to reflect substantial political power resources. When these resources are at a high level they are able to take, and actually do take, action. It should be noted that this study has been subjected to a slashing and rather devastating attack by James Chowning Davies.[111]

Resource mobilization theory does, as indicated above, have the advantage of focusing on what would appear to be some vital determinants of industrial conflict. Surely the prospects for effective collective action are affected by the resources available for it. Surely there are at least some groups of workers who await only the presence of sufficient resources to launch collective action.

A SET OF FACILITATING CONDITIONS

As has been the case throughout this book, it is necessary for us to integrate highly diverse strains of research in order to construct a portion of the integrative theory. For our purposes, the most important area of literature is the modern literature on collective behavior, which offers a great deal by way of facilitating conditions. Although at first blush it appears that the various theories are incompatible, closer examination reveals that they are susceptible of integration.

The classical view that equilibrium exists and must be disturbed by some special strain is clearly at odds with resource mobilization theory. For our purposes, however, this may be an irrelevant disagreement; we are not seeking a complete explanation of industrial conflict in the collective behavior literature. Instead, we are merely trying to draw from it a set of facilitating conditions. These become important only where individual motivation to act aggressively is present.

One could certainly view the frustration-aggression and threat paths of the integrative theory's model to be consistent with classical arguments for strain. Indeed, Smelser's theory includes the notion of relative deprivation. The integrative theory, however, does not presume that there is an equilibrium at any point, although it might be said that a kind of equilibrium is present whenever there is an absence of industrial conflict. That is, it would be perfectly compatible with the integrative theory to have, in a particular case, a constant strain provided by structural conditions that would produce a constant readiness for, and yet an absence of, aggressive action. Individuals might be constantly circulating through the model, stopping short of readiness for aggressive action because of fear or other reasons. This would create a condition of equilibrium in the sense that conflict was absent. It might be that collective aggressive action had failed to occur only because of a lack of sufficient resources to give it a reasonable chance of success. The integrative theory would predict that in such an event, resource mobilization would be the crucial factor for the onset of industrial conflict. On the other hand, it is not plausible to argue that all workers who could potentially engage in industrial conflict would do so if only they had the resources. Not all workers are deprived. Why would contented workers engage in industrial conflict? Given such a condition, it would seem to require some change, a strain, to provide an impetus to industrial conflict. This is a situation Smelser's analysis seems to fit quite well.

The controversy between the classicists and the resource mobilization theorists is not, at base, theoretical. Instead it is an empirical argument over what factors furnish the best explanation of particular conflicts, and the importance in general of particular factors. Consequently, the integrative theory runs afoul of neither approach *theoretically* when it argues that *either* an increase in discontent *or* an increase in resources might spark an instance of industrial conflict in a particular case. If the discontent is present, but the resources absent, it is increased resources that might provide the spark. If resources are present, but discontent absent, an increase in discontent might provide it. In point of fact, both of these theoretical explanations are incomplete. Taken together they can be used to help build a complete theory. As has been argued extensively above, however, the matter is a great deal more complicated than this, and these theories must be supplemented by still other theories.

This writer believes that both classical and resource mobilization statements of facilitating conditions can be made use of. Smelser's conditions of structural conduciveness and the presence of a mobilizer are sound and useable. Resource mobilization theorists have convincingly established the importance of resource availability to collective action. The facilitating conditions set out by Zald and Berger are well reasoned and potentially powerful. Fireman and Gamson's argument for the necessity of solidarity, and their list of its determinants, are also usable. All of these ideas can be used at the collective aggressive action stage of the integrative theory.

It remains for us to inquire whether our list of facilitating conditions can be improved by adding items drawn from the older theories of collective action. Freud's and LeBon's arguments regarding the importance of a leader and the affective nature of group action have been picked up by later writers. The class theory emphasis on solidarity and communication have likewise been absorbed by collective behavior theorists. The Kerr and Siegel condition of common grievances at the same time against the same people, would seem to be a result of the homogeniety of which Zald and Berger speak. It does lend some support to the segment of the model that posits individual readiness for aggressive action by a number of workers at about the same time. Convergence theory also furnishes some support for this portion of the model. The other conditions suggested by Kerr and Siegel—homogeneity, difficulty of exit, and cohesiveness—have been included in the works of such collective behavior theorists as Zald and Berger and Fireman and Gamson. The same can be said for Sayles' conditions of a large group, common tasks, leadership, group cohesion, and much interraction among workers. Dahrendorf's condition of the necessity of a "founder" is similar to the leadership condition of later writings. His political conditions of the political system allowing the protest and his social condition of communication have been included in Smelser's theory. It appears, therefore, that the older collective action literature has been largely absorbed by the newer literature insofar as if relates to facilitating conditions. Although it formed the basis for the newer collective behavior literature, and it enriches our understanding of the whole set of facilitating conditions, we would gain nothing by explicitly drawing from it to construct our list of conditions facilitating industrial conflict.

Table 1 sets out the list of facilitating conditions included in the integrative theory. They are mainly drawn from the collective behavior literature. The one exception is the instrumentality condition, which is attributed to the work of DeCotiis and LeLouarn.[112] This is believed to be an extensive listing, rather than one that can at this time be narrowed to a few major conditions. A pruning of this list

Table 1

FACILITATING CONDITIONS FOR INDUSTRIAL CONFLICT
Love Homogeneous employee group (Zald and Berger) Vertical segmentation (Zald and Berger) Associations in intraorganizational groups (Zald and Berger) Friendship or blood relationship (Fireman and Gamson) Shared superordinate and subordinate relations (Fireman and Gamson) Support among members for conduct of life (Fireman and Gamson) *Hope* Large employee group (Zald and Berger) Possibility of norm modification without fundamental value modification (Smelser) Open avenue for agitation (Smelser) Communication (Smelser) Resources mobilized for collective action (Jenkins and Perrow) Perceived instrumentality (DeCotiis and LeLouarn) *Saliency* Mobilizing event or person (Smelser) Other channels of protest unavailable (Smelser) Difficult organizational exit (Zald and Berger)

will only be possible after it has been used as a tool to analyze industrial conflict in a number of instances. Even more than any other part of the integrative theory, this list is seen as tentative. This is an area where theory will likely adjust to the empirical reality. Indeed, many of these items may be "pet" hypotheses we should "throw away before breakfast," as Konrad Lorenz suggests scientists should do.[113]

The categories into which the facilitating conditions are placed are *love, hope* and *saliency*. This is believed to be the most useful taxonomy for grouping these conditions. It is also, as is the nature of a taxonomy, a statement about the structure of conditions and their essential nature. It does say that collective aggressive action of this type is facilitated by mutual affection among group members, hope of success, and the salience of collective aggressive action as a form of activity. The condition of love goes back, of course, to Freud. This author suspects that this is the crucial condition, under whatever label it is given. As Freud argued, it is probably the love of members of a group for one another that makes collective action ultimately possible.

Having stated the conditions for occurrence of collective aggressive action, we are at the end of our journey through the model. The integrative theory of industrial conflict has been derived and set out. Having started with an examination of the individual human mind and heart, we have worked our way to the level of a particular kind of mass action by groups of human beings in the role of employee.

NOTES

[1]Leonard Berkowitz, *Aggression: A Social Psychological Analysis* (New York: McGraw-Hill Book Co. 1962), pp. 73-103.

[2]John Dollard, Leonard W. Doob, Neal E. Miller, O. H. Mowrer, Robert S. Sears, *Frustration and Aggression* (New Haven: Yale University Press, 1939), p. 33.

[3]Berkowitz, *Aggression: A Social Psychological Analysis*, p. 73.

[4]Ibid., p. 76.

[5]Ibid., pp. 78-79.

[6]Ibid., pp. 85-91.

[7]Ibid., p. 102.

[8]Gustave Le Bon, *The Crowd* (London: Ernest Been, 1952).

[9]Ibid., pp. 28-29.

[10]Ibid., p. 33.

[11]Sigmund Freud, *Group Psychology and the Analysis of the Ego,* trans. J. Strachey (New York: Harper and Row, 1970).

[12]Ibid., p. 13.

[13]Ibid., p. 23.

[14]Ibid., p. 24.

[15]Ibid., p. 35.

[16]Ibid.

[17]Ibid.

[18]Ibid., p. 53.

[19]Ralph H. Turner, "New Theoretical Frameworks," in *Collective Behavior,* ed. M. D. Pugh (St. Paul, Minn.: West Publishing Co., 1980), p. 38.

[20]Floyd H. Allport, *Social Psychology* (Boston: Houghton Mifflin Co., 1924), pp. 292-319.

[21]Turner, "New Theoretical Frameworks," in *Collective Behavior,* ed. Pugh, p. 38.

[22]James Chowning Davies, "Communications," *American Political Science Review* 62, no. 4 (December 1968), p. 828.

[23]David Synder and Charles Tilly, "On Debating and Falsifying Theories of Collective Violence," *American Sociological Review* 39, (August 1974), pp. 610-612.

[24]Ted Robert Gurr and Raymond D. Duvall, "Introduction to a Formal Theory of Political Conflict," in *The Uses of Controversy in Sociology,* ed. Lewis A. Coser and Otto N. Larsen (New York: The Free Press, 1976), p. 148.

[25]Ibid.

[26]Ibid., pp. 148-149.

[27]Ibid., p. 149.

[28]Turner, "New Theoretical Frameworks," in *Collective Behavior,* ed. Pugh, p. 38.

[29]Mancur Olson, *The Logic of Collective Action* (Cambridge: Harvard University Press, 1971).

[30] Ibid., p. 5.

[31] Ibid., p. 21.

[32] Ibid., pp. 61–62.

[33] Ibid., p. 68.

[34] Joseph A. Schumpter, *History of Economic Analysis* (New York: Oxford University Press, 1954), p. 131.

[35] Samuel B. Bacharach and Edward J. Lawler, *Power and Politics in Organizations* (San Francisco: Jossey-Bass Publishers, 1980).

[36] Karl Marx and Friederich Engels, "Manifesto of the Communist Party", in *Marx and Engels Basic Writings on Politics and Philosophy*, ed. Lewis S. Feuer (Garden City, N.Y.: Doubleday Co., 1959), pp. 6–41.

[37] Ibid., pp. 12–14.

[38] Ibid., p. 17.

[39] Ibid., pp. 19–20.

[40] Clark Kerr and Abraham Siegel, "The Interindustry Propensity to Strike—An International Comparison," in *Industrial Conflict*, ed. Arthur Kornhauser, Robert Dubin, and Arthur M. Ross (New York: McGraw-Hill Book Co., 1954), pp. 189–212.

[41] Ibid., p. 191.

[42] Ibid., pp. 191–192.

[43] Ibid., p. 192.

[44] Ibid.

[45] Ibid.

[46] Ibid., p. 193.

[47] Leonard R. Sayles, *Behavior of Industrial Work Groups* (New York: John Wiley and Sons, 1958), pp. 7–8.

[48] Ibid., p. 8.

[49] Ibid., p. 13.

[50] Ibid.

[51] Ibid., p. 95.

[52] Ibid., p. 19.

[53] Ibid., p. 34.

[54] Ibid., p. 39.

[55] Ibid., p. 97.

[56] Ibid., p. 103.

[57] Ibid., p. 43.

[58] Ibid.

[59] Ibid., pp. 70–71.

[60] Clayton P. Alderfer, "Group and Intergroup Relations," in *Improving Life at Work: Behavioral Science Approaches to Organizational Change,* ed. J. Richard Hackman and J. Lloyd Suttle (Santa Monica, Cal.: Goodyear Publishing Co., 1977), p. 237.

[61] Jon Amsden and Stephen Brier, "Coal Miners on Strike: The Transformation of Strike Demands and the Formation of a National Union," *Journal of Interdisciplinary History* 7, no. 4 (Spring 1977), p. 588.

[62] Ralf Dahrendorf, *Class and Class Conflict in Industrial Society* (Stanford: Stanford University Press, 1959), p. 184.

[63] Ibid., p. 185.

[64] Ibid.

[65] Ibid., pp. 185–186.

[66] Ibid., pp. 186–187.

[67] Ibid., p. 187.

[68] Neil J. Smelser, "Theoretical Issues of Scope and Problems," in *Collective Behavior,* Pugh, p. 8.

[69] Ibid.

[70] Ibid.

[71] Neil J. Smelser, *Theory of Collective Behavior* (New York: The Free Press, 1962), p. 290.

72Ibid., p. 9.
73Ibid., p. 278.
74Ibid., p. 284.
75Smelser, "Theoretical Issues of Scope and Problems," in *Collective Behavior*, ed. Pugh, pp. 9–10.
76Turner, "New Theoretical Frameworks," in ibid., p. 40.
77Ibid., pp. 40–41.
78Ibid., p. 36.
79J. Craig Jenkins and Charles Perrow, "Insurgency of the Powerless: Farm Worker Movements (1946–1972)," *American Sociological Review* 42 (April 1977), pp. 249–268.
80Ibid., p. 250.
81Ibid.
82Ibid.
83Ibid., p. 251.
84Ibid., p. 266.
85Ibid.
86Mayer N. Zald and Michael A. Berger, "Social Movements in Organizations: Coup d'Etat Insurgency, and Mass Movements," *American Journal of Sociology* 83, no. 4, (January 1978), pp. 823–861.
87Ibid., p. 829.
88Ibid.
89Ibid.
90Ibid., p. 841.
91Ibid.
92Ibid., p. 842.
93Ibid.
94Ibid., p. 843.
95Ibid.
96Ibid., pp. 843–844.
97Ibid., pp. 844–845.
98Ibid.
99Ibid., pp. 845–846.
100Ibid., p. 847.
101Anthony Oberschall, "Protracted Conflict," in *The Dynamics of Social Movements*, ed. Mayer N. Zald and John D. McCarthy (Cambridge: Winthrop Publishers, 1979), p. 45.
102Ibid., pp. 45–46.
103Ibid., p. 52.
104Bruce Fireman and William A. Gamson, "Utilitarian Logic in the Resource Mobilization Perspective," in *The Dynamics of Social Movements*, ed. Zald and McCarthy, pp. 8–44.
105Ibid., p. 21.
106Ibid., p. 22.
107David Snyder and Charles Tilly, "Hardship and Collective Violence in France, 1830 to 1960," *American Sociological Review* 37 (October 1972), pp. 530–532.
108Ibid., p. 520.
109Ibid.
110Ibid.
111James Chowning Davies, "The J-Curve and Power Struggle Theories of Collective Violence," *American Sociological Review* 39, no. 4, (August 1974), pp. 607–610.
112Thomas A. De Cotiis and Jean-Ives LeLouarn, "A Predictive Study of Voting Behavior in a Representation Election Using Union Instrumentality and Work Perception," *Organizational Behavior and Human Performance*, vol. 27 (1981), pp. 111–112.
113Konrad Lorenz, *On Aggression*, trans. Marjorie Kerr Wilson (New York: Harcourt Brace Jovanovich, 1963), p. 9.

CHAPTER 8

The Integrative Theory in Application

To audience: Well, what's the answer?
All: STRIKE!
Agate: LOUDER!
All: STRIKE!
Agate and others on stage: AGAIN!
All: STRIKE, STRIKE, STRIKE!!!

Clifford Odets, *Waiting for Lefty*

The proof of any theory is in the application. In order to judge its usefulness, one must observe it in use. However elegant or interesting, a theory of industrial conflict has small claim on our attention unless it can produce improved understanding or prediction of industrial conflict. The purpose of this chapter is to apply the integrative theory to several instances of industrial conflict in order to determine whether it does this. This will be performed by first briefly summarizing the theory, then deriving some hypotheses from it, and, finally, examining these several instances with an eye to testing the hypotheses and judging whether the theory improves our understanding. In doing so, perhaps we will better understand the circumstances under which Odets' answer of "STRIKE, STRIKE, STRIKE!!!" is in fact given by workers.

What is proposed in this chapter is not a final and definitive confirmation or denial of the integrative theory, or even of any of its hypotheses. Such confirmation or denial, if it is ever completely achieveable, will come only after much more extensive testing in a very wide range of instances. It is suggested that this is true of all theory, and that it is an illusion to hope that any more than preliminary indication of confirmation or denial can be hoped for in the early testing of any new theory. Patient accumulation of evidence and the tentativeness and amendability of theory is not the least of the lessons we can learn from our cousins in the natural sciences.

SUMMARY OF THE THEORY

The model stated in Chapter 1 is again set out in Figure 2. It is at two levels. The first relates to *individual readiness* for action, the second to the occurrence of *collective aggressive action*. The model starts with general human predispositions. Its end is the occurrence, or nonoccurrence, of industrial conflict in a particular unit of the industrial relations system.

The model begins with the innate human predispositions to pursue social dominance and material outcomes. These predispositions are moderated by an employee's expectations and achievements regarding these outcomes, which derive from his environment and personality. Where a gap is present between expectations and achievements he is likely to act nonaggressively, with a significant degree of

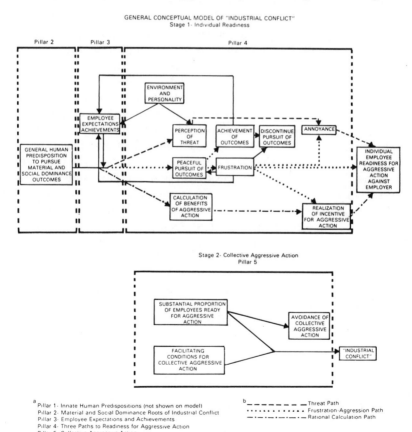

GENERAL CONCEPTUAL MODEL OF "INDUSTRIAL CONFLICT"
Stage 1- Individual Readiness

Stage 2- Collective Aggressive Action
Pillar 5

a Pillar 1- Innate Human Predispositions (not shown on model)
Pillar 2- Material and Social Dominance Roots of Industrial Conflict
Pillar 3- Employee Expectations and Achievements
Pillar 4- Three Paths to Readiness for Aggressive Action
Pillar 5- Collective Aggressive Action

b ――――――― Threat Path
••••••••••• Frustration-Aggression Path
―•―•―•―•― Rational Calculation Path

Figure 2

intensity, to obtain the expected level of outcomes. This action creates the potential for *frustration* and places the employee on the model's central path toward readiness for aggressive action. Two other paths to readiness for aggressive action are also posited. One of these becomes operative when a *threat* is posed or actual harm is done by the employer to an employee's expected level of outcomes. This can lead to annoyance, which is likely to bring on a readiness for aggressive action. The other path comes into play when an individual simply *calculates* that the benefits of aggressive action outweigh the costs, realizes that there is an incentive for such action, and therefore becomes ready for it.

The central path to readiness for aggressive action, which includes a nonaggressive pursuit of outcomes, is somewhat complex. First, the nonaggressive action may result in achievement of the outcomes. If so, this would be expected to lead to at least a temporary discontinuance of their pursuit. If the individual's pursuit is blocked by a failure to obtain these outcomes, this will probably produce frustration. The frustration may lead *directly* to a readiness for aggressive action. This readiness may also come about *indirectly*, either through annoyance or the stimulation of a search procedure which leads the individual to realize that there is some incentive for aggressive action because of a favorable cost-benefit ratio. Alternatively, frustration may lead to a discontinuance of the pursuit of the outcomes. This will be the case when the individual: (1) is very fearful of the consequences of aggressive action; (2) fails to identify the frustration with the employer; or, (3) is predisposed to exit the organization or otherwise withdraw, resigning himself to the result.

The collective aggressive action stage of the model is simpler, at least on the surface. Its argument is that readiness for collective action on the part of individual workers is likely to lead to industrial conflict (collective aggressive employee action) only in the presence of certain facilitating conditions. Collective aggressive action will be avoided if it is inhibited by fear of adverse consequences, or by the fact that it violates strongly held norms or values of the workers.

HYPOTHESES

Several hypotheses can be derived from the theory. They are framed in absolute terms in order to facilitate falsifiability, although the theory itself has been stated in terms of probabilities.

The first hypothesis:

> H₁: In any instance of industrial conflict, material or social dominance roots are present.

might be tested by detailed examination of a number of instances of industrial conflict to see whether either of these roots proves to be present. If it is determined, for example, that wage demands were the subject matter of an instance of union organizing, this would tend to support the hypothesis. If, on the other hand, the sole issue were self-actualization needs of workers, this would tend to disconfirm the hypothesis.

> H₂: In any instance of industrial conflict, an actual or threatened gap between expectations and achievements as to material resources or social dominance is present.

This hypothesis might be tested through the use of objective data which provide reasonable proxies for worker expectations and achievements. This strategy was reasonably successful when used by James C. Davies to test his "J-curve" theory.[1] Davies used past earnings, and their trend, as his measure of material expectations. He used present earnings as a measure of their achievement. In this writer's judgment, the relative deprivation literature shows that this is more likely to work than the direct measurement of perceptions, although it might be possible to use this latter strategy as well.

> H₃: In any instance of industrial conflict there exists either: (1) frustration; (2) threat; or, (3) rational calculation of advantage.

> H₄: In any instance where there is an open and severe threat by the employer to employees' expected levels of social dominance or material outcomes, industrial conflict will occur, given the absence of the inhibiting conditions and the presence of the facilitating conditions.

> H₅: Instances exist where the presence of rational calculation of advantage, combined with an absence of inhibiting conditions and the presence of the facilitating conditions, leads to industrial conflict.

> H₆: In any instance where the following conditions exist, industrial conflict will occur: (1) the peaceful pursuit of expected levels of social dominance or material outcomes; (2) a blocking of the achievement of these outcomes by the employer; (3) ready identification of the employer as the frustrator; (4) the absence of overwhelming fear; (5) the absence of the inhibiting conditions; and, (6) the presence of the facilitating conditions.

Because of its generality, H_3 will be difficult to test. Yet, it is believed to be testable by rigorous, in-depth examination of numerous cases. In order to prove frustration in a particular case, we would have to find that employees were engaged in ongoing response sequences in an attempt to close an expectations/achievements gap, and were blocked by the employer from closing this gap. The unsuccessful pursuit of grievances, or either individual or group attempts to persuade the employer to raise wages, are possible examples of this.

A conclusion that threat is present would require: (1) the discovery of clearly apparent action by the employer in material derogation of expected levels of material or social dominance outcomes; (2) an expression of intent by the employer to take such action; or, (3) actions by the employer that unambiguously reveal such an intention. A wage cut would be an example of this.

Proof of rational calculation would require evidence of objective grounds for a favorable cost-benefit analysis, or perceptual measures showing that such a calculation was actually made. For example, if employees organized where they knew that the union wage was much higher than the nonunion wage (benefit) and there was no employer opposition to organizing (few costs), this might provide evidence that rational calculation had occurred. This is admittedly very difficult to test and might require subjective perceptual measures.

H_4 and H_5 involve the use of measures similar to those used for H_3, with the addition of measures pertaining to the inhibiting and facilitating conditions. The absence of the inhibiting conditions can be only indirectly measured. Anticipation of punishment can be indirectly measured by examining the circumstances surrounding an instance of industrial conflict to ascertain whether there were any grounds for employee perceptions that punishment was likely—for example, a history of the employer discharging union activists. The absence of such a history, or of other grounds for such perceptions, would be evidence of an absence of this inhibition.

Norms contrary to collective aggressive action constitute the other inhibiting condition. Its absence can be inferred indirectly from the presence of conflicting norms. That is, if there is evidence of the presence of norms *supportive* of collective aggressive action, we might infer the absence of norms *contrary* to such action.

The presence of facilitating conditions is also somewhat difficult to measure. There are three constructs involved: *love, hope,* and *saliency*. For each of these, a number of indicators are suggested by the literature. Firm confirmation of the hypothesis would require finding clear indicators of each construct in a large number of instances of industrial conflict.

For the construct *love*, one would be required to find sufficient indicators of affective ties among group members to conclude that a positive affective relationship in fact exists. In a particular case, a large degree of homogeneity, coupled with shared racial or ethnic backgrounds and the existence of social mutual aid organization, might, for example, be sufficient.

Easy communication and the presence of substantial outside resources, perhaps combined with a social system that allowed norm modification without challenging basic societal values, might, for example, serve as sufficient proof of employee *hope* of a successful outcome. The presence of a dramatic leader or event, combined with the existence of few apparent alternative avenues for goal attainment and evidence of difficulty of exit, might, for example, establish the presence of *saliency*.

Up to a point, H_6 is identical to the frustration aspect of H_3. In addition, however, it requires measuring: (1) ready identification of the employer as the frustrating agent; and, (2) the absence of overwhelming fear as a response to frustration. Ready identification of the frustration with the employer might be inferred where the employer openly does the blocking and there are no reasonable grounds for attributing the fault to another source. This might occur, for example, where the employer refuses to give a pay increase in circumstances where economic conditions do not appear to be the cause of this refusal.

The absence of overwhelming fear can only be approached indirectly, at least without the use of perceptual measures. The absence of employer behaviors reasonably expected to give rise to such a high degree of fear may be an adequate proxy for its absence. If an employer does not maintain a brutally oppressive environment or have totally overwhelming economic power, it may be reasonable to conclude that there is an absence of overwhelming fear.

It should be noted that the hypotheses regarding inhibiting conditions state that industrial conflict is predicted only where both inhibiting conditions are absent. That is, either employee norms contrary to collective aggressive action or fear of punishment is expected to lead to avoidance. The reverse is true with respect to facilitating conditions, as love, hope, and saliency are *all* predicted to be necessary for industrial conflict to occur. In the cases of both the inhibiting and facilitating conditions, it is recognized that testing may cause the theory to be amended. Yet, it should be initially stated in the most easily falsifiable form.

H_6 does not include the possibility of employees being personally inclined to simply resign themselves to frustration or to exit the organization. This omission is made for two reasons. First, resignation to the frustration of efforts to achieve just entitlements is believed to be rare. Second, the propensity to do this, as well as the individual inclination to exit, are impossible to measure in the research design that best suits most of the other parts of the theory. Of course, conditions pertaining to the *objective condition* of availability of exit are dealt with under the heading of facilitating conditions in the second stage of the model.

APPLICATION OF THE THEORY

Fortunately for our application of the integrative theory, there are numerous well-documented incidents of industrial conflict to which the theory can be related. These instances are akin to the "natural experiments" utilized by biologists. If one examines them with a careful eye, it is possible to determine whether or not they support or detract from the explanations offered by the integrative theory, and whether the theory clarifies them.

This strategy for testing theory is more congenial to European social science traditions of field research than to the American quasiexperimental techniques, which emphasize the physical or statistical manipulation of variables. It is also akin to the strategy of the case study, upon which the field of industrial relations was founded. This is not currently fashionable in American social science literature; it is nevertheless a sound approach.

The integrative theory will be applied in some detail to six instances of industrial conflict. These instances were chosen to represent a variety of circumstances and to be spread over a period of approximately a century. The chief constraint upon their selection was the requirement that a reasonable amount of data be available with respect to the *reasons for the occurrence* of industrial conflict. Unlike some other studies, we are interested solely in why industrial conflict happened, not in the details of the conduct of the strike or other matters. It is not claimed that these instances represent a random sample of occurrences of industrial conflict. Accordingly, one cannot safely generalize from this study without the addition of evidence from other cases.

Understanding Industrial Conflict: Analysis of Cases

In order to see whether the integrative theory improves our understanding, the following instances of industrial conflict will be considered: the Pullman Strike (1894), a West Virginia Mine War (1920), organization of the Marinette Knitting Mill (1950), the Memphis Sanitation Strike (1968), the Charleston Hospital Strike (1969), and the Minnesota Community College Strike (1979). In this section each of these instances will be discussed in the light of the theory.

The Pullman Strike

The Pullman Strike of 1894 is a useful subject for analysis because its causes have been well documented. It is also an important instance of industrial conflict, and of special interest for our purposes because it is the event that gave rise to James C. Davies' relative deprivation theory.[2]

The background of the Pullman Strike shows its varied roots. It is clear that in 1894, Pullman employees had reached the starvation level.[3] Many workers received from $1.00 to $6.00 in pay to support a family for two weeks. A few received a few pennies for two weeks of work, after rent had been deducted from their pay checks.[4] Wage cuts had been instituted by the Pullman Company in response to the 1894 depression,[5] cuts averaging 25 to 40 percent between September 1893 and May 1, 1894. The cuts affected not only the manufacturing department, which was losing money, but also the repair shops, which were profitable for the company.[6] The situation was considerably exacerbated by the refusal of the company to lower either the rental charges on company houses, or the prices of utilities supplied by the company.[7] One historian has noted "a radical reduction of wages fostered by depression and business conditions."[8]

The Pullman workers were subject to highly oppressive social subordination. While at work they found themselves confronted with company officials who were unfair, arbitrary, and insulting. For example, a female employee described the conduct of her forewoman as "tyrannical and abusive." She said that the supervisor seems to "delight in showing her power in hurting the girls in every possible way." The supervisor had "a few favorites in the room, to whom she gave all the best work, that they could make the most money on." Complaints by employees to the forewoman's superiors were fruitless. They were told that if they did not like the abuse they could leave the job.[9]

Even when the employee left the job, she was confronted with an all-pervasive paternalism. As one newspaper reporter described it:

> The corporation is everything and everywhere. The corporation trims your lawn and attends to your trees; the corporation sweeps your streets, and sends a man around to pick up every cigar stump, every bit of paper, every straw or leaf; the corporation puts two barrels in your back yard, one for ashes and one for refuse of the kitchen; the corporation has the ashes and refuse hauled away; the corporation provides you new barrels when the others are worn out; the corporation does practically everything but sweep your room and make your bed, and the corporation expects you to enjoy it and hold your tongue.[10]

The conduct of the workers in the town itself was very tightly regulated by the company.[11] Spying on employees was quite common, and it was generally believed that the company knew everything that went on, both at work and at home.[12] Contemporary descriptions of the circumstances of the worker are filled with phrases such as "feudalism," "un-American," and "tyranny."

The integrative theory does shed some light on the Pullman Strike's roots. First, it is fairly clear that expectations/achievements gaps occurred with respect to both material resources and social dominance. It is reasonable to assume that the employees expected subsistence, and there had been a wave of prosperity immediately before 1893, probably causing worker expectations to rise.[13] The depression of 1894 caused wages to go down and created real hardship when placed into conjunction with continued high levels of rent and utility charges.[14] It was this increase in achievements followed by a decrease that caused James C. Davies to conclude that relative deprivation was created by a "J-curve" effect.[15]

Expectations as to social dominance, and their failure of achievement, can be seen in the language used by workers and reporters talking about the situation at Pullman. In the society at large, prevailing norms held that all Americans were free citizens and not subject to feudal-style domination. Yet Pullman was "un-American," "feudal," and "tyrannical."

The actions taken by the Pullman workers conform rather nicely to the frustration-aggression path of the integrative model, even though conditions existed that might have moved the workers to react as if threatened, since they had suffered a wage cut that took away existing benefits. Nevertheless, the initial response to both material and social dominance deprivation was to engage in peaceful pursuit of their desired outcomes.

A grievance committee formed by the employees met with George Pullman, the company president. The workers asked for a return to the wage scale that existed prior to the wage cuts of the preceding summer. They complained of a number of "shop abuses" they wanted investigated and resolved.[16] They also asked for a reduction in rent.[17] Pullman declined to grant any of the demands of employees. He professed a great interest in their welfare and argued that it was for the employees' benefit that shops had been kept open in spite of losses. He offered to allow a committee of workers to inspect the company's books in order to confirm the losses being sustained in the company's construction department. He refused to make any revisions in rents on the grounds that they had nothing to do with the wages and that the rents were reasonable. He agreed to investigate shop complaints and further agreed not to discriminate against any of the members of the grievance committee. The committee accepted this explanation. It agreed to go along with the refusal of the company to meet their requests, except for the appointment of a committee to investigate the company books and an investigation of shop abuses.

The workers had been blocked in their attempt to peacefully achieve their desired outcomes. Nevertheless, rather than responding with a readiness to take aggressive action, they discontinued their pursuit of material outcomes. This was apparently based upon their acceptance of Pullman's argument that he was not the source of their frustration. They accepted this argument, or withheld judgment on it, until they could investigate the books. With respect to the social dominance, they agreed to continue peaceful pursuit on the basis of Pullman's promise to have the shop abuses investigated.[18]

The willingness of the workers to remain peaceful was quickly destroyed by company action. The very next day after the meeting with Pullman, three members of the grievance committee were "laid off." The context in which lay-offs had been made by the Pullman Company in the past and the workers' discovery that the action was in retaliation for complaints against the acting superintendent, did tremendous damage to the credibility of Pullman's claims that the workers' frustrations were not the fault of the company.[19] This argument had always been somewhat problematic, as the wage cuts had been instituted by Pullman in the absence of any similar cuts for managers and in the presence of the maintenance of high dividend levels for stockholders.[20]

In addition, the investigation of shop abuses was done in a manner the workers believed one-sided and unfair. Employee grievances were "made light of and treated as trivial and inconsequential." Only the management side was represented in the investigation. Workers left the management office saying that they felt like a "set of fools."[21]

The situation was mixed with respect to inhibiting conditions. The employees certainly had grounds to believe that they might suffer some detriment if they struck. The history of Pullman and his company should have led them to believe that punishment would likely follow if they were unsuccessful. With respect to employee norms contrary to collective action, there is no evidence one way or the other. The Pullman workers were gathered together into a community in the company town of Pullman. They lived near one another and participated in the various social and civic organizations of the town. Social systems that existed at work carried over into community life. The conditions for mutual affection among employees existed.

There were some conditions present that were capable of giving rise to hopes of success. The employee group was of substantial size and forming a union was neither illegal nor contrary to the fundamental values of the society, although George Pullman's basic values were certainly challenged. Communication networks existed, although it was commonly believed by the workers that they were not secure from company penetration.[22] The potential support of the newly formed American Railway Union may have led workers to believe that resources would be available to them and that organizing and striking might produce the wages and conditions they desired.

Saliency was provided mainly by the mobilizing events of the layoffs of activists and a rumor that the company was going to lock out the workers in anticipation of a strike.[23] During the economic downturn that existed at the time of the strike, it is likely that exit was difficult.

The theory can also be used to inquire as to how the strike might have *failed to occur*. It is fairly clear that the relationship between the propensity to pursue material and social dominance outcomes and the eventual occurrence of industrial conflict is rather longlinked. If any link in the chain between the predispositions and the action is missing, industrial conflict is unlikely. For example, if wages had been above subsistence levels and had not been cut below existing levels, it is unlikely that a gap as to material resources would have been present. A similar argument can be made with respect to social dominance outcomes. Had the employees been persuaded to expect nothing but subordinance and so-called "feudal" relations, they might not have rebelled.

It seems clear that the Pullman employees were willing, at one point, to accept the company's explanation. This did cause them to temporarily discontinue the pursuit of these outcomes. Had the Pullman Company made a convincing case and not lost its credibility by laying off grievance committee members, the strike might never occurred.

When one moves to the stage of collective action, it is not so easy to ascertain how the strike might have failed to occur. Perhaps if the workers had anticipated that they might fail to mobilize resources from the outside they might not have struck. Other than that, it seems that the whole set of conditions created by a paternalistic employer favored a strike. Close communication, a shared set of superordinate and subordinate relations outside work, association with others in nonwork organizations, all seem part of a pattern created by the employer in setting up a paternalistic system.

The West Virginia Mine War

The West Virginia Mine War of 1920 is of interest for several reasons. First, it is an especially important event in American labor history: it resulted in the disappearance, at least for a time, of the United Mine Workers Union from the southern coal fields. Second, as it was a particularly violent and almost revolutionary occurrence, it is similar to events studied by students of social revolution. Third, like the Pullman Strike, it is reasonably well documented, having been the subject of intensive investigation over the years.

Like the Pullman Strike, the West Virginia Mine War had both material and social dominance roots. Nonunion miners in Mingo County, West Virginia, and other southern West Virginia counties were not included in a liberal pay increase that had been granted to unionized areas by the United States Coal Commission in early 1920. They also suffered a local wage reduction.[24] Furthermore, between 1918 and 1919 the average annual earnings of coal miners had declined from $1,211 to $1,097.[25]

The West Virginia coal fields were, like Pullman, affected by an all-prevading paternalism, where the company had control over every aspect of a worker's life. The miner's situation was described by one observer as follows: "He cannot escape the dependent position in which it places him. The coal company touches his life at every point. If there is a playground for his children, it is because the coal company has generously supplied it. If the prices charged him for food at the company store are reasonable, it is because the coal company decrees it. If the physical aspects of his life, on the whole, are tolerable, it is because he is fortunate enough to have a beneficient employer."[26]

The company maintained the right to determine what persons a worker could have in his home and to evict him at any time. The company store system also kept the worker heavily dependent on the company. A black miner described the situation as follows: "There is some things that we cannot stand for. I was raised a slave. My master and mistress called me and I answered, and I know the time when I was a slave, and I felt just like I feel now."[27] It is clear that the extent of company control and dominance was one of the crucial issues that led to the strike.[28]

As to a gap between expectations and achievements, it appears that earnings had been increasing for several years before dipping sharply in 1919.[29] This may have created a "J-curve" effect. As to social dominance, the subordination experienced by the miners at work and in the company towns was inconsistent with the status they experienced in the larger society. How much they were dependent upon their employers was dramatically emphasized by the employer response to the first union organizing efforts. This response included firing employees and evicting them from their homes if they showed any inclination to join the union.[30]

Union organizing in Mingo County was immediately prompted by the failure of these miners to obtain the same wage increases given in the northern West Virginia fields, accompanied by a wage cut. The initial organizing was not preceded by any effort to peaceably obtain their goals. Instead, there was a brief spontaneous strike. The union was approached by disgruntled miners. It issued a charter to them. The rapid organizing of several thousands workers immediately followed. The companies responded by firing and evicting suspected union sympathizers. A meeting was held in Mingo County in June, 1920, which attracted 4,000 miners. From this meeting the union attempted to carry to the employers a demand for wages and conditions equal to those in the northern West Virginia field. The employers refused to recognize the existence of the union or to receive its demand. On July 1, the miners struck for the claimed purpose of maintaining the unity of some 2,700 discharged miners.[31]

Inhibiting conditions were not present to any significant degree. Although it would seem that grounds for overwhelming fear of the employers might have been present, Mingo County miners are not known for reluctance to engage in conflict. While it would be an exaggeration to say that they are utterly fearless, the history of "Bloody Mingo" would lead one to believe that they would not be much inclined to be overwhelmed by fear. Norms favoring collective action were common currency in the coal fields. A history of previous strikes, mine wars, and marches is evidence of this.

The Mingo County, West Virginia, miners, like the Pullman workers, lived in company towns. They had common associations in the religious and social organizations of the towns as well as in the "beer joints." Blood relationships formed a wide network among miners in the West Virginia hollows. In addition, the nature of the work lent itself to the formation of close bonds among the miners who worked together, whatever their color or background. Solidarity and cohesiveness characterized the coal miners. They are a classic case of Kerr and Siegel's "isolated mass."[32]

Several conditions gave the miners grounds for hope. There were large numbers of them. Communication networks were strong and secure. Organizing and striking were legal. From the perspective of those who were powerful in the community, however, it would have taken something approaching a modification of fundamental values to accept a union of miners.[33] As to instrumentality, the evidence is mixed. Unionized miners had higher wages. Whether their organizing was likely to produce the same result was more problematic, given the strong resistance to the union by the Mingo County employers. They did have substantial resources mobilized for collective action by the United Mine Workers of America.

Saliency seems to have been provided by a wage cut combined with pay increases for other miners. Local leaders may have also substantially contributed to this. Organizational exit was virtually impossible for miners without leaving their home community and kin. This is generally an especially unappealing option for mountain miners.

It is not particularly difficult to speculate as to how this strike might have been avoided. Obviously the extension of the wage increase given other miners to these miners would have prevented the development of an expectations/achievements gap as to material outcomes. Yet, there was long-standing social dominance deprivation that might have continued to keep the miners in motion. Given the favorable facilitating conditions and lack of inhibiting conditions, the eventual occurrence of industrial conflict seems to have been nearly inevitable.

Organization of the Marinette Knitting Mill

Organizing of the employees of the Marinette Knitting Mill, in Marinette, Wisconsin, took place in 1950. One reason that it is a useful subject for the application of the integrative theory is that it was well documented in a classic study by Bernard Karsh.[34] This study captures many of the subtleties and individual motivations that are not ordinarily available with respect to an organizing campaign.

There were both material and social dominance roots to the Marinette employee's organizing. According to Karsh, "an overwhelming majority of the workers were dissatisfied with their level of earnings."[35] Although there had been recent increases in their guaranteed minimum wages, piece-work rates had remained constant for a number of years. There were also problems with the assignment of work, which affected the opportunities of workers for earnings.

Social dominance problems constantly appeared in statements of employees as to why they had joined the union. Several spoke of being "pushed around."[36] One employee described being sworn at and called a "Polack" by a supervisor who was a cousin of the company's president. The employee believed that the supervisor knew that he was so dependent on his wages that he couldn't quit in response to being "pushed around."[37] Employees recounted occasions on which they had been "bawled out."[38]

There is some direct evidence of an expectations/achievements gap with respect to material outcomes. As one worker said, "All of us have friends who work in other factories around here and my gosh, sometimes when we compare paychecks, we were almost ashamed to show ours."[39] Another employee told the interviewer that he found out what others were making in the same trade, both in other towns and in the community in which he lived, and realized that his wages compared very unfavorably to theirs.

It appears there was also an expectations/achievements gap related to social dominance. Supervisors played favorites and generally gave workers the impression that they were treating them in a highly arbitrary fashion. Most American workers are likely to have expectations of more egalitarian treatment.

One of the most interesting aspects of the Karsh study is his evidence of the peaceable efforts of the employees to obtain desired material and social dominance outcomes. A number of employees said that when work problems arose with their supervisors the supervisors made no effort to solve them. One worker said, "They wouldn't listen to you. They would say, like they would say so many times—'If you don't like it, you know what you can do. There is the door.'"[40] Another employee described an incident where a group of workers went to see the superintendent about holiday pay. The employee stated that he knew that a group of "girls" in another department had been discharged for complaining to the superintendent in a group, but decided to try it anyway. The superintendent told them that the problems with pay came from the fact that they were not working hard enough. This employee, who was spokesman for the group, became very angry. The superintendent told him, "John, if you don't like it, there's the door." The worker's reaction was, "In my mind, that's where the union started for me."[41] There was a regular pattern of workers complaining, sometimes individually, sometimes in groups, and being met by a management invitation to leave if they didn't like their jobs.

A response of overwhelming fear was apparently avoided by the skillful work of the union organizers in keeping the campaign a secret until large numbers of workers were signed up. This may have been the difference between the successful campaign of 1950 and an unsuccessful one in 1947. Furthermore, there was no problem in identifying the employer as the source of the frustration.

Conditions inhibiting collective aggressive action were absent. Fear of punishment for organizing was avoided by the organizers keeping the identity of union adherents secret until the organizing was nearly complete.[42] As noted above, employees at least had the safety of numbers when it became known that they had joined the union. Norms supporting collective action were supplied to many of the semiskilled female workers by their union-member husbands. One worker said that her husband told her to "go out and work with the organizers because the union was trying to do the right thing."[43]

The facilitating condition of love appears to have been present. The Marinette Knitting Mill employees appear to have been composed of highly cohesive subgroups. These subgroups consisted of male skilled craftsmen and female semiskilled workers.[44] Within those subgroups ties of friendship were common. The subgroups were linked together by the union organizers.

Hope of success was provided by several conditions. First, a secure and effective communication network was established by the organizers. Second, in addition to the resources of the union doing the organizing, support was provided by other trade union organizations in the city and by a Catholic bishop.[45] Third, the success of other unions in their community, whose membership included the husbands of the female workers, may have led these workers to believe that the union would be instrumental in producing desired results. Fourth, although fundamental values of the managers were at stake, community values were reasonably consistent with collective aggressive action by workers. Sixth, the employee group was fairly large.

The chief condition giving rise to saliency was the skillful action of the national union organizers. This was considerably enhanced by the work of local leaders who were discovered by the national organizers.[46]

What are the conditions that might have prevented the organizing from taking place? A crucial factor appears to have been relative deprivation as to pay. Had the employees been paid consistently with other workers in the same community, organization would have been less likely. However, there was also a social dominance gap. This, by itself, may well have led the workers to readiness for aggressive action. Closing this gap would have required a major reorientation of the way that the firm operated on the shop floor.

Had the company been able to maintain the climate of fear that prevented earlier organizing, the organizing may not have taken place. Surveillance of the kind practiced by Ford Motor Company and other employers in the 1920s and 1930s might have made it possible for the collective response to have been repressed. This, of course, would have been illegal, and those were the innocent days when it was still believed that the National Labor Relations Act protected workers from this kind of abuse.

The Memphis Sanitation Strike

The Memphis, Tennessee, sanitation workers strike of 1968 was one of the most dramatic strikes in recent history. It involved a conjunction of the civil rights and labor movements and led to the tragic assassination of Martin Luther King, Jr. Unlike the Charleston Hospital Strike the following year, it was successful. Very importantly for our purposes, it was the subject of a thorough study by F. Ray Marshall and Arvil Van Adams, the purpose of which was to "identify the major contributing factors that led to this dispute and its resolution."[47]

The Memphis Sanitation Strike had both material and social dominance roots. It appears, however, that the social dominance roots were the most important. On the material side, the black Memphis sanitation workers were poorly paid. In addition, the incident that immediately gave rise to the strike involved the refusal by the city to pay black sanitation workers for work missed on a rainy day, while paying white workers in similar job classifications.[48]

One has to be greatly impressed by the centrality of social dominance issues to the strike. Even the pay-connected incident involved an affront to the dignity of the black workers. The crucial issue of strike was "recognition."[49] Recognition implied more than the mere technical status of a labor organization. It implied the recognition of the black workers as having dignity and being worthy of dealing on an equal basis with the white city government. It was clearly a matter of black dignity.[50] A constant theme of the strike was the slogan "I'm a Man" that strikers carried on their placards.[51]

The importance of the social dominance issues was stated dramatically by Baxton Bryant, director of the Tennessee Council of Human Relations, who was deeply involved in the strike. When asked to contrast the economic issues of the strike with those involving human dignity, he replied:

> "I think the human dignity issue would override five to one. I don't think the economic issues . . . this is where the mayor made his bad mistake, he didn't see this thing for what it was. This business of 'I'm a Man' I think is one of the most marvelous things. The picture I saw happen illustrates this. The day after Martin was assassinated, and you had the tanks rolling down the street, there was this little black man picketing with a sign 'I Am A Man' walking on the sidewalk with a big old tank with all armaments down. This was all you could see, this little man and the tank. I think it was one of the most beautiful things I've ever seen. Here something had happened to this little man that this tank with all its size and guns didn't scare him. To me, this was the overriding issue. The others were important, but they would never have been settled, and neither will they in America until the first issue is settled—the dignity and acceptance of the individual."[52]

There were expectations/achievements gaps with respect to both material and social dominance outcomes. Materially, workers saw other employees of the city, such as police and fire fighters, receiving raises while they did not.[53] In the incident involving discrimination against them with respect to rain pay, the treatment of white employees probably determined their expectations as to treatment in this respect. With respect to expectations involving social dominance, the civil rights movement, which had made great strides in the South in the 1960s, had raised expectations of blacks in general. In Memphis, in particular, there had been desegregation of schools and considerable progress in the elimination of racial discrimination in employment.[54]

The sanitation workers did attempt to resolve their problems by peaceful means. With respect to the issue of rain day pay, they complained about their treatment and even received some amelioration of it.[55] In addition, prior to the strike call the local union president met with the city's director of public works and wrote a letter to the mayor in an attempt to resolve the issues.[56]

There is no indication that any of the required conditions for discontinuance of outcome pursuit were present. The sanitation workers did not have grounds to be overwhelmed by fear of employer action. They had no problem identifying the city government as a frustrator. This identification was probably facilitated by the presence of a mayor who was perceived to be antiblack as well as antiunion.[57] At the level of collective aggressive action, it appears that there were not powerful inhibiting conditions. The workers might have had some reason to fear employer retribution. There is no indication, however, that the employer intended this. The norms prevailing in the black community were highly supportive of collective action, given the strength of the civil rights movement and its norms of solidarity and collective action by blacks.

The Memphis sanitation workers shared membership in a segregated black community in a southern city. They were homogeneous as to race and social class. They were highly segmented vertically, to use the Zald and Berger terminology. They were all in a subordinate position in a white society. They had available the religious and social organizations of the black community which provided support to the community's members.

The sanitation workers formed a fairly large employee group. Although the strike was illegal, they probably perceived striking as an open avenue for agitation, and as instrumental, given the success of other public employee strikes. They had a solid communication network secure from white penetration. Through the union and the general civil rights movement, resources of considerable magnitude were brought to bear on their behalf. On the other hand, they were in a situation of having to fundamentally modify the values of the local society, which placed a heavy burden upon them. The mayor's insistence that he did not want to be the first southern mayor to recognize a union is some evidence of this.

Saliency was provided by a mobilizing event. The discriminatory treatment regarding rain day pay provided the spark. There also seems to have been an absence of any other channels for the workers to pursue their goals effectively.

What are the conditions under which the strike might have been avoided? It appears that the key to the strike was existing social dominance achievements rendered unacceptable by rising expectations. The civil rights movement was an obvious source of these expectations. The rise of the labor movement among public employees may have been another. Recognition in a broad sense would have avoided the strike; indeed, once this was achieved, the other terms of the settlement the workers were willing to accept were quite modest.

The Charleston Hospital Strike

In 1969, black employees of the Medical College Hospital of Charleston, South Carolina, organized and struck. This received a great deal of national publicity. Like the Memphis strike of the previous year, it was strongly linked to the civil rights movement. It is rather well documented as to causes.[58]

The *organizing* of the Charleston Hospital employees was sparked by a social dominance-related incident. A white supervisor summarily ordered a small group of black nurse's aides and licensed practical nurses to perform patient care without observing the custom of showing them the patients' charts. This attack on their traditional degree of professional respect caused these workers to refuse to perform the work. They left work and were fired. Although the incident was eventually settled by the intervention of black community leaders, it led to the institution of regular meetings by a group of employees.[59]

At the meetings of the original group of employees, the social dominance theme of the civil rights movement, "I am somebody," was prevalent. The organizing of other workers was conducted in secret through an all-black communications network. One leader described their purpose in forming a formal organization to prevent being "picked off one by one." According to her, they were trying to protect their jobs.[60] She couldn't recall when the idea of a union came up, but felt that "It's a union whenever people get together."[61] Contact was made with a local of the Retail, Wholesale and Department Store Workers Union (RWDSU), which represented hospital workers in New York. Hospital management, learning that something was afoot, offered to meet with randomly selected groups of employees and proposed an extra holiday on Robert E. Lee's birthday.

Local 1199 of the RWDSU, the New York hospital workers' local, was at this same time considering expanding its range of organization. An officer of Local 1199 visited Charleston and was overwhelmed with the response of the Charleston workers. Subsequently, the union committed itself to organizing the Charleston hospital employees.

The *strike* was precipitated by the failure of a meeting with hospital management called at the urging of the mayor of Charleston.

This meeting was an attempt by the workers to settle the matter peaceably. Management first attempted to pack the meeting with proemployer workers. When this failed, it refused to meet with worker representatives, frustrating the employees in their attempt at a peaceful settlement. The next day twelve union activists were fired; one day later, the strike began. It involved two demands—union recognition and the return to work of the twelve fired employees.[62]

The hospital strike occurred at a time of broad change in Charleston, which had been economically stagnant since the Civil War. In the late 1960s, the growth of defense-related industries, trade and tourism, meant Charleston was becoming more prosperous, and expectations of hospital workers, as well as other workers, were probably rising. Yet the wages of hospital workers continued to be very low.[63] The civil rights movement had brought to blacks new feelings of self-worth and the expectation of being treated with respect. Yet the black workers in the Charleston hospital could both experience and observe "racial subordination" at their places of employment.[64] The racially based subordination at work was clearly the doing of the employer, but was consistent with practices elsewhere in the community. It was only with the clear emergence of the employer as a frustrator that the organizing and strike occurred.

It would seem that there were grounds for fear which might have been the overwhelming response to this frustration. This, indeed, may have been what the hospital's administrator intended. That it did not occur is a tribute to the courage of these workers.

Some conditions capable of inhibiting collective aggressive action seem to have been present. There were certainly grounds for employees to believe that they would suffer punishment for engaging in industrial conflict. On the other hand, there were strong norms supporting collective aggressive action flowing from the civil rights movement.

Like the Memphis sanitation workers, the Charleston hospital workers were the members of a highly segregated black community. They were segmented vertically into this community. They shared a position at the bottom of society. They participated in the various social, religious, and political groups that made up the black community. These organizations supported them in many areas of their lives. Ties of friendship appear to have existed fairly widely among them.

There were some grounds for hope of success. The communication network was effective and securely shut out white penetration. The employee group was large. Resources were mobilized through the union and national and local civil rights groups. Yet, the burden of fundamentally modifying values was very heavy. The strike as an avenue of agitation was illegal, although it had been used successfully by public employees outside of South Carolina. Furthermore, the instrumentality of the collective aggressive response must have appeared somewhat doubtful, given the strength of the ruling social classes in Charleston.

Saliency was provided by the attack upon customary respect levels, and by the firings and refusals to meet. Mobilization was also provided by some extraordinary local leaders as well as national union leaders and, eventually, national civil rights leaders. It appears that no other effective channels of protest were available.

The organizing might not have taken place if the rising social dominance expectations had been timely met. This was probably the key to the organizing of these workers. The strike might not have occurred if the employer had made some effort to avoid frustrating employee efforts to achieve some amelioration of their conditions. Even in the presence of frustration, if Local 1199 had not been present, or had the civil rights leaders not been available, a strike might not have occurred.

The Minnesota Community College Strike

The Minnesota Community Strike of 1979 was much less dramatic than those previously discussed. It is an example of a strike that took place in the process of collective bargaining. Although it was the first strike of college faculty in the state of Minnesota, it was both authorized by law and conducted by a worker organization extant for a number of years. It was documented by a paper written by John P. Oldendorf, then a graduate student in industrial relations at the University of Minnesota, a community college teacher.[65]

The roots of the strike were entirely material. Salary was the only major issue involved in the negotiations leading to the strike.[66] It appears that an expectations/achievements gap was created by the history of salary determinations for community colleges and by the structure of salaries for college faculty within the state of Minnesota. During the period between the initial organization of community college faculty (1973) and the strike (1979), community college faculty salaries had dramatically improved. Not only had they improved on an absolute basis, but also relative to other groups of university and college teachers in the state. Traditionally, salaries at the University of Minnesota had been the highest in the state, followed by the state universities, and then by the community colleges. In 1979, the average community college salaries and average salaries in the other higher educational institutions were as follows: the University of Minnesota, $22,814; state universities, $19,116; community colleges, $18,404.[67]

In 1973, because of unexpected increases in the cost of living and the inclusion of a cost-of-living adjustment clause in their contract, community college faculty salaries came to exceed those in the state universities. As a result, in the 1975 contract the legislature rejected a cost-of-living adjustment clause and froze community college salaries for the period 1976–1977, in order to reestablish salary differentials among the state systems. In 1977, contract negotiations came to an impasse and the dispute went to arbitration. The arbitrators awarded the community college faculty a generous settlement of an 18 percent pay increase over two years. The legislature rejected this arbitration award and reduced it to the 14 percent increase received by the state university faculty that year.[68] In 1979, the Minnesota Community College Faculty Association (MCCFA) and the state reached an agreement on a 14 percent pay increase over two years. They could not, however, agree on the base to which the increase would be applied. The faculty demanded that the increase be applied to the salary schedule that would have existed if the legislature had not lowered the 1977 arbitration award. The state refused to do this. The MCCFA took a strike vote and received 90 percent support for the strike from those faculty who voted.[69] In accordance with the vote, they struck.

Community college teachers had their expectations raised by the 1977 arbitration award, and by a high inflation rate, which was 13 percent per year at the time of the 1979 negotiations.[70] They attempted to resolve this gap by the peaceable pursuit through collective bargaining. They were frustrated in this by the state's refusal to meet their demands.

There is no reason to believe that any of the conditions for discontinuance of the pursuit of outcomes were present. The teachers had no reason to be overwhelmed by fear of employer retribution, given both the legal and social contexts in Minnesota. The identification of the employer as the frustrator was facilitated by the fact that the employer's argument was that it *would not* pay, not that it *could not* pay.

At the collective aggressive action stage, there were no serious inhibitions. The teachers had no reason to believe that they would be punished for engaging in collective action. Although it might have been the case at one time, in 1979 there were no norms prevailing among college teachers in Minnesota that especially mitigated against their taking the collective action of a strike.

The Minnesota community college teachers formed a relatively homogeneous group. Although separated by distance and fields of expertise, they were united by their common occupation of a special niche in the higher education system. They were segmented from other parts of the system by credentials and their exclusive focus on teaching. Yet they occupied the special position of college teachers in their communities. That some feeling of mutual affection existed among them is shown by the fact that teachers who participated in the strike generally felt that solidarity among community college teachers was very important to them.[71]

The teachers had some grounds for hope of success. The employee group was large. No modification of fundamental values was required. The strike was a legal avenue of protest. Resources were mobilized by their union, and by the Minnesota Education Association, with which they were affiliated. However, they did have problems with communication, given the wide geographic dispersion of the colleges.

Saliency was provided by reaching the stage in the collective bargaining process where a strike was the expected next step. This event provided mobilization. Other channels had proved unavailing, as bargaining had not provided the desired result and the employer had refused to go to arbitration. Organizational exit would have been extremely costly for these teachers, as alternative employment at this level was essentially unavailable.

What conditions might have caused the strike not to occur? It appears that the strike might not have taken place if the expectations/ achievements gap on salaries had been prevented or closed. Had community college salaries been consistent with the terms of the 1977 arbitration award, there would have been no gap between material expectations and achievements. Had the community college teachers been persuaded that their expectations should be a reasonable position relative to other groups of college and university teachers in the state, and that they already possessed such status, they might have had lower expectations. Once an impartial arbitration panel decided that their salaries should be at a certain level, however, is highly unlikely that they could have been convinced that their high expectations were unreasonable. Of course, had the state agreed to meet the community college teachers' demands, there would have been no blocking, and therefore no readiness for aggressive action.

Testing the Hypotheses

This section will systematically apply the hypotheses to the instances of industrial conflict that we have analyzed above. This should provide us with some indication of whether these instances provide any evidence that either supports or detracts from these several hypotheses.

The First Hypothesis

H_1: In any instance of industrial conflict material or social dominance roots are present.

In all of the cases that we have analyzed there were either material or social dominance roots, or both. The Pullman Strike had roots in both material resources and social dominance. On the material resources side, we found low absolute levels of wages, recent wage cuts and high rents, all squeezing the worker economically. On social dominance, there were numerous conditions, such as espionage, an oppressive and arbitrary officialdom, favoritism, and other conditions, which led workers to use terms such as "serfs" to speak of themselves.

In the West Virginia Mine War, there were also both social dominance and material roots. There, however, the material roots may have been crucial, as it was those which led the workers to first take action and organize.

In the Marinette Knitting Mills organizing both material and social dominance grounds existed. There were problems both with earnings and with being "pushed around," which led to union organization.

Both the Memphis Sanitation Strike and the Charleston Hospital Strike had social dominance roots. Although economic matters may have been involved, the issues appear to have primarily related to human dignity.

The Minnesota Community College Strike was entirely economically rooted. This strike appeared more free of social dominance roots than any of the others examined.

The Second Hypothesis

H_2: In any instance of industrial conflict, an actual or threatened gap between employee expectations and achievements as to material resources or social dominance is present.

In all of the cases examined, it would appear that there was a gap between worker expectations and achievements as to material or social dominance outcomes. Our strategy for determining this is similar to the one employed by James C. Davies. This involves identifying and measuring plausible grounds for expectations, along with information on achievements. Although this is hardly as quantitatively rigorous as some other strategies, it appears from our review of the broad relative deprivation literature that it is the most useful approach.

In the Pullman Strike wages were cut below existing levels. Whatever one already has may form the clearest basis for what one expects. A cut below existing levels would almost inevitably create a gap between expectations and achievements. With respect to social dominance, it is fairly clear that the Pullman employees, like most American workers, expected to be treated in something other than an "un-American" or "feudal" way. There had been a long-standing gap at Pullman between worker expectations and achievements in this regard.

In the West Virginia Mine War there had been a decline in earnings after several years of growth. This created a "J-curve" situation: workers expected earnings to rise, but they fell. In addition, other miners received substantial pay increases, giving rise to expectations that the Mingo County miners would receive the same increases. This expectation was not achieved. With respect to social dominance, American workers expect to be treated in a reasonably egalitarian fashion. What the miners described as "slavery" in the mines failed to meet those expectations.

In the case of the Marinette Knitting Mill organizing, employee expectations concerning wages were affected by the earnings of other workers in the community. There is ample evidence that many of the Marinette employees recognized that their wages were substantially lower than those of other industrial workers in the same community. As to social dominance, their expectations were apparently based upon the general belief of American workers that they are entitled to be treated fairly and accorded some dignity. The female workers with husbands who were union members may have had their expectations raised by the better treatment their husbands received.

In both the Memphis Sanitation Strike and the Charleston Hospital Strike social dominance expectations had been increased by the civil rights movement and by generally improving conditions for blacks in the United States. Neither of these groups of workers had seen their social dominance achievements increase in accordance with these rising expectations. The Memphis sanitation worker who carried a placard declaring "I Am a Man," obviously believed that his expectations for being treated with respect and dignity were not being met. The same theme was present in the Charleston case.

The role of the expectations/achievements gap is fairly clear in the Minnesota Community College Strike. Expectations as to salaries had been increased above achievements by the 1977 arbitration award. This may have been exacerbated by the high rate of inflation.

The Third Hypothesis

H_3: In any instance of industrial conflict there exists either (1) frustration; (2) threat; or (3) rational calculation of advantage.

In all of these cases there was frustration. The Pullman Strike, and West Virginia Mine War, and the Charleston Hospital Strike also involved threat.

Frustration

In the Pullman Strike, the workers met with the company president in an attempt to peacefully obtain their desired outcomes. This attempt was frustrated by the company refusing to grant most of their demands and then behaving in a way that made it clear there was no serious chance of their peaceful actions being successful.

In the case of the West Virginia Mine War, the employees attempted to present their demands to the employers prior to striking and were frustrated by the employers' refusal to meet their representatives. Only then did the full-scale strike occur. In the Marinette Knitting Mill organizing, numerous unsuccessful peaceable efforts by individual employees and informal groups preceded the formation of the union.

In the Memphis strike, employees were frustrated when their representatives were unsuccessful in an attempt to obtain the expected rain pay. In the Charleston case, it was only after management frustrated employee efforts by a refusal to meet amd discuss grievances that the strike was called. The Minnesota Community College Strike took place only after the frustration of peaceable efforts to achieve their expected achievements through collective bargaining.

Threat

In the Pullman case, the discharge of several employees who had complained about the superintendent probably constituted a general threat to employee job security. Such a threat to the job itself is a threat to the job-derived outcomes of material resources. Arbitrary termination of the employment relationship is also an extreme assertion of social dominance that threatens existing levels of this outcome.

The discharges in the Pullman case constituted an attack on those who were discharged. They also constituted a threat that what happened to them could happen to others as well. This, of course, is often the message intended by employers who discharge union activists.

The wage cut that occurred in the Pullman case is also the sort of action that would normally constitute an attack. We would, therefore, expect it to cause workers to move along the threat path directly to a readiness for aggressive action. In this case, however, the employees reacted to this as if it were an ordinary event that created an expectations/achievements gap, stimulating only more intense pursuit of the outcome. They took action only after being frustrated in this pursuit. This could mean that the distinction between the threat and frustration-aggression paths of model cannot be made. But hard economic times had caused the workers to lower their expectations as to wages, meaning that a wage cut was a much less severe threat than it would ordinarily have been.

The West Virginia Mine War forms an interesting contrast to Pullman. There, as in Pullman, the spark for the initial organizing was a wage reduction. In West Virginia, however, this appeared to operate, as expected, by the threat path. Unlike the Pullman situation, workers had no reason to lower their expectations, as unionized miners had just been given a wage *increase*. Under these circumstances they moved directly to a readiness for aggression, without first attempting a peaceable solution.

Threat was also present in the Charleston organizing: the attack upon customary deference to workers' professional status and the firing of workers who refused to accept this. Before the strike itself a threat was posed by the firing of the twelve union activists. As argued above, the firings can be viewed as a threat to the whole employee group.

The Fourth, Fifth and Sixth Hypotheses

H_4: In any instance where there is an open and severe threat by the employers to employees' expected levels of social dominance or material outcomes, industrial conflict will occur, given the absence of the inhibiting conditions and the presence of the facilitating conditions.

H_5: Instances exist where the presence of rational calculation of advantage, combined with an absence of inhibiting conditions and the presence of the facilitating conditions, leads to industrial conflict. (Insufficient evidence to confirm or deny in our cases)

H_6: In any instance where the following conditions exist, industrial conflict will occur: (1) the peaceful pursuit of expected levels of social dominance or material outcomes where an expectations/achievements gap exists; (2) blocking of the achievement of these outcomes by the employer; (3) ready identification of the employer as the frustrator; (4) the absence of overwhelming fear; (5) the absence of the inhibiting conditions; (6) the presence of the facilitating conditions.

We have already concluded that either threat or frustration, or both, existed in all of the cases examined. In all there is proof of an expectations/achievement gap. This leaves us with the necessity of speaking to conditions (3) and (4) of H_6, which apply only to it, and to the inhibiting and facilitating conditions shared by both H_4 and H_6.

Condition (3) of H_6, ready identification of the employer as the frustrator, is present in all of our cases. In Pullman it was the realization of this condition that finally brought on the strike. The Pullman employees at first believed the company's assertions that wage cuts were the fault of economic conditions. It was only when the company's claim lost credibility that they struck.

In the Marinette, Memphis, and Charleston cases the workers should have had no difficulty identifying the employer as the frustrator. This was also true in West Virginia, where the employers refused to even meet with worker representatives. In the Minnesota strike the employer's position was clearly that it would not pay, not that it could not pay.

Condition (4) of H_6, the absence of overwhelming fear, is much more difficult to judge. In several cases, Pullman, West Virginia, and Charleston, it would seem that there were strong grounds for fear on the part of employees. Although it seems reasonable to believe that fear is capable of overcoming readiness for aggressive action against the employer, there is evidence to the contrary in our cases.

The inhibiting conditions posited by the theory are, (1) fear of punishment; and, (2) norms contrary to collective aggressive action. Fear of punishment fares rather poorly as an important condition. It would seem that grounds for it were strongly present in some cases; however, it is where these grounds were present that the attempts at organizing and striking were *unsuccessful.*

The absence of norms contrary to collective action fares a bit better. With the possible exceptions of the Pullman and Minnesota strikes, all of our instances of industrial conflict took place in the presence of strong norms favoring aggressive collective action. Even in the Pullman strike, the new American Railway Union may have provided this. In Minnesota, given the local social and political climate, norms contrary to collective aggressive action were probably absent.

As to the facilitating conditions, the results are mixed. Conditions relating to love appear to be crucial. The provision of saliency by mobilizing persons or events is observable in all of our cases. Yet industrial conflict appears to occur even where conditions leading to hope of success are rather weak.

In the Pullman strike the workers had the conditions for mutual affection created by close association in a small company town. The same was true of the West Virginia miners. In addition, the miners had strong blood ties and close bonds arising from the work itself. The Memphis and Charleston workers were part of a segregated and cohesive black community which had become newly sensitized to its common bonds by the civil rights movement. In the Marinette organizing cohesive subgroups existed.

The Minnesota community college teachers shared a special occupation. In this case, however, the existence of love conditions may have been less important, given the relatively routine nature of the incident of industrial conflict. This may generally be the case in a strike at the expiration of a collective bargaining agreement. It may be for organizing that the love condition is of greatest importance.

In Pullman, saliency was provided by mobilizing events that showed the bad faith of the company and by the rumor of a planned lock-out. In West Virginia, repressive company actions and energetic local leadership performed this function. In Memphis, it was an instance of pay discrimination. In Charleston, it was disrespectful treatment, firings, and refusals to meet, along with the work of active local and national union leaders. In Minnesota, it was the reaching of the strike stage of the collective bargaining process.

It was often the case that other channels of protest had either already proved unavailing or simply appeared to be useless. The saliency condition of difficulty of exit is difficult to identify. More information on local labor market conditions would have been highly useful in this regard. Further investigations should probably include such data.

In all of the cases, it appears that the hope conditions of a large employee group, good communication, and the mobilization of resources were present. However, in Pullman, West Virginia, Charleston, Memphis, and perhaps Marinette, the modification of fundamental values was required. In Charleston and Memphis the avenue of agitation was, at least legally, closed.

The effects of instrumentality perceptions are difficult to judge. This may be because of the inappropriateness of this methodology for measuring this. Direct perceptual measures may be required to speak to this.

The absence, or weakness, of hope conditions did not prevent industrial conflict from occurring in our cases. However, in those cases in which hope conditions were missing the industrial conflict was often unsuccessful. It may be, therefore, that the hope conditions chiefly affect the outcome of the instance of industrial conflict rather than its occurrence. It may also be the case that the absence of certain hope conditions reduces the probability of industrial conflict, but does not always prevent it. A different, more conventional, methodology is required to test this last probability.

Conclusions on the Theory's Application

The integrative theory of industrial conflict does appear to be of at least some use in improving our understanding of several instances of industrial conflict. Viewed through its lens, the causes of industrial conflict and the relations among various determinants do seem a bit clearer. It also seems to be the case that the theory's hypotheses do fairly well when tested against the reality of a variety of cases of industrial conflict. It may, therefore, be useful in predicting industrial conflict or its absence.

NOTES

[1]James C. Davies, "Toward a Theory of Revolution," *American Sociological Review* 27, no. 1 (February 1962), pp. 5–19.

[2]James Chowning Davies, "Communications," *American Political Science Review* 73, no. 3 (September 1929), p. 825.

[3]Almont Lindsey, *The Pullman Strike* (Chicago: University of Chicago Press, 1942), p. 90.

[4]Ibid., p. 94.

[5]Samuel Yellen, *American Labor Struggles* (New York: S.A. Russell, 1956), p. 103.

[6]Ibid.

[7]Ibid., pp 104–105; Lindsey, *The Pullman Strike*, pp. 91–94.

[8]Lindsey, *The Pullman Strike*, p. 95.

[9]Leon Stein, ed., *The Pullman Strike* (New York: Arno and The New York Times, 1969), pp. 77–78.

[10]Ibid., p. 24.

[11]Lindsey, *The Pullman Strike*, p. 70.

[12]Stein, *The Pullman Strike*, p. 50; Lindsey, *The Pullman Strike;* p. 64.

[13]Lindsey, *The Pullman Strike,* pp. 30, 85, 86, 90; Yellen, *American Labor Struggles,* pp. 105–106.

[14]Stein, *The Pullman Strike,* p. 33; Lindsey, *The Pullman Strike,* p. 96.

[15]Davies, "Toward a Theory of Revolution."

[16]Yellen, *American Labor Struggles,* pp. 106–108.

[17]Lindsey, *The Pullman Strike,* p. 104.

[18]Yellen, *American Labor Struggles,* p. 108.

[19]Stein, *The Pullman Strike,* p. 36.

[20]Yellen, *American Labor Struggles,* pp. 103–107.

[21]Stein, *The Pullman Strike,* pp. 36–37.

[22]Lindsey, *The Pullman Strike,* pp. 28–29.

[23]Ibid., pp. 122–123.

[24]David P. Jordan, "The Mingo War: Labor Violence in the Southern West Virginia Coal Fields, 1910–1922," in *Essays in Southern Labor History,* ed. Gary M. Fink and Merl E. Reed (Westport, Conn.: Greenwood Press, 1977), p. 107.

[25]Hoyt N. Wheeler, "Mountaineer Mine Wars: An Analysis of the West Virginia Mine Wars of 1912–1913 and 1920–1921," *Business History Review* 50, no. 1 (Spring 1976), p. 83.

[26]Ibid., p. 84.

[27]Ibid., p. 87.

[28]Jordan, "The Mingo War: Labor Violence in the Southern West Virginia Coal Fields, 1910–1922," p. 114.

[29]Wheeler, "Mountaineer Mine Wars: An Analysis of the West Virginia Mine Wars of 1912–1913 and 1920–1921."

[30]Jordan, "The Mingo War: Labor Violence in the Southern West Virginia Coal Fields, 1910–1922," p. 107.

[31]Ibid., pp. 107–108.

[32]Clark Kerr and Abraham Siegel, "The Interindustry Propensity to Strike—An International Comparison," in *Industrial Conflict,* ed. Arthur Kornhauser, Robert Dubin, and Arthur M. Ross (New York: McGraw-Hill Book Co., 1954), pp. 189–212.

[33]Jordan, "The Mingo War: Labor Violence in the Southern West Virginia Coal Fields, 1910–1922," p. 113; Wheeler, "Mountaineer Mine Wars: An Analysis of the West Virginia Mine Wars of 1912–1913 and 1920–1921," p. 88.

[34]Bernard Karsh. *Diary of a Strike,* 2nd ed. (Champaign: University of Illinois Press, 1982.

[35]Ibid., p. 29.

[36]Ibid., pp. 22, 29.

[37]Ibid., pp. 31, 32.

[38]Ibid., p. 41.

[39]Ibid.

[40]Ibid., pp. 32–33.

[41]Ibid., p. 34.

[42]Ibid., pp. 18–22.

[43]Ibid., p. 34.

[44]Ibid., p. 24.

[45]Ibid., pp. 54–56.

[46]Ibid., pp. 21–22, 24.

[47]F. Ray Marshall and Arvil Van Adams, "The Memphis Public Employees Strike," in *Racial Conflict and Negotiations,* ed. W. Ellson Chalmers and Gerald W. Cornick (Ann Arbor: Institute of Labor and Industrial Relations, University of Michigan–Wayne State University, 1971), p. 75.

[48]Ibid., p. 81.

[49]Ibid., pp. 87, 166, 171.

[50]Ibid., pp. 87, 205.

[51]Ibid., p. 177.

[52]Ibid., p. 191.
[53]Ibid., p. 165.
[54]Ibid.
[55]Ibid., p. 81.
[56]Ibid., p. 161.
[57]Ibid., p. 80.
[58]Leon Fink, "Union Power, Soul Power," *Southern Changes* 5, no. 26, (March/April 1983), pp. 1–20.
[59]Ibid., p. 11.
[60]Ibid., p. 12.
[61]Ibid.
[62]Ibid., p. 13.
[63]Ibid., p. 10.
[64]Ibid.
[65]John P. Oldendorf, "The Minnesota State Community College Strike: Spring 1979" (unpublished manuscript, University of Minnesota, 1980).
[66]Ibid., pp. 8–9.
[67]Ibid., p. 5.
[68]Ibid., p. 7.
[69]Ibid., p. 9.
[70]Ibid., p. 7.
[71]Ibid., p. 46.

CHAPTER 9

Making Sense of
Industrial Conflict

theory is based on practice and in turn serves practice—Mao-Tse-Tung,
On Practice, 1937.

In evaluating a theory, the principal question is whether one is any
better off with the theory than without it. It is relatively easy to
string together a theoretical framework of some kind. It is, however,
very difficult to construct such frameworks that "make sense" of the
phenomena addressed. Yet it is only this latter type of intellectual
structure that can usefully "serve practice."

In order to meet such a general criterion of usefulness, a theory
must (1) be coherent and plausible *internally*; (2) work *externally* to
provide explanations for existing findings and improve our understanding of important issues in the field; and (3) predict. The theory's
predictive ability having been considered in the previous chapter,
this final chapter will address itself to the first two requirements.

INTERNAL PLAUSIBILITY OF THE THEORY

In order to conclude that the integrative theory makes sense in
terms of its internal consistency and plausibility, one must be persuaded that each of the five pillars makes sense and that these relate
together in a plausible way.

The first of the pillars is the proposition that innate predispositions do exist in human beings; the second is that material and social
dominance predispositions are among these and are the roots of industrial conflict. Third, the theory is grounded upon the proposition
that a gap between expectations and achievements with respect to
material and social dominance outcomes is ordinarily a necessary
condition for industrial conflict. The fourth pillar is that readiness
for conflict is obtained by individuals operating along any or all of
three paths for readiness for aggressive action: (1) frustration and

254 • Making Sense of Industrial Conflict

aggression, (2) threat, and (3) rational calculation. The fifth pillar proposes that for the aggressive readiness of a group of individuals to be translated into the collective aggressive action (industrial conflict) certain facilitating conditions must be present and certain inhibiting conditions must be absent. If any of these pillars is weak, or if the way they are linked is implausible, the stucture of the theory collapses.

The First Pillar—Innate Predispositions

Acceptance of the proposition that there are innate predispositions that strongly influence human behavior requires one to accept a model of humankind that is at least partly biological. Such a man is not "economic man" who rationally calculates his own pleasure and pain and acts on the basis of this calculus. He is also not "blank paper" man who somehow responds as he has been reinforced to respond. Biological man acts in ways that have been encouraged by the heavy hand of natural selection. When one takes biological man into account, a model of man emerges that includes not only rational calculation and learning by reinforcement, but also behavior according to the "whisperings within."

It is this whole human being who gives institutionally inclined scholars the opportunity to go beyond the limits of the utility theory of the neoclassical economists and the extreme behaviorism of some psychologists. Economic man is clearly conceptualized. He is obviously relevant to many types of human behavior. The same can be said for the blank paper man of the behaviorists. However, the limitations upon these models of man account in major part for the limitations upon their explanatory power. Addition of the biological view may allow industrial relations scholars to leapfrog these schools, and perhaps breathe new life into research in this field of human social behavior.

The logic of natural selection of human behaviors is highly compelling. One has to reject the whole body of biological science in order to reject the notion that natural selection occurs. Furthermore, selection clearly has to do with behavior, as physical characteristics that are not translated into behavior are irrelevant to survival. Behaviors are inherited by all other animals. There is no good reason to believe that man is any different. If one believes that natural selection operates, it seems also that one must believe that behaviors that are inconsistent with survival would disappear as humans engaging in those behaviors would be less likely to pass on their genes.

"Human nature" is defined by characteristics that have been the result of natural selection. These provide "whisperings within" which make certain behaviors attractive to us. As Mary Midgley has argued, to ignore our nature is like "spitting against the wind."[1] It would be difficult to imagine being able to socialize human beings to perform the typical behaviors of, for example, birds or rodents. Yet, it is important to understand that human behavior is not "determined" by predispositions. Human instincts, like those of all higher animals, are "open." They produce behaviors that differ according to the circumstances. They are also balanced by competing instincts. The inclination for aggression is, for example, balanced by the inclination for love and mutual aid.

Those who believe deeply in human reason as "good" are often offended by the notion of human beings operating on some other basis. However, as Konrad Lorenz has suggested, a totally rational man would be a devil, not an angel.[2] As Lorenz also ably argues, unaided reason is like a computer into which no useful information has been fed and that has no motor to make it operate.[3]

One of the chief problems with rational economic man and blank paper man is that they do not tell us what it is that gives pleasure or pain or reinforcement. The rationally calculative view is also inconsistent with the common observation that humans sometimes act without calculating the consequences. This may be because of laziness, instinct, or inability to make calculations with respect to a particular action. Certainly humans act in haste and repent at leisure, at least at times. This being the case, it seems hardly plausible to argue that rationality accounts for all human behavior.

All things considered, a model of man that posits innate predispositions for behavior, along with rational calculation and reinforcement, appears more sensible, usable, and complete than either economic man or blank paper man standing alone. In addition, it is the only view that appears to be consistent with the best scientific knowledge regarding human nature.

The Second Pillar—Material and Social Dominance Roots of Industrial Conflict

The general proposition that industrial conflict has its roots in material resources and social dominance requires two things. First, it assumes that material and social dominance predispositions are relevant to the context of industrial conflict—the industrial relationship. Second, the existence and operation of both material and social dominance roots must be believed.

With respect to the relevance of material and social dominance predispositions to industrial conflict, it is useful to look at the essential nature of the relationship from which this conflict derives. It is, at base, an exchange of a worker's agreement to be on the subordinate end of a social dominance relationship in return for an employer's agreement to provide economic rewards.[4] The employment relationship is rooted both in law and custom. It is reasonably clear that both law and custom dictate a relationship as just described.

The case for a human predisposition to pursue material resources is fairly easy to make. On biological grounds, it would seem that an obvious predisposition of humans, as well as of other animals, is to seek material resources. This is so fundamental for survival that it is hard to imagine how a being without such a predisposition could survive. In addition, as Joseph Schumpeter has argued, the general economic theory about the wish to obtain wealth with as little sacrifice as possible is quite plausible.[5]

The case for social dominance leading to industrial conflict is just as clear but requires a more elaborate discussion. First, it appears rather clear that there is an innate predisposition for the establishment of hierarchies, "pecking orders," among social animals generally. Similar structures can be observed to exist in human social groups. The innateness of social dominance predispositions in human groups is argued for by its universality among humans and our closest relatives and by the plausibility of arguments for the survival function of hierarchies. That hierarchies are universally rational, or universally reinforced, seems unlikely. On the other hand, at least when considered as an open instinct subject to modification according to circumstances, an innate predisposition for social dominance is quite plausible.

One of the effects of seeing the social dominance hierarchy as a product of innate predispositions is that it allows one to see the industrial relationship with a new eye. Insubordination becomes not merely an interference with the rational operation of the firm, but a behavior at odds with a strongly held predisposition of the superior. The behavior of a supervisor in "staring down" subordinates, having "executive bearing," wanting to be "looked up to," wanting to be addressed in terms of deference, receiving high pay in excess of that deserved on a rational basis, and using threats to maintain his or her position, is all fundamental social animal behavior. Use by subordinates of status sex terms such as being "screwed," or "pushed around," a subordinate's pleasure in seeing a foreman get his or her "come uppance" in an arbitration hearing, can be seen as fundamental pieces of social dominance behavior. When these behaviors are seen in this light, they are understood differently than when viewed within other frames of reference. Not only the behaviors, but the intensity with which persons are attached to these behaviors, become more understandable when one sees that these are fundamental "whisperings" that guide our behavior in ways of which we are often unaware.

One finds a great deal of support for the notion of social dominance in the psychology literature. In that literature there is support for both innate predispositions to dominate (or to be free from domination) and subordinance. Sigmund Freud spoke of a "desire for freedom" that is innate with himan beings.[6] The psychological reactance theory of Jack W. Brehm also argues for an innate response to restore freedom if it is taken away.[7] With respect to asserting control over others, Alfred Adler has spoken of a "tendency" toward domination and superiority.[8] This is confirmed by the work of Adolf A. Berle,[9] Rollo May,[10] and David C. McClelland (n Power).[11] It has been argued rather convincingly in the psychological literature that there is a contradictory need for subordinance. This appears clearly from the work of Stanley Milgram.[12] Indeed, Milgram concluded that "obedience is as basic an element in the structure of social life as one can point to."[13] Freud recognized a human "thirst for obedience."[14] This characteristic in human beings who have an "authoritarian personality" has been extensively developed by Eric Fromm and Adorno et al.[15]

Although individuals with authoritarian personalities can be happy as subordinates, others are not. A. H. Maslow discovered long ago that individuals high in "dominance-feeling" are restive in subordinate status.[16] It seems likely that having individuals in subordinate status who have high dominance-feeling would be very likely to produce "status tension."[17] Those with high dominance-feeling might well have high expectations as to social dominance. All things equal, this would make the individuals with these feelings more likely to have a gap between expectations and achievements. It is further true that managers who are high in "n Power," as suggested by McClelland,[18] or "predisposed to dominate," as suggested by Vance Packard,[19] might be inclined to keep the social dominance achievements of their subordinates rather low. Such managers might also be inclined to block attempts by subordinates to improve their social dominance status.

The sociological literature is enlightening with respect to the existence and operation of human social dominance hierarchies. This literature deals with the concept of "authority." Authority entails: (1) subordination of one person's preferences to those of another; (2) "commands"—imperative statements issued by superiors to subordinates; (3) compulsion; (4) the element of "oughtness' or "legitimacy," which involves the subordinate believing that it is "right" that he obey his superior's command; and (5) boundaries. It is interesting to note that the first three elements are consistent with the hierarchies of other social animals. Even the fifth element, boundaries, appears to exist in some animal hierarchies.[20] This, however, is not the case with the element of "oughtness."

It is with respect to the characteristic of "oughtness," or legitimacy, in human hierarchies that we find some especially interesting connections with other parts of the integrative theory. Commands and assertion of dominance that are within the bounds of the superior's "authority" would not be expected to cause an extraordinary amount of status tension. It is when the bounds of oughtness are exceeded that power becomes tyranny and is likely to give rise to resistance. Put another way, the subordinate's expectations with respect to social dominance may be achieved so long as commands fit within the "zone of indifference" or "area of acceptance."[21] If they do not, a crisis of authority may be engendered.[22]

The view that assertions of social dominance outside the range of legitimacy give rise to industrial conflict also links with frustration-aggression theory. That is, even some of the strongest opponents of frustration-aggression theory agree that "unjustified" or arbitrary frustration is likely to lead to aggression. Action that is not within the "zone of indifference" is, by definition, "unjustified." So also are actions contrary to expectations by definition "unjustified" under relative deprivation theory. All of these theories, drawn from different disciplines, come together to support one another at this point.

How can the assertion of social dominance by the giving of commands come to exceed the boundaries of an employee's zone of indifference? This might happen if an employer attempted to control the behavior of an employee beyond the expected boundaries of workspace and work-time. For example, a worker might feel it inappropriate for the employer to attempt to control his personal habits that bear no relation in job performance and are engaged in off work. Closer supervision than that previously maintained might also be deemed illegitimate. This could also be true of a decline in the degree of respect shown to employees by their superiors (as in the case of the Charleston hospital strike) or merely arbitrary treatment. Existing treatment might come to be illegitimate if an employee, because of increased pay or other reasons, gained a higher status in the community in general and perceived this to be inconsistent with the lack of deference at work.[23] Simply living in an egalitarian society might lead an employee to believe that autocratic work relations are illegitimate.[24]

It appears that bureaucratic forms of organization make it less likely that subordinates will perceive commands to be illegitimate. This is because (1) the impersonality of the subordination (to a position rather than to a person), which may be less demeaning; (2) the limited range of bureaucratic authority; and (3) the ideology of efficiency that supports bureaucratic behaviors. As suggested by Reinhard Bendix and others, bureaucracy can be seen as a system of creating expectations of obedience in the work place. In feudal societies the expectations of obedience arose from the general social structure. In an industrial society, subordination at work requires its own justification.[25]

There is an innate predisposition to resist dominance, but there is also one to accept it. The tendency to accept dominance is facilitated by the ideology of bureaucratic authority. However, the tendency to resist may also be facilitated by the bureaucratic ideology where commands are outside the range of bureaucratic legitimacy.

Why is legitimacy a necessary ingredient of a human structural hierarchy? This may be because of the nature of the human animal as a reasoning, imagining beast. Animals such as humans may simply not be willimg to accept mere animal symbols of dominance. As Desmond Morris suggests, these symbols are used, but appear not to be adequate by themselves.[26] The learning, intelligent character of human beings, as described by social learning theorists such as Albert Bandura, perhaps makes it impossible to rely on such symbols.[27] Of course, compulsion (the "primeval canine tooth")[28] is always present in a system of authority as well.

The Third Pillar—Expectations and Achievements

With the exception of cases where individuals move along the rational calculation path to readiness for aggressive action, a gap between the expectations and achievements of workers is a necessary condition for industrial conflict. The occurrence of such a gap is likely to put an individual into rather intensive action to close it. It is the frustration of this action that produces a readiness for aggressive action by means of the frustration-aggression path. As to the threat path, in order to move an individual toward a readiness for aggressive action the threat must be to the individual's *expected* level of achievements.

It is quite important to understand that "expectations" are meant, as defined by Ted Gurr, to be those "values" to which the individual believes that he is *justly entitled.*[29] It is this definition of expectations that places us within the bounds of the strongest area of frustration-aggression theory. There is clear evidence that unjustified or arbitrary frustration is likely to give rise to aggression.[30]

There are a number of sources of employee expectations. These sources include: (1) the achievements of relevant others, (2) the past experience of the individual on these same values, (3) the achievements of the individual on other values or in other settings, (4) achievements of the individual's ancestors, (5) achievements that tradition ascribes to the individual, (6) n Power, (7) dominance-feeling, (8) authoritarian personality, and (9) the individual's past experience in achieving expectations. The salience of expectations with respect to particular outcomes may be determined by: (1) the valence of the particular outcome to the individual, (2) occupation, and (3) the individual's stage on his or her need hierarchy.

It might be useful to consider some examples of how these determinants of expectations could operate in industrial conflict. For instance, achievements of relevant others could lead to an expectations/achievements gap if the wages of those to whom a worker compared himself, those within his "orbit of comparisons,"[31] went up while his did not. As to the individual's own past experience, wages that rise constantly over an extended period, and then drop, can create a gap. This, of course, is the "J-curve" phenomenon observed by James C. Davies.[32] With respect to the individual's achievements in other settings, an individual who has gained high status as a citizen, but remains subject to industrial tyranny, is likely to have an expectations/achievements gap. The achievements of ancestors and tradition can create the same situation, where expectations for equal treatment are high, but the individual's superior begins behaving in a way that implies great dominance.

The person who is high in n Power or in dominance-feeling will experience an expectations/achievements gap at low levels of deference. For such a person, merely being required to call a supervisor "mister" or to park in a less desirable spot than that reserved for supervisors might create a gap. On the other hand, an individual with an authoritarian personality might be willing to tolerate a considerable degree of subordination, and even like it. With respect to the influence of past experience, a worker who has successfully achieved pay increases in the past is likely to feel justly entitled to receive pay increases in the future. On the other hand, a worker who has unsuccessfully tried on many occasions to achieve a pay increase may come to not expect one.

The salience of expectations on particular outcomes might vary. That is, a white collar worker who considers status but not money to be highly valent may not be moved to an intense level of action by failure to achieve the expected level of wages. Also, if a worker is wealthy and has fulfilled needs for food, shelter, and the like, an expectations/achievements gap on wages may not produce intense action.

The Fourth Pillar—Paths to Readiness for Aggressive Action

This pillar contains the proposition that industrial conflict is "aggression." This is argued to be so by definition and also as the only means of capturing the emotive climate that accompanies industrial conflict. It is further argued herein that there is an innate predisposition of human beings to aggress, given certain conditions. Marking the three paths to readiness is an attempt to establish those conditions that might eventually lead to a particular kind of aggressive action—industrial conflict.

The Frustration-Aggression Path

A worker who is intensely pursuing material resources or social dominance at work because of an expectations/achievements gap is predicted to act peaceably, either individually or collectively, to eliminate that gap. If he is blocked (frustrated) in this pursuit, identifies the employer as a source of his frustration, and is not overwhelmed by fear, he is likely to become ready to take aggressive action against the employer.

These predictions are supported by a considerable body of literature on frustration-aggression theory. As noted above, this is not only true of the writings of various apologists for frustration-aggression theory, such as Berkowitz, but also of those of some of its opponents. Even its critics admit that unjustified, severe blocking leads to aggression.[33] This, of course, is precisely what the integrative theory is talking about.

Collective bargaining routinely works in a frustration-aggression mode. Workers articulate their expectations and then try to achieve them peacefully through negotiations. They typically argue for the right to be paid comparably to other workers. It is clear that other workers' pay is important in the expectations-formation process. Employers ordinarily try to persuade workers of their inability to pay. If successful, this would serve to create the perception that any blocking that occurs is not the fault of employers but of outside forces. If, on the other hand, there is a blocking by the employers' voluntary failure to agree, the workers are more likely to engage in a strike.

The Threat Path

Threatening, or actually taking away, the level of social dominance or material outcomes to which the worker believes himself justly entitled is a reasonably clear and noncontroversial path to industrial conflict. For some historical evidence, one only has to look to the many early strikes produced by wage cuts. This was, for example, the case in the classic strike of the Philadelphia Cordwainers.

The Rational Calculation Path

It is reasonably clear that on some occasions workers may simply calculate that aggressive action has more benefits than costs and accordingly become ready for it. It may be that certain workers, such as those in the "strategic" groups identified by Sayles, are more likely to engage in this kind of conduct.[34] Overall, however, it is believed that this path is less likely to be pursued than the others.

It is crucial to the occurrence of industrial conflict that a substantial number of workers become ready for aggressive action at about the same time. They may or may not have reached that readiness through the same path. Indeed, an individual worker may simultaneously pursue more than one path to readiness. Given this readiness, however reached, collective aggressive action becomes possible.

The Fifth Pillar—Collective Aggressive Action

It is the collective aggressive action that we have labeled "industrial conflict" we aim to understand. Although it is engaged in by individuals, it is a collective phenomenon. It is believed not to be, as the convergence theorists hold, simply the sum of individual actions; it is instead a different type of human action. It involves human beings acting in cooperation with one another and not simply moving independently along parallel ruts. In collective action several act as one.

The explanation of action of this type posited by the integrative theory is that it will occur given (1) individual readiness for aggressive action by a number of individuals in a group; (2) the absence of inhibiting conditions; and (3) the presence of facilitating conditions. The inhibiting conditions are relatively straightforward, and are derived from frustration-aggression theory. These are: (1) fear of punishment and (2) holding norms contrary to collective action.

The facilitating conditions are more complicated. A very large body of literature exists on this subject. From that literature I have drawn a list of those conditions that significantly increase the probability of collective action. These can be summarized under the headings of: (1) *love*, (2) *hope*, and (3) *saliency*.

As Freud said long ago, human beings are unlikely to act as a group unless they have some degree of love for one another.[35] The affective relations among members of a group must be positive in order for them to act as a community. Industrial conflict is action by a community, and it requires ties of mutual affection to bind it together. This, I believe, is what is meant by "solidarity." It is also what communication, homogeneity, vertical segmentation, difficulty of exit, friendship or blood relationship, sharing of design for living, and sharing of the same set of subordinate and superordinate relations all have to do with. It may be the absence of this condition that has made organization impossible for members of the desparately poor lumpen proletariat who must spend all their energies on meeting their own individual basic needs. This may also be true for blacks and whites together, and perhaps for women, who may have been more oriented toward the family group than the work group.

Hope of success is probably necessary for, or at least increases the probability of, collective action. This can involve the perceived instrumentality of the action to achieve specific goals, the decreased probability of repression where fundamental values are not challenged, and society's acceptance of industrial conflict as an avenue of agitation. Possessing resources that are mobilized for use by the collectivity is another ground for hope; so is having a large group relatively impervious to outside control.

The remaining facilitating conditions are best placed under the heading of saliency. These include the existence of a mobilizer in the form of a leader, a "founder" in Dahrendorf's terms.[36] Someone must do the work that is required for a collective aggressive response to take place. In addition to furnishing inspiration, the founders do this. Collective aggressive action is also made more salient by the unavailability of other means of protest and the difficulty of escape from the situation by organizational exit.

The Model—Linking the Pillars

The integrative theory essentially holds that industrial conflict is rooted in material resources and social dominance. When an individual employee's expectations with respect to social dominance or material resources are not met, there is a tendency to act with a significant degree of intensity to close the gap between those expectations and their achievement. If this action is blocked by the employer, the individual is likely to become ready for aggressive action. In the alternative, a threat to expected levels of material or social dominance outcomes may lead to such readiness. Also in the alternative, a rational calculation that the benefits of aggressive action exceed the costs may lead the individual to be ready for aggressive action against the employer. This aggressive action is likely to take a collective form in the event that a large proportion of the work group is ready for it, this action is not inhibited, and certain facilitating conditions are present. Possible inhibitors are fear and contrary norms. Facilitating conditions include love, hope, and saliency. Given all of these conditions, collective aggressive action—industrial conflict— is highly probable.

It is suggested that this model is a reasonable explanation of the linkages that lead to, or away from, industrial conflict. These links are all grounded in theory. They are forged from connections provided by the extensive body of literature used to devise the integrative theory. Indeed, it is chiefly the model that performs the integrative function of the theory.

EXTERNAL APPLICATION

Existing Empirical Studies

One strategy for assessing the usefulness and explanatory power of the integrative theory is to try it as a mechanism for analyzing the findings of existing studies. This gives us some notion of whether the integrative theory might be more useful than extant theories in explaining what we already know.

Among the studies considered here are the strike studies and psychology-based studies of union organizing reviewed in Chapter 2. In addition, the literature on "union growth" will be briefly analyzed. This last literature will be discussed as it is presented in a major recent review by Jack Fiorito and Charles R. Greer.[37]

Strike Studies

The strike studies can be placed into three groups: macrolevel, microlevel, and miscellaneous. Although the other groups of studies are believed to be more useful, the macrolevel studies will also be considered in order to see whether some sense can be made of them by considering them in the light of the integrative theory.

Macrolevel Strike Studies

It has been previously argued that a lack of plausible theoretical grounding is one of the main weaknesses of the macrolevel strike studies. If this is the case, it ought to be possible for a sound theoretical framework to at least cast some additional light upon this body of work. Of course, there are severe limitations upon what can be done because of problems with measures and what is believed to be the virtually insurmountable problem of moving from the microlevel to the macrolevel. Nevertheless, it is an interesting challenge to attempt to use the integrative theory to make sense of these findings.

It should be noted at the outset that the greatest strength of strategies utilizing macrolevel variables is that, as Arthur Kornhauser has noted, it may be at the level of society that expectations originate.[38] That is, it is reasonable to argue that the wage expectations of workers are determined, at least in part, by the general economic conditions reflected in macrolevel variables. The integrative theory holds that these expectations are a crucial factor in moving workers toward a readiness for aggressive action. Therefore, at least on this point, there is some conjunction between the macrolevel strike literature and the integrative theory. This notion is also consistent with the arguments of Zelditch et al., that it is the achievements of a "generalized reference group" that determine expectations.[39]

Most of the macrolevel strike studies employ economic variables. Kochan has concluded from a review of these studies that they generally find a positive relationship between the business cycle and the occurrence of strikes.[40] As Kochan notes, this is ordinarily explained in the macrolevel strike literature on the basis of increased union bargaining power in good times. Yet it would seem that increased bargaining power on the part of unions would, by definition, make employers more inclined to agree with union demands and therefore lessen the likelihood of industrial conflict. On the other hand, if one views a prosperous economy as increasing worker expectations in general and not affecting the ability or willingness of all employers to meet those expectations, increasing prosperity might increase the incidence of industrial conflict. It may also be that workers are less fearful of employer retribution in good times, decreasing this inhibition. As argued at length above, things are a great deal more complicated than this. It is, however, interesting that there is some consistency between this macrolevel study result and the integrative theory.

Kochan also concludes that macrolevel strike studies have generally found a negative relationship between real wage growth and strikes.[41] These findings are consistent with a deprivation-based rationale also used by the macrolevel scholars. Real wages going down would, all things equal, also appear to increase the probability of industrial conflict under the integrative model. However, as is the case throughout the macrolevel strike literature, one has the feeling that it is far too simplistic to treat this as a sufficient condition for an increase in industrial conflict.

One of the more frequent findings of the macrolevel strike studies is a negative association between the unemployment rate and strikes. This is consistent with the integrative theory, which argues that worker expectations are affected by their perceptions of the conditions of other workers. If comparable others do not even have jobs, it is less likely that employed workers' expectations would exceed their achievements.

The best of the macrolevel strike studies is by Michael Shalev.[42] Shalev posits a large number of variables, justified on an ad hoc basis, which have relatively plausible rationales. What is lacking, as he concedes, is a model tying them together. This, of course, is what is attempted by the integrative theory. Shalev finds that high product demand and low inventories are associated with higher strike rates. He rationalizes his findings on the basis of greater union bargaining power under these conditions. His explanation, however, runs into the problem that high union bargaining power might equally well be expected to lead to management concessions as to strikes. The effect of a prosperous economy on worker expectations would appear to be a more plausible explanation.

Shalev finds a positive relationship between nominal price rises since the last contract and strikes. He connects price rises with a greater propensity of workers to increase their demands. Again, this propensity can be plausibly tied to increasing expectations or decreasing achievements in real terms. Shalev's findings that greater wage increases by other unionized employees cause more strikes is consistent with the integrative theory's argument that expectations are important and that they are in part determined by the achievements of relevant others. The relationship between declining profits and more strikes is best tied to the employer side of the equation, as he suggests. One would expect declining profits to make the frustration of worker demands by management more likely, as management says "no" with more frequency and more insistence, although this condition might also allow the employer to escape blame for the frustration of outcome pursuit by the employees.

Macrolevel studies utilizing *political* variables are difficult to use because of the weakness of their measures.[43] However, to the extent that we can draw conclusions from these studies, they do seem to provide some support for resource mobilization theory. This theory is incorporated into the integrative model as providing a facilitating condition.

Considering the macrolevel studies in terms of the integrative theory may slightly improve their explanations. Findings gleaned from these studies do appear to be generally consistent with, and analyzable in terms of, the integrative theory. One cannot make too much of this, however, as other findings might also have been consistent with the theory.

Microlevel Strike Studies

The microlevel strike studies have produced more interesting and interpretable results than the macrolevel studies. Kochan summarizes a set of interindustry studies by stating that they have generally found that strikes are more frequent in industries with (1) a lower level of unemployment, (2) a greater proportion of male workers, and (3) a higher proportion of the work force organized.[44] The findings regarding lower levels of unemployment and greater proportions of male workers are explainable in terms of the integrative theory. A low unemployment level in the industry may make it less likely that workers would be inhibited by fear of punitive action by their employers. Losing a job is not so likely where there is a shortage of labor.

A greater proportion of male employees might produce a work force with higher social dominance expectations. Historically, male workers may also have had a higher saliency of material outcomes because of the need to support a family. Furthermore, traditional norms of "lady-likeness" among female employees may have inhibited collective aggressive action by them.

The positive effect on strike rates of a higher percentage of the work force organized is not explainable by the integrative theory because the most obvious reason for this relationship is the greater opportunity for the occurrence of strikes when more workers are organized. The findings of a study by Michael Mauro conducted at the level of the firm are consistent with the integrative theory.[45] Mauro, like the integrative theory, finds expectations to be an important explainer of industrial conflict. Mauro goes on to speak of the diverse expectations of managers and employees, as did some earlier studies, and uses this diversity to explain the occurrence of strikes. This is a logical extension of the integrative theory which is worth pursuing.

One of Arthur Ross' arguments regarding strike trends shares some common ground with the integrative theory.[46] Ross believed that the increasing institutionalization of collective bargaining in many industries would make strikes less frequent. In terms of the integrative theory this can be seen as an increasingly successful use of peaceable means to achieve material and social dominance outcomes desired by employees, although the theory does not speak to whether success will increase.

Robert Stern's interesting study of differences in industrial conflict among cities is somewhat amenable to analysis under the integrative theory.[47] Unlike most other studies, Stern's looks for *patterns* of variables. This would seem to be a good strategy for dealing with such a complex phenomenon. His variables of greatest interest for our purposes are large plant size and "economic vulnerability" (a measure of wage levels in the metropolitan area). A large group of workers is a facilitating condition of the integrative theory. In the integrative theory's terms, high wages in the community would have an upward influence upon worker expectations. In firms unable, or unwilling, to pay high wages, workers might well develop an expectations/achievements gap that would move them toward readiness for aggressive action aginst their employer.

Miscellaneous Strike Studies

Reviewing a large number of miscellaneous strike studies, Kochan concludes that they have a number of findings in common, [48] some interpretable under the integrative theory. For example, the finding that laws protecting the right to strike are associated with more strikes is consistent not only with common sense, but also with the integrative theory's facilitating condition of the availability of the strike as an avenue of protest. However, as illegal strikes occurred in the cases to which we have applied the integrative theory, it is difficult to have much confidence in this as a *necessary* condition.

The relationship between strikes and employer efforts to change bargaining structures may be connected to the threat path of the integrative theory. A change in structure could pose a threat to employees' material resources. The association between employer pattern-leading and strikes may result from an increasing probability of the pattern-leading employer frustrating worker demands. This may be the result of less reliable information about worker expectations being available to pattern-leaders than to pattern-followers. These findings do lead one to believe that an area to which the integrative theory should be extended is the determinants of employer action.

Some of the bargaining-related variables found by Kochan to be significant, such as the vesting of power in negotiators, are arguably related to the ability of the parties to achieve peaceful solutions through collective bargaining and thereby avoid employee frustration. This is very similar to the interpretation I would give the Brett and Goldberg finding that low-strike coal mines were those where peaceful solutions were worked out at the lowest level.[49] The Brett and Goldberg finding that workers strike when they perceive it to be instrumental to get the employer to pay attention to their problems is roughly consistent with the instrumentality condition of the integrative theory.

Union Organizing Studies

Perhaps because the literature is much less extensive, the findings of psychologists studying union organizing attempts have produced clearer and less contradictory findings than the strike studies. It is easier to summarize and work with the variables that have been found to be significant in the organizing studies.

It is relatively clear from these studies that employee "dissatisfaction" is associated with an inclination on the part of a worker to join or vote for a union. Although "dissatisfaction" is not always well defined in these studies, it is reasonably clear that it is at least akin to the existence of the expectations/achievements gap central to the integrative theory. It may be that an expectations/achievements gap is a severe form of dissatisfaction, or is a related construct.

Another fairly clear finding of the organizing studies is that workers are more likely to favor a union if they perceive it to be instrumental to relieving their dissatisfactions. This links to the integrative theory in a number of ways. First, the integrative theory recognizes that instrumentality is an important factor in determining whether industrial conflict will take place. Second, it clearly ties to the rational calculation path to readiness for aggressive action. Third, it is consistent with the purposefulness that is a part of the Berkowitz formulation of frustration-aggression theory. Fourth, it involves identifying the employer as a source of employees' problems, otherwise a union cannot be instrumental in resolving the dissatisfaction. Fifth, it is related to a lack of fear of employer retribution in the event of collective action.

Instrumentality is a useful construct in understanding industrial conflict. It is believed, however, that it must be utilized in the complex manner proposed by the integrative theory in order to provide its maximum explanatory power. Otherwise, one is simply left with rational calculation as an explainer of industrial conflict. This does not appear to be consistent with either the essential nature of industrial conflict or the empirical reality. Linked to a broader theory, instrumentality is a highly useful concept. Standing alone, it is of only limited help in understanding or predicting this phenomenon.

These studies have commonly found that a favorable worker attitude toward unions in general is associated with a higher likelihood of his choosing a union or being favorably disposed toward joining one. In terms of the integrative theory, one can argue that this variable taps a lack of norms contrary to aggressive collective action, which it posits as a condition inhibiting industrial conflict.

There are a few findings with respect to demographics that appear to be fairly consistent across these studies. Generally, it is found that younger workers are more union-prone. In terms of the integrative theory, this may be because they are often the lowest paid workers and have lower achievements. This may be particularly galling to members of a generation reputed to have rather high expectations. The union proneness of blacks and other minority group members may reflect their lower achievements, combined with increasing expectations, norms supportive of collective action and a degree of cohesiveness (love) that comes from strong common bonds.

There is also present in this literature the suggestion that the normal progression of attitudinal and behavioral development is for workers to attempt to peaceably achieve their objectives before turning to organizing.[50] This fits very nicely with the frustration-aggression pattern of the integrative theory.

There has been a recent major review of this literature by Herbert G. Heneman III and Marcus H. Sandver.[51] Heneman and Sandver conclude that the main findings of these studies are: (1) dissatisfied employees are more likely to favor unions; (2) perceived instrumentality of a union increases the probability that the employee will favor it; (3) the larger the size of the election unit, the lower the union victory rate; and (4) employees who view unions more favorably in general are more likely to vote for or support union membership. The third conclusion on unit size is contrary to the integrative theory's facilitating condition of large employee group size. It may be that this facilitating condition is one that should be eliminated from the integrative theory. It may be the case that it is easier for workers to organize themselves in large groups, but that employer resistance is likely to be greater in these same units. It would make sense for employers to be more willing to spend money on union avoidance strategies of various kinds where large groups of employees are involved. Also, there may be a loss of homogeneity in large groups. Perhaps unit size, like organization size, is reflective of such a wide variety of unknown factors that it is useless for analytical purposes.

The need for new theory receives some support from Heneman and Sandver. They argue that "construct clarity would be greatly aided by the development of stronger theoretical frameworks" to support research in this area.[52]

One additional recent study of interest is by Richard B. Freeman.[53] He contends that unions are not organizing very effectively at present because of management opposition and inadequate union efforts. To the extent that management opposition creates increased fear or produces the perception of low union instrumentality, these findings are consistent with the integrative model. Union organizing efforts are connected with both resource mobilization and the presence of a mobilizer, which are facilitating conditions under the integrative theory.

In general, the integrative theory's predictions are consonant with what has been found in the literature on union organizing. However, it must be admitted that this literature poses a major challenge to the integrative theory. It is a challenge because it could be used as a basis for an argument that all that is needed to explain organizing, and perhaps even strikes, is dissatisfaction and instrumentality. Yet it would seem that this explanation is both too simple and too calculative. It is believed that the integrative theory makes the case for the complexity of the phenomenon and the existence of behavioral patterns that cannot be contained under the rubrics of dissatisfaction and instrumentality. These concepts are intertwined with some of the fundamental notions of the integrative theory. They are not, however, the whole story.

Union Growth Studies

A considerable literature on union growth has developed over the years. This literature is of some interest for theorizing about industrial conflict, although its main focus is upon the general growth of the labor movement, not particular instances of organizing. It ordinarily operates at the societal level, although some studies are at the industry level. Even though its level and focus are somewhat different from those of the integrative theory, it nevertheless speaks indirectly to the question of why workers organize.

A major review of this literature by Jack Fiorito and Charles R. Greer[54] breaks down its significant results under the headings' of "employee" and "union" variables. The *employee* variables found to be significant are race, sex, education, and the employee's family responsibilities. Nonwhites tend to be more union prone, perhaps because of their greater need for union protection. This proneness is said to be balanced somewhat by the propensity of unions to discriminate against minorities. The integrative theory's explanation for minority union proneness would be their lower achievements, due to discrimination, their rising expectations in recent years, their solidarity, and norms favoring collective action.

The propensity of males to form unions is explained in the union growth literature by the historically greater attachment of males to the work force. This explanation does have some empirical support. The integrative theory's explanation would largely lie in the area of greater male expectations with respect to social dominance and greater saliency of material resources.

More educated workers have been found to be less likely to organize. This is explained in this literature on the basis of greater individual bargaining power for highly educated workers, a more favorable labor market, and greater identification with management. This is not greatly different from explanations based upon the integrative theory. Educated workers probably have higher achievements. Because of their more favorable opportunities for exit, they have a greater potential for correcting their problems through peaceable individual action. If this is the case, they would be less likely to become frustrated, and therefore less likely to become ready for aggressive action. They might also be likely to opt for exit.

The integrative theory does not have a ready explanation for the finding that workers with greater family responsibilities are more union prone. However, it may be that saliency of economic outcomes is greater for these workers.

The variables labeled as *union* variables that have been consistently found to be important are the "saturation effect" and instrumentality perceptions. The saturation effect refers to the diminishing degreee of organizing success by unions as an industry becomes more and more unionized. It is expected that at some point the union will cease to be as effective because of decreasing levels of organizing efforts by the union and the inherent difficulty of organizing the remaining units. The integrative theory would explain this as a diminishing amount of resources made available for organizing and a lesser amount of leadership to mobilize collective action. The issue of instrumentality has been dealt with previously.

Fiorito and Greer also break down the results of various studies into variables pertaining to the technological context, the market context, and sociopolitical matters. With respect to technological context, it has been found that occupation has an effect on unionization, with white collar workers generally being less union prone. As Fiorito and Greer note, the explanations for this in the literature are not particularly clear. They suggest that perhaps it may be necessary to inquire more deeply into the particular working conditions involved in an occupation in order to find the determinants of union proneness differences. They suggest that factors such as machine pacing, high effort level, and low autonomy are linked with unionism. This is consistent with the understanding suggested by the integrative theory. Occupational differences in social dominance expectations and achievements would be expected to produce differences in the propensity to unionize. It may be that white collar workers generally have greater social dominance and material achievements than do blue collar workers. It may, of course, also be the case that their expectations are higher, which would work in the opposite direction.

The *market context* variable believed by Fiorito and Greer to be most important is changes in employment, particularly in the unemployment rate. The findings are that unions do better in times of low unemployment or of rapid employment growth. These have generally been seen as a proxy for employer resistance to unionization efforts. This explanation has, however, been put in question by the results of some studies. The integrative theory's explanation of this phenomenon would incline mainly toward effects on expectations.

A number of wage-related variables have been investigated. Results regarding money wage changes are somewhat mixed, although the evidence generally seems to be that unions grow during times when money wages are increasing. This is generally explained on the basis of unions being given credit for increasing money wages. The integrative theory would explain the relationship between money wage increases and unionization on the basis of increased expectations and an increasing expectations/achievements gap for those who did not get an increase in money wages. Some studies have found a link between increases in real wages and unionization. The integrative theory's explanation for this would be the same as that given regarding money wages. This is not as convincing an explanation, however, as the effects of real wages on expectations are not as obvious.

Studies showing wage inequity effects on unionization are highly consistent with the integrative theory. This comes very close to finding an expectations/achievements gap and a link between that gap and unionization. This is precisely what integrative theory would predict.

With respect to *sociopolitical* variables, only urbanization appears to have consistent results. The explanations generally given for this are less than convincing. The integrative theory would explain this relationship mainly on the basis of better urban worker access to information about the achievements of others.

The union growth literature is interesting and varied. To a degree it cuts across the strike and organizing literatures. To the extent that there is theory involved in it, it appears to be rooted in a rough type of utility theory. In general, however, the union growth literature uses variables that seem to have been selected in major part because they were available. As is the case with the literature on strikes and organizing, one is left with the impression of a highly fragmented set of studies not organized by any particular model. Indeed, Fiorito and Greer note that "there is no satisfactory model of union growth."[55]

It is not plausible to claim that the integrative theory produces clear and consistent explanations in all cases where this is not achieved by the literatures on strikes, union organizing, and union growth. What does appear to be the case is that it occasionally gives a richer explanation, and one that is tied to a general body of theory to an extent that is not already true. Quite importantly, one finds few glaring differences between the empirical results found by scholars from these various perspectives and the predictions of the integrative theory. While this certainly does not prove the integrative theory to be valid, at least these studies do not establish its invalidity. The very mixed nature of the results of many of these studies is also supportive of the integrative theory's central argument that industrial conflict is a highly complex event. It is a phenomenon not easily understood and predicted by selecting variables on an ad hoc basis—even variables that individually seem to intuitively "make sense." A theory of some kind is needed.

Explaining the Great Upsurges of Unionization

One of the most important problems in the field of industrial conflict and, indeed, in the field of industrial relations generally, is the explanation of the two great upsurges of union organization in the United States. In the 1930's and again in the 1960s and early 1970s very large numbers of workers suddenly organized. A theory that explained these surges of organization would perform a considerable service to the field.

Organizing Mass Production Industry—the 1930s

In the middle and late 1930s, the basic mass production industry of the United States organized. How and why this happened has been much discussed; yet, one searches in vain for any general treatment that explains this important phenomenon in a convincing way.

A good review of these events is provided by a classic book written by Irving Bernstein, *The Turbulent Years*.[56] Bernstein quotes John Steinbeck's *In Dubious Battle* to get to the heart of the matter. One of Steinbeck's characters is a former lumberjack who has been reduced to selling apple crates. He describes the feeling that he senses in the country during the mid-1930s:

> "it's anger," the old man cried . . . "Only it ain't just in one man. It's like the whole bunch, millions and millions was one man, and he's been beat and starved, and he's gettin' that sick feelin' in his guts. The stiffs don't know what's happenin', but when the big guy gets mad, they'll all be there, and by Christ, I hate to think of it." . . . He swayed on his limb and tightened his arms to steady himself. "I feel it in my skin," he said. "Ever' place I go, it's like water just before it gets to boilin'."[57]

Some of the most important instances of worker organization of the 1930s occurred in coal mining, rubber, automobiles, and steel. The coal industry, largely unorganized since the early 1920s, was organized in a matter of a few weeks in 1933. Berkowitz attributes this mainly to the passage of Section 7(a) of the National Industrial Recovery Act (NIRA), which guaranteed the rights of workers to organize and bargain, and the massive campaign launched by the United Mine Workers Union, which utilized the argument that the

popular president, Franklin D. Roosevelt, favored union organization.[58]

The rubber industry was also organized in 1933. According to
Bernstein, the workers' grievances included instability of employment, technological displacement, wage cuts, and a "speed up."[59]
The passage of Section 7(a) of the NIRA had a powerful effect on Akron, the center of the rubber industry. According to Bernstein, it "hit
Akron like a bolt of lightning."[60] A meeting to discuss the NIRA
called by Akron trade unions produced an overflow meeting of 5,000
workers. Within a few months 40,000 to 50,000 workers in the rubber industry in Akron had signed up with the union.[61] As was the
case in other cities during the Depression, the Akron establishment
was demoralized and in disrepute, limiting the ability of employers
to resist unionization.[62]

The steel industry did not organize until 1936–1937. It was organized through a massive and heavily funded campaign by the Steel
Workers Organizing Committee, affiliated with the CIO. This was
during a brief period of economic recovery. The Wagner Act, which
provided workers with protection for organizing, had just been
passed. Powerful national political support for the unions existed
within the Roosevelt administration and also in Congress. Democratic governors had been elected in the major steel producing
states.[63] The revelations of the LaFollette Committee and the
changed political environment deprived management of a great deal
of its public support. The Steel Workers Organizing Committee, led
by Phillip Murray, worked creatively and energetically, operating
very effectively through the existing company-dominated unions.
The union showed that it could be effective by acting through the
company unions and by demonstrating to workers that the union
could "stand up to" their employers.[64]

The auto industry was also organized in 1936–1937. The key to organizing the automobile industry was organizing General Motors.
The keys to that, in turn, were the GM plants in Flint, Michigan.[65]
According to Bernstein, the chief union organizer, Wyndam Mortimer, entered Flint surreptitiously. He organized secretly, working
with workers "one-to-one" to alleviate their fears of employer retribution.

The auto workers' main complaint at this time was the "speed up."
Soon workers began calling "quickie" strikes in response to the
speeded-up assembly line. GM did not punish employees involved in
the quickie strikes. Sit-down strikes occurred in other auto plants.
These also went unpunished and were somewhat effective.

Reading Bernstein's account of the events at Flint, one gets the impression of leaders who were being swept along by the emotions and desires of the workers. Mortimer and other union officials attempted to hold back the Flint workers' desire to have a sit-down strike, trying to wait for a propitious moment. The local union attempted to bargain with GM management but was met with a company refusal to bargain. At about that time, auto workers in Cleveland struck. GM prepared to move some critical auto body dies out of the Flint plants. When this was discovered by the workers and seen as a threat to their jobs, a meeting of the workers in one of the plants was held. The cry went up, "Them's our jobs." In response to an inquiry as to what they should do, the men shouted, "Shut her down! Shut the goddam plant." What followed was the famous and effective Flint sit-down strike, which was a powerful aid to organizing the auto industry.

The organizing of coal, rubber, autos and steel in the 1930s fits the integrative theory reasonably well. In all of these industries there were conditions of longstanding deprivation. The organizing had a strong flavor of aggression. It bears little resemblance to coolly calculated, economically rational action. In the coal industry, it appears that the removal of worker fears of being punished for organizing, combined with the presence of a mobilizer and mobilized resources, was sufficient to produce employee organization. In the rubber industry, wage cuts and the speed-up were added to longstanding deprivations. The speed-up, in addition to having material consequences, might be seen as having to do with social dominance as well. It is extraordinarily demeaning for human beings to feel the lash of the mechanical whip of automation forcing them to work ever harder and harder. The passage of Section 7(a) of the NIRA seems to have served both to remove the inhibiting fear of employer retribution for collective action, and as a mobilizer.

In the steel industry we see the same picture—legal protection of the right to organize removing the fear of victimization, a new supply of economic and political resources from the union and from the federal government, and the mobilizing effectiveness of the union.

In the organization of the Flint auto workers, the organizers operated secretly to avoid the workers' being inhibited by fear. The speed-up provided both material and social dominance roots for worker action. The success of small strikes without employer retribution may have operated to reduce fear. As predicted by the integrative theory's frustration-aggression path, the union first attempted to obtain results peaceably through bargaining. It struck only when this failed. To all these circumstances were added the threat of the removal of machinery from one of the plants—threatening the workers' very jobs. The strike action, which occurred at a very high level of annoyance, was very aggressive in tone and action.

Organizing Public Employees—1960s and 1970s

In the 1960s and 1970s public employees became largely organized. The particular causes of public employee organizing have been the subject of considerable speculation and study, with a set of explanations generally coming to be accepted by students of public employee collective bargaining.[66] Without necessarily accepting these explanations, it is of some interest to examine them in the light of the integrative theory. Assuming that they capture some of the truth of public employee organizing, it would be troubling if they were inconsistent with the integrative theory.

One of the most commonly cited reasons for the organization of public employees in the 1960s and 1970s was their loss of traditional advantages over workers in the private sector. Although public employee wages had never been greatly superior to those of private sector employees, their fringe benefits had historically been better. In addition, their job security had been considerably greater. Beginning in the 1940s these advantages began to slip. By the 1960s they had largely disappeared.[67] In terms of the integrative theory, worker expectations may have been created by their own past experience. When the traditional, and thereby expected, relationship with the achievements of others disappeared, this may have created a gap between their expectations and their achievements.

It is also rather widely believed that authoritarian modes of decision-making in the public sector caused a lack of responsiveness to employee complaints and left the employees "frustrated and helpless, apathetic and angry."[68] The failure of peaceable attempts to close an expectations/achievements gap leading to organizing is, of course, consistent with the frustration-aggression path of the integrative theory.

It is sometimes argued that the 1960s saw a new general acceptance of unionism by society.[69] If this were the case, workers would have been able to engage in norm-modifying activity without bearing the burden of a basic modification of societal values. This is one of the integrative theory's facilitating conditions. It is clearly the case that this period saw increased efforts at organizing public workers by unions. In terms of the integrative theory, this provided outside mobilized resources, communication paths and mobilizers.

It does appear that there was something of a demonstration effect created by social confrontations engaged in by the other social movements of the 1960s.[70] During this period many groups within the society benefited from aggressive collective action. In terms of the integrative theory, this demonstration effect may have heightened employee perceptions of the instrumentality of union action, removed inhibiting fears of employer retribution, and created a set of norms conducive to collective action.

It would appear that the traditional explanations of mass organizing of both mass production industry and public employees are consistent with the integrative theory. This, of course, does not prove the integrative theory, but does remove one possible objection to the theory—that it is inconsistent with major occurrences of industrial conflict or is not at all helpful in explaining them.

Some Unanswered Questions

There are a number of questions pertaining to industrial conflict that have either been troubling scholars of industrial relations for many years or been inexplicably ignored in spite of their importance. Any theory about industrial conflict should inform our answers to these questions or at least provide an organized approach to them.

Why Is Industrial Conflict So Rare?

The relative rarity of industrial conflict is a question that has been little explored but is deserving of attention. It is believed that the integrative theory does shed some light on this question; if nothing else, it points out that the occurrence of industrial conflict is a very complicated matter. A number of things have to fall into place for it to occur, and there are numerous opportunities for it not to occur.

One reason that industrial conflict is so rare is that collective bargaining is a very effective way for employees peaceably to achieve expected levels of outcomes. In terms of the integrative theory, bargaining is a peaceable way of achieving expected material and social dominance outcomes, avoiding frustration, and, therefore, avoiding strikes. Indeed, one can view collective bargaining as serving the same function as ritualized aggression. It very well accomplishes an accommodation between the expectations of the workers and the goals of management without aggressive action being taken. This result is probably facilitated by the collective bargaining practice of dealing with the most common sources of worker expectations, the earnings of comparable others and increases in the cost of living. It may either lower worker expectations or serve as a mechanism for achieving them. In collective bargaining employer representatives predictably argue that the employer is not responsible for any deprivation felt by the employees but is giving them all that it can. Any problems that the workers have are usually laid on the door step of outside economic forces.

The difficulty of organizing is reflected in the integrative theory. A number of things have to transpire at the same time. In addition, it is quite easy to see that there are some points of the model at which favorable conditions are very difficult for a union to achieve. Employer behaviors such as "positive employee relations" are aimed at removing the sources of worker deprivation in the first place. If this is successful, it effectively removes the threat and frustration-aggression paths, and may affect the rational calculation path, to readiness for aggressive action. Many employers, in the Japanese style, are dealing with social dominance problems by eliminating the symbols of dominance, such as reserved parking places and executive dining rooms.

"Negative" actions by employers to defeat unions have historically been aimed at inducing worker fears in order to inhibit the collective aggressive response. In addition, employers have often attempted to increase employee feelings of hopelessness in order to decrease union instrumentality perceptions. Union avoidance specialists typically emphasize the fact that the National Labor Relations Act does not require the employer to *agree to anything* in collective bargaining. This, of course, is a thinly veiled threat not to accord a union any effectiveness in the event that it is organized.

When one is informed by the integrative theory, the *collective* aggressive action stage can be brought into sharp relief. At this stage love, solidarity, among the members of the employee group, may be sufficient to overcome even the most compelling fears of workers. This seems a crucial determinant of organizing. Resource mobilization and mobilizing leaders appear to be especially important in creating, respectively, hope of success and saliency.

What Accounts for Differences in Union Proneness?

An abiding question in the field of industrial relations is why some groups of workers organize rather easily while others do not. It is believed that the integrative theory may furnish some assistance in arriving at the answer to this question, at least with respect to some groups of workers.

In the American industrial system skilled craftsmen, blue-collar industrial workers, and teachers are, at least in many regions, among the most highly organized in the American system. Skilled craftsmen may, as a "strategic" group, be prone to act in a rational fashion and organize when the cost-benefit ratio is favorable.[71] Furthermore, they have generally had less reason to fear employer retribution because of their ability to find alternative work if fired. Most importantly, they ordinarily have a high degree of solidarity. The positive affective character of the relationship among skilled workers has been powerful for generations, providing them with a strong basis for organization. In addition, their instrumentality perceptions may be high, as skilled craftsmen have historically done rather well as a result of unionizing. Indeed, in addition to high wages, they have obtained, through their unions, a degree of control over their work which accords them a high degree of the autonomy aspect of social dominance.

Blue-collar industrial workers in the United States became highly organized in the massive wave of unionization in the 1930s. Substantial deprivation of employed workers (relative to their previous conditions) was present during the Great Depression. As predicted by Marx and Engels, their organization into factories may have provided the facilitating conditions of solidarity and communication.[72] Workers in mass production industry organized once the inhibiting fear of retribution was removed by law. Organization was facilitated by a weakening of management ability to resist, given the social and political climate of the 1930s. Often unrecognized is the existence of class feelings of solidarity among blue-collar workers in the United States. In an industrial area, such as Pittsburgh, working-class organizations such as churches and clubs and social meeting places such as bars have provided the nucleii for the formation of these relationships among workers.

Teachers organized suddenly and dramatically in the 1960s, leading the public employee push to unionization. During this period they were suffering material relative deprivation, as their wages and conditions of work became substantially lower than those of other workers. In addition, the increasing number of male teachers may have created a different set of relevant social comparisons. Males probably compared their wages and conditions to those of males in other occupations. It seems reasonable to conclude that a considerable expectations/achievements gap was created during this period. In addition, a shortage of teachers in the 1960s produced an ability to engage in collective action without being inhibited by fear of losing an irreplaceable job. Teachers have long had a reasonably high degree of solidarity, making organization possible even in the face of strong employer opposition.

Traditionally resistant to union organizing have been southern workers, textile workers, women, professionals, white-collar workers, and very low-wage workers. Many of these categories overlap. Southern workers, for example, are often low-wage textile workers.

The fear of employer retribution is perhaps crucial to the failure of southern workers to organize. In addition, it may be that they are very low on feelings of solidarity, the traditional "independence" of the southern worker. They have, of course, been split along racial lines. Their expectations are often quite low. In addition, in order for them to organize it is necessary to challenge fundamental societal values. Lastly, they may not believe a union to be instrumental in serving their purposes, as the employers appear to be so overwhelmingly powerful. In addition, the ability of the main southern industry, textiles, to pay higher wages, at least given its relatively low level of technological sophistication until very recently, may cause workers to accurately perceive that there is no real prospect of higher wages.

Historically difficulties in organizing women probably stemmed from their lower expectations (particularly with respect to social dominance) and norms contrary to aggressive action of any kind. These explanations seem more reasonable than the traditional one of their limited attachment to the labor force. This view is also consistent with the connection of successful organizing of women in some areas with the rise of the women's rights movement. The history of the "Willmar Eight," and 9 to 5 are testimony to this connection. This movement, of course, has a very high social dominance content.

Professional workers and white-collar workers may not move toward aggressive action for several reasons that are included in the integrative theory. It may be that their achievements are relatively high and their solidarity with their fellows relatively low. There may also be a set of norms contrary to collective action and high availability of exit. All of these reasons offered by the integrative theory seem to have some plausibility for these workers.

While not furnishing any final or complete answers to differences in union proneness of various groups of workers, the integrative theory does at least speak to this question in an organized way.

Why Do "Irrational" Strikes Occur?

One of the questions most commonly asked by students in university industrial relations classes is why employees strike when it is not "rational." It does indeed seem that strikes often occur when the cost-benefit calculations are not favorable for employees.

The conventional explanation is the long-range benefit to the workers of establishing the credibility of their strike threat. While this sounds reasonable, it is neither empirically nor theoretically grounded. Perhaps a better explanation, which is offered by the integrative theory, is that rational calculation is simply not the usual engine of industrial conflict. If strikes ordinarily occur along the threat or frustration-aggression paths of the model, it is hardly surprising that they are not closely connected to cost-benefit ratios.

Why Are Managers So Intensely Antiunion?

The intensity of management opposition to union organizing can probably be better understood when viewed in the light of the integrative theory's arguments. In the first place, the integrative theory sees managers as the objects of aggression. This would lead one to believe that they would be likely to respond with a high degree of intensity and emotionalism. In addition, managers would be expected to be persons with high dominance-feeling and n Power. Union organizing, particularly when related to social dominance, directly attacks these feelings and needs of managers.

Management opposition to unions has traditionaly been explained on the basis of the interests and role of managers. Admittedly, it is ordinarily true that managerial interests are tied to those of the stockholders and the "bottom line." It is also clear that the managerial role is to represent the efficiency interest of the owners. However, neither of these facts explains the intensity and personal animosity involved in the responses of most managers to union organizing. To understand this, one needs to think in terms of aggressive action and the fundamental predisposition of human beings for dominance.

One aspect of industrial relations that is particularly revealing with respect to the operation of social dominance in work organizations is the industrial offense of "insubordination." Insubordination is viewed by managers as a "hanging offense." American labor arbitrators have pretty well accepted the proposition that it is a major offense. Yet, upon reflection, one is hard pressed to rationalize the classification of insubordination along with theft, drug usage, intentional destruction of company property, and other major offenses. The seriousness of insubordination as an offense says something about the fundamental social dominance nature of the industrial relationship. It forms a ground for action that goes beyond the mere need for efficiency.

Why Is Collective Bargaining Structured as It Is?

It is not often asked why collective bargaining follows the sort of formal ritual it does. Studies of collective bargaining assume the traditional framework and then test how human beings operate within it. A more interesting question may be why collective bargaining is framed as it is. The integrative theory offers some explanation. A part of this explanation is that bargaining is perfectly suited to perform the function of peaceable achievement of employee expectations short of aggressive action.

Two of the ever-present arguments in collective bargaining are comparability and employer inability to pay. As previously argued, comparability makes a good deal of sense, since it is what one would expect to form the basis of expectations of workers. Management's customary inability to pay argument obviously connects not only with rationality but also with an attempt on the part of the employer to avoid being identified as the frustrator of employee desires. It is not contended that collective bargaining was intentionally designed to operate as it does. Instead, it is suggested that its *function* as it is now structured serves to avoid individual conflict. Perhaps this is why it survives.

Industrial conflict has long been a puzzling phenomenon. The integrative theory is just one more attempt to try to answer some of the questions that have been, or should have been, asked by scholars over the years. Its ability to make some sense and be somewhat helpful in dealing with these enduring questions does furnish some support for its right to exist.

CONCLUSIONS

John Maynard Keynes states in the preface to his *General Theory*: "Those who are strongly wedded to what I have called 'the classical theory' will fluctuate, I suspect, between a belief that I am quite wrong and a belief that I am saying nothing new."[73] This may be the fix in which the integrative theory finds itself. Because it necessarily implies the inadequacy of existing unidisciplinary explanations, it will likely be seen as "quite wrong" by the adherents to those disciplines. This problem is probably exacerbated by the theory's reliance on some ideas not currently in vogue in the disciplines from which they are drawn. Yet, to an industrial relations scholar it seems that the explanations a la mode do not serve well to deal with the phenomenon of industrial conflict.

Many of the ideas used in the integrative theory are indeed "nothing new." They have been around for a long time. The contribution of the theory is the drawing together of diverse strands of thought and tying them into a single conceptual model in a different way. It is hard to imagine theorizing about an area that has been as much studied as this one without using the ideas of those who have gone before. Perhaps the newest thing about the theory is its attempt to ground itself in a model of humankind not previously used in this context. Since Marx, not many industrial conflict theories have expressly tried to build from such a fundamental level to deal with the question "why."

The integrative theory does clearly stand for several propositions that, to say the least, are not universally accepted. It does not conform to the current fashion of utilizing some version of utility theory as the sole explanation of human behavior. It is, rather, something of a throwback to an earlier intellectual tradition in industrial relations. It is more clearly akin to Thornstein Veblen's "instinct of workmanship" and Selig Perlman's "scarcity consciousness" than to modern superrational economic theory. It posits innate behavioral mechanisms, and in doing so roots itself mainly in biological, not economic, theory. It views strikes and union organizing as acts of aggression, not calculated market transactions. It emphasizes the importance of affective relations among group members in organizing and striking. It considers the occurrence of strikes and organizing as a long-linked, complex matter that requires detailed analysis in individual cases. It also emphasizes the importance of employee expectations and utilizes the notion of relative deprivation. It is, first and foremost, and *industrial relations* theory in that it focuses solely on an industrial relations subject and is interdisciplinary in nature.

NOTES

[1]Mary Midgley, *Beast and Man* (Ithaca: Cornell University Press, 1978), p. 326.

[2]Konrad Lorenz, *On Aggression*, trans. Marjorie Kerr Wilson (New York: Harcourt, Brace and World, 1966), p. 239.

[3]Ibid.

[4]John R. Commons, *Legal Foundations of Capitalism* (Madison: University of Wisconsin Press, 1968), p. 284.

[5]Joseph A. Schumpeter, *History of Economic Analysis* (New York: Oxford University Press, 1954), p. 577.

[6]Sigmund Freud, *Civilization and Its Discontents*, trans. and ed. James Strachey (New York: W.W. Norton and Co., 1961), p. 43.

[7]Jack W. Brehm, *A Theory of Psychological Reactance* (New York: Academic Press, 1966).

[8]Alfred Adler, *Understanding Human Nature* (Greenwich, Conn.: Fawcett Publications, 1927), p. 32.

[9]Adolph A. Berle, *Power* (New York: Harcourt, Brace and World, 1969), p. 62.

[10]Rollo May, *Power and Innocence* (New York: W.W. Norton and Co., 1972), p. 39.

[11]David C. McClelland, "The Two Faces of Power," *Journal of International Affairs* 24, no. 2 (1970), pp. 35–36.

[12]Stanley Milgram, "Some Conditions of Obedience and Disobedience to Authority," *Human Relations* 18 (1965), p. 74.

[13]Ibid.

[14]Sigmund Freud, *Group Psychology and the Analysis of the Ego*, trans. and ed. James Strachey (New York: W.W. Norton and Company, 1959), pp. 13, 59.

[15]Erich Fromm, *Escape from Freedom* (New York: Holt, Rinehart and Winston, 1941), p. 164; T. W. Adorno, Else Frenkel Brunswick, Daniel J. Levinson, and R. Nevitt Sanford, *The Authoritarian Personality* (New York: Harper and Row, 1956), pp. 182, 192, 228.

[16]A. H. Maslow, "Dominance-Feeling, Behavior, and Status," *Psychological Review* 44 (1937), p. 413.

[17]Desmond Morris, *The Human Zoo* (New York: McGraw-Hill Book Co., 1969), p. 41.

[18]David C. McClelland and David H. Burnham, "Power is the Great Motivator," *Harvard Business Review* 54, no. 2 (March-April 1966), p. 101.

[19]Vance Packard, *The Pyramid Climbers* (New York: McGraw-Hill Book Co., 1962), p. 173.

[20]Edward O. Wilson, *Sociobiology*, abgd. ed. (Cambridge: The Belknap Press, 1980), p. 137.

[21]Chester I. Barnard, *The Functions of the Executive* (Cambridge: Harvard University Press, 1962), p. 165; James A. F. Stoner, *Management*, 2nd ed. (Englewood Cliffs, N.J.: Prentice-Hall, 1982), p. 304.

[22]Daniel V. J. Bell, *Power, Influence and Authority: An Essay in Political Linguistics* (New York: Oxford University Press, 1975), pp. 35–69.

[23]Emile Benoit-Smullyan, "Status, Status Types, and Status Interrelation," *American Sociological Reveiw* 9, no. 1 (February 1944), pp. 160–161.

[24]Louis D. Brandeis, "The Fundamental Cause of Industrial Unrest." in *Unions, Management and the Public*, ed. E. Wight Bakke, Clark Kerr, and Charles W. Anrod (New York: Harcourt, Brace and World, 1967), p. 244.

[25]Reinhard Bendix, *Work and Authority in Industry* (New York: John Wiley and Sons, 1956), pp. 2–3; Herbert Marcuse, *Eros and Civilization* (New York: Vintage Books, 1962), p. 82; Ralf Dahrendorf, *Class and Class Conflict in Industrial Society* (Stanford: Stanford University Press, 1959), p. 249.

[26]Morris, *The Human Zoo*, pp. 42–45.

[27]Albert Bandura, *Aggression: A Social Learning Analysis* (Englewood Cliffs, N.J.: Prentice-Hall, 1973), p. 174.

[28]Lionel Tiger and Robin Fox, *The Imperial Animal* (New York: Holt, Rinehart and Winston, 1971), p. 39.

[29]Ted Robert Gurr, *Why Men Rebel* (Princeton: Princeton University Press, 1970), p. 28.

[30]Stephen Worchel, "The Effect of Three Types of Arbitrary Thwarting on the Instigation to Aggression," *Journal of Personality* 42, no. 2 (June 1974), pp. 314–317; James T. Tedeschi, R. Bob Smith, III, and Robert C. Brown, Jr., "A Reinterpretation of Research on Aggression," *Psychological Bulletin* 81, no. 9 (1974), pp. 543–544;

James A. Kulik and Roger Brown, "Frustration, Attribution of Blame, and Aggression," *Journal of Experimental Social Psychology* 15, no. 2 (March 1979), pp. 190–193.

[31] Arthur M. Ross, *Trade Union Wage Policy* (Berkeley: University of California Press, 1956), pp. 53, 74.

[32] James C. Davies, "Toward a Theory of Revolution," *American Sociological Review* 27, no. 1 (February 1962), pp. 5–19.

[33] Robert A. Baron and Donn Byrne, *Social Psychology: Understanding Human Interactions*, 3rd, ed. (Boston: Allyn and Bacon, 1981), p. 139.

[34] Leonard R. Sayles, *Behavior of Industrial Work Groups* (New York: John Wiley and Sons, 1958), pp. 97–103.

[35] Freud, *Group Psychology and the Analysis of the Ego*, pp. 24, 35.

[36] Dahrendorf, *Class and Class Conflict in Industrial Society*, pp. 184–185.

[37] Jack Fiorito and Charles R. Greer, "Determinants of U.S. Unionism: Past Research and Future Needs," *Industrial Relations* 21, no. 1 (Winter 1982), pp. 1–32.

[38] Arthur Kornhauser, "Human Motivation Underlying Industrial Conflict," in *Industrial Conflict*, ed. Arthur Kornhauser, Robert Dubin, and Arthur M. Ross (New York: McGraw-Hill Book Co., 1954), p. 76.

[39] Morris Zelditch, Jr., Joseph Berger, Bo Anderson, and Bernard P. Cohen, "Equitable Comparisons," *Pacific Sociological Review* 13, no. 1 (Winter 1970), pp. 19–26.

[40] Thomas A. Kochan, *Collective Bargaining and Industrial Relations* (Homewood, Ill.: Richard D. Irwin, 1980), p. 251.

[41] Ibid.

[42] Michael Shalev, "Trade Unionism and Economic Analysis: The Case of Industrial Conflict," *Journal of Labor Research* 1, no. 1 (Spring 1970), pp. 133–173.

[43] See, Hoyt N. Wheeler, "Determinants of Strikes: Comment," *Industrial and Labor Relations Review* 37, no. 2 (January 1974), pp. 263–269.

[44] Kochan, *Collective Bargaining and Industrial Relations*, p. 255.

[45] Martin J. Mauro, "Strikes as a Result of Imperfect Information," *Industrial and Labor Relations Reveiw* 35, no. 4 (July 1982), pp. 522–38.

[46] Arthur M. Ross, "The Prospect for Industrial Conflict," *Industrial Relations* 1, no. 1 (October 1961), p. 59.

[47] Robert N. Stern, "Intermetropolitan Patterns of Strike Frequency," *Industrial and Labor Relations Review* 29, no. 2 (January 1976), pp. 218–235.

[48] Kochan, *Collective Bargaining and Industrial Relations*, p. 257.

[49] Jeanne M. Brett and Stephen B. Goldberg, "Wildcat Strikes in Bituminous Coal Mining," *Industrial and Labor Relations Review* 32, no. 4 (July 1979), p. 480.

[50] Thomas A. DeCotiis and Jean Yves LeLouran, "A Predictive Study of Voting Behavior in a Representation Election Using Union Instrumentality and Work Perceptions," *Organizational Behavior and Human Performance*, vol. 27 (1981), p. 116; Robert E. Allen and Timothy J. Keaveny, "Correlates of University Faculty Interest in Unionization: A Replication and Extension," *Journal of Applied Psychology* 66 (1981), p. 585.

[51] Herbert G. Heneman, III, and Marcus H. Sandver, "Predicting the Outcome of Union Certification Elections: A Review of the Literature," *Industrial and Labor Relations Review* 36, no. 4 (July 1983), pp. 535–559.

[52] Ibid., p. 552.

[53] Richard B. Freeman, "Why are Unions Faring Poorly in NLRB Representation Elections?" (paper presented at MIT Union Conference, Cambridge, June 19–23, 1983).

[54] Fiorito and Greer, "Determinants of U.S. Unionism: Past Research and Future Needs."

[55] Ibid., p. 19.

[56] Irving Bernstein, *Turbulent Years* (Boston: Houghton Mifflin Co., 1971).

[57] Ibid., p. 126.

[58] Ibid., pp. 41–42.

[59] Ibid., p. 99.

[60]Ibid.

[61]Ibid., p. 100.

[62]Ibid., pp. 98–99.

[63]Ibid., pp. 448–451.

[64]Ibid., pp. 455–457.

[65]Ibid., pp. 520–521.

[66]Robert E. Allen and Timothy J. Keaveny, *Contemporary Labor Relations* (Reading, Mass.: Addison-Wesley Publishing Co., 1983), pp. 543–545.

[67]Ibid., p. 544.

[68]Ibid.

[69]Ibid., pp. 544–545.

[70]Ibid., p. 545.

[71]Sayles, *Behavior of Industrial Work Groups*, p. 34.

[72]Karl Marx and Friederich Engels, "Manifesto of the Communist Party," in *Marx and Engels Basic Writings on Politics and Philosophy* ed. Louis S. Feuer (Garden City, N.Y.: Doubleday and Co., 1959). pp. 12–14.

[73]John M. Keynes, *The General Theory of Employment, Interest and Money* (New York: Harcourt, Brace and World, 1936), p. v.

INDEX